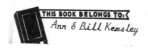

THE MURDERERS AMONG US

THE MURDERERS AMONG US

THE SIMON WIESENTHAL MEMOIRS
EDITED AND WITH AN INTRODUCTORY PROFILE
BY JOSEPH WECHSBERG

McGRAW-HILL BOOK COMPANY
New York · Toronto · London · Sydney

Editor's Note

Because of the unusual content of this book, it has been arranged in a somewhat unusual fashion. Joseph Wechsberg's profile of Simon Wiesenthal appears in four parts, as Chapters 1, 2, 11, and 18. The remaining twenty-two chapters contain Simon Wiesenthal's own narrative of his life and his activities, as told to Mr. Wechsberg.

Contents

THE MURDERERS AMONG US

A PROFILE OF
SIMON WIESENTHAL

I have lived in Vienna for a number of years, and I hadn't been in the city long before I began to hear about Simon Wiesenthal. In 1960, Wiesenthal was identified on the front pages of the papers in Vienna and the rest of the world as *der Eichmann-Jäger*—the Eichmann-hunter—for his role in helping the Israeli government track down Adolf Eichmann, the supreme logistics expert of Hitler's "final solution of the Jewish question." In 1963 Wiesenthal again made news when he pointed out to the embarrassed officials of Vienna's police department that the ex-Gestapo man who had arrested Anne Frank in Amsterdam in 1944 was now a member in good standing of the Vienna force. Numerous other notorious Nazis in Germany and Austria had been apprehended, I knew, thanks to Wiesenthal's dogged sleuthing. I became curious about the man and his bizarre detection agency. Wiesenthal himself, I learned, had been hounded by the Nazis through more than a dozen concentration camps, from his native Poland to Austria, and had survived thanks to a series of near-miracles. Most of his relatives, including his mother, had been exterminated. In 1945, after his liberation, he had volunteered to work for the United States Army in its hunt for war criminals in Austria, and he had subsequently been employed by the U.S. Office of Strategic Services and the Counter-Intelligence

Corps. In 1947, with meager volunteer help, he had set up at Linz, Austria, a small Documentation Center, where he helped his fellow Jews trace missing relatives and where he set about tracing some of the thousands of Nazi killers he knew were still at large. By 1954, denazification seemed momentarily a dead issue in Germany and Austria, and he closed the Documentation Center and went into refugee work. By 1961, after Eichmann's capture and trial, the tide of public sentiment in the former Nazi-ruled lands had again— rather miraculously—changed, and Wiesenthal decided to reopen his Documentation Center, this time in Vienna, and dedicate himself once and for all to tracking down those who, he knew, might soon evade justice as a result of the expiration of laws aimed at punishing them.*

Assigned to collaborate with Wiesenthal on this book, I phoned him during the summer of 1965 to suggest that we meet and to propose that I compile the histories of a few of the most unusual among his hundreds of unusual cases. The voice I heard was soft, warm, and friendly. Wiesenthal laughed easily once or twice. I detected in his German the accents of the farther reaches of the old Austro-Hungarian Empire, where I, like Wiesenthal, had spent my boyhood. I looked forward to meeting this most unusual avenger.

Rudolfsplatz, where Wiesenthal has his office, is a secluded square of nondescript buildings in Vienna's First District. Number 7 was newer than its neighbors. It must have been built after the last war, perhaps rather hastily, for it showed signs of fairly recent construction as well as of recent decay, and there was a damp smell of mortar in the stairway. On the fourth floor, a white door bore a small, inconspicuous sign reading DOKUMENTATIONSZENTRUM, and underneath, the letters B.J.V.N., for *Bund Jüdischer Verfolgter des Naziregimes*—Federation of Jewish Victims of the Nazi Regime. I rang the bell, and heard heavy steps. From the inside a chain was removed, and the door was half-opened. A dark-haired man stood in the door frame, giving me a careful once-over like a guard at a top-secret installation. The atmosphere reminded me of my postwar days as an OSS agent. I gave my name. The man, apparently an assistant of Wiesenthal's, nodded slightly and motioned for me to come in. There were two small rooms, sparsely furnished, with bare

* See Appendix: Statute of Limitations.

cement floors, no carpets, and only the most rudimentary office equipment—file cabinets, desks, a few chairs. Through the windows, I saw the rear walls of other buildings. It was a dark, gloomy place. A narrow white corridor led to a small private office in the rear, and there I met Simon Wiesenthal.

He looked exactly as he'd sounded on the phone, friendly and cheerful, certainly not like a man whose full-time occupation is tracking down murderers. His build is brawny and he stands about five feet eleven. He said that when he emerged from a concentration camp at the end of the war he'd been down to ninety-seven pounds and had looked "like a skeleton with some skin over the bones." He now weighs about twice as much. He has a big, balding head and a longish face with a high forehead. His eyes are thoughtful and, as I soon learned, can become piercing. With his small mustache and his tendency to put on weight, he could be a prosperous merchant, as his father had been, or a successful architect, which he himself was before the Second World War.

Wiesenthal (the name is pronounced VEE-sen-thal, the accent on the first syllable) gives the impression of being a very quiet man until one discovers that the quietness covers a disciplined tension and much suppressed emotion. There is an inner restlessness about him that affects everybody who sees him. He paces the floor with a swaying gait, like a sailor at sea. He seems to carry a heavy weight on his shoulders. He can be a thoughtful, silent listener, but when he begins to talk and gets emotionally involved—which is almost always—he underscores sentences with wide movements of his large arms and his eyes glow with almost hypnotic power. War criminals and district attorneys, cabinet ministers and scholars have learned that Wiesenthal is not an easy man to argue with. He has persuasiveness, a sharp sense of logic, and the Talmudic wit of his forebears—a combination many people have found irresistible. Once, he told me, a prominent German prosecutor said to him, "You fooled me for a long time, Wiesenthal. You look so harmless." Wiesenthal laughed, explaining that his harmless appearance had been extremely useful in the prosecution of harmful crimes.

The private office had the same Spartan atmosphere I'd noticed outside: a large desk with many papers; a couple of chairs; an old, inelegant sofa. The rear wall was lined with bookshelves. Wiesen-

thal has one of the best libraries anywhere on the history, organization, and activities of Heinrich Himmler's SS.* Originally created as
a special guard to protect Adolf Hitler, Himmler, and other Nazi
leaders (SS stood for *Schutzstaffel* or Security Guard), the black-
uniformed, black-booted SS became the Nazi elite after Hitler's
bloody 1934 purge of Ernst Roehm's brown-shirted SA or *Sturmabteilungen* (Storm Troops). The SS became a symbol of terror, a
state within the Nazi state, a privileged group with sinister power.
The SS created the Gestapo (*Geheime Staatspolizei* or Secret State
Police), and later policed the concentration camps. The SS was the
executive of death. Every concentration camp guard was a member
of the SS; camp administration was under the Economic Section of
the SS; in each district of Hitler's Europe an SS general was in
charge of all camps. Wiesenthal rarely deals with crimes committed
by regular army men or Party members. Almost all his "clients," as
he calls Nazi criminals, are SS men. The evil organization is responsible for the deaths of at least eleven million people, mostly innocent, nonbelligerent men, women, and children: 6 million Jews, and
5 million Yugoslavs, Russians, Poles, Czechs, Dutch, French, and
many others.

Wiesenthal makes an important distinction between "war crimes"
and "Nazi (or SS) crimes." In wartime, civilized men do things they
would never do normally. But war cannot justify the deliberate
murder of millions of innocent civilians. Wiesenthal is not concerned
with "ordinary" war crimes. He points out that many Nazi crimes
were committed between 1933 and 1939, long before the beginning
of the Second World War.

Most of the documents on Wiesenthal's desk, and nearly all of his
files and reports, have to do with tragedies that most people would
be glad to forget. Wiesenthal's constant preoccupation with terror
has made him neither despondent nor callous. It is his strength and
perhaps also his weakness that his files are not "cases"; each is to him
a human being. He has not become a bureaucrat; he often suffers
with his victims. A letter or a man's testimony may suddenly bring
back the memory of someone no longer alive or something he personally experienced, and he may start to cry. In such moments he
relives his own tragedy. One of Wiesenthal's toughest problems is

* See Appendix: SS and SA.

that many of his personal experiences and details of his cases tax other people's credulity. He must make the unbelievable believable to officials, prosecutors, and judges by patiently giving them facts and figures.

A few minutes after I'd stepped into Wiesenthal's office, the phone rang. He listened, said to me "New York," and immediately forgot my presence. The voice on the other end of the line sounded highly perturbed. Twice Wiesenthal took a deep breath, as if he were going to interrupt the caller, but then he shook his head and kept listening.

"No, no, *no!*" he said at last. "Even if we found the man we would need documents or at least the testimony of two persons. They would have to remember *exactly* what happened over twenty years ago. . . . Yes, dates and names and detailed descriptions. *Evidence.*" He listened for a while longer and sighed. "*You've* done nothing at all for twenty years; now you want me to perform miracles." Wiesenthal put down the receiver a few minutes later, exhausted. For a while he sat motionless, his face covered with his hands.

"This man and his brother saw their father killed in Auschwitz one day in 1943. They survived, emigrated to the United States, tried not to think of the past. They worked hard and were successful. Now, after all these years, things keep coming back to him. He sees his father in his nightmares, and he wakes up in the middle of the night. He is tortured by a sense of guilt. Did he really do everything he could? Did he perhaps think too much of himself and too little of the old man? As time goes on, the memories grow stronger, more painful. He's consulted a doctor, who couldn't help him. Then he read of my work, and now he's called me up from New York, asking me to find the man who murdered his father. All he knows is the SS man's first name—Hans—and how he looked. Only he and his brother saw how the crime was committed. Since then twenty-three years have passed. I explained to him that at least six thousand SS men worked at Auschwitz—as guards, technical personnel in gas chambers and crematoriums, medics, and office workers. Only nine hundred of them are known by name. Naturally, the SS guards didn't introduce themselves formally to their victims. One third of the known nine hundred were handed over to the Polish authorities. Of the remaining six hundred, about half are known to us: the names and addresses are in my files. But even assuming we could find the man, it would take more than the testimony of the two brothers to make a strong case. Many Nazi criminals have been acquitted, and prosecutors in Germany and Austria are reluctant to ask for an indictment unless they feel they have enough evidence to convince a jury that may well be in sympathy with the Nazi defendant."

I asked Wiesenthal what had made him start his pursuit of Nazi criminals.

He gave a sigh, got up from his desk, and walked up and down, looking at the floor. "A lot of people have asked me that question," he said. "My friends say: 'Why do you torture yourself with these things?' My non-friends put it more succinctly: 'Do you have to rake up the past, piling new hatred upon old?' Why don't I go back to my prewar profession of building houses? I could have gone to America, led a normal life, and made money." He gave a shrug. "It's no use. I'm doing this because I *have* to do it. I am not motivated by a sense of revenge. Perhaps I was for a short time in the very beginning. At the end of the war, when I was liberated after almost four years in more than a dozen concentration camps, I had little physical strength left, but I did have a strong desire for revenge. I'd lost my whole family. My mother had been taken away before my eyes. I thought my wife was dead. I had no one to live for.

"Most liberated camp inmates reacted differently. They wanted to forget so they would be able to live again. They surrounded themselves with a protective shell, trying hard not to think of what had happened.

"Even before I had had time to really think things through, I realized that *we must not forget*. If all of us forgot, the same thing might happen again, in twenty or fifty or a hundred years. I'm told that the people in Germany and Austria don't want to hear about 'these things.' Correct. But the public-opinion polls prove the inverse relationship between prosecution of Nazi crimes and the upsurge of neo-Nazism. The more trials, the weaker the Nazi revival. The trial of Adolf Eichmann in Jerusalem in 1961 was the greatest setback to the growth of the neo-Nazi movement in Germany and Austria. Millions of people who didn't know, or didn't *want* to know, the truth, for the first time had to listen to the facts. Today no one here can

say that he didn't know about 'these things.' If he still sympathizes
with the criminals, he has placed himself unequivocally on the side
of evil. Not many people like to do that."

At the end of the war, he went on, Wiesenthal saw the world populated only by two kinds of people: the white victims and the black
murderers. But the white-and-black phase was short. He was approached by several groups who wanted to create gangs that would
capture and kill their former tormentors; he opposed this idea violently. The Jews must not fight the Nazis with the Nazis' depraved
methods, he said. The Nazis had had their early, secret *Feme*
gangs, devoted to violence and revenge. Jews, he pointed out, must
not lower themselves to this level.

Wiesenthal knew that the Nazi crimes could never be "avenged."
They couldn't be atoned for in a thousand years. Even if all unpunished Nazi criminals were brought to trial, which was unlikely,
this wouldn't begin to balance the enormity of their crimes. Eleven
million dead—including one million dead children. How can the
murder of a million children ever be balanced by earthly justice?

But something *could* be done: the thought slowly emerged during
Wiesenthal's sleepless nights. He might at least attempt to create a
symbolic memorial to the dead and perhaps provide a warning
against future excesses. Obviously, strict accountability for the
crimes was impossible. What sense did it make when a Nazi who
had killed thousands of people got two years in prison—twenty
minutes for each murder? The important thing was to prevent the
commission of mass murder in the future.

In the early postwar months, Wiesenthal still hoped that many
people might have survived the inferno. Perhaps they had escaped,
were hiding out in forests, had changed their names, had disappeared in Russia. Gradually he became oppressed by the enormity
of the apocalypse. It became terrifyingly clear that what the Nazis
had called "the final solution of the Jewish question" had resulted in
the extermination not of tens of thousands, or even of hundreds of
thousands, but of millions of innocent people. But by the time he
knew the truth, the hatred in his heart was gone. Early in 1946, an
SS *Obersturmführer* named Beck (Wiesenthal doesn't know his first
name) was being held by the Americans at Dachau. Wiesenthal
learned that Beck had been the *rara avis,* a decent SS man who re-

fused to torture or kill his prisoners. For this he had been punished by his SS superiors with solitary imprisonment. Wiesenthal rounded up three Jewish witnesses and went with them to Dachau. They testified that no criminal acts had been committed by Beck, and he was released. Later, Wiesenthal discovered that another former Nazi named Werner Schmidt had been fired from a job in Halle when his Party membership became known. Schmidt had helped Wiesenthal in the ghetto of Lwow, Poland, where Wiesenthal lived when the Nazis took over in 1942. He had brought him food and warned him of impending Gestapo actions. Wiesenthal called Halle, had Schmidt cleared, and helped him get his job back.

"People like Beck and Schmidt were living proof to me that a man could come back from the war wearing a white vest, if he wanted to," he says. In German, *weisse Weste* is the symbol of innocence. "Unfortunately, for each man with a white vest there were many who didn't *have* to commit crimes but volunteered for executions and torture. Slowly I learned that between white and black there were many shades of gray: steel-gray, pearl-gray, dove-gray. And there were many shades of white. The victims were not always innocent either. I once talked with a Jewish concentration-camp trusty who had saved his life by taking part in the execution of a fellow Jew. The devilish SS man told him it was either he or the other man. The trusty's defense was that if he hadn't done it, somebody else might have shot the Jew; and he would have died too. I don't accept this: murder is murder, no matter who commits it. Every nation has its collaborators. We Jews had them too; we had perhaps fewer than other peoples, but we are not all angels. It was a typically diabolical touch of the SS to force Jews to kill their own people."

Wiesenthal often remembers his first walk as a free man into the outside world, after living four years behind barbed-wire fences. It was about ten days after his liberation from Mauthausen concentration camp, in Upper Austria, on a warm spring day in May 1945. Still weak and a little dizzy from unaccustomed exertion, he walked to the nearby village. Farmers worked in the fields, children played, the birds were singing. Less than a mile from the horrors of the gas chambers the countryside seemed a peaceful bucolic idyl. The people he met glanced briefly at his emaciated face, at the clothes hanging loosely from his shoulders. They showed no trace of either curiosity or sympathy. Wiesenthal suddenly felt terribly tired. He stepped into a farmhouse and asked for a drink of water. A sturdy, well-fed Austrian peasant woman brought him a glass of grape juice.

"Was it bad over there?" she asked, pointing vaguely in the direction of the low gray buildings across the fields.

"Be glad you didn't see the camp from the inside," said Wiesenthal.

"Why should *I* see it?" the woman said, "I am not a Jew."

Wiesenthal thought about this for a long time. Years of indoctrination had convinced the woman that there were two kinds of people on earth: those like herself, who were here to live, and the "inferior" races, who were here to die. Wiesenthal soon discovered that many people who had done nothing evil were infected by the Nazi theories. He became very angry when people told him, without being asked, that they had "known nothing about these things," or when others volunteered the information that they "had saved some Jews."

"If all the Jews had been saved that I was told about in those months there would have been more Jews alive at the end of the war than there were when it began. I also didn't believe after a while when people tried to convince me that they had known absolutely nothing. Maybe they had not known the whole truth about what went on inside the death camps. But almost all of them had noticed *some*thing after Hitler invaded Austria on March 11, 1938. They couldn't help seeing Jewish neighbors taken away by men in black SS uniforms. Their children came home from school and reported that their Jewish classmates had been thrown out. They noticed the swastikas on the broken windows of plundered Jewish stores. They couldn't ignore the rubble of the synagogues burned down during the night of November 9, 1938.* People knew what was going on, although many were ashamed and preferred to look the other way so they wouldn't see too much. Soldiers and officers on leave from the Eastern Front often talked about Jewish massacres there. People knew much more than they admitted, and that is why today so many have an acute sense of guilt."

* See Appendix: *Kristallnacht*.

Wiesenthal's career as a Nazi-hunter began shortly after his release in 1945, when the War Crimes section of the United States Army in Austria gave him a job helping to track down the SS men who had brutalized him and thousands of others. As Wiesenthal felt his strength coming back, he was able to listen to accounts of Nazi crimes without a feeling of hatred.

"Wiesenthal's wounded soul will never quite heal, but at least it doesn't bleed any longer," one of his friends, a noted Viennese psychologist, said recently. This seems confirmed by Wiesenthal's reaction to the problem of collective guilt, which is now being much discussed in Germany.

"A Jew who believes in God and in his people does not believe in the principle of collective guilt," he says. "Didn't we Jews suffer for thousands of years because we were said to be collectively guilty—all of us, including the unborn children—of the crucifixion, the epidemics of the Middle Ages, communism, capitalism, bad wars, bad peace treaties? All ills of mankind, from the pestilence to the atomic bomb, are 'the fault of the Jews.' We are the eternal scapegoat. We know that we are *not* collectively guilty, so how can we accuse any other nation, no matter what some of its people have done, of being collectively guilty?"

Having made up his mind during that early postwar period to start a search he had no hope of ever completing, Wiesenthal used his architect's training and began to build from the foundations. The first thing he did was to start establishing a historical record while the memory of the eyewitnesses was still fresh. At the end of the war, there were more than 100,000 survivors of the concentration camps, most of them living temporarily in 200 displaced-persons centers in Germany and Austria that had been set up by the Western Allies. With the help of a few friends, Wiesenthal established a network of correspondents in various camps. Their job was to interview each former prisoner and take affidavits concerning brutal SS guards, eyewitness accounts of killings and torture, and other personal experiences. Wiesenthal pointed out the need for exact names and dates; he ruled out hearsay accounts. The signed affidavits were numbered and later filed in the small Jewish Historical Documentation Center Wiesenthal set up in 1947 at Linz, after leaving the service of the Americans.

Even before he set up the Documentation Center, Wiesenthal had collected affidavits concerning Nazi crimes in about a thousand different places. He had obtained photographs of many SS men; these were reproduced and distributed in all DP camps. Often survivors didn't know the names of criminals, but now they recognized them by their photographs. Wiesenthal made an alphabetical card index of all locales of Nazi crimes. A second card index contained the names of all criminals. A third index contained the names of all witnesses. Wiesenthal's files were first used at Nuremberg during the preparation of the trials of Nazi war criminals there; the authorities at Nuremberg reciprocated by sending him their lists of war criminals. Later his files were used at Dachau in 1947 during the trial there before an American military court of SS men who had served as concentration-camp guards. Wiesenthal's cross-index system works very efficiently. When he is informed of a crime that was committed in a certain place, it takes only a few minutes to find the names and addresses of witnesses and the names of implicated SS men. Some witnesses have seen crimes in various places. The names of certain criminals are mentioned in connection with different locations.

Wiesenthal's card index of Nazi criminals now contains approximately 22,500 names. Most of the SS men listed are accused of murder; some are believed to be mass murderers. (His list is small compared to the master list of 160,000 names kept by the Central Agency of State Administrations of Justice for the Prosecution of National Socialist Crimes of Violence, established by the various states of West Germany in 1958 at Ludwigsburg in the Palatinate, in response to a belated recognition among West Germans of the enormity of the Nazi atrocities. The Center has helped initiate prosecutions in more than a thousand cases.)

Wiesenthal's index of criminals has many gaps. On some cards there is only a first name, or the nickname under which some SS man was known among the prisoners. In the Lwow concentration camp one of the most vicious SS guards was called "Tom Mix," after the famous American cowboy movie star. The favorite pastime of

this Tom Mix was to ride his horse through the camp and shoot at
random at prisoners. There are several eyewitnesses to the crimes,
but Wiesenthal hasn't found the man yet because he doesn't know
his real name. In the Cracow concentration camp the head of the
trusties was called *Waisenkind* (Orphan) because he was a criminal
who had been sentenced to life for murdering his parents. The Nazis
released him from prison and made him a trusty in the concentration camp, where The Orphan demonstrated his full talent for brutality. "No one knew his real name," Wiesenthal remembers. "Perhaps
an earlier group of inmates had known it, but they were dead. I remember another trusty in the Grossrosen camp, near Wroclaw, the
former Breslau. When he came into a room full of prisoners they
knew it was the end. The inmates called him The Angel of Death.
Unfortunately, a man cannot be traced by such a name."

Murderers, thieves, and other criminals are usually known by
name to the law-enforcement agencies looking for them. But many
SS men carefully guarded their true identities because, as the war
grew more and more hopeless for Germany, they knew that the day
might come when they would have to account for their crimes. After
the war, many members of the SS and the Gestapo went underground with false papers and lived under assumed names. Even
when Wiesenthal discovers a man's real name, the problem of locat-
ing the man in question remains. Many of his index cards bear a
question mark or the words *address unknown*—a reminder of the
time when mail addressed to Jews in Germany was often returned to
the sender with the same notation.

The Documentation Center in Linz soon became known all over
Europe. Reports and testimony, letters and queries, facts and figures
arrived from many countries. The Israelis gave Wiesenthal their
own list of wanted Nazi criminals. But the most valuable list of
names so far has come from the SS itself. One day in 1961 a former
"client" offered Wiesenthal an SS *Dienstalterliste* (service list) that
contained the names of 15,000 SS men, each with rank, decorations,
special remarks, places of duty. Only forty such lists had been
printed—one for each of the forty Gauleiters who were Hitler's
regional bosses in Nazi-ruled Europe. They had strict orders to destroy the lists at the end of the war. Wiesenthal's "client" had
managed to get hold of one list during the confusion following V-E

Day. He told Wiesenthal he needed money and asked five hundred
dollars for the booklet. Wiesenthal bought the list and doesn't regret
it. Subsequently, several men he had tracked down claimed that
they had never been in the SS. They couldn't deny it when Wiesenthal pointed out their names in the list.

The financing of what newspapers like to call "the Wiesenthal network" is a source of endless speculation among Wiesenthal's "clients" and those who resent his activities. They intimate that various
governments and the sinister power of "international Jewish capitalism" are behind him. The truth is less glamorous. Unlike some fic-
tional secret agents, Wiesenthal does not live on caviar and Dom
Pérignon champagne. When he opened his Documentation Center
in 1947 he had a number of enthusiastic unpaid helpers and he received $50 monthly as a voluntary contribution from Dr. A. Sil-
berschein, a former member of the Polish Parliament who was living
in Geneva. Wiesenthal supplemented his meager budget by writing
articles and doing other odd jobs. Although in the early 1950s West
Germany agreed to pay indemnities to Jews for their losses, for
years Wiesenthal refused to apply for the restitution to which he
was entitled, having lost his home, his business, and all his property
under the Nazi regime—he just couldn't get used to the idea of taking money from the Germans. At last Wiesenthal agreed to do so,
but said he would spend half of the money to finance the Documentation Center. Actually he has used more than half of what he has
received since 1958, when he got his first payment. He paid all his
own expenses for his almost sixteen years of work on the Eichmann
case.

In 1961, after the Eichmann trial in Jerusalem, the Board of the
Jewish Communities in Austria decided to finance a Documentation
Center in Vienna and asked Wiesenthal to take it over. He got $400
monthly. Of this he kept $150 as his monthly salary, spending the
rest on rental, office help, telephones, and postage. The monthly sub-
sidy was withdrawn the following year when the highly outspoken
Wiesenthal had strongly criticized the policies of the Board. He was
again on his own. He founded the Federation of Jewish Victims of
the Nazi Regime, whose twelve hundred members now contribute
small monthly dues. As his work became better known, voluntary

contributions began to arrive on a highly irregular basis. A man in
Australia sent a small check "because you touched my heart." An old
woman in New York sent $2. ("I won't go to the movies for two
weeks, dear Mr. Wiesenthal, but you'll make better use of my
money.") In a small American town a rabbi collected $18 each from
eighteen members of his congregation. (In the Hebrew language,
which expresses numbers by letters, eighteen is the equivalent of
chai, the Hebrew word for "life.") The largest contribution, a check
for $1000, came from an unknown Indian supporter in Calcutta.
Several Jewish communities in West Germany make occasional contributions. The Dutch have set up a special Wiesenthal Fund in the
Netherlands, where his work has drawn much attention. And there
are Friends of the Documentation Center in Brussels, Frankfurt,
Johannesburg, Milan, Munich, and Turin. All gifts are deposited in
a special bank account. Payments for expenses must be authorized
by four officials of a committee that oversees the work of the Documentation Center.

In recent years, the activities of the Center have expanded considerably. The monthly budget is now around $1500. Wiesenthal does
all the important work himself. He is assisted by two secretaries and
by a co-worker who speaks and corresponds in twelve languages,
takes care of the growing files, and handles the rented Xerox machine. The largest single monthly item is the telephone bill; Wiesenthal hates to be anyplace he cannot reach for a phone. He spends
about $150 a month on long-distance calls, usually because it is vital
for him to alert the authorities concerning the whereabouts of a
wanted Nazi before the man's friends alert him that Wiesenthal is
on his trail.

Wiesenthal has learned that information that is for sale is rarely
reliable. Sometimes tips are offered him on the whereabouts of
prominent Nazis hiding out somewhere. These offers come from
shady characters (former Nazis who pretend to have inside information) or from reputable lawyers and businessmen. Wiesenthal is
usually skeptical about the value of such information. Besides, he
says, the amounts asked are much too high for his budget. He still
has a number of unpaid helpers whose expenses he covers for important errands.

"There are four basic facts about our finances," Wiesenthal says.

"First, the Documentation Center has no regular income; I try to have enough money in the bank to keep us going for at least six months, and when the account gets low, I ask my friends to raise some funds. Second, no government and no governmental agency ever gave us a penny. Third, we get no money from Israel, where they spend large amounts on their own investigations of Nazi crimes, but we have friendly and helpful relations with their agencies. Fourth, we get no money from what some of my Nazi 'clients' call 'the Jewish capitalist international.'"

Wiesenthal's own needs are modest. He lives with his wife in a small apartment, sees few people outside his office, and spends most of his evenings at home answering his private correspondence and studying books and files on his favorite subject. He sometimes visits his only child, a married daughter living in Holland. He drives a small English Ford, doesn't drink, and smokes only when he is nervous. A few years ago he began to collect postage stamps in order to relax, but he turned even his hobby to use; stamped envelopes from the Nazi period gave him valuable clues. Once he trapped an SS man who denied having been in Poland at a certain time. Wiesenthal produced a stamped envelope, addressed to the man's family, on which the date was clearly visible. The man was arrested.

Although Wiesenthal feels that he has done much to arouse the public conscience in Germany and Austria, there is one group among whose members—with a few rare exceptions—he feels he can do little along this line. These are his "clients," the former SS men and rabid Party members. After many talks with such people, and years of study and observation, Wiesenthal has concluded that the great majority "either had no conscience to begin with or were able to stifle it completely. Such a man has got rid of his conscience as others get rid of their appendix. *'Befehl ist Befehl'*—'an order is an order.' The Führer commanded and he followed. The Germans have an expression for that kind of obeisance: *Kadavergehorsam,* the total obedience of the dead." The concept of *Befehlsnotstand*—"an order must be obeyed"—is often accepted as an ameliorating circumstance by juries in Germany and Austria. But these juries never demand proof that if a defendant had *refused* to carry out an order he would actually have risked his life. Such proof does not exist. Some men refused criminal orders and were sent to prison or to the front. Those who survived have a clear conscience today.

Three years ago Wiesenthal met Alfons Gorbach, the former Federal Chancellor of Austria, a Catholic who had spent many months at the Dachau concentration camp. Gorbach complained that Wiesenthal was "opening old wounds." "I'm not at all sure this is a good thing," the former Chancellor said. Wiesenthal admitted he was not sure himself. "Perhaps history will decide whether it was a good thing or not," he said. "But I believe it is necessary. Do you want your children and the children of your children to grow up and again become infected with theories of inferior races that must be exterminated like vermin! Don't you want them to become immunized by learning the truth? I believe the young people in Germany and Austria deserve a chance to live without a sense of guilt. The young people know that the older people failed them. Their teachers don't teach unpopular historical facts. Their parents prefer to keep quiet because they hope that in a while 'the whole thing will be forgotten.' But you know, *Herr Kanzler,* that the truth has a curious way of coming back at unsuitable moments. I often talk to young people, and I know that they are getting inquisitive. They've heard and read too much about these things. I feel they have a right to know."

Wiesenthal got his first insight into the mysteries of the SS mind soon after the war, when he obtained some letters SS men on duty in concentration camps had written home to their wives. He remembers a letter from an SS *Führer* who described matter-of-factly how his unit had been ordered to repair a landing strip in Uman, near Kiev in the Ukraine, where a Russian bomb had torn a large crater. The SS mathematicians figured out that the bodies of 1500 people would just fill a crater of that size, whereupon they methodically procured the building material by shooting 1500 Jewish men, women, and children, and throwing their dead bodies into the crater. The bodies were covered with earth, a steel mat was placed on top, and the landing strip was as good as new. All this was described unemotionally, with much technical detail. On the same page of the letter, the SS man inquired about the roses in his garden and promised his wife to try to find a Russian servant girl "who can cook and look after the children."

"He wrote as if reporting that the exterminators had cleaned their apartment while his wife was on her summer vacation," Wiesenthal says. "I've read another letter in which an SS man describes how they killed Jewish babies by throwing them against the wall, and then he goes on to ask whether his own baby got over the attack of the measles. These things are hard to understand. I remember the summer of 1941, when the SS arrived in Lwow. First, they fenced off part of the old town as a ghetto. Next, they pulled out the cobblestones, turning the streets into a quagmire. That was part of the systematic method of creating subhuman living conditions. On rainy days you couldn't cross the street without wading in mud up to your ankles. It was impossible to clean oneself. We must have looked like animals, or phantoms from a nether world. And on the worst days, SS *Führers* and army officers would arrive, with some women, in their big cars, and they would watch us and laugh and take photographs of the strange species of *Untermenschen*. They sent these pictures home, and everybody said 'Look at those Jews! The Führer is right—they aren't even human.' "

Like a surgeon who sees his patient for the first time when he is wheeled into the operating room, Wiesenthal often sees the men he has traced and brought to justice only during the final phase of *his* operation—in court, where he appears as a witness or as an interested spectator. He worked on the case of Adolf Eichmann for about sixteen years, and in the end he knew perhaps more about Eichmann than Eichmann liked to remember himself. But he first saw Eichmann at the opening of the trial in Jerusalem.

Sixteen years earlier, in 1945, when Wiesenthal began to collect material against the man primarily in charge of carrying out "the final solution of the Jewish question," Wiesenthal lived in a rented room at 40 Landstrasse in Linz, the home town of Adolf Eichmann. Just four houses away, at number 32, was the house in which Eichmann had spent his youth. Several times a day Wiesenthal had to pass the doorway through which Eichmann had so often walked, and Wiesenthal always had a slight dryness in his mouth and a constricted feeling in his throat. One day the American captain for whom Wiesenthal was then working told him they were going to search the Eichmann house and asked him to come along. Wiesenthal refused. "I couldn't touch the doorhandle," he says. He still feels strongly about physical contacts with his "clients." After the war, when he searched for SS criminals in various prisons and detention camps, he thinks he may have unknowingly shaken the hands of murderers, and the mere thought makes him uneasy.

Soon after the war, when Wiesenthal worked for various American agencies, he often accompanied American officers on their errands. On several occasions he had personally to arrest SS men accused of crimes. He noticed in their eyes the same expression he'd seen earlier in the eyes of Jews arrested by SS men. But there was an important difference: some former SS and Gestapo supermen went down on their knees and asked for mercy—something the Jews had not done. Wiesenthal had seen many people go to their deaths. Most were afraid; some were so terrified that they had to be supported by others. Some prayed; some cried. But they had never begged for their lives.

Not surprisingly, Wiesenthal is an object of much antipathy among former SS men, and his continued safety is a matter of frequent anxiety to his friends. He has often been threatened and has several times been attacked. Once, when a man burst into his office with a knife, Wiesenthal grabbed an ink bottle and hurled it; the noise alerted his aides, who came to Wiesenthal's rescue. Most would-be attackers use more devious methods, such as anonymous letters addressed *Dirty Jew Wiesenthal, Vienna.* Others specialize in anonymous telephone calls. For a while he received so many threats, mostly at night, that he asked the authorities to monitor his line. A man who had often called him from public telephones was arrested and sentenced to two months in prison.

Wiesenthal considers anonymous threats the hazards of a hazardous profession and takes a philosophical attitude about antagonists who are too cowardly to come forward. "My friends tell me 'Be careful!' " he says. "That's like telling a man to be careful when he boards an airplane. How much can you do for your own safety after you've fastened your seat belt? People who are afraid of planes shouldn't fly. If I worried too much about these things I couldn't function."

In September 1965 Wiesenthal received newspaper reports of a conference of the World Union of National Socialists (WUNS) in Southend, England, at which someone supposedly had put a price of $120,000 on Wiesenthal's head. The Austrian Police investigated the report and asked the British Embassy in Vienna for details. Earlier, a man working for the State Police who had infiltrated a secret conference of various neo-Nazi groups in Salzburg told his superiors that several middle-aged *Kameraden* had suggested to their younger comrades that they ought to "do something about Wiesenthal." For a while Wiesenthal's home and office were guarded by patrol cars and he was accompanied by a police bodyguard. At Wiesenthal's suggestion, the neo-Nazis were informed, through devious channels, that their plans were well known, and that was the end of it.

On another, more serious, occasion, in 1962, Wiesenthal arrived at the Vienna airport from abroad one morning and received a message telling him to call his home at once. He dialed the number. A friend answered the phone and asked him to wait at the airport; the friend would come for him. "No, everything is all right, Simon," the friend said, "but please do not come home."

When the friend arrived at the airport, he told Wiesenthal that at three o'clock that morning his wife had had an anonymous phone call. A woman's voice had said: "Mrs. Wiesenthal, if your husband won't stop raking up the past, my friends are going to get hold of your daughter and you will never see her alive again." A click, and the voice was gone. Mrs. Wiesenthal had collapsed after calling the friend, who had called the police and a doctor. Mrs. Wiesenthal was in bed with a mild heart attack, but she would be all right, said the friend, who had wanted to let Wiesenthal know that everything was under control so he wouldn't have a shock himself when he came home.

"When we drove up in front of the house, I noticed a plain-clothes man on the other side of the street," Wiesenthal says. "My wife was asleep. The doctor had given her a sedative. Our daughter was at home, and I took her in my arms and held her tight for a long time, and then I walked into my room, and sat down, with my face in my hands. I was miserable. For the first time in my life I was not sure whether I should go on—whether I had the right to go on. I don't mind taking a risk but I couldn't expose my family to danger. Besides, hadn't I done enough all these years? Was there any sense in continuing the search? No matter how many Nazis I caught, there would be many more left who would remain unpunished. I argued with myself for a long time, but in the end I knew how the argument would come out. It was no use, I *had* to go on. I remember I held my head in my hands, saying to myself, 'I cannot stop, I cannot stop.'"

Chapter 2

A PROFILE OF
SIMON WIESENTHAL *(Continued)*
Buczacz to Mauthausen

Simon Wiesenthal often says that in his work his worst problem is finding reliable witnesses who will testify accurately as to dates and places. In his own life, this difficulty began before he had heard of a concentration camp or a Nazi. He was born on December 31, 1908, "about half an hour before the end of the year," according to what his mother later told him. The midwife dutifully reported his birth to the registry office in the town of Buczacz, in what was then the easternmost part of the Austro-Hungarian Empire. In time he received his birth certificate, passport, and the many other documents that people in his part of the world always had to have to prove that they existed. When he reached eighteen, in 1926, Galicia had become part of independent Poland, and Wiesenthal registered with the Polish army authorities. He was then a university student, and as such was granted the usual deferment.

The following year, two policemen came to arrest him for trying to evade military service. Wiesenthal said that there must be a mistake, since he'd already registered and had been deferred. The policemen said there was no mistake, because they had proof that he had been born on January 1, 1909. He had not registered in 1927, as he should have, and now was liable for immediate induction. Wiesenthal discovered that after his birth, his mother's father had also registered his birth, but not as of December 31, 1908; he had put down January 1, 1909. His grandfather thought that half an hour would make no difference, and he wanted his grandchild to be the first name in the book for 1909, because that was supposed to bring luck. As it happened, it created considerable difficulty for Wiesenthal, who was told by the Polish authorities that all his personal documents might be proved invalid—that, in fact, he didn't exist at all—unless he was able to prove that he had been born, as he claimed, on December 31, 1908. A Polish magistrate told Wiesenthal he would have to produce two witnesses who would swear an affidavit as to his birth date.

"For the first time in my life I had to find two witnesses who would remember to the minute something that had happened almost twenty years earlier. I began to search and found two neighbors who had lived in the apartment next door to us in Buczacz. Fortunately, they *did* remember the particular night, since it had been New Year's Eve and there had been big excitement when the midwife reported that the Wiesenthal boy had arrived next door. One witness even remembered that the midwife had come in before the lights went out at midnight and people wished each other 'Happy New Year.' The other witness remembered that they'd opened a new bottle of vodka to drink to my health. *That* convinced the magistrate and settled the matter, and my birthday was legally recognized. But suppose it had not been New Year's Eve, but just an ordinary night, and there had been no party?"

In Buczacz, a town of 9000 people, there lived 6000 Jews. The 3,500,000 people of Galicia included 1,700,000 Ukrainians (also called Ruthenians), 1,000,000 Poles, and 800,000 Jews. The Poles and the Jews lived in the urban centers, the Ukrainians in the countryside. There was no love lost among the various groups.

Wiesenthal's father, a successful wholesale commodity dealer, traded in, among other things, sugar. As a boy, Simon loved to go to the warehouse and build houses and castles of white sugar cubes. Young Simon also inherited a propensity toward mysticism, still evident in his thought and speech, from his maternal grandmother, a deeply religious woman. She liked to take little Simon on her visits to famous *wunder* rabbis, whom she asked to bless the child. Wiesenthal still remembers the journey to the famous rabbi of

Czortkov, who lived in a large, rambling farmhouse surrounded by the houses of his disciples. Wiesenthal has no recollection of the pious man, but he will never forget a small window in the attic of the house, behind which he saw the face of a man. His grandmother told Simon that this was "the silent one." One day, it seemed, this man had wound up an argument with his wife by exclaiming "You should burn!" That night his house burned down, and the wife died in the flames. The guilt-stricken man went to see the rabbi, who ruled that he must never speak a word as long as he lived and must pray for forgiveness. Twice a day some food was brought to "the silent one" in his small attic room. For years Simon felt a shiver run down his spine when he thought of the silent sinner behind the dark window.

When Simon was six years old, the First World War broke out. His father, a reserve officer in the Austrian army, joined his unit, and, like many other fathers, never came back from the war. He was killed in action in 1915. That was the year when the Czar's Cossacks arrived in Buczacz on their small, fast horses. The frightened Jewish inhabitants knew what to expect. Many had come from Russia, where pogroms were begun whenever there were internal difficulties and the citizens' attention could be diverted by letting them beat up the Jews and plunder their stores. Many Jews escaped to the West, first to Galicia, later to Germany, finally to Western Europe and to America.

Late in 1915, Wiesenthal's mother took Simon and his younger brother to Vienna, still the capital of the Habsburg monarchy, where he went to public school. In 1917, the Russians retreated from Galicia, and many Jews returned, among them the Wiesenthals. After the Armistice, for three months Eastern Galicia became the independent Western Ukrainian Republic. Then the Polish armies moved in, and the people of Buczacz became Polish citizens. The Polish regime lasted almost two years, until the Polish-Bolshevik war began in 1920. For the inhabitants of Buczacz the unending wars meant a continuous coming and going of military hordes, and constant terror.

"We would get up in the morning without knowing what regime was in power," Wiesenthal remembers. "I was going to the local *Gymnasium*. When we were asked who was now in power we had to look at the picture on the wall above the teacher's table. One week there was a Bolshevik leader, the next there was a Ukrainian, and then it was the Polish Marshal Pilsudski. The Bolsheviks rounded up all *bourgeois* and made them pay ransom. My mother and other Jewish women were ordered to clean the local gymnastics hall, which the Russians had turned into a stable."

The Bolshevik troops were bad, but the Ukrainian cavalry bands were worse. They rode through the town on their small horses like the Cossacks, plundering, raping, and killing. Once they gave the Jews of Buczacz a three-hour ultimatum. They would have to have three hundred liters of *schnapps* by five in the afternoon or they would burn down the Jewish houses. Wiesenthal remembers vividly how the people scurried around trying to collect the liquor. That night the Ukrainians were dead drunk, prowling the streets. The people of Buczacz locked their doors and prayed. After a day or so some people were short of food, but the women were afraid to venture out. Simon's mother sent the twelve-year-old boy across the street to borrow a piece of yeast from a neighbor so she could bake bread. As Simon ran across the street, a Ukrainian came after him on his horse and playfully slashed his thigh with his saber. The boy collapsed and had to be carried back into his mother's house. A doctor was summoned. He reached the house by walking through cellars and back yards, and stitched up the wound. Wiesenthal still has a deep scar running across the upper part of his thigh.

At the *Gymnasium* Wiesenthal fell in love with a pretty, dark-blonde Jewish classmate named Cyla Müller. They were still teenagers, but it was soon taken for granted in town that Simon and Cyla would one day be married. In 1925 Wiesenthal's mother remarried, and the family moved to Dolina, a town in the Carpathian Mountains, where his stepfather owned a tile factory. Simon always spent his vacations there. He loved the countryside, and he liked to ride the horses there and hike through the woods. He had decided to become an architect. After graduating from the *Gymnasium* he tried to get into the Technical University at Lwow, but was rejected since there was a very limited quota for Jewish students.

Wiesenthal spent the next four years in Prague, where he studied at the Czech Technical University and lived some of the happiest days of his life. He was very popular with his fellow students as a stimulating polemicist at student meetings and as an amusing master of ceremonies at social functions. He had an excellent memory for good stories and a talent for mimicry and satire. His brand of humor was particularly liked by his non-Jewish friends, who loved the deeper meaning and the hidden irony in his stories. On his way home for the Christmas and Easter vacations, he would sit up in the train all night long with his friends telling stories; when he arrived home, he was so hoarse he couldn't speak.

In 1936, he married Cyla Müller and opened his own architectural office, specializing in handsome residences. This pleasant interlude lasted until August 1939, when Germany and Russia signed their "nonaggression" pact and agreed to partition Poland between them. On September 1 the Germans started their *blitzkrieg* invasion from the west, and two weeks later the Red Army invaded Poland from the east. By the middle of September, the Red Army was in Lwow, and again Wiesenthal found himself "liberated," as he had been earlier by Russians, Ukrainians, and Poles. The latest liberators had brought along the NKVD, their security police, who went around arresting Jewish "bourgeois" merchants and factory owners, as well as members of the intelligentsia—doctors, lawyers, and teachers. Wiesenthal's stepfather was taken to a Soviet prison, where he soon died. Wiesenthal's mother came to live with him and his wife. His stepbrother, a merchant in Stanislau, was arrested (and later shot by the Russians in 1941 when they retreated before the advancing German armies). The Russians issued many "bourgeois" Jews so-called Paragraph 11 passports, which made them under-privileged, second-class citizens, not permitted to live in larger cities or within a hundred kilometers of any border. They lost good jobs and had their bank accounts confiscated. Proving himself a resource-ful man under pressure, Wiesenthal bribed an NKVD commissar and obtained regular passports for himself, his wife, and his mother. A few months later, all Jews with "Paragraph 11" passports were deported to Siberia, where many died. The Wiesenthals managed to stay in Lwow, but Wiesenthal's days as an independent architect were over. He was glad to find a badly paid job as a mechanic in a factory that produced bedsprings.

Twenty-two months after the German-Russian "nonaggression" pact, on June 22, 1941, Hitler invaded the Soviet Union. Eight days later, the last Red Army units left Lwow and the first German uniforms were seen in the streets of the city. They were worn by Ukrainian auxiliary troops—men who had earlier fled from the Soviet Union to Germany and had been trained there. They celebrated their return to Lwow by starting a pogrom that lasted three days and three nights. When the massacre was over, 6000 Jews had been killed.

On the afternoon of Sunday, July 6, 1941, Wiesenthal was hiding in the cellar of his house, playing chess with a Jewish friend named Gross. At four o'clock, an auxiliary Ukrainian policeman who spoke Yiddish came to arrest them and took them to Brigidki Prison. About forty Jewish lawyers, doctors, teachers, and engineers stood in the courtyard. In the center of the courtyard was a large table covered with vodka bottles, sausage, *zakusky* (Polish *hors d'oeuvres*), guns, and ammunition.

The Jews were ordered to form a long row, face the wall, and cross their arms behind their necks. Next to each man stood an empty wooden crate. A Ukrainian began to shoot. He began at the left end of the long row and shot each man in the neck. After a couple of shots he would step back to the table and have a swig of vodka and some *zakusky,* while another man handed him another gun. Two Ukrainians threw each body into a wooden crate and took the crate away. The shots and the shouts of the dying men were getting closer to Wiesenthal. He remembers that he stood looking at the gray wall without really seeing it. Suddenly he heard the sound of church bells, and a Ukrainian voice shouted "Enough! Evening mass!"

The shooting stopped. The survivors stood trembling, looking at each other incredulously. There were about twenty Jews left. They were led to two large cells where a Ukrainian took away each man's belt and shoelaces. The Jews lay down on bunks and on the floor. Wiesenthal thought of the dead in the crates and almost envied them.

He finally dozed off. Next, he remembers staring into the beam of a flashlight and hearing a Polish voice: "Mr. Wiesenthal, what are *you* doing here?" Wiesenthal recognized one of his former construction foremen, a man named Bodnar. He wore a civilian suit and the armband of a Ukrainian auxiliary policeman. "I've got to get you out of here tonight," Bodnar said into Wiesenthal's ear. "You know what they'll do tomorrow morning."

Wiesenthal asked him also to help his friend Gross, who had an old mother to look after. Bodnar had an idea. He would tell the Ukrainians that he'd discovered "two Russian spies" among the Jews. They would be beaten, would admit everything and sign a statement, and then Bodnar would say he was taking them to the Ukrainian commissar in Academy Street. Wiesenthal and Gross were badly beaten—Wiesenthal lost two front teeth that night—but, after a series of narrow escapes, they reached home the next morning.

Wiesenthal's period of relative freedom didn't last long. A few weeks later the Germans decreed that all Jews must give up their apartments and move into living quarters in a newly created ghetto in the old part of the city. One day an SS man came into the Wiesenthals' apartment with a Polish prostitute. He asked her whether she liked the place. She said, "Yes . . . it will do." An hour later the Wiesenthals were out, leaving everything behind. After a few months in the ghetto, Wiesenthal and his wife were taken to the nearby Janowska concentration camp, while his old mother stayed in the ghetto.

Late in 1941, Wiesenthal and his wife were sent from the concentration camp to a special forced-labor camp that served the OAW, the Ostbahn (Eastern Railroad) Repair Works. The German offensive against the Soviet Union was in full swing, and the vital supply line through Poland had to be kept open. Mrs. Wiesenthal was sent to the locomotive workshop, where she developed skill in polishing brass and nickel. Wiesenthal was ordered to paint swastika-and-eagle shields on captured Russian locomotives. Later he was promoted to sign-painter, a respected profession in the regime of a former sign-painter.

One very cold day, Wiesenthal was painting outside when his top boss, Heinrich Guenthert, walked by. Wiesenthal had no gloves on, and his hands were blue with the cold. Guenthert stopped to talk, and asked him where he'd gone to school. Wiesenthal, knowing that Jewish members of the intelligentsia were given priority on the extermination lists, told Guenthert that he'd gone to a trade school. A

Pole standing nearby said it wasn't true, and that Wiesenthal was an architect. Guenthert asked Wiesenthal why he had lied; didn't he know that liars wound up in the hands of the Gestapo? Wiesenthal admitted the truth. Guenthert, who seemed a decent sort, was impressed. From now on, he said, Wiesenthal would work inside as a technician and draftsman.

Until early in 1942 living conditions in Lwow were bearable, but after Hitler's adoption of "The Final Solution of The Jewish Question" at Wannsee * in early 1942, and after the assassination of Gestapo Chief Reinhard Heydrich in Lidice, Czechoslovakia, on May 28, 1942, a wave of terror swept over Nazi-occupied Europe. In August, thousands of Jews were sent from the Lwow railroad station to the death camps that had by now been set up in Poland. Wiesenthal looked on helplessly on one occasion as the SS crammed old Jewish women in freight cars, one hundred women to a car. They let the cars stand for three days in the blazing August sun while the women begged for water. One of them was his sixty-three-year-old mother. Wiesenthal never saw her again. He later learned that she had died at Belzec. His wife's mother was soon afterward shot by a Ukrainian policeman on the staircase of her home.

By September 1942, most members of both their families were dead. Wiesenthal didn't know about Hitler's plan for the "Final Solution," but he had no doubt that they would all die sooner or later. He had no hope for himself but wanted to save his wife, who, he thought, because she was blonde, might be able to pass for a Pole. Wiesenthal had friends among members of a Polish underground cell inside the Repair Works. Members of the cell planned to blow up the Lwow railroad junction, which would create grave complications for the German war machine, and Wiesenthal thought he might be useful in this project. As a technician, he had relative freedom and was permitted to walk all over the yards. He had set up his office in a small wooden hut, where he began secretly to draw maps of the junction, showing all of its potentially vulnerable points. Wiesenthal spoke to the Polish underground people about his wife. One night a man named Zielinski smuggled her out of the Repair Works and took her to his apartment. Then Szczepanski, an archi-

* See Appendix.

tect from Lublin whose construction firm had worked on several building projects inside the yards, agreed to conceal Wiesenthal's wife as his "sister" in his house in Lublin, where she would take care of his children. But after she had spent a few months in the house somebody denounced her to the Germans. One day she was warned that Gestapo men were on their way to the house. She got away in time returning to Lwow, and one night a Polish underground friend told Wiesenthal that his wife was waiting outside the barbed-wire fence. Wiesenthal hurried to the secluded spot where she stood and seized her hands through the fence. She told him quickly that she was staying for two nights with the old woman who cleaned the toilets at the railroad station, but then she would have to leave. Wiesenthal told her to come back the next night; by then he would have thought of something.

In the morning, Wiesenthal approached his underground friends and proposed a deal. He would give them all the maps he'd secretly drawn if they in turn would give his wife false papers, a job, and a place to live. The underground members said it was a deal. That night Wiesenthal met his wife again at the barbed-wire fence and told her to take the first morning train to Warsaw, where a man would be waiting for her. She was to become "Irene Kowalska" and would be given a job and a place to stay. (Mrs. Wiesenthal lived in a Warsaw apartment with the wife of the Polish poet Jerzy Lec; neither she nor Mrs. Lec discovered that the other was Jewish.) Wiesenthal told his wife that they would keep in touch through a contact named Szatkowski in Lwow. He kissed her hands through the barbed wire fence, and waited till the sound of her footsteps died away.

Wiesenthal remembers the Ostbahn Repair Works as an island of sanity in a sea of madness. The fifty German officials under Heinrich Guenthert behaved correctly toward both Poles and Jews. Wiesenthal's immediate superior, *Oberinspektor* Adolf Kohlrautz, was, like Guenthert, an exceptionally decent man. Both of them, Wiesenthal discovered, were secretly anti-Nazi. Kohlrautz went so far as to allow Wiesenthal to hide two pistols, which he had obtained by clandestine means, in Kohlrautz's desk. Among the Poles, many who pretended to be willing collaborators were ardent underground members.

April 20, 1943, Hitler's fifty-fourth birthday, was sunny, with a touch of spring in the air. Wiesenthal had been up since dawn painting Hitler posters and swastikas for the big SS celebration at the Repair Works. He and two Jewish helpers were finishing a big sign, WIR LIEBEN UNSEREN FÜHRER (We Love Our Führer), when they were accosted by one *Unterscharführer* Dyga, who, because he was from Silesia and had a Polish-sounding name, tried to prove by his brutality that he was more German than a German. He told the three men to come along with him. They put down their brushes and stepped out into the sunshine. *Oberinspektor* Kohlrautz looked at Wiesenthal unhappily, raising his shoulders in a gesture of frustration. Apparently he'd tried to stop the SS man and had failed. Dyga escorted them to the concentration camp two miles away. People in the street hardly looked at them. Wiesenthal wondered whether this was his last walk through the city.

At the concentration camp, many SS guards were drunk. There was plenty of free *Schnapps* and they wanted to forget the bad news from the front. It was a few months after Stalingrad and the SS men were afraid they might soon be sent to the East. Dyga rounded up more Jewish prisoners from sheds and workshops, took the whole group to a spot known as *der Schlauch* (the hose), and told them to wait. Now Wiesenthal knew what was going to happen.

The hose was a six-or-seven-foot-wide corridor between two barbed-wire fences that separated the inner camp from the rest of the installation. At the end of the hose was the sandpit where executions took place. The hose was synonymous with death; no prisoner who walked through the hose had ever come back. Some twenty men and a few women were waiting inside the hose. Most of them Wiesenthal recognized as professors, lawyers, teachers, doctors—the last of the camp intelligentsia. They waited in silence. No one spoke; no one asked "why?" There was no "why?" Only "because." The SS men were going to shoot a few Jews to celebrate the Führer's birthday. A half-dozen SS men appeared, led by one *Unterscharführer* Kauzer, who carried a submachine gun. The prisoners were told to march through the hose, two abreast.

Wiesenthal remembers how they walked. "Each person was walking all by himself. Each of us was alone with himself, with his thoughts. Each was an island of solitude. That was our privilege and our strength."

A heavy April shower broke as they reached the sandpit, which was six feet deep and perhaps 1500 feet long. A few naked bodies from earlier executions were lying there. After one section of the pit was filled, the SS men would throw sand on top of the dead bodies and proceed to the next section. A large truck stood near the pit, its engine running. The Jews were told to take off all their clothes, fold them in neat heaps, and put the clothes on the truck. Later the clothes and shoes of the Jews would be distributed among the poor in Germany by the benevolent ladies of the NS *Volkswohlfahrt*, the National-Socialist welfare organization. The poor would praise the Führer and put on the clothes and the shoes.

The truck drove off. Wiesenthal counted thirty-eight men and six women. They were told to form a single row and step up to the rim of the sandpit. Out of the corner of his eye, Wiesenthal saw SS man Kauzer raise his gun. The rain was stronger now, but not strong enough to drown out the shouts of the dying. Mechanically, Wiesenthal counted the shots: One, two, three, four, five. There was a pause. One man had fallen on the ground instead of into the pit. An SS man stepped up and kicked the body into the pit. Six, seven, eight, nine.

Wiesenthal didn't want to count any longer. From somewhere came the shrill sound of a whistle, and a voice that seemed to reach through time and space.

"Wie–sen–thal!"

Once more, from nearby: "Wiesenthal!!" This time he automatically snapped to attention, heard himself say "Here!" He was told to turn around. Half-blinded by the rain, Wiesenthal saw the face of another SS man, *Rottenführer* Koller, who told him to follow. Kauzer, the executioner, stared at them, puzzled: he had come here to shoot forty-four people, not forty-three. Koller said that he was taking Wiesenthal back and told Kauzer to carry on.

"I staggered like a drunk," Wiesenthal remembers. "Koller slapped my face twice, and that brought me back to earth. I was walking *back* through the hose, naked. Behind me, the sounds of the shooting resumed, but they were over long before I had reached the camp."

The truck with forty-four heaps of clothing stood in front of the clothing shed. Wiesenthal was told to get his clothes and shoes "without disturbing the other heaps." Then he was escorted back through the city to the Repair Works, where Koller delivered him to *Oberinspektor* Kohlrautz. "Here is your man," Koller said, staring suspiciously at Kohlrautz.

"Good," said Kohlrautz. "We need Wiesenthal. These signs must be finished for the afternoon celebration. We need another big poster, with a swastika, white letters, a red background, and the words WIR DANKEN UNSEREM FÜHRER [We thank our Führer]."

Koller left and Wiesenthal was alone with Kohlrautz. For a while he was unable to speak. Kohlrautz told him that he'd telephoned to the camp commander and urgently asked to get Wiesenthal back.

"I'm glad it wasn't too late, Wiesenthal." He smiled. "Come to think of it, it isn't only the Führer's birthday. It's yours too."

Wiesenthal nowadays often cites the examples of Guenthert and Kohlrautz to bear out his argument against collective German guilt. Guenthert was a member of the Nazi Party; he was also a thoughtful man who had endless troubles with the SS because he refused to treat the forced laborers as subhuman. Once Guenthert dismissed two members of his staff because they maltreated Poles and Jews. Guenthert is now an official of the West German Federal Railroads in Karlsruhe, and he and Wiesenthal often meet and talk about the bad old days. In December 1965 Wiesenthal invited his friend to the marriage of his only daughter. "When a man like Simon Wiesenthal, after all that happened, invites a German to join his family, I feel honored," Guenthert has said.

Guenthert remembered that he'd noticed Wiesenthal among the other prisoners "because he always walked with his head up and looked me straight in the eye. The SS men said that Wiesenthal was impertinent. I didn't argue with them, but I admit that I was impressed by the man's erect bearing. He had a thoughtful expression in his eyes, as though he knew that we Germans might one day have to account for all this."

Kohlrautz, too, was a Nazi, but he shared the general manager's contempt for the SS. Between Kohlrautz and Wiesenthal there was a silent mutual bond. It seemed that Kohlrautz respected both Wiesenthal's quiet dignity and his technical ability, and in fact Kohlrautz often turned in, under his own name, technical drawings that had been made by Wiesenthal. He showed his gratitude by pretending not to know that Wiesenthal had concealed the guns in his desk drawer. Kohlrautz often told Wiesenthal what he'd heard over the forbidden BBC news broadcasts and he furtively smuggled food to Wiesenthal's old mother in the ghetto. The two men often had political discussions in Kohlrautz' private office when they were alone. Once Kohlrautz said: "I know about the crimes in the concentration camps. Some day we Germans will have to account for them."

After the war, Wiesenthal found out that early in 1944 Kohlrautz had been transferred to the front. He was killed during the battle of Berlin.

"Too many decent Germans died because they were ordered to fight Hitler's battles and didn't try to evade what they considered their duty," Wiesenthal says. "And too many SS men and Party people survived because they were cowards. The SS fought a safe war in the concentration camps against defenseless men, women, and children."

Late in September 1943 orders were given that the Jewish prisoners who had previously lived at the Repair Works would be sent under guard nightly to the nearby concentration camp, and Wiesenthal decided there would be no next time for him. It was time for him to attempt his escape. Kohlrautz often permitted him to go into town to buy drafting supplies. Wiesenthal was accompanied on his errands by a Ukrainian policeman. If he got rid of the policeman, the rest would be easy. A Polish underground friend, Roman Uscienski, had promised to let him stay at his apartment for a few days. And a Polish girl who worked at the Repair Works said he could hide at her parents' small house in the nearby village of Kulparkow.

That morning—Wiesenthal remembers the date well—October 2, 1943—he asked Kohlrautz for a pass to do some shopping in town. "Kohlrautz looked at me; he knew what I was going to do. He was a swell guy. Some weeks earlier he had asked me, 'Wiesenthal, what are you waiting for?'" Now he wrote passes for me and my friend

Arthur Scheiman, a former circus director. Then Kohlrautz left the office, saying he was going out to find a policeman. I quickly took out the two guns from his desk drawer. Kohlrautz came back with a stupid-looking Ukrainian who had come to Lwow recently and didn't know the city. At the door I turned and looked back, and Kohlrautz lifted his right hand, as if saying good-bye."

Wiesenthal and Scheiman went to a stationery store that had a front and a back entrance, and there they got rid of the policeman. Next they reached Uscienski's apartment, where they celebrated their escape. Scheiman joined his wife, a Ukrainian woman who would conceal him, and Wiesenthal reached Kulparkow, where he spent a month in the attic of the girl's house. Once in a while she came to see him. She said that Scheiman's wife worked as a seamstress and that he had to hide all day long in her clothes closet and listen to the noisily gossiping women. It was nice and quiet in the attic, but one night the girl's mother came up in great excitement. The SS had liquidated the concentration camp, shooting most of the prisoners, but a few had got away, and now the Germans were searching the countryside. Wiesenthal, she said, would have to leave. He got out of the house and decided to try to reach Scheiman.

"The next eight days were almost as bad as the concentration camp," Wiesenthal remembers. "Scheiman and I spent our days squatting on low stools in the left half of a large closet in his house. The other half remained open, filled with clothes. The police twice came into the room, but when they saw the open closet they went away again. The air was sticky in there and we were afraid to cough, and a couple of yards away Mrs. Scheiman's customers were having fittings."

After a week they moved to the apartment of friends who lived on the ground floor of an old house. The floor consisted of sand covered with boards. They removed three boards and dug out the sand, which created enough space for two reclining people and their weapons and papers. In the latter category were a diary Wiesenthal had kept and a list of SS guards and their crimes that he'd compiled, believing that one day it might be useful. The house was often searched, but Wiesenthal and Scheiman were always warned in time and disappeared into their "graves." A Polish friend would put back the boards and push a heavy table on top.

On the evening of June 13, 1944, an alarm was sounded in the street. A German soldier had been shot. SS men and Polish plainclothes men were conducting a search for concealed weapons. Wiesenthal was in his "grave," feeling rather unconcerned, when he heard heavy boots in the room. Suddenly the steps stopped, and the next moment the boards above him disappeared. Two Polish detectives fell on him, pulled him out and pushed him against the wall, while an SS man seized his diary and the list of the SS men. He was taken to the police post in Smolki Square. When he arrived there, he still had his pistol, but fortunately for him it was found by one of the Polish detectives, who stole it, presumably to sell on the black market. If a German had found the gun, he would have shot Wiesenthal at once.

From Smolki Square, Wiesenthal was taken back to the concentration camp. Only a few Jews had survived: tailors, shoemakers, plumbers—artisans the SS still needed for a while. Wiesenthal knew that after reading his diary and his list of SS torturers with specific details, the Gestapo would have enough evidence to hang him ten times.

On the evening of June 15, two men from the Gestapo jail came for him. One was *Oberscharführer* Oskar Waltke, perhaps the most feared man in Lwow. He was a heavy-set man with cold gray eyes and reddish-blond hair. He addressed prisoners as *Kindchen*—"my little child"—with a sneering smile. Waltke, a cold, mechanical sadist, was in charge of the Gestapo's Jewish Affairs Section in Lwow. His specialty was to make Jews with false Polish papers confess that they were Jews. He tortured his victims until they made the admission and then he sent them to be shot. He also tortured many Gentiles until they admitted to being Jews just to get it over with. Waltke's name had been on Wiesenthal's private list, which Waltke must have studied with great interest. Wiesenthal knew that Waltke wouldn't simply have him shot. He would first submit him to his very special treatment. As Wiesenthal was led into the dark courtyard where the truck from the Gestapo prison stood waiting, he took out a small razor blade that he'd kept concealed in his cuff for such a moment.

"Get in, *Kindchen*, quick!" Waltke said.

With two fast movements, Wiesenthal cut both wrists. He got on the truck and lost consciousness. When he came to, he was in a cell of the Gestapo prison hospital, which he shared with a German SS man and a Ukrainian—deserters. An SS doctor told Wiesenthal he had the distinction of being the first Jew ever treated in the prison hospital. Herr SS *Oberscharführer* Waltke had given special orders to speed up Wiesenthal's recovery with a special diet of strong soups, liver, and vegetables, so that he could soon interrogate him. Waltke came in a few days later to look at his protégé.

"That was not necessary, *Kindchen*," he said. "We are not monsters. Now get well so you and I can have a heart-to-heart talk."

The following night, after his two cellmates were fast asleep, Wiesenthal made another suicide attempt, this time by trying to throw his belt around a bar of the high cell window so he could hang himself. But his bandaged wrists were numb, and when he stepped up on the toilet seat to put the belt around his neck, he got dizzy and fell down. His cellmates woke up and called the guards. Wiesenthal was tied into his bunk. He gave up trying to kill himself. On July 16 he was told he would be taken to Waltke the next morning at nine o'clock.

He couldn't sleep all night long. There was the sound of heavy guns, and of planes in the sky. His cellmates said that the Russians were getting near. At dawn the cell door was opened and all prisoners were told to get into the courtyard. Many prisoners stood there in a row. In the middle of the courtyard was a long table with stacks of files. Behind the table with Waltke, Wiesenthal saw an SS man named Engels, who sat with crossed feet, whipping his right leg with a riding crop. He would take up a file, a name would be called out, a prisoner would step in front of the table; Engels would look briefly at the file, but hardly at the prisoner. Then he would say something to Waltke. Still whipping his leg, Engels would point his thumb to the right. The group of people on the right side got larger: Russians, Ukrainians, Poles, and Kalmucks who were sentenced to death.

When Wiesenthal's name was called out, Waltke said to Engels: "That's *him*." Engels gave Wiesenthal an interested glance and said "Aha!" before his thumb dispatched him to the group on the right side.

"We were probably going to be buried in a large mass grave,"

Wiesenthal remembers. "I looked at the others the way some people on an airplane look at their fellow travelers. If there should be a crash, they are thinking, these will be one's companions in death. On the other side of the courtyard I saw a group of Jews. I wished I could be buried with *them,* not with the Poles and Ukrainians, but how could I get there? Suddenly there was a roar in the sky above us, and an explosion shook the courtyard. From Sapieha Street a cloud of fire and smoke went up into the air. The files from the tables were scattered all over the courtyard, and there was terrific confusion. I quickly ran across the courtyard and joined the Jews. A minute later two SS men put us on a truck and brought us back to the Janowska concentration camp."

They were pushed into a concrete pillbox. After a few hours, the Jews were brought before SS *Hauptsturmführer* Friedrich Warzok, the camp commander, a squarely built man with reddish cheeks and cold eyes. He walked past the prisoners and stopped in front of Wiesenthal, whom he greeted as "one of my old guests." He wanted to know how Wiesenthal had escaped. Wiesenthal told Warzok a slightly changed version of the truth, so he wouldn't implicate his friend Kohlrautz. Warzok became quite genial. He told Wiesenthal to come with him, and gave brief orders to shoot the other Jews. At the *Kommandantur,* Warzok introduced Wiesenthal to the other SS man as "the lost son who has come back."

"You thought I would have you shot, like the others, didn't you?" he asked Wiesenthal. "Here people die when *I* want them to die. Back to your old barracks. No work, and double food rations for you."

Wiesenthal walked through the camp, unable to comprehend anything. Warzok, who was responsible for the death of at least seventy thousand people, had let him live, with double food rations. Nothing made sense any longer. At the barracks there were thirty-four men and women left—thirty-four out of the 149,000 Jews of Lwow. After threatening to have them shot, Warzok surprisingly told the prisoners that SS *Brigadeführer* Katzmann had decided to let them live. They were going to leave Lwow together, the prisoners and their guards. They were marched through the city, which was under heavy artillery fire. At the railway station, they were pushed into a freight car already crammed with Poles. Someone said that the SS would gas them in the car, but when the door was opened once more and an SS man named Blum put in a small black dog and a cage with a canary in it and threatened to shoot them all if anything happened to the animals, Wiesenthal knew they would not be gassed. The SS men loved their animals.

The next morning they arrived in the city of Przemysl, where Warzok informed them that he had sold his prisoners, as "non-German forced laborers," to the Organization Todt—the state-controlled company that built fortifications and the like. He told them to forget that they had been in the concentration camp and to forget that they were Jews. Anyone who talked about what had previously happened would be shot, he said. The evacuation would continue toward the west. The Jews would get the same food, *Schnapps*, and cigarette rations as the SS guards.

"Now we understood why Warzok had spared us," Wiesenthal says. "As long as the SS had someone to *guard*, they might get out of front-line duty. We thirty-four Jews became the life insurance for almost two hundred SS men. We were all going to be a happy family. Warzok said we would try to reach the woods of Slovakia, where we would hide until the war was over."

In the town of Dobromil there was no more railroad, and they started to march. The highway was crowded with civilians running away from the Russians, and in the opposite direction came columns of apathetic German soldiers, marching toward the front. When a convoy of *Volksdeutsche* (Germans who had lived in Poland) tried to overtake them, Warzok stopped the convoy of horse-drawn vehicles and requisitioned thirty of them. The wretched *Volksdeutsche* were permitted to keep ten vehicles. Now on each wagon sat one Jewish "laborer" and a half-dozen SS men "guarding" him. As they reached the last bridge leading across the San River in Poland, there was mounting confusion. The Russians were rumored to be close, and ahead of Warzok's convoy was a Wehrmacht column, blocking all traffic. If the troops crossed the bridge first, the SS might be trapped.

Warzok knew what would happen to him if he fell into the hands of the Soviets. He drove up to the head of the *Wehrmacht* column, pointed his gun at the major in charge, while another SS man covered the other officers with his submachine gun. Warzok ordered his SS men to pass the *Wehrmacht* column. As they did so Wiesenthal saw the German major looking pale and furious while Warzok kept his gun pointed at him. On the western side of the bridge, Warzok ordered some German army engineers to blow up the heavily dynamited structure. The SS men were safe, but the *Wehrmacht* column was captured by the Soviets. (Wiesenthal later described this experience to several ex-*Wehrmacht* officers. They had at first refused to help him in his investigation of SS men because, they said, that would violate "the spirit of comradeship" [*Kameradschaftsgeist*]. "After they heard the story, they usually helped me," Wiesenthal has said drily.)

In Grybow, a Polish city, Warzok ordered Wiesenthal to paint a large sign reading SS BAUSTAB VENUS. It was put up in the middle of a large field, surrounded by the vehicles and the horses. This was the headquarters of the nonexistent "SS Construction Staff Venus." Long columns of dejected-looking German soldiers marched by, saw the sign, and obviously wondered what the people of Baustab Venus were going to construct. So did the people of Baustab Venus. After a while they moved farther west again. There was little to eat, and small groups of Jews and SS men were sent out into the countryside to steal food. In the village of Chelmiec, Warzok's men surrounded a church during mass, arrested all men, women, and children, and brought them back. Wiesenthal understood: Warzok needed a more realistic balance between prisoners and guards. In the town of Neu-Sandec, Warzok took Wiesenthal out into the countryside and asked him to survey the terrain; they were going to build tank barriers.

"I thought Warzok had gone mad. There was a steep, narrow dirt road leading up a hill, where it ended. The engineer in me became alive. I told Warzok that the road led nowhere. What was the sense of building antitank defenses? He slapped his gun holster and shouted, 'Did I ask you for your military opinion?' And then I understood. For a while we built defenses against tanks that would never come. Then the Russians came closer, and we moved again, this time to the Plaszow concentration camp near Cracow, and there two of Warzok's SS men, Dyga and Wurz, took most of the Jews to the nearby woods and shot them, in another display of Warzok's brotherly love. He is still around somewhere, and I hope I'll find him."

On October 15, 1944, several thousand inmates of the Plaszow camp were moved to the Grossrosen concentration camp, near Breslau (now Wroclaw, Poland). There were about six thousand Polish and Jewish prisoners in Grossrosen. Wiesenthal heard rumors about the battle of Warsaw. He had tried unsuccessfully to get a message through to his wife there. He didn't know then that his wife had received a message from Lwow in August 1944: "Wiesenthal was arrested by Gestapo man Waltke, cut his wrists, and is dead."

One day a group of Poles from Warsaw were brought to the Grossrosen camp. It was shortly after the Warsaw uprising. One of the men was said to be from Topiel Street. Wiesenthal's wife had lived at 5 Topiel Street. He talked to the man and cautiously inquired about the people in Topiel Street. Had the Pole by any chance known a certain "Irena Kowalska" at Number 5? Wiesenthal had learned not to trust his fellow men, even in the concentration camp. He didn't tell the Pole that "Kowalska" was his wife.

The Pole said he remembered her well; he himself had lived at Number 7, next door. "My friend, *no* one in Topiel Street survived," he said. "The Germans surrounded one house after another with flame throwers, and afterwards they blew up what was left of the houses. There is no hope, believe me. Topiel Street is one large mass grave."

Early in January 1945 the Red Army was near Grossrosen. The prisoners marched all the way to Chemnitz (now Karl-Marx-Stadt in East Germany), from there across fields and through woods to Weimar, and to the nearby Buchenwald concentration camp. It was terribly cold and there was much snow. Thousands of prisoners died, and many who fell exhausted were shot by SS guards. Wiesenthal didn't stay long in Buchenwald. On February 3, 1945, 3000 prisoners were put on trucks, 140 people on each open truck. They stood on the trucks for hours and days; many were dying of hunger and thirst.

"The dead stood quietly among the living," Wiesenthal remembers. "We would throw them out of the trucks, but the civilian population protested, and the SS men warned us we would be shot if we threw the bodies out along the highway. We placed the stiff bodies on the floor of the truck, like wooden boards, and sat on our dead comrades."

On February 7, the convoy from Buchenwald arrived at the railroad station at Mauthausen in Upper Austria. There was a rollcall. Of the 3000 people who had left Buchenwald three weeks earlier, 1200 were still alive; 180 of these died on the walk from the station to the Mauthausen concentration camp, just four miles away.

Wiesenthal well remembers the terribly cold, clear night, with the grating sound of frozen snow underfoot. Each step was a major effort. He happened to be walking next to a Prince Radziwill, one of whose relatives later married the sister of Mrs. John F. Kennedy. Their arms were linked and they tried to support each other, but at last they couldn't go on and fell down in the snow. Wiesenthal heard a voice shout "Are you alive?" and then there was a shot, but the SS guard's hands must have been cold, for the bullet hit the snow between him and Radziwill. The column moved on in the darkness, and Wiesenthal and Radziwill just lay there. After a while it became comfortable and almost cozily warm in the snow. Wiesenthal remembers that he slept a little, but then he was being lifted up and put on a truck, on top of some dead bodies. Later he was told that the camp authorities had sent out trucks to collect the bodies so that the villagers of Mauthausen, going to work in the morning, wouldn't be bothered by the sight of so many dead. Apparently he and Radziwill were almost frozen stiff, and it was assumed that they were dead. But when the truck arrived in the courtyard of the camp crematorium and the bodies were taken down, the prisoners assigned to the detail noticed that the two men were not quite dead. Fortunately no SS men were present, and it was quite dark in the courtyard. The prisoners carried Wiesenthal and Radziwill to a nearby shower room, took off their clothes, and put them under the cold water. There the two men regained consciousness. From the shower a narrow corridor led to the camp barracks, and the two were smuggled into a room, weak and dizzy but alive.

Wiesenthal was not expected to live long, however, for the camp authorities assigned him to Block VI, the "death block," with other prisoners who were not able to work and were expected to die. His weight was down to about a hundred pounds. The daily diet was two hundred calories—one bowl of foul-smelling soup. Most people lay apathetically on their bunks, unable to sit up or walk. Wiesenthal ascribes his survival to his willpower and to the help of a Polish trusty named Eduard Staniszewski, a coffee merchant Wiesenthal had known in Poznan. Staniszewski brought him a small piece of bread once in a while. He would sit down on Wiesenthal's bunk, and they would talk about what they were going to do when the war was over. They knew it couldn't last long because they heard the sound of American planes in the sky. Staniszewski said he would like to go back to Poland and open a beautiful coffee house, and he suggested that Wiesenthal, the well-known architect, should draw up the plans for the establishment.

"He brought me paper and pencils and I began to draw," Wiesenthal says. "It helped me to forget where I was and took my mind off the dead and the dying people around me. I made detailed drawings for the coffee house. I even designed costumes for the waiters. Lying on my bunk, I drew so many plans that they made up quite a book. Staniszewski was very happy and brought me more bread. We talked for hours about the colors of the rugs and the shape of the tables. He took the plans with him. I met him several years ago, and he told me he still had them. Unfortunately things didn't work out for him, and the coffee house was never built."

Wiesenthal was lying in room A, known as the "better" place. When a man became so weak that he was expected to die immediately, he was taken to room B. But the death rate was high even in room A. There were two or three men to one bunk, and sometimes Wiesenthal woke up in the morning and saw that one of his bunkmates was dead. Even the hard-boiled SS guards wouldn't enter the room because it smelled so of sickness and pus and death. Every morning an SS man would stop at the door, shouting, "*Wie viele sind heute nacht krepiert* [How many died last night?]?"

"Sometimes," Wiesenthal says, "we in room A thought we were the last men alive on earth. We had lost touch with all reality. We didn't know whether anybody else was still alive. And we weren't really very wrong. Almost 3000 prisoners died in Mauthausen *after* the Americans liberated us on May 5, 1945."

Chapter 3

SIMON WIESENTHAL'S
NARRATIVE

It was ten o'clock on the morning of May 5, 1945, when I saw a big gray tank with a white star on its side and the American flag waving from the turret. I stood on the windswept square that had been, until an hour earlier, the courtyard of the Mauthausen concentration camp. The day was sunny, with a scent of spring in the air. Gone was the sweetish smell of burned flesh that had always hovered over the yard.

The night before, the last SS men had run away. The machinery of death had come to a stop. In my room, a few dead people were lying on their bunks. They hadn't been taken away this morning. The crematorium no longer operated.

I do not remember how I'd got from my room into the courtyard. I was hardly able to walk. I was wearing my faded striped uniform with a yellow *J* in a yellow-red double triangle. Around me I saw other men in striped dungarees. Some were holding small flags, waving at the Americans. Where had they gotten the flags from? Did the Americans bring them? I shall never know.

The tank with the white star was about a hundred yards in front of me. I wanted to touch the star, but I was too weak. I had survived to see this day, but I couldn't make the last hundred yards. I remember taking a few steps, and then my knees gave way and I fell on my face.

Somebody lifted me up. I felt the rough texture of an olive-drab American uniform brush against my bare arms. I couldn't speak; I couldn't even open my mouth. I pointed toward the white star, I touched the cold, dusty armor with my hands, and then I fainted.

When I opened my eyes after what seemed a long time, I was back on my bunk. The room seemed changed. There was only one man on each bunk, no longer three or four, and the dead had been taken away. There was an unfamiliar smell in the air. It was DDT. They brought in big kettles with soup. This was *real* soup, and it tasted delicious. I took too much of it—my stomach wasn't used to such nourishing fare—and I got violently sick.

The next days went by in a pleasant apathy. Most of the time I dozed on my bunk. American doctors in white coats came to look at us. We were given pills and more food—soup, vegetables, meat. I still was so weak that a friend had to help me when I wanted to go out. I had survived, I didn't have to force myself to be strong any longer; I had seen the day I'd prayed for all these years, but now I was weaker than ever. "A natural reaction," said the doctors.

I made an effort to get up and walk out alone. As I shuffled through a dark corridor, a man jumped at me and knocked me down. I collapsed and lost consciousness. I came to on my bunk, and an American doctor gave me something. Two friends sat next to me. They had picked me up in the corridor and carried me to my bunk. They said that a Polish trusty had beaten me. Perhaps he was angry because I was still alive.

People in room A said I must report the trusty to the American authorities. We were free men now, no longer *Untermenschen.* The next day my friends accompanied me to an office in the building that had formerly been the camp headquarters. A handwritten sign WAR CRIMES was on the door. We were told to wait in a small anteroom. Somebody brought me a chair, and I sat down.

Through the open doors, I saw American officers behind desks who interrogated SS men who stood at attention in front of them. Several former prisoners worked as typists. An SS man was brought into the room. Instinctively I turned my head sideward so he wouldn't see me. He had been a brutal guard; when he walked through the corridor and a prisoner did not step aside quickly and snap to attention, the SS man would whip the prisoner's face with the riding crop he always carried. The sight of this man had always brought cold sweat to the back of my neck.

Now I stared; I couldn't believe it. The SS man was trembling, just as we had trembled before him. His shoulders were hunched, and I noticed that he wiped the palms of his hands. He was no longer a superman; he made me think of a trapped animal. He was escorted by a Jewish prisoner—a *former* prisoner.

I kept staring, fascinated. I didn't hear what was said as the SS man stood before the American interrogator. He could hardly stand at attention, and there was sweat on his forehead. The American officer motioned with his hand and an American soldier took the SS man away. My friends said that all SS men were being taken to a big concrete pillbox, where they were to be kept under guard until they were tried. I made my report on the Polish trusty. My friends testified that they had found me lying unconscious in the corridor. One of the American doctors also testified. Then we went back to our room. That night the trusty apologized to me in front of our comrades, and extended his hand. I accepted his apology but did not give him my hand.

The trusty wasn't important. He was already part of the past. I kept thinking of the scene at the office. Lying on my bunk with my eyes closed, I saw the trembling SS man—a contemptible, frightened coward in his black uniform. For years that uniform had been the symbol of terror. I had seen apprehensive German soldiers during the war (the soldiers, too, were afraid of the SS men), but never a frightened SS man. I had always thought of them as the strong men, the elite, of a perverted regime. It took me a long time to understand what I had seen: the supermen became cowards the moment they were no longer protected by their guns. They were through.

I got up from my bunk and walked out of the room. Behind the crematorium, SS men were digging graves for our 3000 comrades who had died of starvation and exhaustion after the arrival of the Americans. I sat down, looking at the SS men. Two weeks ago they would have beaten me half-dead if I had dared look at them. Now they seemed to be afraid to walk past me. An SS man begged an American soldier for a cigarette. The soldier threw away the cigarette that he'd been smoking. The SS man bent down, but another SS man was faster and got hold of the butt, and the two SS men began to scuffle until the soldier told them to get away.

Only two weeks had gone by, and the elite of the Thousand Year Reich were fighting for a cigarette butt. How many years had it been since we had been given a cigarette? I walked back to my room and looked around. Most of my comrades were lying apathetically on their bunks. After the moment of exhilaration many of them suffered attacks of depression. Now that they knew they were going to live, they were aware of the senselessness of their lives. They had been spared—but they had no one to live for, no place they could go back to, no pieces they could pick up.

I had to do something so I wouldn't succumb to such apathy. Something had to keep me from having nightmares when it got dark, and daydreams in the daytime. I knew exactly what I could do, and what I *had* to do.

I went to the War Crimes office and offered my services. I hoped they wouldn't notice my appearance. The American lieutenant listened to me and shook his head. What could they do with me? He said I had neither training nor experience.

"And, incidentally, how much do you weigh?" he asked.

I lied. "Fifty-six kilos [123 pounds]."

The lieutenant laughed. "Wiesenthal, go and take it easy for a while, and come to see me when you *really* weigh fifty-six kilos."

Ten days later I'd gained some weight. Now I put on some make-up. I'd found a piece of red paper and used it to redden my pale cheeks. A friend asked me whether I was going out to look for a bride.

"Some people won't like that bride," I said.

The lieutenant must have sensed how much the job meant to me, for he said I could start at once, and assigned me to a Captain Tarracusio, a former Russian aristocrat who had emigrated to the United States in 1918 from the province of Georgia. He had taught international law at Harvard University.

I accompanied Captain Tarracusio on his errands, looking for SS guards from Mauthausen who were hiding in the nearby countryside. A few times Tarracusio asked me to carry out arrests myself.

I'll never forget our first case. We drove to a small house where an SS man named Schmidt lived. He had been one of our guards, an insignificant little man who looked as anonymous as his name. I walked up to the second floor, found him, and arrested him. He didn't even try to resist. He was trembling. So was I, but for a different reason. I was weak from getting up the stairs and from the excitement. I had to sit down for a while.

Schmidt helped me as we walked down the stairway together. He could have easily tried to run away. If he'd given me a slight shove, I would have fallen down the stairway, and he might have escaped through the back of the house.

But Schmidt didn't even think of running away. On the contrary, he held me by the arm and helped me down the stairs. It was absurd—like the rabbit carrying the hunting dog. He sat down in the jeep behind Captain Tarracusio and me, and he pleaded for mercy. He was crying. He said he'd been one of the little fish. Why pick on him? He'd done nothing bad. He'd acted strictly under orders. He swore that he'd helped many prisoners.

I said to Schmidt: "Yes, you helped the prisoners. I've often seen you. You helped them on their way to the crematorium."

Then he didn't say any more. He just sat there, hunched on the back seat, with his twisted, trembling fingers, until we reached the camp and handed him over to the War Crimes people.

Schmidt was my first "client," and there were many others in the weeks that followed. You didn't have to go far. You almost stumbled over them. During the next months I helped line up some of the testimony used at the war crimes trials in Dachau before a U.S. military court some months later.

After the establishment of the four military zones of Austria in 1945, Mauthausen became part of the Soviet zone. Our War Crimes group moved to Linz, in the U.S. Zone. Many of the former inmates of Mauthausen were brought to a Displaced Persons camp that had been set up in the public school in Leonding, a small town near Linz.

A little boy named Adolf Hitler had spent his first school days in this school. We slept on cots in a classroom whose windows looked out on a small house that was the former home of Hitler's parents. They were buried in the cemetery at the end of the road. I didn't particularly like the view from the room and moved out of the school after a few days. I rented a modest furnished room in the Landstrasse in Linz. Not much of a room, really, but from the window I could see a small garden.

I spent the mornings at the War Crimes office and the afternoons at the newly established Jewish Committee in Linz (later expanded into the Jewish Central Committee of the U.S. Zone in Austria), of which I became vice-chairman. The Committee set up a makeshift office in two small rooms.

The rooms were always crowded. In the months after the war our visitors were human wrecks who always seemed to be wearing somebody else's clothes. They had sunken cheeks and bloodless lips. Many said they had been at Mauthausen. We recognized each other by stories of SS men we all knew or by memories of friends who had died. Some of them acted like people who had just survived an earthquake or a hurricane and cannot understand why they have been saved while everybody else has died in the disaster. They would ask each other: "Who else is alive?" One couldn't understand that one had survived, and it was beyond comprehension that others should still be alive. They would sit on the steps to the office and talk to one another. "Can it be that my wife, my mother, my child is alive? Some of my friends, some of the people in the town where we lived?"

There was no mail service. The few available telphone lines were restricted to military use. The only way to find out whether someone was alive was to go and look. Across Europe a wild tide of frantic survivors was flowing. People were hitchhiking, getting short jeep rides, or hanging onto dilapidated railway coaches without windows or doors. They sat in huddled groups on haycarts, and some just walked. They would use any means to get a few miles closer to their destination. To get from Linz to Munich, normally a three-hour railroad trip, might take five days. Many of them didn't really know where to go. To the place where one had been with his family before the war? To the concentration camp where the family had last been heard of? Families had been torn apart too suddenly to make arrangements for the day when it would be all over.

In Jaroslav Hašek's immortal *The Adventures of the Good Soldier Švejk* the hero makes a date with a friend to meet him at a certain beerhouse in Prague "on Wednesday after the war is over." But the

First World War had been a *gemütlich* affair compared to the apocalypse we few had survived. And yet the survivors continued their pilgrimage of despair, sleeping on highways or in railroad stations, waiting for another train, another horse-drawn cart to come along, always driven by hope. "Perhaps someone is still alive. . . ." Someone might tell where to find a wife, a mother, children, a brother—or whether they were dead. Better to know the truth than to know nothing. The desire to find one's people was stronger than hunger, thirst, fatigue. Stronger even than the fear of border patrols, of the CIC and NKVD, of men saying "Let's see your papers."

The first thing we did at the Committee in Linz was to make up lists of known survivors. People who came in to ask for someone were asked where *they* were from. They were nomads, vagabonds, beggars. But once upon a time they had had a home, a job, savings. Their names were put on the list of some town or village. Slowly the lists grew. People from Poland, Czechoslovakia, or Germany brought us lists. We gave them copies of our lists. We worked long into the night to copy these lists. Early in the morning, the first people would arrive to look up names. Some waited all night to get in. Behind a man another waited for a glance that might mean hope or despair. Some people were impatient and there were brawls. Once two men began to scuffle because each wanted the same list. In the end they tore up the precious piece of paper. Another time two men started to argue, their eyes glued to the list in the hands of a third man. Each wanted it next. Suddenly they looked at each other and gasped, and the next moment they were in each others' arms. They were brothers and each had been trying to find the other for weeks.

And there were moments of silent despair when someone discovered that the person he was looking for had been there only a few days before, looking for him. They had missed each other. Where should one look now? Other people scanned the lists of survivors, hoping against hope to find the names of people they had seen killed before their very eyes. Everybody had heard of some miracle.

I hardly ever looked at the lists. I didn't believe in miracles. I knew that all my people were dead. After the Pole from Warsaw had told me what had happened in Topiel Street, I had no hope that my wife was alive. When I thought of her, I thought of her body lying under a heap of rubble, and I wondered whether they had found the bodies and buried her. In a moment of illogical hope I wrote to the International Committee of the Red Cross in Geneva. They promptly answered that my wife was dead. I knew that my mother did not have a grave; she had died in the death camp of Belsec. I hoped that at least my wife might have a grave.

One night, when I had nothing else to do, I looked at a list of survivors from the Polish city of Cracow and found the name of an old friend from Buczacz, Dr. Biener. I wrote him a letter. I told him that my wife's body might still be lying under the ruins of the house in Topiel Street. I asked him to go to Warsaw and look at what was left of the house. There was no mail service to Poland, so I gave the letter to a man who specialized in getting things through Czechoslovakia to Poland.

I didn't know that a miracle had indeed happened. My wife told me all about it later. When the German flamethrower squads had closed in on Topiel Street, in the darkness and confusion my wife and a few other people had managed to get away. For a while they hid. After the battle of Warsaw, the few survivors were driven together by the Germans and assigned to forced-labor transports for Germany. My wife was sent to a factory in Heiligenhaus, near Gelsenkirchen in the Rhineland, where they made machine guns for the *Wehrmacht*. The Polish laborers were decently housed and fed, and the Gestapo left them alone. The Germans knew that the war was lost.

My wife was liberated by the British, who marched into Gelsenkirchen on April 11, 1945. (That day I was lying on my bunk in the death block of Mauthausen.) My wife went to the British authorities and reported that she was Cyla Wiesenthal, a Jewish woman from Poland. Six women in her group turned out to be Jewish, but they had not known of each other. One of them told my wife that she was going home.

"Home?" asked my wife. "Where is home?"

"To Poland, of course. Why don't you come with me?"

"What for? My husband was killed by the Gestapo in Lwow last year. Poland has become a large cemetery to me."

"Have you proof that he's dead?"

"No," said my wife, "but . . ."

"Don't believe it. Now, suppose he were alive: where is he likely to be?"

Cyla thought it over. "In Lwow, I would think. We spent the years before the war there."

"Lwow is now in the Soviet Union," said her friend. "Let's go there."

The two women left Gelsenkirchen in June 1945. (At one point on her journey, we later discovered, my wife had been less than thirty miles from Linz.) After an arduous trip, they reached the Czechoslovak–Polish border at Bohumin. They were told that a train left that night for Lwow. They got on the overcrowded cars and arrived in Cracow, Poland, in the morning. It was announced that there would be a four-hour stop.

At the Cracow railroad station somebody stole my wife's suitcase with everything she owned. That was her homecoming. To cheer her up, her friend suggested that they walk into town. Perhaps they would meet someone they had once known. The beautiful old city of the Polish kings looked deserted and ghostlike that morning. Suddenly my wife heard her name called out, and recognized a man named Landek, who had been a dentist in Lwow. (Landek now lives in America.) For a while they exchanged hectic questions and unfinished sentences, as always happened when survivors met. Landek had heard that Simon Wiesenthal was dead. He told my wife to talk to Dr. Biener. He might know more.

"Dr. Biener from Buczacz?" asked my wife. "Is he in Cracow?"

"He lives five minutes from here." Landek gave her the address and hurried away.

When they came to Dr. Biener's house, my wife asked her friend to wait downstairs. She walked up the stairway with a heavy heart. On the third floor she saw a sign reading BIENER and rang the bell. The door was opened. For a moment she saw Dr. Biener's face and heard a muffled cry. Then the door was quickly shut again.

"Dr. Biener!" my wife shouted, banging her fists against the door. "Open up! It's Cyla. Cyla Wiesenthal from Buczacz!"

The door was opened. Dr. Biener was pale, as if he were seeing a ghost.

"But—you are dead," he said. "I just got a letter . . ."

"I'm very much alive," my wife said angrily. "Of course I *look* half-dead, after spending the night on the train."

"Come in," Dr. Biener said hastily, and closed the door. "You don't understand. Yesterday I had a letter from your husband. Simon writes that you died under the ruins of a house in Warsaw."

Now my wife got pale. "Simon? But he's dead. He's been dead for over a year."

Dr. Biener shook his head. "No, no, Cyla. Simon is alive, in Linz, Austria. Here, read the letter."

They called my wife's friend from downstairs. She was not at all surprised. Hadn't she told Cyla that her husband might be alive? They sat down and talked, and when they remembered the train it was much too late. If my letter hadn't reached Dr. Biener the day before, if my wife hadn't met Landek, if Dr. Biener hadn't been at home, the two women would have gone back to the station and continued their journey to the Soviet Union. My wife might have been sent into the interior of the USSR, and it would have taken years to find her again.

My wife stayed in Cracow, and tried to get in touch with me. Dr. Biener knew several illegal couriers who would carry letters for a fee, with no guarantee of delivery. She wrote three letters and gave them to three men working different routes. I received one of them, from a man who had come to Linz by way of Budapest—which is quite a detour.

I'll never forget the moment when I saw Cyla's handwriting on the envelope. I read the letter so many times that I knew it by heart. I went to see the OSS captain for whom I was then working and asked him to give me travel orders to Cracow. He didn't like the idea of my going to Poland. He said I might never be able to come back. He suggested we think it over until next morning.

I didn't go to the Jewish Committee that afternoon. I was happy and perhaps feeling a little guilty at being a happy man among so many unhappy people. I wanted to be alone. I knew a peasant not far from where I lived who had a few horses. I thought of my summer vacations in Dolina, where I loved to ride horses. I asked the peasant to let me have a horse for an hour. I forgot that I was a little older and not yet in good physical condition. I mounted the horse.

Something went wrong. I suppose the horse sensed at once that I was still weak. I was thrown and landed in a potato field with a broken ankle.

I had to stay in bed. That settled the matter of my projected journey to Poland. I asked a Jewish friend, Dr. Felix Weisberg, to go to Cracow and gave him a letter for my wife. He promised to bring her back to Linz. My OSS friends made out the necessary travel documents for her, so she would have no difficulty in getting into the U.S. Zone of Austria.

They were fine travel documents, but unfortunately my wife never received them. Crossing Czechoslovakia on his way to Poland, Dr. Weisberg was warned that there was an NKVD roadblock ahead, with "very strict controls." He got nervous; if the Soviet secret police found any American *dokumenty* on him, they might arrest him as a spy. He destroyed the documents. Too late he realized that he had also destroyed my wife's address in Cracow. As it turned out, the NKVD didn't even search him. In Cracow, he went to the local Jewish Committee and put a notice on the bulletin board. Mrs. Cyla Wiesenthal, the wife of Simon Wiesenthal, was asked to get in touch with Dr. Felix Weisberg, who would take her to her husband in Linz.

My wife saw the notice the next morning and went to see Dr. Weisberg. She was not the first visitor. Two other women were already there, each claiming to be the one and only Cyla Wiesenthal. A lot of people in Poland were trying to get to Austria, hoping they might later try to get to America. Poor Felix Weisberg had a trickier problem than the mythological Paris. Weisberg didn't know my wife. In all the excitement preceding his sudden departure, I had foolishly forgotten to give him her exact description. He faced the unpleasant possibility of bringing back the wrong Mrs. Wiesenthal. Weisberg told me later that he'd asked each of the three women to describe how I looked. Two seemed rather vague, but one knew a lot of details, naturally. Also, Weisberg admitted to me, he'd liked her best. He decided to take a chance and bought false travel papers for her in the black market.

One evening, late in 1945, I was early in bed as usual. My broken ankle still gave me a lot of trouble. There was a knock at the door. Felix Weisberg came in, confused and embarrassed. It took him quite a while to explain how he'd foolishly thrown away the American documents, and his dilemma over three women each claiming to be Mrs. Cyla Wiesenthal.

"I brought one of them with me. She's waiting downstairs. Now, don't get excited, Simon. If she isn't your wife, I'm going to marry her myself."

"You?"

"Yes, my word of honor. You're under no obligation whatsoever. To tell the truth, I thought it safest to bring the one I liked best. That way, I knew even if she was not your wife, I would——"

But then she came into the room, and Felix Weisberg, God bless him, knew that he could not marry her.

We moved into a larger apartment. The following year our daughter Paulinka was born in Linz. I kept working for various American agencies—the War Crimes Commission, later the OSS and the CIC. Our efforts were often frustrated by a lack of cooperation among the Allied powers.

The hardest stand was taken by the Soviets, who summarily arrrested both genuine Nazis and people who were denounced as Nazis, and shipped them to the Soviet Union. Also, in the Soviet Zones of Gemany and Austria, "People's Courts" pronounced swift, severe judgment on presumed Nazi criminals. The Soviet authorities got efficient help from local Communists who had infiltrated the police. But most of the Nazis caught there were "little fish." The Nazi Party *Bonzen* (bigwigs), the leading SS and Gestapo criminals, had escaped to the West before the end of the war. There they hoped to be treated more leniently by the Western Allies. Their hope was fulfilled.

In the West, the French took the toughest line—not unnaturally, since they had directly suffered under the Nazi occupation. Gradually, however, the tough French line was noticeably softened as former Vichyites joined the French occupation forces in Germany and Austria and managed to throw sand into the works of justice.

The British policy toward Nazi criminals was neither clear nor coordinated, not the same in Germany as in Austria, and often paradoxical. The British often overlooked important Nazis hiding out in their zones, but they handed over Nazis with a criminal record to the Soviets or, for instance, to the Yugoslavs, when it was evident that the Nazis had committed crimes in the USSR or Yugoslavia. The British were short of experienced investigators; denazification was carried out ineffectively. The British had their own problems in Palestine and in their colonies and were less interested in clearing up the Nazi mess than were the Americans.

The Americans, in accordance with their national temperament, went from extreme to extreme. First, they created the policy of "automatic arrest." All SS men, Gestapo members, important Nazi Party people, sympathizers and collaborators were rounded up and put in detention camps, where they got ample food, medical care and cigarettes, and were told to wait, while investigators interrogated them and separated the sheep from the goats, the criminals from the inactive hangers-on. Different compounds in the detention camps were set up for SS men and less implicated Nazis, for higher-ranking Wehrmacht officers, for non-German collaborators (Hungarians, Slovaks, Croats). I spent much time in these camps as an investigator for the War Crimes Commission, the OSS, and the CIC, and I know how well the internees were treated. For a long time the internees had more food than the civilian population.

I also noticed the subtle ways in which the internees began to go to work on the Americans. Self-styled "Soviet experts" among the men who had been in the Soviet Union began to involve the American investigators in political discussions. Some were asked to write special reports for members of various competing American intelligence agencies. I knew American officers who wrote long reports on the basis of such information without bothering to check their sources. In 1946 and 1947, the Americans released many Nazi criminals who were much later arrested by the German and Austrian police. Many local police officials had been victims of the Nazi regime. Some had been sent to concentration camps; they knew more about the Nazis than the Americans who were separated from the Nazi internees by insurmountable barriers of language and mentality.

Basically, though, as long as those Americans who had won the war in Europe were around, denazification was carried out impartially. But eventually these men went home and were replaced by others who had been stationed in the United States or the Far East. They didn't understand the Nazi problem, which seemed to them already part of history. Many of them made no effort to speak German and depended on German and Austrian girl interpreters. They often became victims of the Nazis' best secret weapon—the *Fräuleins*. A young American was naturally more interested in a pretty, complaisant girl than in one of "those SS men," whom everybody wanted to forget like a bad dream. These Americans thought we who were intent on seeing justice done were eye-for-an-eye avengers and alarmists, who would always see the world through a barbed-wire screen. An American captain who had an important job in the re-education of Germans once told me: "There'll always be people with different viewpoints. At home we have Democrats and Republicans. Here you have Nazis and anti-Nazis. That's what makes the world go round. Try not to worry too much about it."

Chapter 4

THE KNIFE

It was difficult not to worry; I could see where such an attitude would eventually lead. While more detailed facts about Nazi crimes were becoming available and the full horror of genocide was becoming apparent, I realized with a sense of frustration that it was getting harder to deal with the criminals.

My work kept me occupied all day until late at night. When I went to bed and tried to sleep, things I'd read and heard during the day would fuse with memories of the past. Often, after a bad dream, I woke unable to separate the dream from reality. I've had many letters from other survivors of concentration camps who are also tortured by their dreams. One who had seen his mother killed in Auschwitz and who is now in a neurological clinic near Bremen once wrote to me: "Please help me. There must be a drug against bad dreams. Haven't they got drugs against everything now? If I wouldn't dream any more, I might get well again. . . ." One night in September 1947, after one of these bad dreams, I heard the sound of fists on the door. I sat up in bed. My heart was beating fast. I could never forget that sound of fists on the door.

I switched on the light and the nightmare was gone. I was a free man, here in Linz, with my wife and daughter. I got up and walked to the door. Through the peephole I saw Misha Lewin, head of the association of former Jewish partisan fighters in the Soviet Union. Misha seemed a tough man who always wore boots and shouted, but he was really a sweet fellow who had kept his sense of humor. Two men were with him. "Open up, Simon!" he called. "We've got news for you!"

They came in, and Misha introduced Mair Blitz and Moses Kussowitzki. They'd been with him during the war, when groups of Jewish partisans fought with the Red Army against the Germans. At the end of the war they returned to their native Poland, did not find their families—murdered by the Nazis—and came to Austria.

"These boys have hooked the big fish," Misha said. "Eichmann!" He looked at me triumphantly. "Go on, tell him."

Blitz and Kussowitzki were living in Camp Admont, the largest displaced-persons center in the British Occupation Zone of Austria. Admont is in northwestern Styria, in a lovely high valley surrounded by mountains. Some two thousand people, mostly Jews from Poland and the Baltic states, were staying temporarily amid the beautiful Alpine landscape, clad and fed by the British, but they weren't particularly enjoying their free vacation. A few had found work in the neighborhood, and some made a few schillings in the black market. But most were waiting impatiently to go to Palestine with one of the illegal transports that were then being channeled through southern Austria and Italy.

It was the week before Yom Kippur, the Day of Atonement. The devout Jews in Camp Admont had been preparing for the high holiday. According to Orthodox ritual, men and women would say their prayers; each man would sacrifice a cock and each woman a hen—a symbolic representation of Abraham's offering as recounted in the Old Testament.

Unfortunately, poultry was scarce in Austria. Blitz and Kussowitzki, resourceful young men, decided to go around among the peasants in the vicinity, trying to barter a few cans of the food and chocolate they'd been given by the British for a couple of chickens.

They spoke only Yiddish, a fact that somewhat complicated the negotiations with the peasants of Styria. When they asked for a *Huhn* (chicken), a farmer misunderstood and brought them a *Hund*—a small Dachshund in a sack. Another peasant shook his head and said he couldn't help them. All chickens were numbered and controlled by the authorities since eggs were strictly rationed. He wouldn't want to risk a fine.

"Try the fellow up on the hill there," said the helpful peasant. "He's got a large place, at least two thousand chickens. Don't know, though, whether he won't have you thrown out. He hates all Jews. They say he was a big Nazi."

The boys looked at each other. They had had the same thought. "That must be *him*," Blitz said. Kussowitzki nodded. They no longer sought chickens that day. Instead, they went straight to the local British Field Security Service (FSS) post in Admont and got the border-crossing permits for "family visits" they needed to travel to the nearby U.S. Zone. They took a train to Linz, some hundred miles away, and reported their findings to Misha Lewin, who decided that I was the man to see.

"And here we are," Lewin said. "Let's not waste a minute. We've got to get Eichmann." All of us were obsessed with Eichmann, even then known as the most vicious Nazi criminal still at large, probably hiding in the British Zone of Austria. I had recently opened my Documentation Center in Linz, and almost every day people who thought they'd seen Eichmann somewhere came to see me. The trail led from an internment camp in Bavaria into the British Zone of Austria. There it seemed to have vanished.

"What makes you think he's Eichmann?" I said.

"The man has two thousand chickens, he hates the Jews, he was a big Nazi. Why shouldn't it be Eichmann?" Blitz asked me with Talmudic logic. He didn't convince me, but I decided to go along with them. I was quite sure the man wasn't Eichmann, but he might be another big Nazi.

The next morning I obtained travel permits to the British Zone for Lewin and myself. We drove there with the two former partisans. The big farm was located in the village of Gaishorn, about twelve miles from Camp Admont. I had no official status, and decided to ask the Austrian police for help. We stopped in front of the field gendarmerie post in Gaishorn, an old chalet.

Two old peasants in short leather pants sat in the anteroom, chatting and killing time. It was very *gemütlich*. The post commander was an old man with a drooping white mustache, probably a relic from the good old Habsburg days. We asked about the big farm on the hill. He got up and looked at a local map on the wall. "Must be Gaishorn 66. Belongs to Murer. He was in Poland and Russia during the war. He's very popular around the village."

I was stunned. "Murer? *Franz* Murer?

"That's right," said the old man. "Know him?"

I managed to shake my head. We walked out quickly. For a while no one spoke. All of us had heard of Murer. In the past two years I had collected the testimony of many refugees about Franz Murer, Deputy Kommissar for the Wilna district in Lithuania, where 80,000 Jews had lived before the war. Exactly 250 were alive when the Nazis got through with them. Before the war, Wilna had been called "The Jerusalem of Lithuania" because of its Jewish community's contributions to literature, science, philosophy, and the arts. Celebrated Jewish musicians, among them Jascha Heifetz, had come from Wilna.

Murer was known among the refugees as "the butcher of Wilna," the man mainly responsible for the extermination of the Jews in Wilna. I've seen people's faces go white many years later when his name was mentioned.

We drove to Camp Admont. I knew that several survivors of Wilna were among the displaced persons there. I told the camp committee what my errand was. They announced by loudspeaker that persons who had knowledge about Franz Murer from Wilna should report to me at once. Seven people came to the small office. When we told them that Franz Murer was living on a farm only a few miles away, some of them became hysterical. A woman broke down; Murer had killed two people before her eyes. A man whose mother had been murdered by Murer became so overcome by emotion that he had to be taken out. Everybody was shouting at the same time. I told them to calm down. All would have a chance to talk, I said.

Some of the stories were too vague to be used in court, but some were quite accurate—and terrible. One witness remembered the day Murer had personally ordered the inhabitants of a street in the ghetto of Wilna loaded onto trucks, driven to the nearby Ponary Woods, and shot by Lithuanian auxiliary police. Another man gave evidence that Murer had ordered two houses in a ghetto street dynamited. Told that there were still women inside, he had said "Never mind" and had the houses blown up.

Other witnesses testified that Murer, a complete sadist, had repeatedly stripped and beaten people. The only way to fend off his tortures was to buy him. The Jews in the ghetto had repeatedly collected jewelry, silverware, and paintings and given them to Murer. When the bribes were acceptable, he would order the donors to pack their contributions into wooden boxes that were sent to his home in Austria.

One day in January 1942 Murer confiscated a Catholic convent in Wilna and a model farm run by the nuns. The nuns and a few monks were later "liquidated" in Ponary. In 1945 their bodies were dug up by Jewish exhumation teams who had orders to burn the remains and remove all traces.

The testimony included the description of an incident I shall never forget. If you happen to be the father of a child, you will understand why. It seems that two groups of men had been waiting at the ghetto exit. One was to be marched off to work. The other group was to be executed in the Ponary Woods. Among this group was seventeen-year-old Daniel Brodi. His father stood in the work group, helpless. When Daniel thought he wasn't observed, he slipped out of the death group and quickly ran over to his father in the other group. Murer saw him. He took the boy by the neck and struck him hard. Daniel fell to the ground. Then Murer took out his revolver and shot Daniel in front of his father.

I took down four affidavits, had the signatures certified, and went back to the Gaishorn gendarmerie. I gave the elderly post commander the statements without a word. He seemed aghast as he read on. Once he lifted his eyes in a helpless gesture to the wooden Madonna on the wall. He told two of his officers to go up the hill and arrest Murer. Then he notified the British Field Security Service post. According to Military Government law, all war criminals had to be handed over to the occupation authorities.

Lewin, the ex-partisans, and I went with the gendarmes to the farm on the hill. We were told to wait some distance away. It was a nice-looking place, prosperous and peaceful, well kept with trees and flowers. The gendarmes said that Murer lived there with his wife and two grown sons. He had several people working for him. The gendarmes went into the house—just in time, as they told us afterward. Murer had been about to clear out. Two packed suitcases stood near the door. His overcoat and hat were lying on a chair. Murer seemed to have been warned, perhaps by the two old peasants we'd met at the gendarmerie post. He was quite impertinent with the policemen and told them it was a damned nuisance to bother him. This was late in 1947. The shock of defeat that had paralyzed the big Nazis after the war was wearing off.

He was a sturdy mountain peasant with a longish hard-bitten face, a long nose, a protruding chin, and reddish hair. He was thirty-five at the time of his arrest. Nine years earlier he had joined the Nazi Party, been selected for training in the *Ordensschule,* where the SS elite was groomed, and had been sent to Wilna. There he became master over life and death, mostly death. But no one in Gaishorn would believe *that:* Franz Murer was a nice man and a helpful neighbor. The old police-post commander told me that Murer had been born in nearby St. Georgen. He had bought his farm before the war. Everybody liked him. No one would bother such an upright citizen with unpleasant questions after his return from the war.

I've been asked how a man could dare live so close to a camp housing people whose families he had murdered. For one thing, the displaced-persons center had not existed when Murer returned. Wilna was far away, 2500 kilometers to the east. He considered it highly improbable that he would ever meet any survivors. When they put up the center, he knew there was danger if he stayed, but to move away would raise suspicion. He decided to stay. That would convince the people that his conscience was clear.

The Austrian gendarmes turned Murer over to the British FSS soldiers, who brought him by jeep to the central prison in Graz, the capital of Styria. I went back to Camp Admont and spent the night writing a comprehensive survey of the whole case, including the affidavits of the witnesses. The people in the camp were excited. They couldn't understand how Murer could have lived nearby all the time and not have been found by the British. I was not particularly surprised. In recent months I'd asked the British authorities several times for assistance in tracking down war criminals I suspected of hiding out in their zone, but had never received any help from them. That was why I had gone to the Austrian authorities; I had been afraid the FSS might bungle the job.

At that time the British were doing all they could to stop refugees from coming into Palestine. The Jewish settlers were fighting a merciless guerrilla war against the forces of the British mandatory power and there was much bloodshed and bitterness on both sides. A while earlier I had testified before a joint Anglo-American commission on the tricky problem of Jewish immigration into Palestine. The Americans had listened to me with obvious sympathy; the British sat with stolid faces. These were the troubled months before Israel became an independent nation. The British authorities in Austria were more concerned about the illegal transports to Palestine than about Nazi war criminals in their zone.

The next morning I drove to the FSS post in Admont, an old two-story house with wrought-iron balconies. A friendly-looking British sergeant asked me what I wanted. I handed him the memorandum on the Murer case. His behavior changed at once. He put my paper aside without reading it and asked me why I had gone to the Austrian gendarmerie instead of reporting at once to the FSS. I hadn't gone through channels. Had I been in the British Zone before? Had I instigated the arrests of other persons? He must have been informed of my arrival, for I saw that he had a whole questionnaire in front of him. He asked me about my work in Linz, about the Documentation Center. And then he asked me *the* question he'd been waiting to ask all the time.

"What do you know about the illegal transports to Palestine by way of Italy?"

"Sergeant, I came here to discuss the case of Murer."

"In this place," he said, "I ask the questions and you tell me the answers. Who heads the Irgun Zwai Leuni in Austria?"

Members of the Irgun—a Jewish extremist organization that believed in violence—had a few days earlier derailed a British military train near Mallnitz, south of Bad Gastein, causing the death of a British soldier.

I refused to answer and got up. The sergeant barred the door.

"Am I under arrest, Sergeant?"

"No, but you're going to answer my questions."

I was still silent.

"All right. You're going to stay here until afternoon, when the Major is coming over from Graz."

So here I was in custody, having just helped the British to catch an important war criminal they should have caught long ago. They didn't seem to care. They were obsessed with the problem of the Palestine transports. Everybody knew about these transports, which were ignored by the French, tolerated by the Soviets, encouraged by the Americans, and observed by the British with a growing sense of frustration. It was silly to ask me such questions: they knew much more about the transports than I did.

At noon the sergeant came in and asked whether I wanted something to eat. I didn't even bother to answer. Suddenly there was a noise outside; the sound of many voices, first disconnected, then forming a chant: "We want Wiesenthal! We want Wiesenthal!"

I stepped to the window. The street was full of people; there must have been several hundred of them, and they were in an angry mood. The FSS men didn't help matters by barricading the entrance and posting two machine guns on the balcony.

The crowd became furious. Among them were tough partisans, men like Blitz and Kussowitzki, who were not afraid of machine guns. Later I was told that a DP from Camp Admont had been at the FSS post when I came in and heard my interrogation by the sergeant. He had run back to the camp and alerted the people there, who decided to come and "liberate" me.

A young lieutenant came into my room. He said this was *rather* a nuisance, that things were getting out of hand, and would I mind stepping out on the balcony to tell the people that I would soon return to the camp?

I refused. "I didn't ask the people to come here. Why don't you step out yourself and talk to the crowd?"

The lieutenant was getting nervous. If the incident became known at higher headquarters, he might have trouble with his superiors.

The lieutenant called up his major in Graz. I was asked to come to the phone. The major spoke German.

"What's the matter, Herr Wiesenthal? Why are you discourteous to my men?"

"Sir, I came here to talk about Murer. They want other information that I refuse to give. They've kept me here for hours."

"We know all about your activities, Herr Wiesenthal."

"If you think I did anything wrong, why don't you have me arrested?"

There was a pause, and then the major asked me to hand the receiver over to the lieutenant. I was taken into the other room, and a minute later the lieutenant came in and said I was free to leave.

Outside, a terrific shout of triumph went up in the air when I stepped out of the house. Some people lifted me on their shoulders and carried me back toward the camp. The Austrians stared with open mouths, and some actually followed the crowd. This, they thought, was *Hetz*—real fun. Maybe it was a demonstration against the occupiers. Some waved at me with great enthusiasm. Back at Camp Admont, Blitz and Kussowitzki had procured some *Schnapps* to celebrate the arrest of Murer. I was almost happy that night.

Several weeks went by. Murer, in prison in Graz, claimed he was innocent. It was, he said, a case of mistaken identity. Then disturbing rumors reached me from Graz that the British were considering Murer's release. I had some friends on the staff of the International Military Tribunal in Nuremberg. I made a few urgent phone calls; as a result the British were officially asked to hold Murer as a potential witness. In the meantime I mailed circular letters to all displaced persons camps in Austria and Germany, asking for witnesses who could come forward and testify against Murer. At that time it was not difficult to find such witnesses. I had correspondents in many camps, and I received many depositions from camp committees. Several people came to see me at my office in Linz, made and signed their statements. The material was forwarded to the British authorities in Graz.

In December 1948, the British extradited Murer to the Russians. His crimes had been committed in an area that was now part of the Lithuanian Soviet Socialist Republic. The trial of Murer took place in Wilna in the spring of 1949. The depositions of all witnesses in Austria were sent to the Soviet authorities, who had also collected their own witnesses. Murer was found guilty of "killing Soviet citizens" and sentenced to twenty-five years at hard labor. I thought this was the end of the case.

After the Austrian State Treaty of 1955, the Soviets agreed to return all Austrian prisoners of war, including convicted war criminals, to Austria. This, however, was not to be a general amnesty; according to the terms of the treaty, Austria pledged to bring these criminals to trial in its own courts. I saw the list of prisoners repatriated by Russia, and the name of Murer was not on it. Either he had not been released by the Russians because his crimes were considered too serious or he was dead.

After Eichmann's capture in May 1960, I needed some data on Murer to complete my files. I called the gendarmerie post in Gaishorn and asked for some details on Murer's arrest in 1947. The official in charge said he didn't know anything about the case, and suggested that I call him back in a while. He said he would ask Murer about it.

"What? Isn't Murer dead?" I asked.

"Not at all. He came back four years ago, and he's lived on his farm here ever since."

I thanked him and put down the phone. I had to take a deep breath. Murer was free. I called up various officials at the Ministry of Justice and wanted to know why Franz Murer's name had not been on the list of repatriated war criminals. They were embarrassed. Some pretended they had nothing to do with it. At last I was told that Murer's name had been left out "inadvertently"—a bureaucratic mistake.

I began to investigate what had happened to the other war criminals who had been repatriated after the State Treaty. Of 200 persons on the list only three of them—all top SS men—had been put on trial by the Austrians. Of the three, Hermann Gabriel and Leopold Mitas were sentenced to life imprisonment, Johann Pöll to twenty years in prison. Mitas had been set free after two years, Pöll after eighteen months. Only Gabriel—one out of 200—was still in jail. All other trials had been quashed by presidential decree.

And Murer? He was back on the farm, a respected member of the Catholic People's Party. He had been elected chairman of the District Agricultural Chamber. He had made public speeches and had once decorated several farmers in the presence of a member of the government.

I wrote to the Austrian Minister of Justice and asked what he intended to do about Murer. I was asked to forward "the relevant material" to Section XI of the Ministry of Justice. I submitted thirty-two sworn affidavits. When nothing happened for weeks, I telephoned Section XI. A high-ranking official familiar with the case informed me that the material could not be used against Murer since it had already led to his conviction in Wilna.

I said that he had served only part of his sentence in Russia.

"Yes, I know," was the answer, "but Murer spent seven years in a Soviet jail. We consider Russian prison sentences to be three times as hard as our own. That would make Murer's sentence twenty-one years, wouldn't it? And even if an Austrian court sentenced him to life, he would, according to our laws, be let off for good behavior after twenty years. Since he has already served twenty-one years by our reckoning, why put him on trial again?"

The bureaucrat sounded quite pleased with his exercise in the higher arithmetic of Austrian justice.

"That means," I asked, "that in this country Murer is not considered a convicted criminal?"

"No—not in Austria."

"So, theoretically, he might be elected Federal President?"

The high-ranking official was audibly annoyed. "Why do you have to harass a man who has already done penance?"

"I don't think we understand each other. Human life is too short to expiate the crimes Murer committed in Wilna. I'm not looking for vengeance—only for justice. Murer was sentenced to twenty-five years. According to the terms of the State Treaty, he should have been tried before an Austrian court."

The official was silent for a while. Then he said: "All right. If you can produce new evidence, Mr. Wiesenthal, we are going to take action."

Austrian courts subsequently refused to consider evidence collected in 1947, evidence that was claimed to have led to Murer's conviction in Russia. When I pointed out that Murer had only served part of his sentence, there was icy silence from the Ministry of Justice. I was asked to get new evidence. It meant starting all over again. I would have to find new witnesses—eighteeen years after Murer had been in Wilna. It wouldn't be easy. If there were any survivors, they wouldn't want to testify after all these years; they would want to forget, and be left alone.

I contacted the associations of former residents of Wilna that had been formed in Israel, Canada, the United States, South Africa, and

New Zealand. The files in our large Documentation Center in Vienna were accurate, and up-to-date enough for us to find other witnesses. I wrote these people asking for information about *specific* crimes in which Murer had been *personally* involved. I told the prospective witnesses that general accusations, no matter how moving, would be useless.

The response was astonishing. I received over twenty new depositions with specific statements. Wolf Fainberg, now a resident of Vineland, New Jersey, wrote about a day in December 1941 when he was stopped at the ghetto entrance in Rudnicka Street by Murer and his assistant, Hering. They asked Fainberg for his pass. While Hering examined the pass, a ten-year-old hunchback Jewish girl came walking down the street. Murer said to Hering: "Look what *Mist* [misfits] you're keeping in the ghetto," drew his pistol, and shot the child. Fainberg left. In the evening, people who lived in the street had told him that the little girl had died at once. "I can still see the scene, I shall never forget it," Fainberg testified. "Murer had on a brown uniform, and Hering wore a leather coat."

Isak Kulkin, who now lives in Franel, California, wrote about an execution of six Jews in the ghetto at the end of 1942:

> The six men were hanged in the former stockyard. I witnessed the execution from a nearby window. One of the victims fell to the ground because the rope had snapped. He threw himself at Murer's feet and asked for mercy. Murer gave orders that he be hanged a second time.

Szymon Bastocki, a former resident of Wilna, now of New York City, testified about a day in March 1943 when Murer assembled women and children in the square of the local labor camp and told the police to tear the children away from their mothers and load them on waiting trucks.

> Babies were thrown through the air like parcels. Heart-rending scenes took place, but Murer remained inflexible. One woman clasped her child to her chest and fought the SS men. They threw the mother and child on the truck. She was a pharmacist who had studied in Berlin. She cried, *"Ist das die deutsche Kultur?* (Is this German civilization)?" Murer ordered her taken off the truck and told his adjutant, Martin Weiss, to shoot

her right away. Her body was left hanging on the barbed-wire fence.

The new evidence was submitted to the Austrian Ministry of Justice. Several weeks went by and no action was taken. Murer was on his farm in Gaishorn, enjoying life, freedom, and the strange fruits of Austria's political system. There would be elections soon, and the two big parties didn't particularly like the idea of a trial that might irritate over half a million former Nazis in Austria. They were, after all, half a million votes.

It was one of the situations when a direct appeal to the conscience of the world seemed the only way of getting things done. On February 2, 1961, the Jewish Congregation in Vienna announced a press conference on the subject "The Murderers Among Us." I gave the representatives of the world press detailed information on the case of Franz Murer.

A few weeks later, the story of the Wilna ghetto was mentioned at the Eichmann trial in Jerusalem, where Dr. Mark Dvorzecki, a distinguished author from Wilna who now teaches at Bar-Ilan University in Tel Aviv, told what happened in his home city. His story was printed in newspapers all over the world.

As more editorials appeared on the Murer case and public pressure mounted, the authorities had to act. Murer was arrested and charged with seventeen individual cases of murder. Murer's arrest caused disorders in Gaishorn, where friendly peasants gathered to protest. They marched to nearby Liezen and threatened to storm the seat of the provincial government. Fiery speeches were made in defense of their fellow citizen, Murer. A protest delegation was sent to the Ministry of Justice in Vienna.

The trial by jury against Murer opened in Graz on June 10, 1963. The indictment charged him with having committed "murder by his own hands" in fifteen specific cases; later the public prosecutor added two more cases. Over a dozen witnesses had arrived from Germany, Israel, and the United States. One of the most important witnesses for the prosecution was Jacob Brodi, before whose own eyes Murer had shot his son Daniel at the exit of the Wilna ghetto. Brodi was now sixty-eight. After the war he had emigrated to America, and he now lived alone on a small isolated farm in New Jersey. He was a lonely man. He didn't want to see people, led a simple life, and had refused to accept the German restitution money to which he was entitled. Twenty years had gone by since the day he had seen his boy killed by Murer, but the passage of time had not helped Brodi to forget. Every day and almost every night he saw the scene at the entrance to the Wilna ghetto.

When I first wrote to ask him to come to Graz to testify, he flatly refused. He explained he couldn't bear the thought of facing the murderer. I wrote him several letters. I said we owed it to our dead to tell the living what had happened. *Die Zeit,* a respected German weekly, had just protested "against the new wave of distrust" and defended the new generation, "which knows Nazi crimes only from the history books." The apologists were working overtime. I explained to Brodi that his silence would no longer help his boy, but it might help to save boys of Daniel Brodi's age who knew these crimes only from the history books. A courtroom with a jury, a judge, a prosecutor would make the defendant look real, not like a character out of a history book, certainly not like a hero. There was no answer. I didn't expect to hear from Brodi again. The day before the trial he sent me a cable. He would take a plane and would be there in time.

Four days later I met Jacob Brodi in his room at the Hotel Sonne in Graz, where all witnesses had been put up. He was a tired man with white hair and deep circles around his eyes. With his sunburned, wrinkled face, he looked more like an American farmer from the Middle West than like a refugee from the Wilna ghetto. I told him I was glad he had come. He would be a key witness. His testimony couldn't fail to sway the jury. The trial was not going well, from the prosecution's point of view. After four days, Murer still cynically denied everything. One witness after the other had stepped forward and identified him, but Murer said they were making a mistake; they were taking him for somebody else. He had never so much as touched a Jew. He had never seen a dead Jew. He was innocent, victim of a monstrous error.

Now Brodi said to me: "I hear that Murer's two sons sit in the front row of the courtroom with his wife and sneer at the witnesses."

I nodded. The boys thought this was a great show. They laughed and grimaced. Two foreign newspapermen who covered the trial were so shocked that they asked the presiding judge why he failed to call the boys to order. He told the correspondents that he hadn't seen the boys.

Brodi said quietly: "They'll stop sneering when I am called to the stand." He looked at me piercingly and said: "I didn't come here to testify. I came to *act*." He opened his waistcoat and pulled out a long knife. Brodi spoke without emotion, a man who had made up his mind. "I was able to obtain a plan of the courtroom. I know that the witness stand is close to where Murer sits. Murer killed my child before my eyes. Now I'm going to kill him with this knife before the eyes of his wife and children."

I could see that he was deadly serious. He said he'd thought about it for the past twenty years. He no longer believed in human justice, he said. He had lost faith in God's justice. He would take justice into his own hands. He was not afraid of the consequences. His life was finished anyway. It had been finished that day in the ghetto twenty years ago.

I said: "If you try to kill Murer, you will be treated like a murderer yourself."

"Yes. But great lawyers will come to my defense."

"That's beside the point. No matter what your motives are, the world will call you a murderer. The Nazis are just waiting for such a thing to happen. They will say: 'Look at these Jews who always talk so much about justice. They accuse Murer of murder, and they are murderers themselves. So Murer killed Jews, and a Jew killed him. What's different about that?' That's the way they will argue."

Brodi gave a shrug, unconvinced.

"Think of Eichmann," I said. "He could have been executed without a trace in Argentina. But the Israelis knew it was necessary to drag him across the ocean and risk antagonizing world opinion and being accused of violating international law. Why? Because Eichmann *had to be tried*. The trial was more important than the defendant. Eichmann was already a dead man when he entered the courtroom. But the trial would convince millions of people—those who knew nothing, or who did not *want* to know, or those who knew deep in their hearts but wouldn't admit it even to themselves. All of them saw the seedy, bald man in the glass box who had engineered the 'final solution'—the killing of six million people. They heard the evidence, they read the newspapers, they saw the pictures. And at long last they knew not only that it was true but that it was much worse than anyone could imagine."

Brodi shook his head. "I am not here for the State of Israel. I am not here for the Jewish people. I came here as the father of my murdered child." He stared at me out of hard, pitiless eyes. I wished desperately that he had been able to cry. But perhaps he couldn't cry any more.

I said: "If you try to harm Murer, all our work will have become useless. We cannot achieve our purpose by using *their* methods. You've read the Bible, Jacob Brodi. You know the Commandment: 'Thou shalt not kill.' I want Murer, not you, to leave the courtroom as a convicted murderer."

He shook his head.

"Words, Mr. Wiesenthal, nothing but words. It's so easy for you. Your child was not murdered. My boy was murdered. I told you I did not want to come. You said it was necessary. Well, I am here now. And you know why I came."

I turned away. I couldn't bear the expression in his eyes. I talked for a long time, although I do not remember exactly what I said. I talked about myself: Why I had decided to do what I had done for the past twenty years—because someone had to do it, for our children and for *their* children—but not out of hatred.

"I still cry sometimes, Mr. Brodi, when I hear what happened to children in the concentration camps," I said. "I did cry when I heard about your boy. Because he could have been my boy. Your child was also my child. Do you really believe I could go on with my work if I didn't feel that way?"

I grasped his shoulders. Suddenly Jacob Brodi put his head on my shoulder. I felt a convulsion go through his body. He cried. We stood there for a while, without saying a word. When I left his room a few minutes later, I carried his knife with me.

Jacob Brodi was called to the stand the following day. He never glanced at Murer. He told his experience in a toneless voice, as though it had happened to someone else. It was very quiet in the courtroom. Even Murer's boys sensed what this lonely man went through during his testimony. They didn't sneer at him. The defense didn't want to question Brodi. He was dismissed. After he left the courtroom, Murer got up and once more said that the witness must have been mistaken. Murer had not shot the boy. Maybe it was someone else.

The trial lasted a week. Foreign journalists sensed that the mood in the courtroom was definitely in favor of the defendant. Some jurors, dressed in the traditional green loden costumes, watched Murer with unconcealed sympathy. Some tried to follow the proceedings fairly, but they seemed to be in the minority. The leading paper in Graz supported the arguments of Murer's defense attorneys. He was said to have received many sympathetic letters from political friends.

The audience was pleased when the defense succeeded in confusing one witness. He became carried away by emotion as he told the court what had happened and mixed up a detail. Another witness was not certain about a date. He described one of Murer's crimes, and then Murer proved conclusively that he had not been in Wilna at that time. Naturally, the testimony of these people was discredited.

Among the witnesses for the defense was Martin Weiss, Murer's former assistant in the ghetto. Weiss had been brought to Graz from Straubing prison in Bavaria, where he was serving a life sentence for mass murder. When Weiss pointed out that "some Lithuanian officers wore uniforms similar to Murer's," there was a satisfied murmur among the audience.

The testimony of the witnesses for the prosecution was received with icy silence. (I was called "manhunter" by Murer's lawyer.) Israel Sebulski, now living in Munich, told the court that his fifteen-year-old son had been mercilessly beaten by Murer, and as a result had lost his mind and the use of his legs and was now in an institution. Mrs. Tova Rajzman of Tel Aviv swore that Murer had shot her sister because she had taken a piece of bread from a Polish woman. In his rage, she said, he had later killed three other women and a man who happened to be standing nearby. As Mrs. Rajzman recalled the scene, she was overcome by the memory and began to scream.

"Don't scream in the courtroom!" said Hofrat Dr. Peyer, the presiding judge.

"Forgive me, Your Honor," said Mrs. Rajzman. "But it was terrible. My sister's blood spilled over my feet."

"Couldn't it have been somebody else who did it?"

"No, Your Honor. It was Murer. I remember him from the time he first came into the ghetto. He beat me in the street. When he walked through the ghetto, everybody had to step down from the pavement, and then had to bow and take off their hats."

Dr. Schumann, the prosecutor, had prepared himself thoroughly for his task. He had studied Murer's files in Frankfurt and Munich. In his summing-up speech, he pointed out that the witnesses had identified Murer beyond any doubt. He appealed to the jury to pass judgment on the defendant as they would on the murderer of their own children.

"In at least six cases there is no reasonable doubt about the defendant's guilt," said the prosecutor. "I want you to know that this trial has already badly hurt the illusion of us Austrians being a *Kulturvolk.*"

After four hours, the jury returned a verdict of "not guilty." In Austria, the exact count of jury votes is announced in the courtroom. The foreman of the jury said that in two of the seventeen cases there had been a tie of four to four. He had cast his ballot in favor of Murer.

I was not in Graz that day. Reporters later told me that the people in the courtroom had cheered and applauded when Murer's acquittal was announced. Some had brought in flowers while the jury was still deliberating. Now they rushed up to Murer with the bouquets.

An American diplomat who visited friends in Graz the following day and wanted to send flowers to his hostess was told in three florist shops that there was nothing left. Everything had been bought up for the trial. Murer left the courtroom a triumphant hero. He was seen being driven off in the Mercedes of Rudolph Hochreiner, a Nazi who had been indicted for the murder of nine Jews and had been acquitted.

There was a storm of indignation throughout Austria. With few exceptions, the Austrian press is anti-Nazi and democratic. Newspapers representing nearly all political groups denounced the verdict as a *Justizskandal,* a travesty of justice. In Vienna, Catholic students pinned yellow stars on their chests and marched in protest through the streets, shouting "Murer is a murderer! Murer must be punished!" Afterward they attended a service of penitence in

Michaeler Church to express remorse for the crimes committed by Christians against Jews.

The prosecutor appealed the verdict. Austria's Supreme Court has granted an appeal with respect to one charge: a case I had discovered in which Murer had been seen committing a murder by two different witnesses. The witnesses knew nothing of each other, now live in different parts of the world, but described the same scheme independently. Murer will be tried once more. Justice may still prevail.

I met Jacob Brodi in the lobby of a Vienna hotel a few days after Murer's acquittal. He looked through me as if I hadn't been there. I understood. I may have saved Murer's life. It is not a very pleasant thought, but there was nothing else I could have done.

Chapter 5

THE SECRETS
OF *ODESSA*

[Late in 1947 I began to trace the escape routes of missing top Nazis who had vanished and were now on the Wanted lists of several nations. I knew that all prominent SS leaders and Gestapo members had received from the RSHA * toward the end of the war false personal documents bearing new names, but I was much less interested in names than in routes. It was essential to find out where they had gone, how they got there, who had helped them, and who had paid for all this.

Few prominent Nazis had tried to escape toward the Soviet Union, where they wouldn't be sure of a friendly welcome. The exception was Heinrich Müller, former RSHA boss and today perhaps the most wanted Nazi leader of all—and one of the biggest unsolved postwar mysteries. He may have found refuge in Russia, but I doubt that he is still alive. A Nazi criminal knew he couldn't expect much help in England and Scandinavia. If he wanted to escape, he had to go south.

I took a map of the world and drew a fine pencil line for each top Nazi whose escape route I knew. Three main routes emerged. The first led from Germany to Austria and Italy, then to Spain. The second pointed to the Arab countries in the Near East, where Nazi ex-

* See Appendix: RSHA, *Reichssicherheitshauptamt.*
78

perts are now highly esteemed in many fields. (Characteristically, the Arab edition of Hitler's *Mein Kampf* does not contain the author's rather unflattering remarks about "Semites," among whom he included Arabs.) The third route connected Germany with certain countries in South America. Until the fall of the Perón regime in 1955, Argentina was the promised land for high-ranking Nazis. Today Paraguay is the fashionable refuge for the SS elite.

Next I transferred the details of known escapes to smaller-scale maps of central and southern Europe. Many transports had gone from certain German cities—Bremen, Frankfurt, Augsburg, Stuttgart, Munich—to the Allgäu, a secluded wooded region in southern Bavaria, conveniently close to the borders of both Austria and Switzerland.

Many routes seemed to converge in Memmingen, a medieval town in the heart of the Allgäu. There the routes branched off in two directions. One continued to Lindau on Lake Constance, where it once more divided into two lines, one going to Bregenz in Austria, the other to nearby Switzerland. The main route led from Memmingen to Innsbruck and across the Brenner Pass to Italy. Later I found out that the Nazis called the north-south route the "B-B axis," a code name for Bremen-Bari. All this was obviously no coincidence. A few individuals or possibly a whole organization seemed to have arranged these escapes. As it turned out, it was an extremely efficient clandestine organization that had all the money it needed—and it needed plenty.]

At the Nuremberg trial I met a German who was there as a witness. I shall call him Hans. He was—and is—an outspoken anti-Nazi who now lives in Germany and must be protected. Hans was recommended to me by American friends. He had been a member of the *Abwehr.** Like many *Abwehr* men, he had been a high-ranking officer with an impressive family background, who regarded the criminal elements in the Nazi Party's *Sicherheitsdienst* (SD) ** first with contempt and later with fear. The rivalry between the counterintel-

* See Appendix: *Abwehr.*
** See Appendix: *Sicherheitsdienst.*

ligence services of the Wehrmacht and the Party ended, not unexpectedly, with a massive defeat of the *Abwehr*. Admiral Canaris,
head of the *Abwehr*, died in a concentration camp; many *Abwehr*
members were executed. The survivors never forgot the humiliation,
and some of them have been among my most reliable helpers.

A few weeks after our meeting in Nuremberg, when Hans had
been rather reticent, I met him again at the Hotel Goldener Hirsch
in Salzburg. This time he spoke frankly; I suppose he'd investigated
me in the meantime. We talked about the political situation. Hans
was pessimistic, and very critical of the Allies.

"I can see what's going to happen. Now that some of the top
Nazis have been sentenced, most of the lesser criminals will be released by the Allies after a token sentence. No one wants to bother
with that Nazi riffraff. Just wait—in no time they will be in big positions again, and no one will be able to touch them, because you cannot punish a man twice for the same crime."

This turned out to be a prophetic statement.

"The Allies made a mistake when they decided to clean up Germany," Hans said. "Commendable, but hopeless. They will never
understand the Nazi mentality. How can they? Instead they should
have given the job to the decent Germans. There *are* such Germans
—although after the war all Germans were considered bad Germans. German courts should have tried the SS criminals. German
judges would have been able to penetrate the twisted minds of the
defendants. They would have sentenced those found guilty. Now it
is too late. The Nazis have learned to deal with those 'innocents
abroad.' The Nazis' secret weapon is the pretty girls of Germany
and Austria. The crisis is over, and the Nazis are getting cocky
again. You would be surprised how much talk there is in Nazi circles
about a future Fourth Reich. The big shots are abroad, plotting
again. They live safely in certain countries that have no extradition
treaties with Germany."

Obviously Hans knew more than he was telling me. I tried to
draw him out. He might be able to give me some answers I needed.

"How did the big Nazis get away?"

"Didn't you ever hear of Odessa?" Hans asked.

I said (rather naïvely, I now realize): "In the Ukraine? Yes, I
was there before the war. A lovely city."

"No, no." Hans was impatient. "*ODESSA*, written in capital letters. The secret escape organization of the SS underground."

A lot of things I'd heard began to make sense now. I remember how Nazis told each other that somebody "went to Odessa," and I had wondered about it.

"*ODESSA*," Hans continued, "has a remarkable record of getting SS criminals and Gestapo members out of the country. It has even helped them escape from prison."

That night Hans told me the complete story of the astonishing organization. It had been set up in 1947. The name stood for *Organisation der SS-Angehörigen*—Organization of SS Members.

"At the end of the war, there were no such secret organizations, although many Allied experts assumed so," Hans said. "The big Nazis lived in hiding. Or they reappeared under false names. Then the first committees were set up, presumably to act as liaison between Nazis in prison and their relatives. These committees had the blessing of the churches and of the Allies. They were said to be strictly charitable institutions. In fact, many people who never had any Nazi records acted as voluntary helpers."

Hans laughed. "A good joke, really, when you look at it now. Under the very eyes of Allied officers and decent Germans, valuable contacts were established between the Nazis in prison and new underground groups outside. The committees forwarded letters from the prisoners to their relatives. Unfortunately, no expert bothered to read the letters carefully, although there was still censorship. No one seemed to care. But one must not underestimate the Nazis. They had had enough time to prepare for their defeat. They had established their secret codes long before the collapse of the Third Reich. When they were released from prison, after a few months or after a few years, they were at once taken over by the new underground groups. The main underground network was called *Spinne*—'spider.' So much for those in prison. But there were many others who had been released from Allied internment camps without trial or who had never been arrested because there was so much confusion that their true identity remained hidden. For some time, anyway. But later they were getting nervous. They didn't want to hang around until it was too late and the awful truth about their crimes became known. They had to get away. The Nazis decided that the time had come to set up a world-wide clandestine escape network."

ODESSA was the answer. Instead of the former B-B (Bremen-Bari) axis, *ODESSA* ran two main routes of escape, from Bremen to Rome and from Bremen to Genoa. Hans didn't know where the *Verteilerkopf* (main distribution center) was situated; possibly in Augsburg or Stuttgart, but perhaps as far away as Argentina. Among *ODESSA*'s prominent travelers were Hitler's deputy, Martin Bormann, and Adolf Eichmann.

In a surprisingly short time *ODESSA* built up an efficient organization of couriers, whom they found in unlikely places. They used Germans who had been hired to drive U.S. Army trucks on the autobahn between Munich and Salzburg for *The Stars and Stripes,* the American Army newspaper. The couriers had applied for their jobs under false names, and the Americans in Munich had failed to check them thoroughly. It was a brilliant idea. The Military Police would never bother to search one of these trucks. The driver would hand them a few issues of the newspaper and cross the German-Austrian border near Salzburg, while a couple of Nazi fugitives were hiding behind bundles of *The Stars and Stripes.* Sometimes the trucks also carried forbidden neo-Nazi literature, mimeographed leaflets, reports about "significant incidents" between Americans and Russians.

I made a report to the CIC in Salzburg, and two of the truck drivers were arrested. But much harm had already been done. Scores of wanted Nazis had been spirited out of Germany.

ODESSA was organized as a thorough, efficient network. Every forty miles an *Anlaufstelle* (port of call) was set up, manned by at least three and not more than five people who knew only the two nearest ports—the one from which fugitives were brought and the next, where they were later delivered. *Anlaufstellen* were set up along the entire Austrian-German border, particularly in Ostermiething in Upper Austria, Zell am See in the Salzburg district, and Igls, near Innsbruck in the Tyrol. In Lindau, close to both Austria and Switzerland, *ODESSA* had set up an "export-import" company with representatives in Cairo and Damascus.

Hans' information was confirmed to me the following year by an Austrian police official in Bregenz, who told me a lot about the illegal transports that came from nearby Lindau. Bregenz and Lindau, on Lake Constance, where the borders of Germany, Austria, and Switzerland meet, were the perfect spots for people who wanted to get away in a hurry. The Austrian official said that the illegal transports were no secret to the German, Austrian, and Swiss police officials—or to the local French occupation authorities, who seemed to wink at them.

"Did you ever hear of Haddad Said?" asked the police official.

"No."

"A German traveling on a Syrian passport who organizes many transports that come from Lindau through Bregenz."

"Where is his base of operations?"

"In Munich and Lindau, from which places Haddad Said channels the groups through Bregenz. We cannot stop them. They have valid border permits. From there they cross the Swiss border, just a few miles away. Once the fugitives are in Switzerland, they get on the next train to Zurich or Geneva, and there they take a plane and fly to the Near East or to South America. All of them have valid passports, visas, and lots of money."

"Can't you do anything about these transports?" I asked.

"What can *we* do? These people are just passing through and we are glad to get them out of our territory. Their documents are in order. The trips to Switzerland are often camouflaged as family visits. The fugitives are accompanied by women and children who have been recruited among the local people in Lindau. They pose as relatives. The women get a little money and do some shopping in Switzerland. A few days later the women and children return, minus the men. No one asks any questions. This Haddad Said has useful friends in high places."

"But what about the French occupation authorities?"

He shrugged. "This is what really bothers the anti-Nazis among us. Maybe Haddad Said has connections there too. I've heard that similar transports are also tolerated by the Americans and the British in *their* zones. . . . Who would have thought that this could happen less than four years after the end of the Second World War?"

Later—too much later—I found out that "Haddad Said" was SS *Hauptsturmführer* Franz Röstel, one of the main organizers of *ODESSA*. He now commutes between a German settlement in Uruguay and Spain's Costa Brava, where many former SS *Führer* and Party *Bonzen* (bosses) have lovely vacation homes. The scenery is beautiful, the climate excellent, the risk minimal.

I discovered later that *ODESSA* also ran a so-called monastery route between Austria and Italy. Roman Catholic priests, particularly Franciscan friars, helped pass the fugitives down a long line of "safe" religious houses. Doubtless the priests were prompted by a sense of Christian compassion; many may have done the same thing for Jews during the Nazi regime. Of the eight thousand Jews of Rome, half were hidden during the Nazi occupation in the convents and houses of religious orders, and they survived. Several dozen were hidden in the Vatican. Many found refuge in the homes of Italian neighbors who never knew the meaning of anti-Semitism. (About a thousand Roman Jews, two thirds of them women and children, died in Auschwitz.)

As I found out more about the operations of *ODESSA*, I realized why the Allied intelligence services knew nothing about it. The men who ran *ODESSA* had overlooked no detail. The *Anlaufstellen* were well camouflaged—an inconspicuous inn, a deserted hunting lodge in the woods, an isolated farmhouse near the border. There the travelers would stay a few hours, days, or weeks, until the next stretch of the route was clear. Although ordinary German and Austrian citizens were not permitted to travel in the military occupation zones without special permits, *ODESSA's* experts were able, to get border permits for all occupation zones.

Ironically, a similar method of travel was also used by the illegal transports of *Bricha* (the Hebrew word for "escape"), which at the same time channeled Jewish refugees through Austria to Italy and from there to Palestine. Sometimes the two organizations used the same facilities at the same time. I know a small inn near Merano, in the Italian Tyrol, and another place near the Reschenpass between Austria and Italy, where illegal Nazi transports and illegal Jewish transports sometimes spent the night without knowing of each other's presence. The Jews were hidden on the upper floor and told not to move; the Nazis, on the ground floor, were warned to stay inside.

A *Bricha* courier once explained to me how this could happen. "We were all hiding like thieves in the night. Everybody was told to keep to himself. When one saw strangers, one quickly moved away. It must have amused our contact people—professional local smugglers who were on good terms with the police and the border guards. They didn't care *whom* they channeled across—so long as they got paid."

ODESSA had contacts with professional smugglers in all frontier areas and valuable connections with the Spanish, Egyptian, Syrian, and certain South American embassies in various European capitals. They kept in touch with the special German section of the "Social Assistance" organization of Spain's Falange, which took charge of "passengers" in Spain and sent them on to South America. Others were taken to Genoa, and there boarded ships for South America. All this cost money, and somebody had to pay for it. Somebody did. The story of the money behind *ODESSA* begins much earlier than *ODESSA* itself. In the spring of 1946 (when I was still working for the OSS) an American officer brought a large rucksack to our office in Linz and took out a thick, dark-blue file. He reported that he'd taken the documents from an *Oberst* Keitel at the Ebensee SS internment camp near Bad Ischl.

Neither the Americans nor I realized that this was one of the most amazing documents that had fallen into Allied hands since the end of the war. The documents concerned Nazi capital, not Nazi crimes, and I was only interested in Nazi crimes. I looked at the documents, thinking that they should go to the U.S. Property Control people. That was another of my beginner's mistakes. Since then I've learned that money often leaves a track to a murderer's lair.

The file contained the minutes of a top-secret meeting of Germany's leading industrialists on August 10, 1944, at the Hotel Maison Rouge in Strasbourg. Hitler and the Gestapo knew nothing of the meeting. It was just twenty days after the abortive *putsch* against Hitler of the twentieth of July. The people who went to Strasbourg knew that their lives might depend on keeping their plans a secret.

The Rhine and Ruhr industrialists who had been among the early followers of Hitler's bandwagon in 1933—among others Emil Kirdorf, the coal baron; Kurt von Schroeder, the Cologne banker; Fritz Thyssen, the steel magnate; Georg von Schnitzler, of IG Farben; and Krupp von Bohlen—were also among the first who deserted. By the time the Allied invasion of Europe had started, the smart money in the Rhine and Ruhr area was betting on Hitler's defeat. It was agreed that long-range preparations would have to be made to safeguard assets from Allied confiscation and to salvage the German potential for the future.

The first step was to prevent funds, deposits, patents, blueprints of new weapons from falling into the hands of the Allies. Early in 1944, the top Nazis began to transfer large funds and looted property into neutral and nonbelligerent countries. At a time when ordinary citizens were sentenced to death for smuggling out a one-dollar bill, the top men in Germany's industries set up enterprises abroad under cover of legitimate business deals. Front men abroad began to invest the money in their own names. No traces must lead back to Germany.

A report issued by the U.S. Treasury Department in 1946 mentioned 750 companies set up all over the world by Germans with German money: 112 in Spain, 58 in Portugal, 35 in Turkey, 98 in Argentina, 214 in Switzerland, 233 in various other countries. The report is not complete. Today I know that it is harder to trace the transfer of funds between three or four big banks on earth than to trace an atomic secret. It is almost impossible, owing to the traditional secrecy of bankers, to find what happened to money that was sent, say, from Germany to a Swiss bank, from there to South America to Spain or Portugal, or possibly back to Liechtenstein or Switzerland.

Many years later—one day in January 1966—I had a conversation in my office that proved my earlier suspicions well-founded. The widow of a former SS *Obersturmbannführer* (lieutenant colonel) came to see me in Vienna. She reported on some neo-Nazis who had threatened her because she refused to have anything to do with them, and then she told me an interesting story. In the fall of 1944, half a year before the end of the war, her husband was approached by his SS superiors. They knew that he had a small account with the Dresdner Bank. They wanted the number of his account and his signature on two blank sheets of paper. He did as he was told.

At the end of the war, all German banks came under control of the Allies, who set up a *Haupt-Treuhänder* (trustee) for the administration of all former Nazi assets. One day the trustee notified the former *Obersturmbannführer* that there were two accounts in his name: one for 12,000 marks, and one for 2,600,000 marks.

"Naturally my husband knew of the 12,000 marks," said the woman. "But he had no idea where the money in the big account had come from. He told them that he'd been told to sign a blank document, and he wondered who now had his signature. If they put so much money into the account of an orinary lieutenant colonel, how much must they have put in for the Nazi *Bonzen?*"

I told the woman it was a good question, but it would be very hard to find the answer. Banking secrets are still among the best-kept secrets in the world. To me it proves that before the war ended the Nazis set up large, hidden funds for the building of a Fourth Reich.

According to the file the American officer had produced in 1946, such matters had been discussed at the memorable meeting at the Hotel Maison Rouge in August 1944. The German industrialists knew that the war was lost. The Western Allies were approaching Paris. The industrialists did not share the romantic illusions of the Nazi Party bigwigs, who talked vaguely of secret weapons that were not yet fully developed, of winning the race for the atomic bomb. The executives knew what the score was and acted accordingly. It would be necessary *at once* to create a "technical network" all over the world that would be able to coordinate all future efforts.

Among those present were representatives of the Rochling concern, Krupp, Messerschmidt, the Goering Werke in Linz, top officials of the War Ministry and the Armament Ministry. A candid statement was reported:

"Germany has already lost the Battle of France. From now on Germany's industry must prepare for the economic postwar campaign. Every industrialist must seek contacts with firms abroad, each for himself, without creating attention. And that is not all. We must be ready to finance the Nazi Party, which will be forced to go underground for some time."

To carry out the decisions of the Strasbourg meeting, German industrialists began to transfer various assets, under cover of legitimate business deals, to secret bank accounts and to business enterprises in Spain, Turkey, and South America. Sylvano Santander, who is now the Argentine ambassador in Spain, was a member of the official commission that investigated Nazi activities in Argentina after the ouster of Perón. He once showed me a list of Argentine enterprises that had been financed by the Nazis. Careful records were kept of all transactions. The German industrialists at the meeting wanted to be sure that no front man abroad who had ever received German funds could later deny having received them. It was decided that copies of all records would be hidden "in various lakes in the Alps" where they might be fished up later during "underwater research."

The minutes of the meeting say: "The Party leadership expects that some members will be convicted as war criminals. Thus preparations must now be made to place the less prominent leaders as 'technical experts' in various German key enterprises. The Party is ready to supply large amounts of money to those industrialists who contribute to the postwar organization abroad. In return the Party demands all financial reserves which have already been transferred abroad or may later be transferred, so that after the defeat a strong new Reich can be built."

There is no record of who was meant by "the Party." It couldn't have been Hitler or Himmler; they knew nothing of the meeting. An interesting statement was made by a Dr. Boss of Speer's Armament Ministry—the man primarily responsible for the production of war matériel, who had been in secret opposition to the Nazi Party since 1942: "The German concerns must set up research institutes and technical offices that are seemingly independent. Such offices should be set up either in big cities, where they won't create attention, or in small villages near lakes and water-power stations, where they can be camouflaged as 'research institutes.'"

As a result of the Strasbourg conference, enormous amounts of money were transferred abroad. *The ODESSA organization was financed from such sources.* Additional income was derived from the illegal trade of *ODESSA* enterprises shipping scrap metal to Tangier and Syria or sending weapons that had come from American ammunition depots in Germany and were "transferred" through *ODESSA* couriers to the Near East.

And *ODESSA* did many other things. Its contact men procured import and export licenses and shipped strategic goods through holes in the Iron Curtain. (One such hole was Vienna, from which materials were sent to nearby Czechoslovakia.) *ODESSA* was an organization of resourceful pros.

In July 1965, I attended a conference of the *Union Internationale des Résistants et Déportés,* held—not purely by accident—in the same room of the Hotel Maison Rouge in Strasbourg where in 1944 the Nazi industrialists had made their plans. The purpose of our conference was to organize the tracing and tracking down of the invisible but considerable Nazi assets.

At this conference I formulated six main questions that so far remain unanswered:

1. Who decided priorities—specifically, who should be taken overseas with the help of *ODESSA?* There must have been a long waiting list, and a lot of jockeying for position.

2. Who selected the names of women and children who survived Nazis who had died, had escaped, or were in prison? Such families would be supported from secret funds. How much should they be given?

3. Who pays for the prominent lawyers who often defend men accused of Nazi crimes? Most of the defendants have no apparent means of paying for their own defense.

4. Who organized a massive legal-aid effort for German war criminals convicted in the Soviet Union and released to Germany after Konrad Adenauer intervened in behalf of imprisoned Germans in Moscow in 1955? We have evidence that some of them, after their arrival from the Soviet Union at Camp Friedland, near Göttingen, received the addresses of West German lawyers and were ordered to report to them.

5. Who finances certain German publishers who specialize in neo-Nazi propaganda literature?

6. Who finances the meetings of former Nazis in various cities of Europe? One took place recently in Milan. The participants arrive from all over Europe with their travel and hotel expenses paid.

Finally, I asked: Who pays for the subversive activities of neo-Nazi groups in various countries?

There are some leads, but they are hard to follow up. I know a man who has no personal fortune but who "contributed" 60,000 marks to a neo-Nazi publishing enterprise; obviously it wasn't *his* money. We have the name and address of a former German industrialist who lives in Switzerland and controls a small bank that was popular with top members of the Nazi Party prior to the Second World War. The bank has changed its name; the industrialist hasn't changed his convictions. We know of large capital transfers from South America and Switzerland to Ireland, where German firms have set up branch offices. Former Nazis have bought properties and estates.

And we know something about the Nazi "treasure" that was (and perhaps still is) hidden in the former "Alpine Fortress"—the Nazis' redoubt in the lovely Aussee region in Austria.

The first rumors about a Nazi "treasure" in the Aussee region reached the American authorities in 1946, while I was still working for the OSS. It was hard to separate the facts from the fiction that was printed in the illustrated magazines. Certain facts were known, though. In Salzburg, a Dr. von Hummel, a former aide of Martin Bormann, was arrested as he tried to get away with five million dollars' worth of gold. Near the Schloss Fuschl in Salzburg (which had belonged to Ribbentrop and is now an elegant guest house) a farmer found a crate containing several pounds of gold coins.

After I started the Documentation Center in Linz in 1947, rumors and reports concerning the Nazi treasure arrived every week. Four years later, after sifting all available material, I wrote a series of documented articles. I concluded that millions of counterfeit English pound notes were lying at the bottom of the Töplitzsee, one of the lakes in the region. The Americans were not interested in costly diving experiments. Nor were the Austrians interested so long as the Americans were around.

Eight years later, in the summer of 1959, the Hamburg magazine *Stern* got permission from the Austrian authorities to organize a diving expedition. A team of divers and underwater television cameramen investigated the bottom of the Töplitzsee for two months. They brought up fifteen boxes. At least a dozen more were found too deeply embedded in the mud to be rescued. All cases but one contained counterfeit Bank of England notes.

The Aussee region in the northwestern corner of Styria, which the natives call *Ausseerland,* was part of the so-called Nazi Redoubt, where the Germans would supposedly make their heroic last stand. Goebbels named it *Alpenfestung* (Alpine Fortress). This part of the fortress fell, rather ingloriously, on May 9, 1945, when Major Ralph Pierson and five American soldiers arrived in the village of Altaussee in one tank and one jeep. No shots were fired. A week earlier Berlin had fallen. Twenty-four hours earlier V-E Day had been proclaimed.

Early in 1944, almost 18,000 people had lived in the region. At the end of the war, nearly 80,000 people lived there. Allowing for a few thousand German soldiers, who were the 60,000 civilians who had arrived during the last year before the collapse of the Third Reich? To the American authorities this was not an academic question, because it was known that many top Nazis had moved there, many under assumed names. As early as Christmas 1944, Nazi Party people began to send their families there, as well as their loot and the records they wanted to hide. Nazi collaborators from Romania, Hungary, Bulgaria, and Slovakia also arrived. Gestapo Chief Ernst Kaltenbrunner moved into a house in the town of Altaussee. The RSHA,* the SD,* and the Abwehr * brought their secret documents and assets—gold, money, and narcotics.

To deceive the local populace, a few SS hospitals were built. Many shipments of gold and narcotics arrived in ambulances marked with the Red Cross. Adolf Eichmann came with staff members of his section IV B 4 * and with twenty-two iron boxes which probably contained documents and gold—a transport that later played an important role in the tracing of Eichmann's movements.

After March 1945 the SS, in its methodical way, began to make records of the assets transported there. Only one detailed list fell into the hands of the Americans. I saw a copy. The list concerns assets of the RSHA, sent by Ernst Kaltenbrunner from Berlin to Altaussee:

50 kilograms of gold bars
50 cases with gold coins and gold articles, each case weighing
    100 pounds
2,000,000 American dollars
2,000,000 Swiss francs
5 cases filled with diamonds and precious stones
1 stamp collection, worth at least 5,000,000 gold marks

Later we found evidence that during the first days of May 1945 the Reichsbank's special department that handled loot from concentration camps had sent several boxes containing "tooth gold" to Aussee. (Collections of gold teeth were sent by the camp cashiers to a central depot at Oranienburg concentration camp and from there to the workshops of Degussa, a firm that melted the gold down into

* See Appendix.

bars.) Some Degussa gold was later found in the Tyrol in the form of camouflaged gold bricks, in the roofs of houses, after one overloaded roof had collapsed. The gold was requisitioned by the French occupation authorities.

The most valuable part of the loot was also the best known: art treasures taken from the museums of France, Italy, Belgium, Denmark, and Holland, which were stored in an old salt mine near Altaussee. There the local *Gauleiter*, SS *Führer* Eigruber, conceived an idea of how to "protect" the loot. The Germans had found seven dud bombs dropped by U.S. Air Force planes. German experts disassembled the bombs, reloaded them, put in new fuses, and concealed them in crates marked CAUTION! MARBLE! DO NOT TILT! which were placed alongside the paintings. Eigruber's plan was to set off the bombs just before the Americans arrived. Afterward American bomb fragments would be found near the wrecked art treasures, and this would prove that the Americans had barbarically destroyed the art works. Fortunately, members of the Austrian resistance got there before it was too late and guarded the paintings until the Americans arrived. American experts removed the fuses, and the paintings were later returned to their rightful owners. Their value has been estimated at more than two and a half billion dollars.

I frequently went to Altaussee after August 1945, when I found out that Eichmann's wife lived there. The region was full of strange rumors. Waiters, taxi drivers, and hotel porters seemed to work for an invisible espionage network. A friend in Altaussee always knew about my arrival an hour *before* I got there. I went to the secluded house that had been inhabited by Gestapo Chief Ernst Kaltenbrunner, who had been captured and was later sentenced to death in Nuremberg. The house belonged to an elderly Viennese woman, Frau Christl Kerry, who moved back in during the winter of 1945. During the next two years, strange things occurred around that house. Shadows appeared in the dead of night, and Frau Kerry heard noises as if people were digging outside. The next morning she would find large, square holes in the ground, as if chests or boxes had been removed.

A peasant named Joseph Pucherl found two iron boxes in a rubbish heap. He turned them over to the authorities. They opened the boxes and found 10,167 gold coins. One day in 1946 two unknown men arrived at the shore of the Töplitzsee and fished up a wooden box. Later the Austrian police confirmed that the box had contained printing plates for counterfeit dollars. In June 1950 several automobiles arrived at the shore of the lake of Altaussee. Several men who had earlier shown French identification papers put on diving gear and went into the lake. They departed later with twelve iron boxes. Still later the Americans found out that the divers had been German, not French. The CIC never discovered what was found in the lake.

These are facts, unexplained facts—not rumors. Other puzzling facts: at least seven people died in mysterious circumstances in the region of the lakes. Two bodies found in an abyss of the nearby Dead Mountains were identified as those of two former employees of a Nazi naval research station at Töplitzsee. In 1955, another German who had once worked there was found dead after a fall from a rock. On the night of October 5, 1963, a young man from Munich named Alfred Egner dove 200 feet down in the Töplitzsee. He had been hired by two Germans, who were waiting in a boat near the shore. When Egner didn't come up, the two Germans became panicky, drove back to Munich, and reported the boy's death to his father. One of the Germans was a former SS officer named Freiberger, who had worked during the war for the German espionage apparatus in Switzerland. The other was a Dr. Schmidt who had been convicted in 1962 in West Germany for unauthorized dealings in gold coins. The Austrian police found Egner's wallet, which he had left on shore with his clothes before diving into the lake. The wallet contained three 1905 Austrian gold coins. Egner's father revealed that his son had been diving in the Töplitzsee before.

Until then, the Austrian authorities had shrugged off all happenings around the lakes of the region as "accidents" or "baseless rumors." After Egner's death, when the papers claimed a connection between this latest "accident" and Nazi "treasure," the area around the lake was roped off, and the Austrian authorities began an official search. After several weeks of diving operations, they found the body of Egner, several cases containing counterfeit English banknotes, engraving plates for five-pound notes, and parts of weapons.

Experts have estimated the assets the Nazis managed to hide in various parts of the world at $750 million and perhaps as high as a billion dollars. The list of people authorized to dispose of these funds has been called the most important unsolved secret of the Third Reich. Six such lists are said to exist, two of them in the safe-keeping of certain banks. Two may have been in the hands of the people who organized *ODESSA* in 1947. On the basis of all available information, I agree with American experts who studied the whole problem after the war and believe that one of the six master lists is still lying at the bottom of the Töplitzsee. On October 23, 1963, I told Franz Olah, then the Interior Minister of Austria, about this. If some Nazi assets were ever recovered in the region, I asked that they be used for further restitution for survivors of Nazism, not for "the financing of antidemocratic institutions."

In September 1964 I was invited by the government-controlled CTK news agency in Prague to go there and study the contents of four iron-bound chests that had been brought up by divers from the bottom of Černé Jezero (Black Lake) near Budějovice (Budweis) in southern Bohemia. The Czechoslovak authorities had obtained precise information about the origin of the chests. Prisoners working for the RSHA in Berlin had loaded them on trucks in the morning of April 13, 1945. One of the former prisoners now lives in Czechoslovakia. He remembered that RSHA chief Heinrich Müller had personally supervised the loading.

The convoy of trucks left Berlin and went through Dresden and Prague to Budějovice. Several chests were dumped into Black Lake. The other chests were taken to the Chiemsee estate of Dr. Rudolph Schmidt, the private physician of Rudolf Hess. They were presumably later dumped in the Chiemsee—not far from where the U.S. Army now runs a popular recreation center. The Chiemsee has not yielded any of its secrets.

The chests in Prague contained:

A detailed secret report about the assassination of Chancellor Dollfuss

A list of Gestapo agents in several European countries

The diary of the daughter of Prince Hohenlohe-Langenberg, who was the host, in 1938, of Lord Runciman, the British mediator in the Czechoslovak crisis

Various documents about the fight against the Communists

A report of German espionage activities in Italy

Documents about the activities of German Ambassador Otto Abetz in France

The most important document was the list of Gestapo agents in European countries. I was told in Prague by an official who had seen the list that many of these men now occupy official positions in their homelands. Many live in Western and in Eastern Germany. The Czechoslovak government later handed over to the Yugoslav government a list of 1800 Yugoslav Gestapo agents. I was also told by the same source that the Russians were given a copy of all names on the master list.

Perhaps the most interesting document I saw personally in Prague was the official *Kriegstagebuch* (war journal) of the SS division *Das Reich*. This journal had been found earlier in Castle Zasmuky, near Prague. It openly records mass executions of Jews in Austria and other Nazi-occupied countries. The journal supplied evidence for the trial of Himmler's aide SS General Karl Wolff, who claimed before the court that he hadn't heard about the executions until "much later." But copies of all entries in the *Kriegstagebuch* had been sent to Himmler as early as 1941. All had gone through the hands of Karl Wolff. He was sentenced to fifteen years in prison.

Chapter 6

EICHMANN
THE ELUSIVE

[I saw Adolf Eichmann for the first time on the opening day of his trial in the courtroom in Jerusalem. For nearly sixteen years I had thought of him practically every day and every night. In my mind I had built up the image of a demonic superman. Instead I saw a frail, nondescript, shabby fellow in a glass cell betweeen two Israeli policemen; they looked more colorful and interesting than he did. Everything about Eichmann seemed drawn with charcoal: his grayish face, his balding head, his clothes. There was nothing demonic about him; he looked like a bookkeeper who is afraid to ask for a raise. Something seemed completely wrong, and I kept thinking about it while the incomprehensible bill of indictment ("the murder of six million men, women, and children") was being read. Suddenly I knew what it was. In my mind I'd always seen SS *Obersturmbannführer* Eichmann, supreme arbiter of life and death. But the Eichmann I now saw did not wear the SS uniform of terror and murder. Dressed in a cheap, dark suit, he seemed a cardboard figure, empty and two-dimensional. Later I told First Procurator Hausner that Eichmann should have worn a uniform. That would have re-created the real identity and true image of the Eichmann the witnesses remembered. They too seemed a little puzzled by the shabby little civilian in the glass cell. Hausner said that emotionally

I was right but that the idea was not practical. It might have given the aura of a show trial, a masquerade. The Israelis were aware that they had been under the continuous scrutiny of the whole world since they had captured Eichmann and brought him across the ocean, and they wanted to avoid unnecessary criticism. I had one other suggestion, also obviously impractical. Fifteen times, after each item of the indictment, Eichmann was asked whether he was guilty. Each time, he said "Not guilty." This procedure, too, seemed inadequate to me. I thought that Eichmann should have been asked six million times, and he should have been made to answer six million times.

By committing the perfectly incredible crime, the Nazis had hoped to get away with it before the bar of history. Future generations wouldn't believe that such a thing could have happened. *Ergo,* the Nazis deduced, history would one day conclude that it had *not* happened. The crime was of such a scope that it was inconceivable.

After weeks in the courtroom I was oppressed by a growing sense of unreality. The courtroom was a gloomy, fortified island in the busy, sunlit city of Jerusalem. The island was guarded by soldiers with submachine guns. The spectators were searched for weapons. When I left this fortress of retribution and walked out into the sun of Israel, children were playing in the street, people were coming home from work, young couples were in love, women carried shopping bags. They seemed totally unaware of the tragedy that was being recalled in the courtroom. I remember being annoyed about the seeming indifference of these people, but I know it was absurd to blame them: almost all of them had lost a relative or a friend because of the little man in the glass cell. Life went on; life was stronger than the defendant in the courtroom, with the forest of six million dead behind him.

Eichmann's capture came at the right moment psychologically. Had he been caught at the end of the war and tried in Nuremberg, his crimes might now be forgotten. He would have been only another face among the defendants in the dock. At that time, everybody was glad that the nightmare was over. Until the trial of Eichmann, there were millions of people in Germany and Austria who pretended not to know or didn't want to know about the enormity of the SS crimes.

The trial did away with such self-deception; after it, no one could claim ignorance. Eichmann, the man, didn't count. He was dead the moment he entered the courtroom. But millions of people read about him, heard the story of the "Final Solution" on radio, and saw the courtroom drama on the television screen. They heard Eichmann's colorless voice, saw his impassive face. Only once did he come close to something resembling emotion, on the ninety-fifth day of the trial, when he said: "I must admit that I now consider the annihilation of the Jews one of the worst crimes in the history of mankind. But it did happen, and we must do all we can to prevent it from happening again."

I've since talked to many Germans and Austrians about the trial. Almost all of them were impressed by the judicial procedure. They realized that the incredible crime had happened. They had to re-examine their consciences. And perhaps some of them came to the same conclusion as Eichmann—it must never happen again.

The Eichmann trial proved the inadequacy of human law. The criminal codes of all civilized nations know the definition of murder. The lawmakers were thinking of the murder of one person, or two, or fifty, or maybe a thousand persons. But the systematic extermination of six million people blasts the framework of all law. It is like the explosive force of an H-bomb—something people don't want to think of. Eichmann understood this very well. In Budapest he said to some friends in 1944: "One hundred dead is a catastrophe. Five million dead is a statistic."

As an architect I learned to build houses according to certain structural rules. I knew that my houses would not withstand an earthquake above a certain force. The "Final Solution of the Jewish Question" was the kind of earthquake for which there were no building rules.

Nearly everything about Eichmann remains incomprehensible. I spent years searching his personal history to find something that might explain why he became what he was. I didn't find anything. Eichmann came from a religious, quiet family. His father, a member of the Presbyterian church, once spoke as the guest of honor at the synagogue in Linz, when the head of the Jewish Community there, Benedikt Schwäger, was awarded a high Austrian decoration.

Unlike Hitler, Eichmann had no unpleasant experiences with

Jews. He was not jilted by a Jewish girl or swindled by a Jewish merchant. He was probably honest when he said, at the trial, that he'd only done his job. He said he wouldn't have hesitated to send his own father into a gas chamber if he'd been ordered to do so. Eichmann's great strength was that he treated the Jewish problem unemotionally. He was the most dangerous man of all—a man with no human feeling. He once said he was not an anti-Semite. But he certainly was antihuman.

Late in April 1945, Eichmann was with the Jewish Council members in Theresienstadt concentration camp, when he saw Rabbi Leo Baeck, one of the leaders of modern Jewry, walk by. Eichmann said he was surprised that Rabbi Baeck was still alive. No one said a word; everybody was afraid Eichmann might issue an order sending Baeck to his death. But Eichmann was in a benevolent mood that day, and he did nothing about Rabbi Baeck. However, as he took his leave, he said amiably to the Jews around him: "Let me tell you something. Jewish death lists are my favorite reading matter before I go to sleep."

He took a few of the lists from the table and walked out.]

The search for Eichmann was not a "hunt," as it has been called, but a long, frustrating game of patience, a gigantic jigsaw puzzle. His capture was achieved through the cooperation of many people, most of whom didn't know each other, in several countries. Each added a few pieces of the puzzle; I was able to contribute some significant pieces.

About four weeks after my liberation, while I worked for the War Crimes Commission in Linz, I met Captain Choter-Ischai of the Jewish Brigade, who had come there to channel former concentration-camp inmates into Palestine. He asked me whether I had heard of Adolf Eichmann. I said I'd heard the name from Hungarian Jews at the Mauthausen concentration camp. It meant nothing to me; I was more interested in people whose crimes I had witnessed.

"Better look up the name," said the Captain. "Unfortunately, he comes from our country. He was born in Palestine."

At the War Crimes office, I went through the lists and found the name Eichmann. He was said to have been active in Austria, Czecho-slovakia, France, Greece, Hungary. No first name was given, only his rank: SS *Obersturmbannführer*.

On July 20, 1945, in Vienna, I met a slim, dapper man named Arthur Pier. He wore an inter-Allied fantasy uniform that looked like (and was meant to look like) a confusing combination of American, British, and French sartorial elements. Arthur, who is now known as Asher Ben Nathan and is Israel's first Ambassador to the West German Federal Republic, was then in charge of *Bricha*. He gave me a copy of a list of war criminals that had been made up by the Jewish Agency's Political Department. Dated June 8, 1945, it described Eichmann (no first name) as "married, one child, nickname· Eichie . . . high official of Gestapo H.Q., Department for Jewish Affairs, member of the NSDAP." Under *place of birth* it said "allegedly Sarona, German Templar colony in Palestine." Under *languages* the record gave "German, Hebrew, and Yiddish." This was confirmed to me by several Mauthausen alumni who told me they had heard that Eichmann spoke Hebrew and Yiddish "fluently."

The next bit of information came from Captain O'Meara, then my boss at the Office of Strategic Services, for which I was working after the War Crimes people had left Linz. The Captain was much interested in Eichmann, whom he called "head of the Jewish branch of the Gestapo," and he asked me to work on the case. I wrote the name in a little black book in which I kept a private "wanted" list of my own. On my travels I made it a habit to ask people I met about the names on my list.

The OSS office was at Landstrasse 36 in Linz. I lived just two houses away, at Landstrasse 40. One night in July I sat in my room, looking over my lists, when my landlady came in. Frau Sturm was always interested in the names on the list. Perhaps it was just curiosity—or perhaps she wanted to find out whether she should warn certain people. While she pretended to make my bed, she glanced over my shoulder.

"Eichmann!" she said. "That must be the SS General Eichmann who commanded [*kommandierte*] the Jews. Do you know that his parents live in our street, at Number 32, just two houses away?"

I thought it was absurd that Frau Sturm should know more than the investigators of the Political Department of the Jewish Agency.

But Frau Sturm was right, just as she was right when she said that Eichmann had "commanded" the Jews.

In the morning I spoke to one of my volunteer helpers, a man from Linz I shall call Max. He said Eichmann must be one of the local Eichmanns, known as "Elektro" Eichmann, because his father had been manager of the electric streetcar company and now owned an electrical appliance store. Max said that one of the Eichmann boys had been with the SS.

I said: "According to my information, Eichmann is a Palestinian German, a member of the Templars."

"Nonsense," said Max. "I remember the *Spitzbube* [rascal] well. I'll look him up at the police station."

There was no record at the Linz police station of Adolf Eichmann. It was the aftermath of the war, and the Austrian bureaucracy had not yet picked up the pieces.

The following day—I believe it was July 24—two members of the OSS searched the house at Number 32, which belonged to the Eichmann family. I didn't go with them. The search yielded nothing. Eichmann's father admitted that his son Adolf had been with the SS, but he knew nothing else. Adolf had rarely been home on leave and he never discussed his activities with the family. He had not returned from the war. His last message had been received from Prague, "several months ago." Adolf, his father revealed, had been born in Solingen, Germany, and had come to Linz as a little boy. He now had three children. Was there a picture? Herr Eichmann shook his head. He told the OSS men that his son had never liked to be photographed. They didn't believe it, but ultimately it turned out to be true.

I corrected the information on the Jewish Agency's "Wanted" list and sent it back to Arthur Pier in Vienna.

On August first, Max came to me, excited. He'd just heard rumors that Eichmann was hiding in Fischerdorf, a part of the lovely village of Altaussee. The address was Fischerdorf Number 8. We called up the CIC in nearby Bad Aussee and asked them to search the house. The CIC asked the Austrian police to do it. Somebody made a mistake—whether by accident or design will never be known—and the gendarmes went to Number 38 instead of Number 8. They didn't find Eichmann at Fischerdorf Number 38, although it happened that an SS *Hauptsturmführer* named Anton Burger was hiding there, with a nice collection of guns and ammunition. The Austrians arrested him.

We called up the CIC again. This time an American went to Fischerdorf Number 8, where he found a Frau Veronika Liebl, who admitted that she was the "former" wife of Adolf Eichmann. She'd divorced him in Prague in March 1945, she said, and had resumed her maiden name. She had not seen him since and had no picture of him. She'd come to Altaussee on April 25, lived first at the Seehotel, later at the Parkhotel, and now rented accommodations at Number 8, which belonged to a Herr Wimmer. Her three boys—Klaus, Dieter, Horst—were with her. In Linz, we discovered that Eichmann had been there in September 1944, meeting with Amin el Husseini, the Mufti of Jerusalem, who was responsible for the murder of many Jews. Eichmann had also met with Gestapo Chief Ernst Kaltenbrunner, a native of Linz and great friend of the Eichmann family.

I went to Altaussee and spoke to Frau Maria Pucher, who owned the Parkhotel. She admitted that Adolf Eichmann had stayed there "around May first." One night he had broken into the clothes closet of Frau Pucher's deceased husband and had taken a civilian suit. He hadn't even bothered to give her any money, Frau Pucher grumbled. Later, when she was interrogated by the CIC, she seemed afraid to say very much. Another man in Altaussee confirmed to me that he had seen Eichmann there on May 2 or 3, and that Kaltenbrunner was "quite angry" when he heard of Eichmann's presence in Altaussee and told him "to get the hell out." This was the first time I noticed that even Eichmann's friends wanted no part of him after the war. His former colleagues rightly guessed that he was too hot to touch.

Two or three other people also claimed to have seen Eichmann the first days of May. The CIC went back to Frau Eichmann-Liebl to confront her with this testimony. She stuck to her earlier story. She had not seen Eichmann since their divorce in Prague. She refused to tell the CIC why she had divorced her husband. Obviously somebody was lying.

I wasn't much of an investigator in those early days, but I thought that the clue to the Eichmann mystery could be found around

Altaussee. I went there several times and talked to various people. The problem was to separate fact from rumor. It became apparent that Eichmann and several SS men had come to the region with a convoy of trucks and trailers early in May. The convoy had passed through Altaussee and gone to Bla Alm, a mountain retreat several kilometers away. The innkeeper there remembered the convoy. He told the CIC that the SS men had unloaded twenty-two boxes in his barn. He'd not been present, but later he'd heard that the boxes contained "documents." Other people said they also contained jewels and gold. The innkeeper couldn't remember any details and refused to sign a statement. He, like others we'd talked to, seemed afraid to be interrogated.

A few days later I met a man called Stevens, an American who was working nearby in Bad Ischl. (I'm not sure this was his real name; some Americans worked under assumed names in the region.) Stevens had met several people who had seen Eichmann in Altaussee early in May. He knew about the convoy and the boxes. He told me they contained gold that had "belonged" to the *Reichssicherheitshauptamt*—gold that had been melted down from the gold teeth and wedding rings of concentration-camp victims. Stevens said the convoy had come from Prague. We agreed that Eichmann probably knew where the gold was hidden.

Early in 1946 the name of Adolf Eichmann appeared on the Austrian 'Wanted" list: No. 1654/46. The same list also contained the names of his staff members Guenther, Krumey, Abromeit, Burger, Novak, and others. One of Eichmann's former staff members, Josef Weisel, spent a year in prison in Vienna until the police learned about his war crimes. Weisel had worked for Eichmann in Prague and later in Vienna, where Eichmann had his office at the former Rothschild Palais. Weisel admitted he had seen Eichmann the last time in Prague, "probably in February 1945," where Weisel had received false papers. All members of Eichmann's staff had orders to meet around Ebensee "at the end of the war." In Ebensee, near Bad Ischl, there had been a German concentration camp (later turned into a special Allied internment camp for SS men).

Gradually we were able to reconstruct the exact journey of the Eichmann group from Prague to Budweis (Budějovice, in Bohemia) and from there to Austria, where they arrived late in April. There were rumors in Vienna that Eichmann might have tried to pass as a Jew and submerge in one of the Displaced Persons camps. The rumors started after a Gestapo member was apprehended in a Jewish DP camp near Bremen, and an SS man was caught living with a Jewish woman in another camp. Several people who had returned from the Theresienstadt concentration camp reported that Eichmann had studied Hebrew with a rabbi. These people were certain that he had already then prepared his escape. There were about a hundred thousand people in two hundred DP camps in Austria and Germany, and it would not be easy to screen them for Eichmann. We didn't have his photograph, and obviously he might have changed his name. A search was made of the camps. Although Eichmann was not found, several other SS men were discovered hiding out as Jews in various DP camps. Back in 1943, when my Polish underground friend Biezenski had helped hide my wife as a Polish woman, he had said to me: "Some day the Nazis will try to save their lives by passing as Jews." History had come full circle.

In December 1946, while attending the first postwar Zionist Congress, I met Dr. Rezskö Kastner, a former member of the Jewish Committee in Budapest, which had negotiated in 1944 with the SS to save Hungarian Jews from deportation. Himmler thought the lenient treatment of the Hungarian Jews would give him an alibi that might save him after the collapse of the Third Reich. He ordered Eichmann to carry on the negotiations, but Eichmann (who knew that nothing would save him) sabotaged Himmler's orders. Dr. Kastner described Eichmann to me. In Budapest, Eichmann had given strict orders that no one must ever take his picture. Once he heard that an admiring SS man had photographed him. Eichmann traced the man and had the negative and all copies destroyed. Kastner said it was not true that Eichmann spoke Hebrew and Yiddish: "He knew just a few Yiddish words and used them the way non-Jews do when they tell Jewish jokes. Once he was terribly mad after he'd received a Hebrew letter from a Hungarian rabbi. He tore up the letter and screamed he would punish the rabbi for testing his knowledge of Hebrew. He had created the legend of his Palestinian origin to show the Jews that he knew them well and was too smart for them."

By February 1947 I had almost the complete list of Eichmann's staff members. I had interrogated Anton Burger, the SS man the Austrian gendarmes had arrested in Fischerdorf while looking for Eichmann. Burger confirmed that Eichmann had been in Aussee in May.

During the trials at Nuremberg, I studied thousands of documents there, and among them I found a statement by SS *Obersturmbann-führer* Dr. Wilhelm Höttl, a member of Department VI of the RSHA, who had known Eichmann well. In the spring of 1945, Eichmann had told Höttl in Budapest: "The number of killed Jews is almost six million, but this is top secret."

The files in Nuremberg contained many orders by Eichmann to his staff members in France, Holland, Greece, Croatia, and other countries. In many German-occupied countries his orders had gone directly to high-ranking officials of the German Foreign Office. I saw a letter that had been written by the German ambassador in Croatia, Kasche, who was negotiating with the Croatian government concerning "the purchase of Jews." The Germans offered thirty reichsmarks per person, delivered at the railroad station. Other German embassies in Bucharest, Sofia, and Budapest also carried on a lively correspondence with Eichmann about the annihilation of Jews.

I spent a week in Nuremberg, reading day and night. Eichmann emerged as the top executive of the annihilation machinery. He constantly asked and was given large funds for building more gas chambers and crematoriums, and financed special research institutes investigating lethal gases and methods of execution. I spoke to several SS prisoners who had known Eichmann. Several thought that he had killed himself, but that was wishful thinking. Eichmann, I decided, was the type of man who could extinguish a hundred thousand people with a stroke of his pen but was too much of a coward to shoot himself.

In the fall of 1947 I returned to Nuremberg, and there a member of the staff named Ponger showed me the transcript of the interrogation of Rudolf Scheide, a German who had been employed at various American internment camps. One paragraph explained why we hadn't found Eichmann right after the war in the Aussee region. He had gone to a safer place: an American camp. Rudolf Scheide had testified on November 6, 1947, that "between May 20 and 30" he had been at Camp Berndorf, near Rosenheim, Bavaria, from which place all SS men were later transferred to a special SS camp in Kemanten, and then, on June 15, 1945, to a camp at Cham, a very old town in the Black Forest. Scheide had been in charge of this camp, which had contained about three thousand SS men. Scheide had told the Americans:

> At that time [the middle of June 1945] an SS Führer, who called himself Obersturmführer *Eckmann,* came to me asking that he be carried on our lists under this name. He admitted that his real name was Obersturmbannführer *Eichmann.* At that time the name "Eichmann" meant nothing to me. I indicated to him that it was his own private business what he did with his name.

At the camp Eichmann served on a construction group assigned to work in the nearby town. Every morning the company marched into town under American escort, and every night it returned to camp. On June 30 Scheide found out what Eichmann had really done during the war and informed a CIC man assigned to the camp. When Eichmann's group returned that night, he was not among them. According to Scheide, "escape was possible only with the help of comrades." There was much excitement among the Americans in Nuremberg because of Scheide's testimony. Actually, such escapes were not unusual in the early postwar months. Many internees managed to get away while they were with some such working group. The Allies just didn't have enough troops to guard hundreds of thousands of SS men. The German leader of Eichmann's group was interrogated but denied knowing Eichmann's true identity. At any rate, we now had proof that Eichmann had been alive on June 30, 1945—a fact that was later of great importance.

My search for Eichmann became known in Linz. I was called the "Eichmann-Wiesenthal" who was looking for the son of the "Elektro-Eichmann." Many people came to see me or sent me tips, and I rather foolishly followed up each, pursuing clues any young policeman might have discarded. I had no experience. Besides, I always hoped that the search for Eichmann might lead to the accidental arrest of other Nazi criminals. Once a doctor in Munich wired me and suggested that I come there at once because he had "important information about Eichmann." I went. The doctor was a gaunt, nervous man who had survived the war but had lost his parents in concentration camps and hadn't recovered from the shock. One of his patients, a woman whose name he wouldn't tell me, was living with a man who called himself Friedrich. Friedrich, she told the doctor, was terrified every time the doorbell rang, paced his room all day long, and often complained that "too many Jews are still alive." He would tell the woman that "Germany lost the war because of the Jews. They should *all* be killed." He would go out only at night, and he warned the woman not to talk about him to anyone, because he had "powerful" friends. The search for Friedrich wasn't successful; when we found his address at last, he had disappeared. Much later I found out that he'd been a minor SS *Führer*.

The Friedrich case was a waste of time but it gave me the idea of trying the *"cherchez la femme"* angle in the Eichmann case. It might well be that Eichmann, like so many other SS leaders, had been involved with women, and we might find out something about him through a woman. A member of Eichmann's staff, SS *Führer* Dieter Wisliceny, had been sentenced to death in Bratislava, the capital of Slovakia, and was trying to save his neck by turning informer on his former boss. Wisliceny claimed to know more about Eichmann than anyone else, and he gave us the addresses of several women Eichmann had been involved with. The social background of Eichmann's conquests was as diversified as that of Don Giovanni's women in Mozart's opera. Eichmann's women ranged from a Hungarian baroness to some peasant girls. He might be hiding with any one of them. We tried to trace some. Meanwhile, I asked Arthur Pier to keep Eichmann's wife under observation in Altaussee. Sooner or later, I believed, Eichmann would try to get in touch with his family.

I thought that one of Eichmann's former women friends might have something we needed very much—a picture of him. Arthur agreed, and he had just the man to do the job for us. Manus Diamant was a survivor of the concentration camps who had lost his whole family. He wanted to help us, and he happened to be a handsome young man. Arthur decided to make Manus "Herr van Diamant," a Dutch collaborator and former member of the Dutch SS Division *Nederland* who didn't dare return to his homeland. We hoped that he might become a romantic success with the lonely grass widows of jailed or hiding SS men. He said he would try to get acquainted with Eichmann's wife, and also with some other women who had known Eichmann.

Van Diamant played his part well. He became acquainted with quite a few SS ladies, though not with Frau Eichmann, who wouldn't talk to anyone. He did become friendly with the three Eichmann boys, and often took them out in a rowboat on the lake of Altaussee.

When Diamant told me about his boatrides with the Eichmann boys I sensed that he was going through a great emotional dilemma. He had seen thousands of children such as Eichmann's in the camps who had been shot, starved to death, or sent to gas chambers. And now here he was alone in a small boat with the boys of the man who had organized the death of all the children.

One afternoon I walked with Manus along the lake. He said that he was going to take the Eichmann boys out in a boat tomorrow. His voice was unnaturally tense. I thought I'd better talk to him before it was too late. I said I felt what he was going through. He'd lost his family, and there had been children among them.

"Two boys and a girl," he said, not looking at me.

"I understand, Manus. But remember, we Jews are not Nazis. We don't wage war on innocent children. And if you think you could really hurt Eichmann by—having an accident out there, you are wrong. Some time ago two of our people came to me with a plan. They wanted to kidnap Eichmann's boys—that would be easy—and announce that the boys would be killed unless the father would give himself up to the authorities. I had many arguments against their plan, but they accepted only one. I convinced them that a man who unemotionally ordered the death of one million children would show no emotion for his own. Even if he were deeply hurt by their plan, he would not save the boys by giving himself up. He is not that kind of man."

Diamant didn't answer. I hoped I'd been able to convince him. I talked it over with Arthur, who agreed to relieve Diamant from his assignment in Altaussee. Instead, he was asked to investigate several of Eichmann's former girl friends and to try to bring back a photograph of their elusive lover. The Hungarian baroness had gone to South America; another woman had been killed during the raids on

Dresden. Late in 1947 we found a girl in Urfahr, a northern suburb of Linz, across the Danube. She had known Eichmann well.

Manus became acquainted with her, was invited to her place, found a "family album," and discovered a photograph of Adolf Eichmann made in 1934, thirteen years earlier. The girl didn't want to give Manus the picture, but later she succumbed to his charms. He jubilantly brought me the photograph, was relieved of his assignment, and went back to a more normal life. We made copies of the picture, which was also put on the "Wanted" notice for Eichmann.

One day late in 1947, I had a telephone call from Bad Ischl. My American friend Stevens asked me to come there at once. It was urgent; he didn't want to say more on the phone.

In Bad Ischl, Stevens told me that Frau Veronika Liebl had applied to the local district court for a *Todeserklärung* (declaration of death) of her divorced husband Eichmann "in the interest of the children." At that time all courts in Austria and Germany were deluged with such requests. Until a woman was able to prove that her husband was dead or declared dead, she could get no pension and could not remarry. The courts issued such delarations perfunctorily, without close investigation. One day much later, the "dead" husband might show up, very much alive, after years in a Soviet prisoner-of-war camp or because he'd been in hiding.

When Stevens told me the news, I was too shocked to speak. We looked at each other in silence, aware of the enormous significance of this information. Once Adolf Eichmann was officially declared dead, his name would automatically disappear from all "Wanted" lists. Officially, he would no longer exist. His case would be closed. The world-wide search for him would come to an end. A man presumed dead is no longer hunted. It was a smart move. I was convinced that Eichmann himself had engineered it with the help of his wife.

In my thick Eichmann file I had the testimony of SS *Sturmbannführer* Höttl, who had sworn an affidavit in Nuremberg that he'd seen Eichmann in Aussee on May 2, 1945. Other witnesses had seen him the day before in Camp Ebensee, near Bad Ischl. We decided that Stevens would talk to the judge and try to find out more about Frau Eichmann's application. The judge told Stevens that a

Karl Lukas, residing at Molitscherstrasse 22, Prague 18, had sent in an affidavit that he had been present when Eichmann was shot dead during the fighting in Prague on April 30, 1945. Stevens told the judge that Eichmann was a wanted Nazi criminal and that he had been seen in Austria, very much alive, *after* the day when he was allegedly killed in Prague. The judge was flabbergasted and at once promised Stevens to extend the usual two-week term for such cases to four weeks. Until then Stevens had time to submit proof of his statement.

I sent one of my men to Prague. Nine days later, I had the information that Karl Lukas was married to Maria Lukas, whose maiden name was Liebl. She happened to be the sister of Eichmann's wife. Lukas, at that time working for the Czechoslovak Ministry of Agriculture, was therefore Eichmann's brother-in-law. We also discovered that Lukas was in touch with a Frau Kals in Altaussee, who turned out to be another sister of Eichmann's wife. The police found their correspondence. Apparently the whole family was conspiring to prove that Adolf Eichmann was dead. (After Eichmann's capture in 1960, I notified the Czechoslovak authorities about Lukas' affidavit, and he was at once fired by the Ministry of Agriculture.)

Back in Bad Ischl, I gave the information to Stevens, who went to see the judge once more. The judge assured Stevens that he would throw out the application. Summoning Frau Eichmann, the judge made it clear to her that he would notify the district attorney if she tried any such deceptions again. She left in dismay.

Today I believe that the most important thing I was able to contribute to the search for Eichmann was destroying the legend of his alleged death. Many SS criminals will never be caught because they have had themselves declared dead and have lived happily ever after under new names; some of them have probably married their own "widows." One such was Hitler's top euthanasia expert, Professor Dr. Werner Heyde, who, after he had been declared officially dead, remarried his former wife. He was later caught and committed suicide in prison.

Early in the summer of 1948 I was again in Nuremberg. The Americans told me a photocopy of Eichmann's personal file had at last been found. Enclosed were two photographs. One showed Eichmann in civilian clothes; in the other he was in uniform. The latest had been made in 1936. Eichmann's superiors had given him some excellent reports. He had, they said, shown *"grosse Fachkenntnisse auf seinem Sachgebiet"*—"considerable experience in his special field." Nowhere was it said that the "special field" was genocide. The three pictures of Eichmann—two from his file and one from the girl friend—were the only ones the Israelis had in 1960 when they caught Eichmann in Argentina.

The most interesting document I found in Eichmann's personal file was a short *curriculum vitae* he had written himself. Dated "Berlin, July 19, 1937," it said:

> On March 19, 1906, I was born in Solingen, Rhineland. As a child I came to Linz where my father was then director of the streetcar and electrical power company. I went to public school, had four classes of *Realschule* [secondary school] and two years at the Federal School for Electrical Engineering. From 1925 to 1927 I was a salesman at the Upper-Austrian Electrical Construction Company. I left at my own wish to become the Upper-Austrian representative of the Vacuum Oil Company in Vienna. I was fired from my job in June, 1933, when they found out that I had secretly joined the NSDAP. The German Consul in Linz, Dirk von Langen, confirmed this fact in a letter which was enclosed in my personal file at the SD Hauptamt.
>
> For five years I was a member of the German-Austrian *Frontkämpfervereinigung* [an anti-Marxist political oranization]. I joined the Austrian NSDAP on April 1, 1932, and also joined the SS. During an inspection of the Upper-Austrian SS by the Reichsführer-SS [Himmler] I swore the oath of allegiance.
>
> On August 1, 1933, I was ordered by the Gauleiter of Upper-Austria, Comrade Bolleck, to start my military training at Camp Lechfeld. On September 29, 1933, I was assigned to the SS liaison office Passau. On January 29, 1934, I was ordered to join the Austrian SS in Camp Dachau. On October 1, 1934, I was transferred to the SD Hauptamt Berlin, where I am now on duty.
>
> (signed) *Adolf Eichmann*
> SS Hauptscharführer.

A remarkable case history of a fifth-column careerist. During the entire period described in Eichmann's *curriculum* all Nazi organizations were illegal in Austria. This didn't prevent the Nazis from building up a military organization with its own camps, training centers, and regular inspections by Himmler.

Everybody knew what Eichmann had done. I wanted to know what had made him do it. I talked to people in Linz who had gone to school with him. They told me the usual funny stories about teachers and the tricks they'd played on them, but when I inquired about their classmate Eichmann, they would fall silent. They knew I was "hunting" Eichmann, and they didn't even like to admit that they had known him. They seemed afraid to talk. One man said that the prosecution of war crimes should be left to "the proper authorities." What legal right did I, a private citizen, have to go after Eichmann? I didn't bother to answer. The man was one of those Austrians who had comforted one another before the end of the war by saying "If we win, we'll be Germans. If we don't win, we'll be Austrians. Either way, we can't lose."

I tried to find people who had known Eichmann during his illegal SS years in the early 1930s. None would talk to me. There was one man—not a Party member—who had often been in the Eichmann house and knew the family well. He had read about Eichmann's crimes in the newspapers and simply refused to believe them. It couldn't be the same Adolf, who had always been such a quiet, clumsy, colorless fellow and who often seemed to get stupidly struck on one idea. The man didn't realize how well he'd characterized Eichmann—how right he was and at the same time how wrong.

I had studied books about the psychology of crime, about motivation and the early childhood of criminals, but I had made a mistake: I thought of Eichmann as an ordinary criminal, which he was not. In his case, the early childhood, the environment, the problems that usually lead to crime didn't exist. As a salesman for the Vacuum Oil Company, he had had some business with Jews, but no unpleasant experience. There had been only eleven hundred Jews in Upper Austria when Eichmann and his friend Ernst Kaltenbrunner, who later became Hitler's Gestapo chief, were illegal SS men in Linz. Eichmann never showed any aggressive feelings toward the local Jews. He was just another obedient, rather colorless *Hauptscharführer* (sergeant). Even at the SD Hauptamt * in Berlin they weren't sure what to do with him.

* See Appendix.

He was assigned to collect material on "the world-wide conspiracy of the Freemasons." He began to read up on the Freemasons and became something of an expert on the subject. He wrote long studies on what should be done to fight the "conspiracy." The Masonic movement stimulated his interest in the Jewish problem. He became convinced that the Freemasons were a sort of Jewish sect that wanted to dominate the world.

Eichmann began to set up a card index of prominent Jewish Freemasons. His superiors praised his *Gründlichkeit* (application), and Eichmann became even more thorough in his "research." After a while, he became so interested in the Jewish problem that he abandoned the Freemasons altogether and devoted his whole effort to studying the Jews. He read countless books and surprised his superiors with his encyclopedic knowledge of Judaica and of Zionism. He became a Gestapo observer at Jewish meetings, and was sent to study the Jewish quarters of various cities. I've spoken to Jews who remember Eichmann from these days. All of them say that he was different from the usual SS rowdies. He was unyielding in attitude but icily polite. Among the documents I found in Nuremberg is an application from Eichmann for "special funds" to enable him to study Hebrew with a rabbi. Although he pointed out that the lessons would cost only three marks, a real bargain, his bosses turned him down. But Eichmann was now known at the SD Hauptamt as "the leading expert on Jewish problems."

At that time, in the mid-1930s, an official Nazi solution for "the Jewish problem" had not yet been formulated. The Nazi bosses agreed that the Jews would have to leave Germany, but the concentration camps were considered no solution. Hitler and his associates were convinced of the universal and omniscient power of *"Weltjudentum"* (World Jewry), and it was solemnly decided that the best way to lick the Jews was to find out more about them so that they could be licked with their own weapons. Weren't the Jews the gray eminences standing behind thrones and ruling over governments? Eichmann decided to meet the Jews on their own home ground. In 1937 he went to Palestine, accompanied by an *Obersturmführer* Hagen. I found many documents about this fateful journey. Eichmann got into Palestine by using a falsified press card identifying him as a staff member of the *Berliner Tageblatt*.

Before he left, many Jews in Germany were arrested as hostages for Eichmann, whose name they had never heard. Eichmann spent exactly two days in Palestine. He visited the German Templars' colony of Sarona, near Tel Aviv, and a Jewish settlement. From there he went to Cairo to meet Amin el Husseini, the Mufti of Jerusalem, a notorious Jew-hater and Nazi sympathizer. After this Eichmann wanted to return to Palestine, but the British mandatory power wouldn't let him in, and he went back to Berlin. One of Eichmann's brothers in Linz told a friend of mine that for some time the family considered Adolf a Zionist, because he often discussed the possibility of a large-scale Jewish emigration from Germany to Palestine. His forty-eight-hour stay in Palestine later gave Eichmann the idea of creating the legend that he was from Palestine and hence knew all about the Jews. He succeeded so well with this myth that in 1944 some Jews in Budapest thought he'd been a student of rabbinical philosophy.

I've tried to find out exactly when Eichmann turned from a theoretical expert on the Jewish question into an executioner. Perhaps it was a gradual development. When he came to Vienna in the fall of 1938, he was still politely talking about "forced emigration." The big change came in November 1938, when the Nazis ordered the destruction of Jewish shops and synagogues to avenge the killing by a Jew of a Nazi diplomat in Paris.* The orders to Vienna from Reinhard Heydrich, the Gestapo chief, specifically asked that Eichmann be notified. Eichmann had found his "mission." Eyewitnesses later reported that he was seen going from one synagogue to the next, personally supervising their utter destruction. It was said that he "helped with his own hands" and seemed "exhilarated."

Several days later the leaders of the Jewish community in Vienna noticed that when Eichmann summoned them, he no longer asked them to sit down in front of his desk. They were told to stand up, three steps away, at attention. In 1939 Eichmann went to Prague, summoned the President of the Jewish community there, and told him: "The Jews must go—but fast!" When he was told that the Jews of Prague had lived there 1100 years and were indigenous, he shouted: "Indigenous? I'll show you!" The following day the first shipment of Jews left for a concentration camp.

* See Appendix: *Kristallnacht*.

By 1941, in Hitler's world there was no more room for the Jews. After the Wannsee Conference * early in 1942, at which the Nazi bigwigs evolved their "final solution"—mass murder—Eichmann was ordered to carry out Hitler's and Himmler's orders. In the spring of 1945 he told a staff member in Budapest: "I'll happily die with the certainty of having killed almost six million Jews."

I had been wrong to look for a motive in his earlier life. There was no motive, no hatred. He was simply the perfect product of the system. When some of his underlings couldn't go on with the job of mass murder, Eichmann told them: "You're betraying the will of the Führer." He would have done the same job if he'd been ordered to kill all men whose name began with P or B, or all who had red hair. The Führer was always right, and it was Eichmann's job to see that the Führer's orders were carried out.

In the spring of 1948, I was able to reconstruct exactly Eichmann's journey at the end of the war. He had arrived at the Theresienstadt concentration camp on April 20 and stayed until the twenty-seventh. The following day he was in Prague, on the twenty-ninth in Budweis, on May first at the Ebensee camp near Bad Ischl, and on the second in Altaussee, where he stayed until May 9. Afterward he voluntarily hid in American internment camps until the end of June, when he escaped from the camp at Cham. Then for a while he hid somewhere in North Germany. That was later confirmed by two prominent SS men. One was Hoess, a former commandant of Auschwitz, who remained in touch with Eichmann in North Germany. From their Eichmann went to stay with an uncle in Solingen. Once the British authorities came to interrogate Eichmann's uncle while Eichmann was hiding in the house. The uncle told them nothing, but Eichmann decided he would go back to the Aussee region, where he felt safer than he did anywhere else.

One of my closest co-workers in these months was a former German *Wehrmacht* major. He had been reluctant to help me, saying "I must not dirty the uniform" and invoking the spirit of *Kameradschaft,* comradeship. I told him that comradeship ends where crime

* See Appendix.

begins. I would not save my own comrades who had committed crimes in a concentration camp, I told him. The major visited several comrades in Germany and talked to many SS men. When he came back to Linz he told me that Eichmann was "the most hated man among the SS because he gave the SS such a bad name." The consensus of all SS men and Eichmann's former comrades was that he was hiding somewhere in the Aussee region. In nearby Gmunden, the Nazi underground organization *Spinne* had its headquarters.

I never doubted that Eichmann's wife and father always knew where he was, though they never received any letters from him. After the war there was strict postal censorship, and the CIC intercepted the correspondence of Frau Eichmann in Altaussee and Eichmann's father in Linz. There were no suspicious messages, no letters in personal code. When all former Nazis were ordered to register in 1947, three members of the Eichmann family admitted Party membership. Father Eichmann had joined in May 1938, two months after the *Anschluss*. Brother Otto had joined the Party and the SA that year. Brother Friedrich had joined Party and SA in 1939. The Americans investigated them but there were no grounds for prosecution. They were *Mitläufer,* unimportant hangers-on.

Frau Eichmann's family was in a different category. Her relatives in Czechoslovakia had become prosperous during the Nazi regime. Every month Frau Eichmann received a postal order for a thousand schillings (forty dollars) from her father-in-law, but we assumed that she also got money from other sources, perhaps from her own family.

On December 20, 1949, a high-ranking Austrian police official came to see me at the Documentation Center in Linz and suggested that we compare our files on Eichmann. The Austrians believed that Eichmann was hiding around the village of Grundlsee, two miles or so from Altaussee. There are some isolated houses in Grundlsee, which is located on the shore of the four-mile-long lake of that name. I told the official that several months earlier one of my men in Altaussee had observed a black Mercedes with an Upper-Austrian license plate that had come from the direction of Grundlsee and stopped for a few minutes in front of Fischerdorf Number 8, where Frau Eichmann lived. A man in a trench coat "who looked like a Jew," as my man said, had spent a few minutes in the house and departed again in the black Mercedes. It might have been Eichmann.

The police official agreed. They were certain that Eichmann kept in close touch with a Nazi underground cell in Styria. His former staff member Anton Burger, who had been found when the police searched the wrong house for Eichmann, had escaped from Camp Glasenbach in 1947 and now acted as a courier between Eichmann and the underground. Each cell consisted of five people; each of them knew only five other underground members. They had contacts with another neo-Nazi organization known as *Sechsgestirn* (Six Stars). The Austrian police hoped that Eichmann's arrest might break up the whole network.

The official came back the next day. The police had found out that Eichmann was going to spend New Year's Eve with his family in Altaussee. They planned to raid the house while he was there, and they asked me to come along. The plan had to remain absolutely secret. New Year's Eve was my birthday. I couldn't think of a nicer birthday gift than Eichmann's arrest.

At that time a young Israeli was a frequent visitor at our Documentation Center. He had emigrated from Germany as a child with his parents to Palestine, had fought in the Israeli Army during the war of independence, and was now on an educational trip in Europe. He had the burning enthusiasm of the citizen of a very young nation, and was fascinated by the work of the Documentation Center, especially by the Eichmann case. I told him—rather foolishly, I now realize—that we might soon have Eichmann in prison. When he heard that I was going to Altaussee where Frau Eichmann lived, he asked me to take him along. "You can always use two strong arms there," he said. We left on December 28. We stayed at the Erzherzog Johann Hotel in Bad Aussee, two miles from Altaussee. The Austrian police had six detectives posted in various inns. I warned the young Israeli not to walk around and, above all, not to talk to people. I didn't know that he went to a night club that evening, where he had a good time and told the girls that he was from Israel. They were properly impressed. No one in Bad Aussee had ever seen a freshly baked Israeli.

On the morning of December 31, I met the police officer in charge. His men would be at their assigned posts at 9 P.M. They were already guarding the road from Grundlsee to Altaussee, and the house where Frau Eichmann lived. Back at my hotel I told the young Israeli not to leave his room before midnight. I would get in touch with him when we had good news. At nine o'clock I joined the police officer and another man. There were New Year's Eve celebrations in all the inns and hotels and in many homes—voices, music, and loud laughter. We alone were waiting to have our celebration. The detective went to a telephone, called Fischerdorf Number 8, and asked for Frau Liebl. After a while a woman's voice said: "Is that you? Will you surely come tonight?" The detective quietly put down the receiver. We looked at each other. So Frau Eichmann was expecting someone. Well, we would give him a proper reception.

At ten o'clock I accompanied the police officer on his rounds. We inspected the detectives at all posts and looked into the inns along the road. It was very cold, and we were shivering. We went back to the Hotel Erzherzog Johann for a cup of hot tea. I opened the door of the hotel tavern, and stood transfixed. The young Israeli sat at a large table, drinking with a group of local people, and talking about the heroic achievements of the Israeli Army.

The police officer was irritated.

"I don't like it. If word gets around that a young Israeli is in town, it may—"

"It's past ten," I said. "Nothing can go wrong now."

"I certainly hope so," he said sharply.

At half past we left again. When we came to the next inn, the detective reported that people were talking about the Israeli who had come to Bad Aussee. At the next place they were already talking about the group of Israelis that had arrived. The police officer glared at me but said nothing. I cursed myself.

Eleven o'clock. If Eichmann wanted to be with his family at midnight, he would soon have to leave Grundlsee. We waited twenty more minutes, which seemed like twenty years. No one spoke. At half past eleven, a detective came running from Grundlsee and said something to the officer.

The police officer gave me an I-told-you-so look. "I'm afraid it's all over. It seems that Eichmann was warned."

I stared at him, unable to say a word. He asked the detective to repeat his report.

"At half past eleven two men approached on the road from Grundlsee. It is quite dark there, but I could see them against the white background of the snow. They were about a hundred fifty meters from me—I was hiding behind the trees along the road. Suddenly another man came running from Grundlsee and shouted something. They stopped and he joined them, and a few seconds later all three ran back."

The officer saw how miserable I was. "Don't take it so hard. We now know the group of houses where they came from. We have no warrants to search the houses, and I cannot do such a thing without higher orders, but we've got Eichmann covered. I'll leave two men here and return to Linz and ask for further instructions." He shrugged and said: "Maybe it was a mistake to bring the young Israeli here. Or maybe Eichmann was warned for another reason. I don't know."

At ten minutes past midnight we came back to Bad Aussee. The streets were full of noisy people. Happy drunks shouted "Happy New Year!" There were the sounds of music, of glasses being broken. I didn't want to see anyone. I went up to my room and lay down on my bed without taking off my clothes. I was thoroughly miserable. My birthday gift had been just a hundred fifty meters away. We'd lost him, and now we might never get him.

A week later the Austrian police officer informed me that they had given up the search. They had received reports that Adolf Eichmann had disappeared from the Aussee region.

1950 was a bad year for an "Eichmann hunter." The Cold War had reached its climax, and the former Allies were dug in on both sides of the Iron Curtain. The Americans had their hands full with the war in Korea. No one was interested in Eichmann or the Nazis. When two Nazis met during these months they would say "A new wind is blowing!" and slap each other on the back. Sensational news stories about Eichmann appeared in the sensational newspapers. He was seen in Cairo, in Damascus; he was said to be forming a German legion for the Arabs; and so on. I knew these stories were pure fiction. A man who had always hated to be photographed would not appear in the limelight.

The large Eichmann file was still on my desk. I could hardly bear to look at it. I was convinced that Eichmann was no longer in Europe. The unsuccessful raid on New Year's Eve must have convinced him that it was too dangerous to stay. Probably *ODESSA* had taken good care of him. It seemed probable that he was hiding in the Near East, where he had friends and admirers in the Arab world. There was nothing I could do now. Most of my unpaid co-workers had left to start a new life. The Americans who came to Europe these days were not interested in Eichmann. When I started to talk about him, they looked bored or gave me speculative glances. One indicated I might be suffering from a persecution complex.

"You cannot run after a phantom, Wiesenthal. Why don't you forget the whole thing?" I was told.

In January 1951 I met a former *Abwehr* member, whom I shall call Albert and who had some acquaintances among *ODESSA* men. Albert told me that Eichmann had been seen in Rome late in the summer of 1950, a few months after he'd left the Aussee region. Eichmann had probably been channeled there through the monastery route. Albert was going to Rome and would try to find out what had happened. I could hardly wait for his return. He came to see me again in February.

"There are different accounts of Eichmann's escape. All agree that he reached Rome with the help of a Croatian committee run by former friends of Ante Pavelic, the leader of the collaborationist Croatian government. Naturally Eichmann didn't stay at a hotel in Rome. We believe he was hidden in a monastery. There he received a Vatican identity card, which he had to have if he wanted to get a visa to a South American country."

"Are you sure it's South America? Didn't he go to the Near East?" I said.

Albert shook his head. "Most Nazis who found temporary asylum in Rome were later sent to South America. We believe that Eichmann joined a group of several people, probably under an assumed name. These group transports go to Brazil and Argentina."

I didn't have the resources to look in Brazil or Argentina for a man whose present name I didn't know and whom I couldn't even describe exactly because the latest photograph of him had been taken fourteen years before. My only hope remained Eichmann's family. Some day he would try to establish contact with his wife in

Simon and Cyla
Wiesenthal in 1936.

A prewar photograph of
Adolf Eichmann.

LEFT:
Simon Wiesenthal in
the first displaced persons'
synagogue, in 1946.

BELOW:
"Unmasked." One of the
photo montages made by Wiesenthal
in Mauthausen in early 1945.

RIGHT:
The deceptively
peaceful countryside surrounding
Castle Hartheim.

BELOW RIGHT:
Castle Hartheim,
the euthanasia "sanatorium" and
school for experiments
in scientific murder.

Alkoven O.Ö.
Luftbild Nr. 3

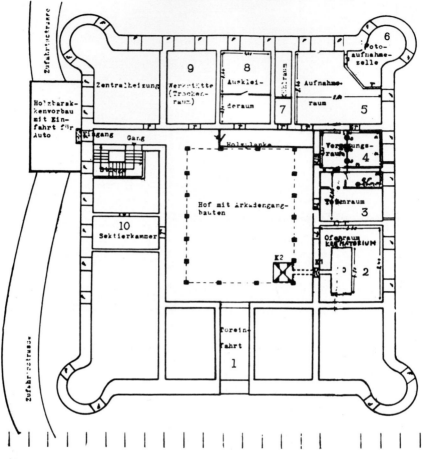

SCHLOSS HARTHEIM 1:200

ABOVE:
The floor plan of Castle Hartheim:
1. entrance; 2. oven room (crematorium);
3. morgue; 4. gas chamber; 5. reception room;
6. photographing room; 7. refrigerated room;
8. disrobing room; 9. workroom;
10. dissection room.

RIGHT:
The photograph which led Frau Keller
to attempt suicide.
It shows her husband participating in a mass
execution of Ukrainian Jews.

PHOTOGRAPHS ABOVE, LEFT TO RIGHT:
S.S. *Scharführer* Schonbach,
a member of the special
execution group in the
Janowska concentration camp.

Kurt Wiese, who was imprisoned
after the war as having been
personally responsible for the deaths
of at least two hundred Polish Jews.

Karl Silberbauer, who led
the party of Gestapo men
sent to arrest Anne Frank
and her family.

Franz Stangl, commander of the
Treblinka concentration camp.
Of its 700,000 inmates, about
40 are known to be still alive.

Dr. Karl Babor, a member of
the "Selection Committee"
at the Grossrosen concentration-
camp crematorium.

RIGHT:
Urns containing the ashes of
Jews cremated in the
Austrian concentration camps.

Simon Wiesenthal speaking at a memorial meeting before the coffin containing the ashes of Austrian Jews was taken to Israel.

Simon Wiesenthal attending a trial of Nazi war criminals in Vienna in 1958.

Simon Wiesenthal and his daughter Pauline at Mauthausen in 1961.

Altaussee, where the children were going to school. Some day he might try to get them all over to South America.

In the fall of 1951, after I'd sold a series of articles about Eichmann's gold and the treasure hunters of Altaussee to several magazines, a man came to see me. My secretary handed me his visiting card: *Heinrich von Klimrod.* A slim, well-dressed man of military bearing came in, bowed correctly, and asked whether he could talk "openly" with me. I asked him to sit down.

"We've read your articles and are impressed by your knowledge of this delicate subject. We would like to propose a deal."

I asked who *we* were.

"You permitted me to be frank. I represent a Viennese group of former SS men. Our mutual interests converge at one point. We know that you are a fanatical idealist. You want to find Eichmann to bring him to justice. We, too, want him—for a different reason. We want Eichmann's gold. I believe we could establish a useful collaboration."

I was speechless. He was suggesting that I should help him to get the gold that Eichmann and his men had taken from the fingers and out of the mouths of millions of Jews who had gone to the gas chambers. Perhaps he misunderstood my silence, for he went on. "We see no reason why so many shady characters living around Altaussee should get rich while many of our SS comrades are living in poverty. We want to be fair partners. We know a lot about Eichmann's escape. We know that two priests, Father Weber and Father Benedetti, helped him while he was in Rome. We know the Capuchin monastery where he was hiding. We don't know Eichmann's present name but we have many comrades in South America who would help us. Well, is it a deal?"

I was playing for time and asked Klimrod what he was doing now.

"I am a partner in an import-export firm. We have very good relations with the Russians. We have been able to ship strategic material to the Communist countries despite the American embargo. You may have heard about the Nationale Liga, a group of former National Socialists cooperating with the Communists. We don't belong to the Liga, but we have our fingers in many pies. You would be well advised to accept our proposal. You don't need Eichmann's gold. You Jews have plenty of money. You'll get Eichmann and we'll have his gold."

I turned down the flattering offer, but it was not easy to make him understand why. We just didn't operate on the same wavelength. I told him that I couldn't go into partnership with a group of former SS men who were cooperating with the Communists. I couldn't make a deal about the gold that didn't belong to me and didn't belong to Eichmann either. For all I knew, part of the gold may have come from my eighty-nine relatives who had been killed by Eichmann's men.

After Easter, 1952, a friend called me from Altaussee. Frau Eichmann and her sons had disappeared. The three boys had not returned to school after the holiday.

I informed the Americans and the Austrian police. Everybody was wondering why Frau Eichmann had taken the children out of their classes in the middle of the school year. Without proper report cards they would not be accepted by any other school in Austria or Germany.

The Austrian police discovered that somebody had dug up something from the ground near the house Fischerdorf Number 8. To this day it is not known whether it was gold, documents, or something else. I began to check on who had issued Frau Eichmann a passport. She had been listed as *Veronika Liebl, German citizen* in Altaussee. Through the intervention of the *Deutsche Fürsorgestelle* (a German welfare organization) in Graz, the German consulate there had issued German passports to Veronika Liebl and her three sons.

The monthly rent was still being paid for the house in Altaussee, and all the furniture was still there, but this didn't fool the neighbors. Some told me that the Eichmanns had gone to Brazil. Others claimed they'd heard that Frau Eichmann had gone to Sindolfheim in Bavaria, "to live with her mother." As usual, the rumors in Altaussee were never substantiated. No one had seen Frau Eichmann in Brazil, and she'd never been in Sindolfheim, and there the matter rested.

Back in 1948, when I'd been suffering from insomnia and had gone to see a doctor, he suggested that I do something at night to take my mind off my troubles, and that's how I began collecting postage stamps. My hobby has since given me many pleasant hours and helped me to meet people in many countries. It even gave me a new clue in the Eichmann case when I was at the end of my wits.

Late in 1953, I met an old Austrian baron in the Tyrol, who invited me to his villa near Innsbruck. We were both ardent philatelists and the baron wanted to show me his collection. I spent a pleasant evening with him, admiring his stamps. Afterward we had a bottle of wine and talked. The baron was a decent old man, a life-long monarchist and devout Catholic. He listened with deep interest when I told him about my work. He knew of some big Nazis in the Tyrol who were back in high positions, "as though nothing had changed." It was shocking, he said.

The Baron got up and opened a drawer full of envelopes, which he had saved for their unusual stamps. While looking through the pile he told me of a friend in Argentina, a former German lieutenant colonel who had not gone higher in the Wehrmacht because he was known as an anti-Nazi. Last year he had gone to Argentina, where he now worked as an instructor in Perón's army.

"He just sent me a letter," said the Baron, handing me the envelope. "Beautiful stamps, aren't they? I asked him whether he met any of our old comrades down there. Here is what he writes:

> There are some people here we both used to know. You may remember Lieutenant Hoffmann from my regiment, and Hauptmann Berger from the 188th Division. A few more are here whom you've never met. Imagine whom else I saw—and even had to talk to twice: *dieses elende Schwein Eichmann, der die Juden kommandierte* [this awful swine Eichmann who commanded the Jews]. He lives near Buenos Aires and works for a water company.

"How do you like that?" said the Baron. "Some of the worst criminals got away."

I said nothing, afraid that the Baron might notice my excitement. This was no Altaussee rumor; this was a fact. I casually asked to look at the letter, pretending to be interested in the new Argentine stamps. I reread the passage about Eichmann and memorized each word. Later, in my hotel room, I wrote the words down as I remembered them. My elation was short-lived, though. Suppose we found a man who looked like Eichmann living near Buenos Aires and working for a water company—improbable though this was—how could we get him? What could I, a private citizen half the world away, do? The Germans were a strong political force in Argentina * where Perón's army was being trained by Germans, Argentine industries were run by German experts, and Argentine banks supported by millions in German capital.

Eichmann must have felt quite safe in Argentina, or he wouldn't have sent for his family. Perhaps he had powerful friends there. Otherwise he wouldn't dare live in a city with more than 200,000 Jews when there was always the danger of his being recognized.

I realized that my work as a private investigator had now come to an end. From here on more powerful people would have to take over. Arie Eschel, the Israeli consul in Vienna, had asked me to prepare for the Jewish World Congress a complete report on the case. I wrote a report that began with the first mention I'd heard of Eichmann and ended with the passage from the letter the Austrian baron had received. I added Eichmann's photographs, copies of his personal letters, samples of his handwriting. I sent one copy to the Jewish World Congress in New York, the other to the Israeli consulate in Vienna.

There was no answer at all from Israel. Two months after I'd sent off the material, I got a letter from New York. A Rabbi Kalmanowitz (whom I'd never met) wrote that he had received the material and "would appreciate Eichmann's exact address in Buenos Aires." I replied I would send a man to South America if they would defray his travel expenses and give him $500. Rabbi Kalmanowitz wrote that they had no money.

It was time to give up. Obviously, no one cared about Eichmann. The Israelis had more reason to be concerned about Nasser. I closed the Documentation Center in March 1954, had all files packed— there were many boxes, weighing exactly 532 kilos—and sent them to the Yad Vashem Historical Archives in Jerusalem. I kept only one large file for myself, the Eichmann file.

Five years later, on the morning of April 22, 1959, I was going through the Linz newspaper *Oberösterreichische Nachrichten*. On a

* See Appendix.

back page there was an obituary notice for Frau Maria Eichmann, Adolf Eichmann's stepmother. Underneath were the names of the survivors. Adolf Eichmann was not among them, but the last name was Vera Eichmann. People usually don't lie when they write obituary notices. It said "Vera Eichmann." Apparently Frau Eichmann had been neither divorced nor remarried. I cut out the obituary notice and put it on top of my Eichmann file.

Late in August 1959, a telephone call from Linz reached me in Murten, Switzerland, where I was spending the holidays with my family. I was told that several people had seen Adolf Eichmann in Altaussee. There was no error possible. A few weeks earlier the German magazine *Stern* had carried out a diving operation in the lake of Töplitzsee, arousing public interest in the sunken "Nazi treasure" in the lakes of the region. I reported the news to the Israeli ambassador in Vienna and decided to return at once. My wife was unhappy; she said, quite rightly, that we still had twelve days of vacation all paid for. Why did we have to leave? I said we *had* to leave. I couldn't stay in faraway, peaceful Switzerland. I wouldn't have enjoyed it.

Times were changing again. In recent weeks, the Israeli papers had published new stories about Eichmann, reporting on his crimes and speculating on his whereabouts. There were also many trials of Nazi criminals in Germany and Austria these days. My letter to the Israeli ambassador had arrived at the right moment. He sent it to Jerusalem and gave a copy to the Federation of Jewish Communities of Austria in Vienna. They informed the Austrian Minister of the Interior. He asked the authorities to get in touch with me. Eichmann was still on the Austrian "Wanted" list.

After my return to Linz I talked to my friends. Of course it wasn't Adolf Eichmann who had been seen in Altaussee, but one of his brothers—the usual Altaussee rumor. But things began moving now. Two young men from Israel, whom I shall call Michael and Meir, came to see me. There was great interest in the case there; they asked me to continue where I had left off in 1954. In Frankfurt am Main, the prosecutor in charge of preparing the trial of SS men from Auschwitz told me that Eichmann led the list of all accused criminals and asked for my cooperation. Before I realized what was happening, I was deeply involved once more in the Eichmann case.

I reread the whole Eichmann file. The question was whether Eichmann still lived in Buenos Aires. I went to the Tyrol, hoping to get from the old Baron the name of his friend in Buenos Aires who had written the letter six years ago. But the Baron was dead, and his stamp collection had been sold.

Next I sent one of my men to see Frau Eichmann's mother. Frau Maria Liebl was not very friendly to the visitor, but admitted that her daughter had married a man named "Klems" or "Klemt" in South America. She said she had no address for them and she received no letters. She asked my man to leave her alone.

I sent what little information I had to Israel. On October 10, 1959, I had a message from there. They had investigated in South America and found the address of Frau Eichmann. who was said to live "in fictitious marriage" with a German named Ricardo Klement. I was sure that it was a real marriage—that Frau Eichmann lived with her husband Adolf Eichmann. Otherwise the Eichmann family in Linz wouldn't have listed her as Vera Eichmann in the obituary notices. The Eichmann boys lived in Buenos Aires with their parents. It occurred to me that they would probably be registered there at the German embassy, since they would soon reach military age. I asked a friend to make a cautious inquiry. He notified me that the Eichmann boys had indeed been registered there, under their real name. (An embarrassed official later claimed that he "had not known that these were the sons of Adolf Eichmann.")

On February 6, 1960, the *Oberösterreichische Nachrichten* in Linz published the obituary of Eichmann's father, Adolf Eichmann, who had died the day before. Among "daughters-in-law" it said again "Vera Eichmann." I sent the clipping by airmail to Israel. Adolf Eichmann had been devoted to his father. I was sure that his brothers would notify Adolf of their father's death. There was at least an outside chance of Eichmann's coming to attend the funeral. I was told that the funeral would take place in five days "because the family expects relatives from abroad." I knew that one of Eichmann's brothers, Emil Rudolf, lived in Frankfurt am Main.

Michael and Meir had not told me what the Israelis hoped to do in Buenos Aires—but they had to get the right man. They urgently needed a picture of Adolf Eichmann as he looked today. We had no recent picture; but perhaps one could get something that might be almost as good. Two days before the funeral, I went out to the cemetery and looked at the location of the grave. I thought what I had in mind could be done, especially on a dark winter day. I took a train to Vienna and talked to two friends, expert photographers, at the Presseklub. I asked them to come to Linz and photograph the whole Eichmann family while they stood around the grave during the funeral. I told them it was essential that they remain unseen.

They did a fine job. Hiding behind large tombstones at a distance of about two hundred yards, they made sharp pictures of the members of the funeral procession, although the light was far from perfect. That night I had before me enlarged photographs of Adolf Eichmann's four brothers Emil Rudolf, Otto, Friedrich, and Robert. Emil Rudolf, the brother from Frankfurt, whom I'd never seen before, was pointed out to me. Otto, Friedrich, and Robert I knew. Adolf had not come to the funeral.

The photographers left. I was alone with the pictures, turning them over, comparing them. I took out of my file the old picture of Adolf Eichmann that had been made in 1936, twenty-four years ago. Next to today's pictures of the four brothers, Adolf looked like a younger brother. I took out a magnifying glass and studied the features of the five brothers. Many people had told me that Adolf Eichmann most closely resembled his brother Otto. Looking at the photographs through the magnifying glass I suddenly understood why so many people had sworn they'd seen Adolf Eichmann in the past years in Altaussee when they had seen one of his brothers. They all looked very much alike. The family resemblance was astonishing. I was thinking about the problem of the Israelis in Argentina. The photos of Eichmann they had were now twenty-four years old. They had no fingerprints. Years ago I'd heard rumors, probably emanating from the SS underground, that Eichmann had had plastic surgery performed on his face. He was said to have been in a motorcycle accident and acquired a scar on the forehead just below the hairline. Eichmann's former subordinate, Wisliceny, had mentioned the scar in his description of Eichmann. This had been confirmed by the testimony of Krumey, another Eichmann aide, at Nuremberg. Looking at the pictures in front of me, I was sure that even plastic surgery could not basically alter Eichmann's face.

If "Ricardo Klement" in Buenos Aires was identical with Adolf

Eichmann, his face must have gone through the same evolution as the faces of his four brothers. I cut from the photographs the faces of the four brothers who had been at the funeral, and the face from the old picture of Adolf Eichmann. I shuffled the faces like playing cards and threw them on the table. Somehow a composite face emerged: perhaps Adolf Eichmann.

When the young Israelis, Michael and Meir, came to see me again, I performed the Eichmann card trick. "This is how he must look now. Probably closest to his brother Otto. All five brothers have the same facial expression. Look at the mouth, the corners of the mouth, the chin, the form of the skull."

Michael shook his head, staring at the pictures. "Fantastic!" he said.

Meir grabbed the pictures. "May we take them with us?"

Suddenly they were in a hurry. I didn't want to detain them, not for a second. I didn't hear from them, so I assumed that they didn't need my help. There was nothing else I could do.

On Monday, May 23, 1960, Prime Minister David Ben Gurion told the Israeli *Knesset* (Parliament) that Eichmann had been caught and was now in an Israeli prison. A few hours later, I had a short cable of congratulations from the Yad Vashem in Jerusalem.

Some time after the capture of Adolf Eichmann I met one of my former "clients." He had once been a prominent SS man. Now he often comes to my office for a quiet chat about the bad old days. He came in that day, clicked his heels, shook hands with me, and said: "Congratulations, Herr Wiesenthal. *Saubere Arbeit* [Nice work]." He meant it, too.

Chapter 7

ALEX

[I first saw Jewish collaborators in the ghetto of Lwow; and later I saw them in various concentration camps. There were some shocking cases, and when I talked about the problem after the war, many Jews were perturbed. Perhaps they had expected the Jews to be immune from corruption. Like all races, we have had our saints and our sinners, our cowards and our heroes. When I began work as an investigator for various American agencies, it didn't take me long to discover that there were members of various Jewish organizations whose war records had been, to say the least, doubtful. Quite a few of them had been members of a *Judenrat*—Jewish Council—one of which had been set up by the Germans in each ghetto and each concentration camp.

The hardest duty of the Jewish Councils in the ghettos had been deciding which names should be put on "transport lists" for the death camps. The Nazis had established certain criteria for inclusion (health, age, and so on), but in typically diabolic fashion they often left the final selection to the Jews themselves. Some members of the Jewish Councils did the only thing they could in the circumstances: they followed the Nazi regulations to the letter. Others became corrupt, accepted favors, and juggled the names, hoping against hope that they might save their own lives. Perhaps the next transport

129

would be the last, and if one avoided getting on *this* list, he might be saved. There were other Jews who collaborated with certain Nazi agencies, or bartered others' lives for their own. Some Jews were concentration-camp trusties. Sometimes they helped their fellow inmates; sometimes they didn't.

These people should have kept silent after the end of the war, should have tried to fade away. Instead, many of them joined the postwar organizations formed by Jews in Germany and Austria— possibly out of a belated sense of repentance, perhaps because they thought they would feel safe. Naturally, the truth came out sooner or later. They were recognized by survivors who had not forgotten, had to be handed over to the Allied authorities, and scandals followed.

The members of the Jewish Central Committee in the U.S. Zone of Austria elected me vice-chairman and put me in charge of the legal and political department. I was responsible for my fellow workers and wanted people with clean records. I made a rule that no Jew who had had any function of authority during the Nazi regime—whether or not he'd been accused of any wrongdoing— could have any place in a postwar Jewish organization. This rule was approved by the American authorities and became known, not very favorably, as the *Lex Wiesenthal* among people with bad consciences who didn't like me very much for pushing it through. When I talked to Jewish groups about the problem, I told them about my childhood memory of the Jew who had cursed his wife and, when she died, had been forbidden ever to utter a word, spending his life as "the silent one" in the house of the great rabbi of Czortkov. "Any Jew," I said to these people, "whose mouth ever delivered a Nazi-given order for the persecution of other Jews must be forbidden ever to speak again to other Jews."

The Americans agreed to a proposal I made for setting up a Jewish Committee that would act as a disciplinary commission, investigating cases of Jewish collaboration. The committee pronounced thirty Jews guilty of collaboration with the Nazis and five guilty of collaboration with the Soviet NKVD. As a result of the latter collaboration, Jews had been sent to Siberian prison camps. The committee had no official authority; its verdicts were merely symbolic. If the "convicted" people objected to our actions, they had the right to go to the regular Austrian courts and protest. Not one of those convicted made such an appeal. In Israel, collaborators were investigated by the regular authorities and sentenced by the courts.

Ever since, I've been suspicious of Jews who claim they saved someone. A man who had the power to save also had the power to condemn. The SS and the Gestapo were not welfare organizations. They wanted a list of so many people to put on the train next Tuesday—and not one person less. There was no room for bargaining. The people were to be there at 12:30 A.M. next Tuesday, not 12:40. When one man appeared before our committee, a witness testified that the accused had taken him off the transport list.

"Please be lenient with him," said the witness. "He saved my life."

"Whose name did he put on the list instead of yours?" I asked him.

The witness did not answer. The accused was pronounced guilty.

I apply the same strict standard to people who offer to help me with my work. Their record must be blameless. A few have asked me to check up on their past. Alex was one of them.]

He was very nervous when he came into my office one day in 1958. He wore dark glasses—for no apparent reason, since it was an overcast day. The man was clearly bothered by a secret. He was tall and reddish-blond, in his late thirties. Standing in front of me, he gave a helpless shrug. He didn't know how to start. "I'm afraid it's a strange story," he said.

I asked him to sit down, closed the door, and offered him a cigarette. Many people who come to see me think that theirs is a strange story. It always is, from their point of view, and it often is from mine. Years ago, young men from the Austrian provinces used to come to see me because they thought that I represented the Israelis. They were not Jewish, but wished to volunteer their services for the Israeli Army. I asked them why they wanted to go. I secretly hoped to find one who might be doing it out of a sense of guilt or because he sought to make some sort of moral restitution. I was wrong. They certainly were not motivated by idealism. Some had spent several years in the *Wehrmacht* and couldn't get used to the boredom of civilian life; they wanted excitement. Others frankly asked: "How much will they pay me?"—Modern *condottieri* who would fight for anybody who paid their price. I had to tell them that I represented no one and that, besides, the Israelis seemed well able to take care of themselves.

Some visitors came to tell me involved stories of how their old Aunt Martha had helped some Jewish neighbors "before they were taken away." She had been promised some silver or a couple of candlesticks. Then the Gestapo had taken everything away. Now they wanted money from "the Jewish organizations that should have funds for people who helped the Jews."

Once an elderly tailor with a small Hitler mustache came to ask advice on how to get "restitution for the Jews." That's what it said in the paper. To him it meant "restitution for damage caused by the Jews." His was a clear case, he said. Back in 1938 he'd made a new suit for an old Jewish customer of many years standing, Herr Kahn, who was suddenly arrested and taken away to a concentration camp. Inexcusably, Herr Kahn had failed to settle his bill before being dragged away.

"He should have paid me for the suit," the tailor said. "After all, he'd ordered it, hadn't he? It wasn't *my* fault that he couldn't use it."

I had to explain to him that one didn't wear new suits in a concentration camp.

He was stubborn. "There's a restitution law, isn't there?"

"No law is perfect. Apparently the lawmakers never considered such an eventuality," I said. But I couldn't convince him. He left muttering that he would go to complain to the *Behörden*—the authorities.

The young man with dark glasses who now sat across from my desk didn't seem to belong in such a category. I sensed that it hadn't been easy for him to come see me. I pretended not to observe him. He took off his glasses.

"No one knows I came to see you," he said, as though it were important not to be seen in my office. "Only my uncle, and he won't tell anyone. I mean the man whom I call 'Uncle.' He said it was all right for me to talk to you. He's very sick. . . . May I start at the beginning?

"My father was an engineer. Before the first War the family must have been quite wealthy. I hardly remember my grandfather, who was an industrialist. Father often talked about *his* grandfather, whose photograph hung in the library in an oval frame. I often looked at it—a dignified man with a white beard, a watchchain across his waistcoat, and a skullcap. Father told me his grandfather had been a well-known scholar." He paused. "He was a rabbi."

I admit that I looked at my visitor with astonishment. Any Nazi *Rassenforscher* (racial researcher) worth his salt would have unhesitatingly called the young man a hundred-per-cent Aryan. He had "the typical oblong Nordic skull," the gray-blue eyes, and the straight nose the Nazis had considered reserved for "Aryans." I thought he looked more Aryan than a great many professional Aryans it had been my misfortune to meet.

"Yes, my grandfather and my father were Jews. My mother was a Christian. I get my blond hair and blue eyes from her. I was brought up a Catholic, although my mother wouldn't have minded if I had been raised a Jew. They thought it would be easier for me in life if I weren't a Jew. I was born in 1922. When Hitler invaded Austria in March 1938, I was sixteen years old."

He spoke less haltingly now.

"Suddenly I had become a *Halbjude* [half-Jew]. I didn't quite understand what that meant, but my parents did. They knew what had happened to half-Jews and to quarter-Jews in Germany in the past four years. My father had studied the Nuremberg laws. I was the only child, and they loved me very much. Father spent as much time with me as his work permitted. Whatever they did, they always thought of me first."

He was silent. For a while he just sat there.

"My parents discussed the problem of my *Halbjudentum* with their best friend, the man I call 'Uncle.' He was a well-known doctor in Vienna. He and my father had been close friends since their student days. My uncle was not Jewish. That day, when he came to our house, I sensed that something of great importance had been discussed in my father's library. I was called in. They were very tense, and my mother was crying.

"Father looked very pale. He asked whether I understood the Nazi laws, that I was *Halbjude*. I nodded, not particularly concerned—I was sixteen and more worried about my next Latin exercise at the *Gymnasium*. Father explained to me that as a half-Jew I would have to leave the *Gymnasium*. That came as a shock to me. He said I would perhaps have to work in a factory. I said no one could force me to do that.

"He gave me a sad look and said: 'Oh, yes, they can. They can do other things—make life miserable for you.' I knew who *they* were, of course. We had a few of them in my class. Nazis.

"Father said: 'We must find a way of protecting you. Mother and I do not matter. We've lived our lives. But you have everything ahead of you. It's worth the sacrifice, believe me. We've discussed all this with Uncle Franz, and here's what we are going to do. Mother will report to the authorities that you are not . . . well, that you are not my son. That she and Uncle Franz . . .' He stopped for a moment, unable to go on, and then he said: 'She will report that you are *their* child, and Uncle Franz will confirm it.' "

My visitor looked straight ahead. "I was completely confused. My mother stopped crying and said, very quietly: 'Of course, Father is your real father. I shall tell them a lie. We must because it's for you, for your future.' "

"I said: 'Mama, I don't understand. What have *I* got to do?' Then Uncle Franz, who sat there with tears in his eyes, said: 'There's only one thing you must do now, and that is to listen to your parents' advice. Don't worry—it will be all right.' "

My visitor was staring straight ahead, perhaps seeing the scene in his father's library again.

"And so I was an Aryan. I don't know how they went about it. Mother probably made a statement which was signed by Uncle Franz. I was going to keep my name. If Uncle Franz had wanted to adopt me officially, he would have needed his wife's consent, but the whole thing had to remain a secret. He was married and had children, and there might be problems if he talked to his wife about this."

I wondered why he had come to tell *me* his story. Such Aryanizations had been quite common at that time. Other desperate Jewish parents tried to protect their children. It was a moving story, but not an unusual one.

He said quietly, "In 1940 I volunteered—for the *Waffen* SS."

I was shocked. "The SS!"

"It was Uncle Franz' idea, and I agreed. Stories had got around about atrocities against the Jews. Nothing certain was known, but many things were whispered. We assumed they wouldn't harm a Jew whose son had volunteered to fight with the *Waffen* SS—even though I was no longer officially his son. Well, I was trained with an SS division in Germany. In the spring of 1941 we were sent to the East. In June came the surprise attack against Russia. Our division had the honor of being among the first to cross the Soviet border.

"I was deep in Russia when I received a short letter from my mother. She'd divorced Father. That was all she wrote. She knew, of course, that all mail was being censored. A few months later I went home on leave. Mother told me what had happened. One day she'd been summoned to the Gestapo. They started to shout at her. Didn't she know that the mother of an SS man must not stay married to a Jew? When she said she would never divorce her husband, the Gestapo *Kommissar* said she'd better think it over, or they would make life difficult for me. Might even make me a Jew again, if she knew what *that* meant. Of course she knew. It was the dirtiest kind of blackmail."

He got up and paced back and forth in front of my desk.

"My father had agreed at once. He'd already put his entire estate in Mother's name. We cried, all of us. Father couldn't live at home any more. He had a small, shabby rented room nearby. The next day I had to go back to the front. A few weeks later *they* came for him. Neither my mother's divorce nor my fighting in the *Waffen* SS saved him. He was deported with other Jews. That was all I knew. We were then in the area of Leningrad. There were rumors that many civilians were being executed, especially Jews. I didn't believe it because I didn't *want* to believe it. Certainly these people were spies and saboteurs and partisans, as we'd always been told. Well, perhaps there were a few Jews among them. But they weren't executed *because they were Jews*. That was the official version and I swallowed it. You know how it was, Herr Wiesenthal. If you didn't want to believe these things, you were always trying to find a plausible explanation."

He sat down. "Perhaps I would still believe it today if I hadn't been wounded and sent to the nearest SS hospital. They took good care of us. Only three men in one room. The two other patients were SS men who had been guards in a concentration camp. They told me what had happened to the Jews there. They didn't tell me everything, but enough to give me sleepless nights. From there I was transferred to a large base hospital in Riga, Latvia. I was in a small room with another SS man who was recuperating from a nervous breakdown. He told me he'd collapsed after weeks of shooting women and children. He couldn't take it any more. They'd told him they would shoot him if he talked about it—but he had to tell it to someone.

"So now I knew the whole truth. There was no getting away from it. Lying there in my bed, I thought of Father, whom I'd always loved. Everything came back to my mind. Little things: how on Sunday mornings he took me for a walk and then we went to a *Konditorei* and he would buy me some sweets but said we mustn't tell Mother, because she would be cross when I came home without any appetite for the noon meal she'd cooked. We were like conspirators. There was nothing Father wouldn't have done for me. And here I was, a member of the *Waffen* SS, the Führer's elite troops, and I couldn't help my own father. I didn't even know where they had taken him, whether he was ill. . . . I couldn't pursue my thoughts to the end. I knew he was in one of these camps, but I didn't want to know it. I prayed to God that He should never let me know."

He got up, stepped to the window and looked out. Anything so he wouldn't have to look at me, at anybody.

"As soon as I was released from the hospital, I volunteered for front-line service. They said I was crazy. I was entitled to easy rear-area duty. I said no, I wanted to go back to my unit. There I volunteered for patrol duty. At the first opportunity, I let myself be captured by the Russians. I could not fight any longer on the side of *these* people."

He turned and looked at me. "I suppose some people would despise me for it. Perhaps I've done everything wrong."

He waited, expecting me to say something. He was a Jew who had become an SS man. He'd worn on his uniform collar the symbol of the mass murderers of his own people. What could I say? What could anyone say?

He nodded, as though my silence didn't surprise him.

"I spent six years in various Russian prisoner-of-war camps. I kept my secret to myself. At long last, in 1955, I came back to Austria. My mother had died. Father had disappeared, 'somewhere in the East,' with millions of other Jews. There was only my 'Uncle' in Vienna."

His voice was hard. "He wanted to help me. He asked me to come and live with his family for a while. I didn't want to be there. I didn't want to talk to him. I was empty inside. All feeling had been drained. He tried to explain to me that he and I had meant the best. We hadn't saved my father but that wasn't our fault. At least I had been saved. If they hadn't Aryanized me I would now be dead too.

"I said maybe it would be better if I were dead. What was the sense of living? I'd learned nothing, I had no hope. . . . May I have another cigarette, please?"

He lit the cigarette with trembling hands. I told my secretary that we were not to be interrupted, and I got up and asked him to come and sit next to me on the sofa.

"You know why I came to see you?" he said. "I don't belong anywhere. Am I an SS man? Am I a Jew? Am I a *Halbjude?* Do I belong to the persecutors or am I one of the persecuted?"

"If your story is true—and I have no reason to doubt it—then you are one of those who were persecuted. Like so many of us, you've lost your parents. You tried to save your father. . . ."

He shook his head. "It's no good. To the Jews I'll remain a damned SS man. For the others I'll always be a dirty Jew. If I tell the truth, I'll remain the eternal enemy, the bad guy."

He jumped up. "I'll tell you why I came to see *you,* Herr Wiesenthal. I feel I am a Jew. For myself, and for you, I am a Jew. But for the outside world, I *could* remain an SS man and help you with your work. No . . . don't interrupt me. I've discussed it with Uncle Franz. I told him I had read about your work and that I was going to offer you my help. He understood, and he agreed at once. This is the only thing I feel I can do, where I could be of *some* use."

I said nothing.

"You don't trust me? I know it's hard to believe such a fantastic story. Well, I've brought you all the information about myself. It's all in here, beginning with the name of my Jewish grandfather and ending with the date of Father's deportation and my own return from the Soviet Union." He handed me two typewritten pages.

"You check every detail. Send your people to the police— anywhere. I'll gladly pay for it. Then if you are convinced that I have told you the truth, write me. Here is my address. I want to work for you. It's like paying off a very tiny part of the interest on an enormous debt. A token payment, but a payment just the same."

I asked him what he was doing.

"I'm a traveling salesman. The job gives me a chance to get around in Austria and Germany, and later in other parts of Europe. I'm not married. So you see, I *could* be useful."

Two weeks later he sat across from me once more. I told him we'd checked everything.

"You told me the truth, just as I expected. No man would use his dead parents to trick me."

"Not even an SS man?"

"Let's hope not. Now I've got to tell you something that you don't know. I checked on the deportation of your father. The transport he joined went to Riga. . . . Yes, it is quite possible that he was in the vicinity while you were lying in the hospital."

This seemed to stun him. I suppose he saw himself again in the hospital room in Riga, next to the SS man who broke down under the pressure of having to kill people.

He swallowed hard and said: "Herr Wiesenthal, let us start—the sooner the better. I've *got* to do some work for you or I'll go crazy."

I showed him some files, told him about our investigations. As a member of an SS *Kameradschaft* (veteran's group), he wouldn't have to pretend; he would just continue to play his wartime role a little longer. His credentials were first-rate. He did very well. He was accepted by the *Kameraden,* who respected him for his "radical" views, and he became one of the boys. He was a "good German"—a bad German who had remained bad.

Alex and I never meet in public. In his notes he calls me Felix. We meet where we are sure not to be seen by other people. He reads all the books about the Second World War and the Nazi regime he can lay his hands on. He often sees things through the eyes of the man who has been on the other side. Sometimes we discuss a case from both viewpoints and a proper perspective emerges.

One day he said to me: "I would like to be a Jew again. Officially, for the whole world. That's where I belong."

I wasn't surprised. I said, yes, he did belong to us. He had proved it. I also told him he could do more for us, at least for a while, if he remained "one of them."

"I would like to live in Israel. There I might really be able to forget the past."

"But what about the people there who are unable to forget the past, Alex? One day you might make a mistake and tell them what you once were. They might not understand. I don't want you to get hurt again—though for a different reason."

We decided to postpone the decision. Alex is still one of my most valuable assistants. How well he plays his part I discovered a while ago. I was informed that some former SS men in a provincial capital of Austria had been heard threatening to kill me. I passed on the information to the Austrian State Police, who put a couple of operatives on the job. Privately, I also asked Alex to inquire.

Two weeks later, the Chief of the State Police showed me the men's report. They had infiltrated the *Kameradschaft* in that city and attended several meetings. The report said that the most dangerous SS man present was one XY, traveling salesman, a tall man with gray-blue eyes and reddish-blond hair, former member of the *Waffen* SS: "one of the incorrigible types with radical views who should be watched."

Alex, of course.

Chapter 8

THE TRAIN WAS
LEAVING IN
THREE MINUTES

Alex played an important part in the case of Kurt Wiese. It began for me unexpectedly one night early in July 1964. I had been listening to the evening news. At the end of the broadcast there was a short pause. Then the German announcer said, in his breezy style: "Ladies and gentlemen, here is an important announcement from the Cologne police: Kurt Wiese, under indictment for war crimes, has escaped from the apartment in Cologne where he has lived for the past two years. He had been arrested, but was out on bail pending his trial. He'd been ordered to report to the prosecutor's office every third day. When he did not report for a week, detectives went to look for him. They were told by neighbors that Wiese had not been seen for several days. . . ."

The announcer's professionally cool voice betrayed no interest as he asked his listeners to report "useful information" to the prosecutor's office in Cologne or to the nearest police post.

I turned off my radio. Another Nazi criminal had escaped. Who cared? Quite a few had escaped during the past few months. Most listeners forgot the name of the fugitive as soon as they turned off their dials. They'd never heard of Kurt Wiese, an obscure metalworker at the local Ford automobile plant.

I had often read the name of Wiese in certain records at our

Documentation Center. I knew that he was accused of having killed, in 1942 and 1943, at least two hundred people (among them eighty Jewish children) in Grodno and Bialystok, Poland. Wiese had been arrested in Cologne in 1963. He was inexplicably released a few months later after bail had been set at 4,000 marks ($1000). A German newspaper wrote that this was the equivalent of "twenty marks of bail for each murder."

I wrote a letter to the *Frankfurter Allgemeine Zeitung* on July 13, 1964, protesting the frequency with which such war criminals were released on bail and deploring the ease with which a number of them had escaped.

After Wiese had committed his crimes, Grodno and Bialystok had, of course, been occupied by the Soviets. At a press conference in Vienna, I talked to Vladimir Gawilewski, bureau chief of the Russian Tass News Agency. Gawilewski promised to write to the Soviet Union for material on Wiese. When he brought me the material, later on, he said: "I know you're going to use it. If I give it to the West Germans, they may just bury it in their files." Actually, I later gave the material to the German authorities. So far as I know this was the first time the Soviets had cooperated with the West in the prosecution of such a case.

The Soviet files contained a list of Wiese's crimes, with names of witnesses and their testimony. Briefly, in the summer of 1942 Wiese had shot a man named Slep who had tried to leave the ghetto without a permit. He had shot a woman named Adassa Kletzel, who "attempted to take a small piece of bread into the ghetto." In November 1942 he "personally hanged a woman named Prenski and two men named Schindler and Drukker." Later, the record said, he had shot an unnamed girl, whose offense was that "she was playing with a cat."

When Ghetto No. 1 in Grodno was liquidated, in February 1943, Wiese and other members of the Gestapo shot the entire personnel of the Jewish ghetto hospital, about forty people. The chief prosecutor of the Byelorussian SSR informed me that the main witnesses, men named Zhukovski and Klowski, would get permission to come to Germany to testify against Wiese—the first case in my experience in which such permission had been granted.

According to our information, Wiese had also killed twenty Jews

with his submachine gun in December 1942, at the fence of Ghetto
No. 1. The commander of Ghetto No. 2, an SS man named Streblow,
had been present. During the shooting Wiese had wounded one of
the Jewish ghetto guards. The man ran away and collapsed in the
court of a nearby house. Wiese ran after him, saw him lying on the
ground, and shot him through the head.

In January 1943 Wiese stopped a group of forced laborers near
the ghetto entrance and searched them. One man was carrying a
piece of white bread. Wiese shot him on the spot. Three days later
he searched a man named Kimche and found a piece of meat in the
man's pocket. He took him to the guardroom and shot him. In February 1943 he had been actively engaged in the forced expulsion of
the last Jewish survivors from Grodno.

The list is not complete. Wiese's activities after 1943 are still being
investigated.

I cannot explain what made me assume that Wiese had escaped
to Austria. It was pure hunch, but I've learned to trust my hunches.
They've turned out to be as useful as the patient search for clues, the
stubborn tracking down of witnesses after twenty years, and meticu-
lous deduction. Around Grodno, many SS units had been made up
of Austrians and Germans. I assumed Wiese would try to get into
Austria and contact former comrades there. They might help him
and hide him and later channel him to a "safe" country in South
America or the Near East.

I called Alex. The SS *Kameradschaft* has local organizations in all
large cities and many small ones in Austria and Germany. The members meet often in inconspicuous inns or shabby beerhouses (we
have an extensive list of these places in Austria). They like to en-
hance their meetings with a ritual of secrecy, like boys in a hideout.
Often they meet in the *Extrazimmer* (back room) of an obscure
joint under the benevolent protection of the proprietor, who keeps
outsiders away. Sometimes a waiter acts as guard—for some reason
a great many waiters are ardent Nazi sympathizers. In certain
places a pianist entertains the innocent customers in the front room
with a medley of waltzes. If a stranger approaches the danger zone,
the pianist alerts the comrades with a code *leitmotif*.

Such secret-society tricks usually seem superfluous, because the
comrades often do nothing worse than reminisce about the wonder-

ful past, read lovely illegal sheets printed in Austria and Germany, and hope for a wonderful Nazi future. Most of them are pathetic, prematurely old men who drink a lot of beer and speak an idiom as outmoded as the bombastic language of Hitler. But they are well organized, and their network is always ready to conceal fugitives and channel them toward safer destinations. They have members everywhere and probably a sort of code. They believe they are ready for *Der Tag*—The Day—if and when it comes.

Alex called me from Innsbruck in the evening. He indicated very cautiously (one never knew who was listening in) that he'd heard some news about "the goods," and was going to Graz, the capital of Styria. Innsbruck, Graz, and Salzburg are the favorite ports of call for Nazi fugitives in Austria. In these cities there are well-organized cadres of helpers. Salzburg, only a few miles from the German frontier, is particularly popular. In summer long columns of motorists pass the Walserberg border station in both directions. Customs inspections are perfunctory. German citizens need no passport—a driver's license or a simple identification card is sufficient.

The following night Alex called me from Graz. His voice was tense with excitement.

"One of the *Kameraden* here told me that a man who pretends to be a refugee from the Soviet Zone of Germany has just arrived in town. 'When a man escapes from the Soviets, we must help him,' the *Kamerad* said. . . . Could it be the fellow we're looking for?"

"How did he come to Graz?"

"They say he arrived by way of Czechoslovakia. He is waiting for his wife to follow him and hopes to go with her to West Germany, where they have relatives."

"Something is fishy, Alex. If he really came from Czechoslovakia, he wouldn't have come to Graz. He would have come to Vienna, Linz, or Salzburg."

"That's what I thought. Maybe I ought to take a look at the fellow."

I said: "Maybe he isn't the man we're looking for. But it could be somebody else who is interesting."

"One of the comrades put him up for the night. This morning the man spent an hour with Herbert Berghe von Trips."

"Trips!" I said. "Then it *must* be the man we're looking for." I couldn't explain over the phone to Alex that the pieces of the puzzle were beginning to fall into place. Trips was a Gestapo *Kommissar* during the war and had been the last commander of Pawiak Prison in Warsaw. He is mentioned—not very honorably—in *Behind the Walls of Pawiak*, a report by a Polish writer named Leon Wanat about the atrocities committed in the prison. There is a file on Trips in my Documentation Center. And there is also a file at the Austrian Ministry of the Interior.

"And where is our man right now?"

"A certain Hubert Zimmermann," said Alex, "who limps heavily with his right leg, left Graz about an hour ago. But I know where he—"

There was a click. Alex must have hung up. I waited for a while. There was no call. And I couldn't reach him; I didn't know where he was.

Alex called me early the next morning.

"Sorry I couldn't finish my report last night. I spoke from a hotel in Graz. Just then a *Kamerad* came in. Now I am speaking from a public telephone on the highway to Semmering."

"What are you doing at Semmering?" (Semmering is a famous mountain resort, sixty miles south of Vienna, popular with the Viennese and with foreign visitors. There are hotels large and small, beautiful paths through the woods, ski lifts, and various amusements.)

" 'Hubert Zimmermann' is registered at a large hotel at Semmering, where he is being taken care of by an old friend named Eberhard Gabriel. I've heard that Zimmermann will be in Vienna tomorrow—I don't know what for."

Very interesting, I thought. SS *Standartenführer* (Colonel) *Herbert* Zimmermann had been the commander of both Wiese and Trips during the war. I later found out that he'd asked Wiese to thank Trips, who had testified in Germany about his former commander and had not incriminated Zimmermann, following the SS slogan *My honor is loyalty*. (SS *Standartenführer* Zimmermann, under indictment in Germany, committed suicide in January 1966.)

It is easy to change *Herbert* into *Hubert*. My first thought was that Zimmermann had given Wiese his own identity card, but later a German prosecutor told me: "Sometimes the Nazis make mistakes, but in this case it was purely an accident that Wiese had papers in the name of Zimmermann. They were not Herbert Zimmermann's papers. Maybe he just liked the name."

But it was no accident that Wiese went to the Semmering hotel, where a former SS man named Eberhard Gabriel happened to be night concierge. Gabriel knows all kinds of people. He is also popular with hotel guests who happen to be Jewish.

Alex reported the next day from Semmering. Trips had come for "Zimmermann" in his car, and both had driven to Vienna. I called the Ministry of the Interior and asked Dr. Josef Wiesinger there whether the German authorities had requested the Austrians to look for Wiese. No such request had been made. No warrant for the arrest of Wiese had arrived in Vienna. I gave Dr. Wiesinger a description of Zimmermann-Wiese I'd received from Alex. Wiese was tall, fifty years old, wore a dark-gray suit and glasses. He had a limp in his right leg, from a wound suffered in the war. He should be easily recognized.

During the next few days "Zimmermann" stayed at Semmering, but he made three trips to Vienna, where he always managed to lose himself. I assumed he was meeting comrades there, perhaps trying to get money and a visa for his journey to a safe country.

In the early morning of Tuesday, July 21, a hot and humid day, Alex called me from Semmering. He had to see me at once.

When I drove up, Alex was waiting nervously.

"We've got to work fast, or Wiese is going to get away forever. He's gone to the Egyptian Embassy in Vienna twice. Apparently he has a stolen passport. He had some trouble with the Egyptian officials. They were reluctant to issue him an Egyptian visa in Vienna. Also, they don't want him to take a plane from Vienna to Cairo. Instead, they suggested that Wiese take a train to Belgrade and go to the Egyptian Embassy there. There are frequent flights from Belgrade to Cairo. So that's the setup. Wiese plans to leave for Graz this afternoon on the four-oh-five express from Semmering. From Graz it's easy to get to Belgrade."

It was already after ten o'clock, which gave us less than six hours to get Wiese arrested. If he succeeded in getting out of Austria he would join other Nazi criminals who have been indicted for mass murder but cannot be brought to trial. Egypt will not extradite them.

I told Alex to return to Semmering and keep an eye on Wiese. I drove back to Vienna and called up Dr. Wiesinger at the Ministry of the Interior. I told him that Kurt Wiese was at a certain Semmering hotel, where he'd registered as Hubert Zimmermann, that he had a false passport, had been promised a visa to Egypt, and was going to take the afternoon express to Graz.

Wiesinger was cautious. "Before I can do anything, we must have the particulars of the fugitive from an official source in Germany which my officers can compare with your description. Try to get me the information at once."

I put through an urgent call to the *Bundeskriminalamt* (Federal Criminal Agency) in Wiesbaden. I asked to speak to the official in charge of the Wiese case, told him what had happened, and asked him to give me the exact wording of the fugitive's official description.

The man in Wiesbaden hesitated. He didn't have the Wiese file at hand. Besides, he was not permitted to give out official information "to either individuals or private organizations." Again and again I've run up against such obstacles because I have no official capacity.

"It's now twelve-thirty," I said. "If we wait another three hours, you will never get Wiese. You published a warrant for his arrest, didn't you? Can't you read the description on the warrant for me?"

"I'm not permitted to do that, Herr Wiesenthal. I'll try to get the description to the Austrian Interpol."

"But—"

"I'm sorry, but that's the only way of doing it."

I called the Austrian Ministry of the Interior again and asked Wiesinger to call Cologne. There he could certainly get an official description. Wiesinger's people called Cologne. After a long delay they were told that the prosecutor was not at his office. They called the prosecutor in nearby Dortmund. No luck. Wiese was having all the luck. It was almost three o'clock; just one hour left to get him.

I called Dr. Wiesinger again. "If you don't send your men to Semmering now, it will be too late. A man accused of mass murder is going to get away forever."

"I know," he said. "But I can't arrest a man who has a valid Ger-

man identity card in the name of Zimmermann only because you
claim he isn't Zimmermann but Wiese. He has committed no offense
against Austrian law. Two of my men are alerted. As soon as word
comes from Germany, we'll proceed, if the information tallies with
yours."

There was nothing for me to do but wait. Even if the police left
Vienna now, they would hardly make it to Semmering.

At three-eighteen, the phone rang in my office. When I heard
Wiesinger's voice, I nearly jumped up out of my chair.

"Interpol contacted me just after your call. Your information was
correct. The man is Wiese. I've sent two officers to Semmering.
They're driving a police car with a siren, and they have a chance of
getting there just in time."

I looked at my watch. "It's twenty past three."

"I told them to board the train without being noticed. We don't
want too much excitement at the Semmering station. . . . I'll call
you back when I have word."

The next hour was endless. At twenty-five minutes past four
Wiesinger called. His men had arrested Kurt Wiese.

Alex came back to Vienna that afternoon and told me what had
happened. He had stayed around the hotel lobby, then followed
Wiese and Gabriel to the Semmering railroad station.

"The train arrived from Vienna. You can imagine how I felt when
I saw Wiese shake hands with Gabriel and get on the train. I knew
the train was leaving in three minutes. I wondered whether to get
on and do something foolish. At that moment the two detectives
arrived. The train was already moving, but they managed to get
aboard the last coach. I heard a whistle and saw the train disappear
into the Semmering tunnel."

The rest of the story I heard from the two detectives. They waited
until the train had gone through the tunnel and was approaching
the next station, Mürzzuschlag. Then they walked through the train
until they came to a compartment containing a solitary man. His
right leg was stretched out. They watched him quietly. Once the
man got up to take a newspaper from the rack above. He limped
with his right leg.

The train was slowing down for Mürzzuschlag. They entered the
compartment and stepped in front of the man.

"Herr Wiese," said one of the detectives.

They caught him unaware. He forgot, nodded, then shook his head; and suddenly there was fear in his eyes. He tried to say "My name is——"

"We know, Herr Wiese. You're traveling under the name of Hubert Zimmermann. Let's see your identification card, please."

Wiese handed them the card. He was very pale. The train came to a full stop.

"You're under arrest, Herr Wiese," said one of the officers. "Let's get out."

They brought him to Vienna by car, where Wiese made a complete confession. It tallied exactly with the information Alex brought me from Graz, where Wiese had told the *Kameraden* the story of his escape.

He had come from Cologne to the German city of Lindau, near the Austrian border, by car. A German woman drove him there. Wiese, a perfect *Kavalier*, didn't tell the police her name, and he'd been careful to prepare an alibi for her. About a hundred yards before the border, Wiese had got out of the car, taking along his suitcase.

There was a small kiosk there where a girl sold newspapers, cigarettes, and candy. Alex later went to see the girl, and she remembered the scene well.

"He seemed nervous when he came into the kiosk," she said. "He was tall, dark-blond, about fifty years old, and he limped heavily with his right leg. He wore glasses and had on a dark suit.

"He asked for a paper. I thought his hands were shaking when he put down his suitcase. Perhaps, I thought, the suitcase was heavy and he'd carried it a long time, or he was nervous because he was trying to smuggle in a few cigarettes," the girl had told Alex. "The smugglers' bad consciences are written all over their faces."

Alex nodded. He didn't tell the girl that the man indeed had a bad conscience—but not because he was trying to smuggle cigarettes.

"When he gave me the money for the newspaper, I noticed his big strong hands," continued the girl in the kiosk. "He said he was trying to get to Bregenz, on the other side of the frontier in Austria, and he asked me whether many cars came by here. I thought he was broke. I told him he'd certainly find a ride to Bregenz if he waited a while.

I said it was better to wait than to walk up to the frontier post carrying that suitcase. They might ask questions. Might even ask him to open the bag. But when he was in a car they wouldn't bother. Traffic was heavy and they didn't have time to look into each car.

"While I talked, I saw a car with a German license plate approaching. I told him to try it. He thanked me, took the suitcase, and stopped the car. A woman sat behind the wheel. He talked to her—probably asked her to be taken along—and I saw that she nodded. Then he walked around the front of the car, waved at me, and got in, and the car continued toward the Austrian border."

It was a fine alibi. The girl in the kiosk would testify that Wiese had stopped a car and was given a ride by a woman he'd presumably never met before. Wiese himself told the story to the *Kameraden* in Graz. They had been much impressed by the brave German woman who took such a chance.

"There are still some decent German women who will help a comrade in need," an old former SS *Führer* shouted. "Not whores, like the rest of them! I tell you, *Kameraden,* there is still hope for a better future. . . . Let's have more beer."

Another round of beer was brought, and they solemnly drank to the better future.

Wiese did not betray the name of the German woman but he was less chivalrous about his *Kameraden* in Graz. He gave the Austrian police the names of all those who had helped him. All are now under indictment. Each wondered who had betrayed Wiese to me. Each, I heard later, suspected his *Kameraden.*

Testimonial recognition of Simon Wiesenthal's assistance to the U.S. Army's War Crimes Group in Austria, in connection with the Group's investigation of conditions at the Mauthausen Concentration Camp.

WCID #16, 7708 WAR CRIMES GROUP,
APO 174, US Army,
5 February, 1947.

TO WHOM IT MAY CONCERN:

This is to certify that Mr. Simon Wiesenthal, President of the Members of the International Concentration Camp Organization, has given invaluable assistance to this organization in securing evidence for use in the Mauthausen Concentration Camp case.

Mr. Wiesenthal has given up much of his own free time to facilitate the work of this organization in Austria, and has also effected expeditious liaison with other groups for the rapid consummation of our mission here.

Mr. Wiesenthal has proven himself to be honest and sincere at all times and is definitely deserving of any assistance rendered him in the furtherance of his work in Austria.

W. L. WRIGHT
Lt. Col., CAC,
Commanding.

Authorization of Simon Wiesenthal's confidential mission granted by the OSS in Austria.

HEADQUARTERS
DETACHMENT A-1, O S S, AUSTRIA
c/o II CORPS MSI, CIC
APO 19, U.S. ARMY

Date___20 August 1945___

TO WHOM IT MAY CONCERN:
The bearer___Ing. Wiesenthal Simon___, is working on confidential investigative work for this Organization. Kindly let him move freely in American-occupied Austria and in case of any inquiries please contact this office.
Expiration Date___27 August 1945.___

EUGENE F. O'MEARA
Captain, CAC
Commanding Officer

Telephone: Token 23314
Address: Landstrasse 36, Linz

Simon Wiesenthal's request to the U.S. Military Government's office in Austria for permission to obtain and keep firearms in his home against possible attacks on himself. The request was granted by the U.S. Provost Marshal and the Assistant Director of Displaced Persons.

To Provost Marshal
through S.5 Section

For a long time now I have been receiving threatening letters at home and at office: their contents is in direct connection with my journalistic work.

In 1945 I worked by turns in War Crimes Office at Mauthausen, in C.I.C. 65 Division and O.S.S.

Throughout that time I contributed to the rounding-up and arrest of quite a number of Nazis, who after a temporary internment in Glasenbach have been set free. In connection with the Dachau process I organized for the War Crimes J.D.16 several hundreds of witnesses. I presume that the threatening letters are stemming from the family circles of the prosecuted-and-executed war criminals.

This is why I apply to you for the permission to get a rifle or a tommy-gun for the protection of my home.

Respectfully Yours

Simon Wiesenthal

Recommend approval of above request for a rifle only for the protection of the home of Mr. Wiesenthal.

ROBERT R WRIGHT JR
Capt   Inf
Asst Director of
Displaced Persons

27 February 1948

Recommend approval of above request for a rifle only for the protection of the home of Mr. Wiesenthal.

SIDNEY B PAINE
Maj   CMP
Provost Marshal
Upper Austria

2 March 1948.

Chapter 9

THE MAN WHO
COLLECTED BLUE EYES

[The Nazi regime succeeded in corrupting members of every profession in Germany, including physicians—men who had sworn the Hippocratic Oath. The Hitler regime had created its own kind of medical science. The physicians who practiced in the concentration camps didn't attempt to heal patients, but acted on the theory that the most effective remedy for a headache is to cut off the patient's head. Invalids and others unable to work were sent to the gas chambers; prisoners showing symptoms of contagious diseases were shot, as were others who had had contact with them. Often medical men injected poison or air into their victims' veins. When a trainload of prisoners arrived at a camp, a doctor stood by, arbitrarily separating those who looked healthy from those who did not, signaling those who looked well to one side—a temporary reprieve—and those who did not to the other side—the crematorium. Worst of all, the camps became weird laboratories where mad scientists used human beings instead of white mice and guinea pigs. Much has been written about the tests that were carried out with incredible callousness not only by doctors but also by chemists and experts from many leading German drug companies. In Auschwitz there was a special "experimental block" where prisoners had to submit to tests ordinarily made only on animals.
154

After the war, I met a young Jew whose left arm looked like a multicolored chessboard. The doctors in Auschwitz had put some stuff on a two-inch square of his skin. After a few days of terrible pain, the skin became dark-blue. The doctors cut out that piece of skin and put something else on another part of his arm. This time the reaction was yellowish and the pain was worse. The experiments were continued for months. When he complained about the pain, the doctors told him he should consider himself lucky. "As long as we're working on you, you'll at least stay alive," one doctor said, laughing.

I met another boy whom the scientists of Auschwitz, after several operations, had successfully turned into a woman. He was then thirteen years old. After the war, a complicated operation was performed on him in a West German clinic. The doctors restored the man's physical masculinity, but they couldn't give him back his emotional equilibrium. He began to drink, showed criminal tendencies, and was arrested—which surprised no one who knew his history. He is six feet three and looks healthy, but he is broken inside; the doctors say that he will never be normal again. Also at Auschwitz, a group of doctors and chemists worked on a new, simplified method of sterilization. They wanted to find "an act of surgery" that would be so easy to perform that quacks and barbers could do it; the new method would be used on the Slavs and other peoples whose procreation was not in the interest of the Nazis.

It is no secret that some of these doctors are still practicing medicine—in Austria, Germany, Egypt, Africa, South America. We have a file of their names and some of their addresses. Perhaps the worst of the lot is Dr. Josef Mengele, the former chief doctor at Auschwitz, who specialized in what he called "the science of twins" and who tried to artificially create children with Aryan features and blue eyes.]

The name of Dr. Josef Mengele was known to all former concentration-camp inmates, even those who had never been in Auschwitz. Mengele had thousands of children and adults on his conscience; in 1944 it was he who determined which of thousands of

Hungarians at Auschwitz would live or die. He particularly hated gypsies (perhaps because he looked like one) and ordered thousands killed. I have the testimony of a man who had seen Mengele throw a baby alive into a fire. Another man testified that Mengele once killed a fourteen-year-old girl with a bayonet.

In 1959 I asked my friend Hermann Langbein, general secretary of the International Auschwitz Committee, with whom I had worked on several cases, whether he happened to know Mengele's address. Langbein said: "In 1954 Mengele filed a suit for divorce against his wife in Freiburg, Breisgau, their last place of common residence, and exchanged several letters with his lawyer, Dr. Hans Laternser. I got his address in Argentina at the time—don't ask me how."

I learned from various sources that in the past years Dr. Josef Mengele had used these assumed names: Helmut Gregor-Gregori, Fausto Rindon, José Aspiazi, Ernst Sebastian Alvez, Friedrich Edler von Breitenbach, Walter Hašek, Heinz Stobert, Karl Geuske, Fritz Fischer, Lars Ballstroem.

At the time of his divorce, Mengele was practicing medicine in Buenos Aires under the name of Dr. Helmu Gregor-Gregori. He had since been married again—to the widow of his older brother Karl, who had been killed in action in the war. I asked Langbein whether the West German authorities had tried to get Mengele.

"On July 5, 1959, the Freiburg prosecutor issued a warrant for his arrest. Then the Bonn Foreign Office asked Argentina for his extradition. The Argentinians claimed that Mengele could not be found at the address indicated. We must try to get his latest address."

Langbein had known Mengele in the concentration camp and described the doctor to me—a small, swarthy, dark-haired man with a slight squint in the left eye and a triangular cleft between his upper front teeth. He stood five feet six. "He's fifty-three now and getting bald," said Langbein. "He's a natty dresser. In Auschwitz he always wore sharply creased uniforms, shining boots, and white gloves."

Langbein told me that once Mengele came into the children's block in Auschwitz to measure the boy's heights. "He became very angry when he found many of them too small for their age. He made the boys stand against a doorpost marked with nails for each age group. If a boy's head didn't reach the proper nail, Mengele gave a sign with his riding crop. The child was taken away to the gas chambers. More than a thousand children were murdered at that time."

Mengele is a Doctor of Philosophy (University of Munich) who studied Kant's *Critique of Pure Reason* and simultaneously swallowed the racial rubbish of the Hitlerian philosopher Alfred Rosenberg. He is a Doctor of Medicine (University of Frankfurt) who sacrificed thousands of children—twins from all over Europe—by using painful injections to try to change the color of their brown eyes to blue. (Both universities have deprived Mengele of his academic degrees.)

Mengele had a theory that human beings had pedigrees, like dogs. He was convinced of his mission to breed a super-race of blue-eyed, blond "Nordic" people, and of his duty to kill "biologically inferior specimens." In Auschwitz, his surgical ward was impeccably clean, his syringes always sterilized. He often used the syringes for injecting phenolic acid, benzine, or air, which killed his patients within a few seconds. Mengele was the perfect SS man; he would smile at pretty girls while he sent them to death. In front of the Auschwitz crematorium he was once heard to say "Here the Jews enter through the door and leave through the chimney."

I felt, as the West German authorities did, that Mengele's capture would make a strong impact on millions of people when the details of his crimes become fully known in court. The West German government offered a reward of sixty thousand marks (fifteen thousand dollars) for him. Next to his friend Martin Bormann (one hundred thousand marks—twenty-five thousand dollars), Mengele is the Nazi fugitive with the highest price on his head.

After talking to Langbein, I contacted a friend in Buenos Aires to whom I gave the doctor's last two known addresses. On December 30, 1959, my informant in Buenos Aires notified the German Embassy there, at my request, that Mengele was now residing under his own name at Vertiz 968, Olivos. He apparently no longer thought it necessary to hide his identity.

I gave the new information to Langbein, who called up the prosecutor in Freiburg. Files were exchanged between the embassies, the foreign ministries, the ministries of justice, and the prosecutor's office. Early in January 1960 an urgent official request—the second —for Mengele's extradition was cabled from Bonn to Buenos Aires. A few weeks later the German Embassy in Buenos Aires was informed that the Argentinian Procurador de la Nación might raise the objection that Mengele's offenses could be considered political rather than criminal. Most countries, especially in Latin America, do not extradite people for political offenses. Although the Argentinian authorities admitted that the evidence against Mengele was very strong, they couldn't overcome the psychological attitudes that make extradition almost impossible throughout South America.

Traditionally, most Latin American countries have a strong conception of political sanctuary. The political situation in these countries sometimes changes abruptly; political leaders may have to run for their lives—usually by applying for sanctuary in the embassy of another Latin American country. Many of these leaders believe that by granting demands for the extradition of Nazi criminals they might create a dangerous precedent. South American countries rarely even extradite murderers. The "guest" is always protected. In certain countries, a man will not be extradited after spending as little as two days in the country. The example of Mengele does not mean that there is widespread sympathy for the Nazis throughout South America, but that there is widespread antipathy toward extradition.

Meanwhile, Mengele had been informed by his relatives in Germany that a warrant for his arrest was being issued in Freiburg. In May 1959, eight weeks before the Freiburg indictment was published, Mengele went to Paraguay, where he had made friends during an earlier visit. One of these friends was Baron Alexander von Eckstein, a Baltic Russian who is said to be close to Paraguay's German-descended President, General Alfredo Stroessner. Eckstein sponsored Mengele's naturalization as a citizen of Paraguay. Eckstein and another witness, a German businessman named Werner Jung, testified (falsely) that Mengele had lived in Paraguay for five years, as that country's naturalization laws require. On the basis of this testimony, "José Mengele" was granted Paraguayan citizenship on November 27, 1959, by governmental decree 809.

A few days after his naturalization Mengele returned to Argentina. There he learned that the West German government had made the second urgent demand for his extradition. In Buenos Aires the matter remained in the hands of the Procurador de la Nación, who made no move—and during the next six months the Procurador gave no indication that he planned to make any. Argentina was apparently going to remain just as passive as it had in the case of Adolf Eichmann. In fact, I can reveal here that if Argentina had extradited Mengele early in 1960, Eichmann's abduction would not have taken place in May of that year.

Mengele was not certain that his brand-new Paraguayan passport would protect him. He thought it might be safer to leave Buenos Aires. He went to Bariloche, a beautiful resort in the lake district of the Andes, where many wealthy former Nazis have elegant villas and large estates. Bariloche is conveniently close to the frontier of Chile, another favorite refuge of many Nazis.

A mysterious incident occurred in Bariloche. (I cannot give the source of my information, but I can vouch for its reliability.) Among the tourists in Bariloche at the time was a Miss Nora Eldoc from Israel, who was visiting her mother. The two women had been in Auschwitz, where Miss Eldoc had been sterilized by Dr. Mengele. It was mere coincidence that she came to Bariloche at a time Mengele was there. She was then forty-eight, still attractive, and had many friends in town. One evening, in the ballroom of a local hotel, she suddenly found herself face to face with Mengele. The local police report does not say whether he recognized her. Mengele had "treated" thousands of women in Auschwitz. But he did notice the tattooed number on her lower left arm. For a few seconds the victim and the torturer stared at each other silently. Eyewitnesses later testified that no word was said. Miss Eldoc turned and left the room.

A few days later she did not return from an excursion into the mountains. The police were notified. Several weeks later Miss Eldoc's bruised body was discovered near a crevasse. The police made a routine investigation and ascribed her death to a mountain-climbing accident.

After Eichmann's abduction, the irate Argentine government complained, claiming that it would have handed over Eichmann voluntarily. This seemed doubtful, to say the least, and I informed the wire services and the leading newspapers of the world what had happened in the case of Mengele. These revelations may have convinced some people in Buenos Aires that something would have to be done about Mengele. At any rate, in June 1960 a warrant was issued for his arrest by the Argentinian authorities. It came too late. On the day of Eichmann's capture, Dr. Mengele had slipped across the Brazilian border and disappeared once more. Not for long, though. One day in April 1961, a man I'll call Johann T. came to visit me. Johann is an elderly German who once was a member of the Nazi Party and still keeps in touch with his former *Kameraden*. Yet Johann, whom I have known since the end of the war, has on several occasions given me information that has proved accurate and useful. I know that Johann does not help me because of a sense of guilt or because he wants to atone for the crimes committed by the Hitler regime. He is not particularly fond of Jews, but he is a man of character. Although he is still an ardent German nationalist, he has a very personal reason for his attitude toward the Nazis. In 1942, his niece Linda, a pretty, blond, blue-eyed girl was taken against her will to a so-called *Lebensborn* castle—an official Nazi breeding camp where young Aryans, male and female, were brought together to produce super-Aryans—precisely the sort of place Mengele might have invented. There Linda gave birth to a baby whose father she couldn't identify, since he could have been any one of a dozen young SS men who had been with her in accordance with the program. Johann never got over this insult to human dignity. He once told me he would never stop hating the Nazis for their perverted race theories. When he came to see me in 1961, I hadn't seen him for years. His hair was white now, but his feelings were unchanged.

"I've got good news for you," he said. "I know where Mengele is. I hope you catch him. His trial would open the eyes of many people." He looked at me. "Last week I met two Germans; one is an old acquaintance. They had just returned from Egypt, where they saw Mengele a few weeks ago."

"Johann, so far as we know, Mengele is still somewhere in South America," I said.

"He *was* there, but he left last month. It seems he was getting worried. He had the feeling that he was being followed by Israeli agents." Johann winked at me. "Maybe he was—or maybe it's just a case of bad conscience. I wouldn't wonder if he lost his nerve after Eichmann's capture. Anyway, he decided that Cairo would be safer for him."

"And how do the Egyptians feel about him?"

"They gave him the cold shoulder. Nasser wants to stay on good terms with both the United States and the Soviet Union. Perhaps he is worried about adverse publicity if it became known that Egypt was sheltering a man like Mengele. At any rate, the Egyptians suggested that Mengele should leave the country as soon as possible. The German group in Egypt, under a former *Obersturmbannführer* Schwarz in Alexandria, who handles such delicate operations, rented a yacht and took Mengele and his wife to the Greek island of Kythnos. It's a tiny island near Crete, ideally located, because hardly any regular boats go there."

"Is Mengele going to stay there?"

"The Germans promised to have him and his wife taken off the island as soon as it could be arranged. You haven't got much time, Wiesenthal. If you move fast, you might get him on Kythnos."

I was about to leave for Jerusalem to attend the Eichmann trial. If I notified the Greek authorities through normal diplomatic channels, several weeks would be lost. This time, as often in the past, I chose to take a nonroutine approach. I called up the editor of a large illustrated magazine in Germany, with whom I had cooperated before. The magazine wanted the story; I wanted the man. Through Langbein we called Athens to contact a Dr. Cuenca, a noted scientist who had been forced during the war to work in Auschwitz as a "medical attendant" under Mengele. I explained that we would have to move fast and in secrecy. Cuenca told us that regular passenger ships stop at Kythnos only twice a week. It was decided that a reporter from the German magazine would go to Kythnos by way of Athens. If he found Mengele in Kythnos, he would telephone Cuenca, who would come there and identify the doctor. If he was the wanted man, Cuenca would notify the Greek police. Everything would be strictly legal. The Greek authorities would certainly extradite Mengele.

The reporter arrived in Kythnos by boat forty-eight hours later.

There were only two large buildings on the island, a monastery and a small inn near the harbor. The reporter entered the latter and asked the innkeeper whether he'd had any guests lately.

"A German and his wife. They left yesterday."

"But there was no passenger steamer yesterday," said the reporter.

"A white yacht came into the harbor. The German and his wife went aboard and the yacht left again, in a westerly direction."

So they had been twelve hours late.

"Are there any other Germans on this island?" asked the reporter.

The innkeeper shook his head. "They were the first two guests we had this year. It's too early for tourists. They usually start coming in May."

The reporter showed the man a batch of photos. Without hesitating the innkeeper picked a picture of Mengele. Two monks who happened to come in also agreed that this man had been there only yesterday.

We had lost another round.

Later, when I met Johann again, I asked him whether Mengele might have been warned that the German reporter was coming to Kythnos.

"I don't think so."

"Who went to fetch Mengele in Kythnos?"

"Some Spanish friends picked up Mengele and his wife on their yacht. This man has friends everywhere. It is appalling what people will do out of a misguided sense of solidarity. I don't know who they are, but I know they brought him to Barcelona. Do you know that he once even dared to go back to Germany?"

"To Germany? But there is a warrant out for his arrest."

"Mengele has *very* good friends in Germany. I know that he came to Günzburg some time in 1959 to attend his father's funeral. He stayed there several days. Naturally he didn't go to a hotel, and he didn't want to stay at home. He lived at the English Institute Convent School."

"And no one went to the police to denounce him?"

"In Günzburg, everybody depends, one way or the other, on the Mengeles. I am sure the police did not know he was there."

When it became known that Mengele had been in Günzburg in 1959, Public Prosecutor Rahn told a press conference in Frankfurt that the town of Günzburg "acted like a group of conspirators to help the Mengele family." Afterward the Mayor, Dr. Seitz, had protested. But then a paper reported that Dr. Seitz happened to be the notary for the Mengele family. There were accusations and counter-accusations. According to the press, a legal official in Günzburg said that one town harbored "a group of old Nazis who skillfully throw sand" into the machinery of democracy. A former Mayor, Michael Zehetmeier, told a Swiss newspaper: "In this town no one will tell anything even if they know a lot." This was Günzburg, a quaint medieval town of twelve thousand people on the banks of the Danube in Bavaria. Günzburg is proud of its lovely Renaissance castle, its Rococo church, its market square with its old houses, and its largest enterprise, the farm-machinery factory of Karl Mengele & Sons. Mengele's father had founded the firm about the turn of the twentieth century. The family had become wealthy; the Mengeles had long been Günzburg's first citizens. A considerable percentage of the town's inhabitants are employed, directly or indirectly, by the Mengele firm. In Buenos Aires, after the war, Mengele & Sons acquired a fifty per cent interest in Fadro Farm KG, SA, a new local assembly plant for German-made tractors. The Argentine company was founded with a capital of a million dollars.

Josef Mengele was born in this lovely old town on March 16, 1911, and grew up as the crown prince of the ruling local family. In the 1920s he went to nearby Munich, where he began to study philosophy. There he met Adolf Hitler, during the early beerhall days, and became a fanatical follower of the Führer. People in Günzburg who remember Mengele as a young man told me that he suffered from his physical appearance. He wanted to look like an Aryan— which he didn't, by any stretch of imagination.

Mengele enlisted early in the war, joined the *Waffen* SS and served as a medical officer in France and Russia. Veterans of the *Waffen* SS dissociate themselves from the ordinary SS, claiming the *Waffen* SS had nothing to do with concentration camps and the cruel aspects of the Hitler regime. However that may be, in 1943 Mengele was appointed chief doctor at Auschwitz. Himmler and Inspector General Glucks, who was responsible for concentration-camp personnel, picked the right man.

Mengele's race-purification experiments reminded me of the testimony of Hitler's aide, SS *Obergruppenführer* von der Bach-Zelew-ski, in Nuremberg. In the summer of 1941, when the Mufti of Jerusalem left Iraq after an unsuccessful fascist-style *Putsch* there and escaped to Germany, the leading Moslem anti-Jew wanted to meet his opposite number in Germany. Hitler was shown a picture of the Mufti. He refused to receive him. He said he was not going to meet a man "who looks like a Jew."

"But, *mein Führer*," von der Bach-Zelewski said, according to his testimony, "the Mufti has blue eyes."

The Mufti was received.

I have now been able to retrace Mengele's movements quite exactly. At the end of the war he went home to Günzburg. His family and friends, unaware of his career at Auschwitz, greeted him as a good soldier who had done his duty. Many people knew that he'd worked in "one of those camps" but no one asked any questions. Even later, when the rumors began to float around, people kept quiet. Günzburg was in the U.S. Zone of Germany, but the Americans brought no charges against Mengele, because they didn't know what he'd done. It was another proof of the total confusion that existed among the various military and civilian authorities in Germany in the early postwar years.

For five pleasant years, Mengele led a quiet life in Günzburg, often visiting Munich and other places. No one bothered him. Only in 1950 did his name begin to be mentioned at various Nazi war-crimes trials. Some of his former colleagues and subordinates, among them his former SS chauffeur, began to talk about things he'd done at Auschwitz.

Mengele thought it was time to disappear. He had powerful friends in the *ODESSA* organization. In 1951 he escaped via the Reschenpass-Merano route to Italy, and went from there to Spain and later to Latin America. Sometime in 1952 he arrived in Buenos Aires with various sets of false papers, and began to work as a doctor without a license. He didn't worry; he was on the friendliest terms with the police of Dictator Juan Perón. He called himself Friedrich Edler von Breitenbach, and he had many friends among local Nazis.

Perón's regime ended on September 16, 1955, when the dictator went into exile. Suddenly the Nazis were afraid they might no longer be officially protected. A general exodus to Paraguay began. Mengele went to Asunción, the capital, but he later returned to Buenos Aires, where life was more pleasant. He no longer dared practice medicine illegally, so he took over the management of the family firm's local office.

Ten years had gone by since he had come back from the war. No German tribunal had opened proceedings against him. Mengele must have felt that it was no longer necessary to hide under an alias. He took up residence in Buenos Aires under his own name. And that was how we tracked him down there two years later, in 1957, when his name appeared as chief defendant in a German trial that was being prepared against Nazis who had been at Auschwitz.

In 1962, some months after Mengele had given us the slip on Kythnos, I learned that he had returned to South America. His wife and son remained in Europe. Frau Mengele lived in Kloten, near Zurich, Switzerland. I got in touch with a Swiss lawyer, who learned that she had rented a small house at 9 Schwimmbadstrasse—close to the airport. Not a very quiet place (the planes came in over the roof of the house), but convenient for her husband, who could be home a few minutes after arriving at the Zurich airport, without the risk of being seen by many people. I wanted to go there and find out more about the couple, but the Swiss police don't like inquisitive foreigners in their bailiwick. I therefore asked a Swiss friend to visit Frau Mengele.

He later told me that the house was an inconspicuous brownish villa in a modern development. He'd rung the bell. A small woman, about fifty and "rather pretty," opened the door. When she saw a stranger, she appeared distrustful. She asked him what he wanted.

My friend explained that he came from the insurance company. "The policy for your house is due. The premium must be paid."

"I am a new tenant. I know nothing about this policy." Frau Mengele tried to shut the door. My friend quickly put his foot in the aperture.

"Excuse me, Madame, aren't you Frau Vogelbauer?"

"No. She's the woman who rented the house before me. Better go and see the landlord."

"I'd just like to take a quick look at your place to find out for my company whether any repairs are needed."

The German *Hausfrau* in Frau Mengele became alive. She told my friend there was a leak in the bathroom and asked him to come in and take a look.

The apartment was modern, comfortable, clean and cool. My friend saw no trace of a man's being around. Frau Mengele seemed to live alone. Later I discovered that her son Karl-Heinz was then studying at Montreux.

That night I met a Swiss official in Zurich, told him of our investigation, and asked him to inform the Swiss police. I didn't want to harm Mengele's wife. I only asked that her house be watched so we would know if Mengele happened to drop in. Probably as a result of my intervention, the Swiss federal authorities expelled Frau Mengele from Switzerland several weeks later, in July 1962. The Swiss didn't want to have the problem of extraditing a Nazi criminal, nor did they want to become involved in a war-crimes trial. Frau Mengele left Zurich and moved to the lovely town of Merano in the Italian South Tyrol. She still lives there, in a secluded house, comforted by the presence of many former Nazis.

By now Mengele had gone back to Asunción. He would have preferred to live in Buenos Aires, but the warrant for his arrest was still out there. From the family firm's branch, though, he received enough money for a comfortable life.

Mengele had good reason to feel safe in Paraguay, and he was comforted by the country's history. Paraguay gained its independence in 1811, and was a dictatorship from 1815 to 1840. It fought Brazil, Argentina, and Uruguay from 1865 to 1870, and eventually adopted a democratic constitution. By that time the population had shrunk to 28,000 men and nearly 200,000 women. Paraguay needed immigrants to work its soil. Greeks, Poles, Italians, and Japanese came, and so did many Germans. Ever since, Paraguay has attracted German settlers, especially following the First World War. Today there are more than thirty thousand people of German descent in the country. The population is now almost two million, but the influence of the German minority is considerably greater than its proportion of the population. Germans have key positions in Paraguayan commerce and trade. The President, General Alfredo Stroessner, is the grandson of a Bavarian cavalry officer. Stroessner himself was born in Paraguay, but he seems to be attached to his German heritage. His presidential guard consists of goose-stepping six-footers.

About a thousand Jews now live in Paraguay. One of them is an old friend of mine from the Mauthausen concentration camp. He had been in Auschwitz, and had known Mengele. I met him in Milan in 1964 and talked about Mengele. He seemed apprehensive. "Please don't do anything drastic, Simon," he said. "The leaders of our Jewish community in Asunción have received many anonymous letters. If Mengele should be kidnaped, the letters threaten that 'not one Jew in Paraguay will survive.' That may be a stupid joke—but some of our people are worried, and I don't blame them."

"What about the police?"

"An outsider who doesn't know Paraguay won't understand how very strong the German influence is in our country. The Nazi ideology of race is still very much alive there, so is the old Nazi principle of *Sippenhaftung* (racial discrimination). The Jews of Paraguay would collectively be made responsible for anything that happens to Mengele."

"That's silly," I said. "We've known for years all about Mengele's second wife, and his son Karl-Heinz. He is a nice, serious boy. I know where he lives, whom he sees, what he does. It wouldn't occur to me to make him responsible for the crimes of his father."

"Of course you wouldn't. We don't do such things. But that doesn't mean that they might not do them."

He said goodbye to me and went off, a deeply worried man. I thought of him for a long time. Twenty years after the end of the nightmare there were still people for whom the nightmare still existed.

In July 1962 the Bonn government had asked the Paraguayan authorities to check on Dr. José Mengele, living at Fulgencio Morena 507 in Asunción. Several months later, the authorities notified the West Germans that Mengele was a citizen of Paraguay with "no criminal record."

Mengele didn't stay long in Asunción. His friends told him that he would be safer in one of the German colonies on the upper Paraná River, in an area where Paraguay, Brazil, and Argentina border one another. The river that forms the frontier is lightly patrolled. It is easy to cross it and enter Brazil. Mengele moved to an estate near Encarnación belonging to Alban Krug, a wealthy farmer in his sixties who has been described as a man with a violent temper and violent political ideas. On his journeys Krug is escorted by four heavily armed bodyguards. Mengele stayed two years at the Krug estate. He helped with the harvest and treated patients in Encarnación under the alias Dr. Fritz Fischer. Late in 1963 he became restless again.

I knew that it would be impossible to trace all the movements of a man who was protected by so many people in various parts of the world. Instead, I decided to watch the movements of the people closest to him—in this case, his wife and his son. Frau Martha Mengele kept pretty much to her home in Merano; Karl-Heinz was still in Montreux. Shortly before Christmas 1963, a letter mailed in Montreux informed one of my friends in Austria that Karl-Heinz Mengele had just gone to Milan, where he would stay at a certain hotel. He had told his classmates he was going there to meet some relatives from overseas. The letter was posted on December 22, but because of the rush of Christmas mail, it reached me on the morning of the twenty-eighth. I took the first plane to Milan. At the hotel I was told that a man carrying a Spanish passport in the name of Gregor-Gregori had stayed there. He had left two days earlier.

The third round occurred a few months later, one night in March 1964. Mengele was spending the weekend at the Hotel Tyrol near Hohenau, a prosperous German settlers' colony in eastern Paraguay. The Hotel Tyrol is the favorite meeting place of the local society— good food, good beer, a good rhumba band. General Stroessner comes there for a weekend once in a while. So did Mengele.

It was a hot, dark night. Half a dozen men had trailed "Dr. Fritz Fischer" to Suite 26 of the hotel. I later met some of them. They had formed a Committee of Twelve; they were twelve survivors of Auschwitz. Some had become wealthy, and had donated considerable money for the purpose of bringing to justice some of their former torturers. Unfortunately, the committee's methods were not as good as its intentions.

I was later told what had happened: six committee members had drawn the assignment of going to South America. They were to seize Mengele alive and bring him to Frankfurt am Main, where preparations for the Auschwitz trial were being made. A few minutes before 1 A.M. the men entered the lobby of the Hotel Tyrol, ran up the stairway, and broke open the door of bedroom number 26. It was empty. The hotel owner informed them that "Herr Dr. Fischer" had left in a hurry ten minutes earlier, after getting a telephone call. He had been in such a hurry that he hadn't even bothered to take off his pajamas. He had put his suit on over them, raced down the stairway, and disappeared into the night.

Mengele was still odd man out.

The Auschwitz trial was to begin in Frankfurt in 1964. Dr. Fritz Bauer, the chief prosecutor, told the press that "José Mengele," believed to be somewhere in Paraguay, was identical with the former concentration camp doctor. The Bonn government made a last determined effort to get the chief defendant extradited. On July 16, 1964, Eckhard Briest, the German ambassador in Asunción, once more presented a formal demand for Mengele's extradition during an audience with President Stroessner.

President Stroessner became furious and banged his desk. "If you continue with this," he shouted, "I shall break off diplomatic relations with the German Federal Republic!" Briest explained that he had received specific instructions about Mengele from Bonn. The President said: "Not another word, Mr. Ambassador! I shall not tolerate such things any longer!"

An account of the meeting appeared several weeks later in the German news magazine *Der Spiegel*. After Stroessner read his airmail copy of the issue, he realized that he might have gone too far. He consulted his advisers. Foreign Minister Raoul Pastor urged the President to get rid of Mengele. Pastor pointed out that Paraguay had just obtained a three-million-dollar development loan from Bonn, and might get more. It would be unwise to antagonize the West German government.

For a week, Mengele's fate was in the balance. He came to Asunción, and shortly afterward an inscription in black paint appeared on the wall of the German Embassy: JEWISH EMBASSY! HANDS OFF MENGELE! THIS IS AN ORDER!

Perhaps it was. Once again General Stroessner decided to keep *his* hands off Mengele. It was decided that Mengele should return to eastern Paraguay. He would live in a heavily guarded area into which no foreigners were permitted. In Caracas, Venezuela, the case of Mengele was later discussed at a conference of Interpol, the international police group. Dr. Frederico Nicholas Fernández, Interpol director in Rio de Janeiro, said he'd been informed that Mengele was hiding in the jungle near the Paraguayan border. But Paraguay is not a member of Interpol, and direct intervention was impossible, he said. Dr. Fernández was right. Mengele now lives as a virtual prisoner in the restricted military zone between Puerto San Vincente on the Asuncion-São Paolo highway and the border fortress of Carlos Antonio López on the Paraná River. There he occupies a small white shed in a jungle area cleared by German settlers. Only two roads lead to the secluded house. Both are patrolled by Paraguayan soldiers and police, who have strict orders to stop all cars and shoot all trespassers. And just in case the police should slip up, there are four heavily armed private bodyguards, with radios and walkie-talkies. Mengele pays for them himself.

The West German government still wants Mengele, and there is still a reward of $15,000 for him.

Chapter 10

EPILOGUE TO
ANNE FRANK'S DIARY

[On August 1, 1944, a fifteen-year-old girl named Anne Frank, who had been hiding from the Gestapo for the preceding two years with her family and some friends in an attic in Amsterdam, confided to her diary

> . . . If I'm watched to that extent, I start by getting snappy, then unhappy, and finally I twist my heart round again, so that the bad is on the outside and the good is on the inside, and keep on trying to find a way of becoming what I would so like to be, and what I could be if . . . there weren't any other people living in the world.

Those were the last words Anne Frank wrote in her diary. Three days later there came on the door the sharp knock the occupants of the attic had dreaded for years. The door was broken down and five men in German uniform entered, led by an SS *Unterscharführer*: a Dutch informer had tipped them off. The people in the attic—Anne Frank; her father, mother, and sister; another couple and their son; and a dentist—were arrested and sent to concentration camps. Only one of the eight survived. Otto Frank, Anne's father, who now lives near Basel, Switzerland, later told the world what had happened that morning.

171

"The SS man picked up a portfolio and asked me whether there were any jewels in it. I told him there were only papers. He threw the papers, and Anne's diary, on the floor, and put our silverware and a candlestick used to celebrate Hannukah (the Jewish Festival of Lights) into his brief case. If he had taken the diary with him, no one would ever have heard of my daughter."

Anne Frank died in the Bergen-Belsen concentration camp in March 1945. A year later her father returned to the attic of the Amsterdam house. The diary was still lying on the floor, where the SS men had thrown it.

The Diary of Anne Frank roused the conscience of the civilized world. It was the story of a normal, average girl who wrote about her private little problems ("Mummy sometimes treats me just like a baby, which I can't bear") against the background of life under the constant threat of terror ("I'm very afraid that we shall be discovered and be shot").

The *Diary* was translated into thirty-two languages, became a stage play and later a motion picture. It stirred the hearts of millions of people, especially young people. Many German youths now go to Bergen-Belsen every year to pray for Anne Frank.]

At half past nine one night in October 1958, a friend called me in great excitement in my apartment in Linz. Could I come at once to the Landestheater?

A performance of *The Diary of Anne Frank* had just been interrupted by anti-Semitic demonstrations. Groups of young people, most of them between fifteen and seventeen, had shouted "Traitors! Toadies! Swindle!" Others booed and hissed. The lights went on. From the gallery the youthful demonstrators showered leaflets upon the people in the orchestra. People who picked them up read:

> This play is a fraud. Anne Frank never existed. The Jews have invented the whole story because they want to extort more restitution money. Don't believe a word of it! It's a fake!

The police were summoned and took down the names of several demonstrators, students at local high schools. Then the performance continued. When I arrived at the Landestheater the play had just ended, but there was still much excitement. Two police cars were parked in front of the theater, and groups of young people stood around discussing the incident. I listened to them. The consensus seemed to be that the demonstrators had been right. This whole Anne Frank business was a fraud. Just as well that somebody had the guts to show those Jews what they thought of them.

Many of these young people had not yet been born when Anne Frank went to her death. And now, here in Linz, where Hitler had gone to school and Eichmann had grown up, they were told to believe in lies and hatred, prejudice and nihilism.

The next morning I went to the police and looked at the names of the arrested youths. It wasn't easy—they had powerful friends, and their parents wanted to quash the whole thing. After all, it wasn't really serious, they said; just a few young people raising hell and having fun. I was told that the names of the students would be given to their schools for disciplinary action. No one was punished. The boys in Linz didn't matter, I thought, but something else did. A few weeks earlier, a Lübeck high-school teacher, *Studienrat* Lothar Stielau, had publicly declared that Anne Frank's diary was a forgery. He had been sued by the girl's father, and three experts had confirmed the authenticity of the diary. According to the *Frankfurter Allgemeine Zeitung* the defendant had for "six hours haggled about the wording of a confession. . . . The youth of Germany should be protected from such an 'educator.'"

The disorders in Linz seemed more serious to me because they were symptomatic. These young rowdies were not guilty; but their parents and teachers were. The older people were trying to poison the minds of the young generation because they wanted to justify their own doubtful past. Many of them were trapped by their heritage of ignorance, hatred, and bigotry. They hadn't learned anything from history. My experiences during these past twenty years have convinced me that the people of Germany and Austria are divided into three groups. There are the guilty ones who have committed crimes against humanity, although sometimes these crimes cannot be proved. There are their accomplices—those who haven't committed crimes but knew about them and did nothing to prevent them. And there are the innocent people. I believe it is absolutely necessary to separate the innocent people from the others. The young generation is innocent. Many of the young people I know are willing to walk the long road toward tolerance and reconciliation. But only if a clean and clear accounting is given will it be possible for the youth of Germany and Austria to meet the young people on the other side of the road—those who remember, from personal experience or from the reports of their parents, the horrors of the past. No apology can silence the voices of eleven million dead. The young Germans who pray at the grave of Anne Frank have long understood this. Reconciliation is possible only on the basis of knowledge. They must know what really happened.

A few days after the demonstrations in Linz, I gave a lecture on neo-Nazism at the headquarters of the Vienna archdiocese. The discussion that followed lasted until two in the morning. A professor reported an incident that had happened to a friend, a priest who taught religion at the *Gymnasium* in Wels, not far from Linz. The priest had been talking about Nazi atrocities at Mauthausen. One of the students stood up.

"Father, it's no use talking about those things. We know that the gas chambers of Mauthausen served only for the disinfection of clothes." The priest was shocked. "But you've seen the newsreels, the photographs. You saw the bodies."

"Made of papier-mâché," said the boy. "Nothing but clever propaganda to make the Nazis look guilty."

"Who said that?"

"Everybody knows it. My father could tell you a lot about these things."

The priest had reported the incident to the boy's school principal. An investigation was started, and a survey made in the region. More than fifty per cent of the students in that class had parents who had been active in the Nazi movement. Their fathers loved to tell their sons about the heroism and glory of their past—how they had joined the Nazi Party in Austria in the early 1930s (when it was illegal), had helped blow up trains and bridges, had printed and distributed illegal literature against the Dollfuss government. Later the fathers had become proud SS men. It is not easy for young people to grow up in such an environment and remain unaffected by it. Their fathers had been afraid, and quiet, during the early postwar years, but in the late 1950s they were once more talking nostalgically about the great past. The boys would listen excitedly. Their schoolteachers, many of them former Nazis, did nothing to challenge the glorious stories told by the students' fathers.

I read *The Diary of Anne Frank* several times. I read it as a member of the human race, whose dignity had been gravely hurt; as a Jew who had lost six million of his own people; as a man who had decided to live for the dead, who wanted punishment, not revenge; and as the father of a girl who was just as old as Anne Frank was when she wrote her diary. It was only the will of God that my girl was not born early enough to suffer the fate of Anne Frank. Yet Anne Frank had not suffered more than a million other children. Her book had appeared when people were becoming indifferent to the tragedy of the past, when many said that they didn't want to hear about it any more, that one must stop hating. The words of a child had torn down a wall of moral apathy. Her last scream had broken through a world-wide barrier of callousness. She was no longer an anonymous body in a mass grave. She had become everybody's child.

Two days after the incident at the Landestheater, I was with a friend in a coffee house in Linz. Everybody was talking about the incident. Could the boys be blamed for the sins of their elders? Certainly they were not responsible.

A group of *Gymnasium* students sat down at the next table. My friend called over a boy whose parents he knew well.

"Fritz, were you at the theater during the demonstrations?"

"Unfortunately not, but some boys in my class were there. Two were even arrested," Fritz said proudly.

"What do you think about it?" my friend asked.

"Well—it's easy. There is no evidence that Anne Frank lived."

"But the diary?" I said.

"The diary may be a clever forgery. Certainly it doesn't prove that Anne Frank existed."

"She's buried in a mass grave in Bergen-Belsen."

He gave a shrug. "There is no proof."

Proof. One would have to produce proof—irrefutable proof that would convince these young skeptics. One would have to tear one single brick out of the edifice of lies that had been constructed, then the whole structure would collapse. But to find that one brick . . .

Something occurred to me. I said: "Young man, if we could prove to you that Anne Frank existed, would you accept the diary as genuine?"

He looked at me. "How can you prove it?"

"Her father is alive."

"That proves nothing."

"Wait. Her father reported to the authorities that they were arrested by the Gestapo."

"Yes," the boy said impatiently. "We've heard all that."

"Suppose the Gestapo officer who actually arrested Anne Frank were found. Would *that* be accepted as proof?"

He seemed startled. The idea had never occurred to him.

"Yes," he said at last, reluctantly. "*If* the man himself admitted it."

It was simple: I had to find the man who had arrested Anne Frank fourteen years before. Tens of thousand of people had been taken away all over Europe by nameless little men, the anonymous handymen of death. Even in the concentration camp we didn't always know the names of our torturers. They were aware of the possible consequences and tried to camouflage their identity.

There was almost nothing to go on. The diary ended abruptly when Anne Frank had been taken away. Anne's father, Otto Frank, had owned the export firm of Kolen & Co. After the Nazi confiscation of all Jewish property in Holland, a Dutch employee of Kolen & Co., Paul Kraler, had taken the firm into trusteeship. He had helped the Franks hide in the attic of the building in Prinzengracht, where the firm had its offices.

In an appendix to the diary, Kraler recalled that after the arrest of the Franks he tried to intervene on their behalf at the Amsterdam Gestapo headquarters. He had spoken with the officer who had arrested the family, a Viennese SS man who, he said, was named Silvernagl. The intervention had not been successful. Kraler's report caused ironic comment among the Austrian Nazis. It was naturally well known that the name Silvernagl did not exist in Austria— further proof that the Anne Frank story was a fake.

I had very little to start out with. I knew that the SS man was Viennese or at least Austrian—many Austrians abroad call themselves Viennese. He must have been an SS man of low rank, since his job was to arrest people—SS *Schütze*, SS *Rottenführer* or, at the most, SS *Unterscharführer*.

That narrowed it down. The *v* in Silvernagl was probably Kraler's error; it could have been Silbernagel, a common name in Austria. Seven people named Silbernagel were listed in the Vienna telephone directory; almost a hundred more were in various city registers. The name was also well known in the provinces of Carinthia and Burgenland. If at least I knew the man's first name!

I continued to search. Among all the Silbernagels there must have been one who had held a low SS rank during the war and had served in Holland with the Gestapo. Names were investigated and eliminated. Rumors were sifted, facts checked. It was a long, tedious process, and I had to be extremely careful. If I implicated an innocent man, I might be sued for libel.

When the police want to find a murderer who has committed a crime, they can stop all cars and ask all the drivers for their licenses and no one can protest. I couldn't do that. I found eight men named Silbernagel who had been Nazi Party members or SS men and were of the right age. One of them, a former *Obersturmführer* (a high rank, which automatically excluded him from my list), is now a prominent functionary in Burgenland. In any event, he had never been in Holland.

I asked a friend to contact private detective agencies and inquiry offices. He told each of them that he had been asked for a credit by a man named Silbernagel; always a different Silbernagel, to be sure. He said he wanted to check on the man's record during the Nazi era. We got much information, but none seemed to point to the man I was looking for. Once I asked a bank for the credit rating of a man named Silbernagel. Banks do a thorough job, but once again the result was negative. Two more Silbernagels were found to be former Nazis, but that was hardly a startling discovery. I came close to giving up the search, but then I remembered the arrogant face of the boys in Linz. I wanted them to go to their fathers and tell them: "You lied, Anne Frank did exist. What other lies did you tell me?"

In 1963 I was invited to appear on the Dutch television network. In Amsterdam, I went to the Anne Frank House, now a memorial, and I touched the walls the girl had touched. I talked to the custodian of the house. He said he'd often wondered about the man who had taken the girl and her family away. No one had any idea who it had been. He'd asked people and they had just shrugged.

"Nineteen years is a long time," he said. "It seems hopeless."

"Nothing is ever hopeless," I said. "Just suppose that I found the SS man who arrested her, and that he confessed that he had done it?"

The man gave me a long glance. "Then you would have written the missing epilogue to Anne Frank's diary."

For a while I thought I should go and see Otto Frank, Anne's father. He *might* remember the man who had come for them on the morning of August 4, 1944. He *might* be able to describe him to me. Any lead would help. The SS man must have changed in all these years—but there might be *something* to recognize him by.

I did not contact Mr. Frank. I admit it was not only my reluctance at upsetting this man who had suffered so much, at forcing him to search his memory once again. Something else bothered me. Suppose Mr. Frank asked me *not* to do anything about it? Could I comply with his request? I'd met other people who had not wanted me to search for the people who had killed their fathers and mothers and children. They said they couldn't bear it. "What's the use?" they asked. "You cannot bring back the dead. You can only make the survivors suffer."

I was still wondering what to do when I read in the papers that Mr. Frank, at a meeting in Germany, had spoken out in favor of forgiveness and reconciliation. The German papers praised his magnanimity and tolerance. I respect Otto Frank's point of view. He has revealed the ethics of a man who doesn't just preach forgiveness but also practices it. But I am above all concerned with the practical and legal aspects of the case. Time and again I saw how tolerance and forgiveness were misunderstood by the Nazis. The fact that the father of Anne Frank had pardoned the murderers of his child was cited as an important argument in favor of ending the prosecution of all Nazi crimes. "What is good enough for Otto Frank should be good enough for anyone," it was said. "If he forgives, then all ought to forgive." Mr. Frank's conscience permits him to forgive. My conscience forces me to bring the guilty ones to trial. Obviously we operate on different ethical levels; we follow different paths. Somewhere our paths meet, and we complete each other.

I remember a discussion I had after the war with a Catholic priest. He said: "We must forgive them. They will come before the High Tribunal of God."

"Father," I said, "why is it that the very criminals who don't believe in God always try to avoid human justice and prefer to await God's reckoning?"

He had no answer.

Presently friends in Holland told me that the SS man I was looking for might not be named Silbernagel but Silbertaler. Several people called Silbertaler had lived in Vienna before the war, but they were Jews and had disappeared. I found three non-Jewish Silbertalers in Vienna and elsewhere in Austria, but none had been active Nazis. I began to realize that it was highly improbable that I would ever find the one historical witness I needed. I began to wonder whether this witness was still alive.

On my next visit to Amsterdam I happened to talk to two friends, both familiar with the case of Anne Frank. They were Ben A. Sijes of the Dutch Institute for War Documentation and a Mr. Taconis, a high-ranking Dutch police official. Many names were mentioned in the course of our conversation—SS leaders Wilhelm Harster, Alfons Werner, Willy Zoepf, Gertrud Slottke, and others who had worked for Eichmann. In our line of work, one criminal leads to another. There were new leads, new names I'd never heard of. As I got ready to leave, Taconis said he had some "travel literature" for me, and he smiled. He brought me a photostatic copy of the 1943 telephone directory of the Gestapo in Holland. There were about three hundred names in it.

"Read it on the plane," he said. "That will keep you awake."

"On the contrary. Looking through a telephone directory has a soporific effect on me. When I'm in a hotel room in a strange place, I usually look through the local directory. Always makes me sleepy."

The flight to Vienna lasted about two hours. I settled back in my seat and looked through the Gestapo directory. I was almost asleep when I turned to the page headed "IV, *Sonderkommando.*" Under "IV B 4, *Joden* [Jews]" I read:

Kempin

Buschmann

Scherf

Silberbauer

I was wide awake. Section IV B 4 had handled the roundup and transport of Jews to death camps. If anyone had tipped off the

Gestapo about Jews hiding out somewhere in Holland, the report would inevitably reach Section IV B 4 in Amsterdam. All of a sudden the plane seemed to be very slow. I could hardly wait to get to Vienna. I knew that most officials of Section IV B 4 had been recruited from police forces in Germany and Austria, mostly among the *Kriminalpolizei* (detectives).

Back home, before I could take off my coat I opened the Vienna telephone directory. My heart sank. There were almost a dozen people called Silberbauer. Probably there were many more in other Austrian city directories. If I had to investigate each of them, as I had the Silbernagels and Silbertalers before, years might go by. I had reached the stage where some deductive thinking was needed. I couldn't investigate everyone named Silberbauer. I decided I would look for a man of that name who had worked (or was still working) for the Vienna police. It was like solving an equation with many unknown factors with the help of one known factor. I had to start from a definite premise if I wanted to build a structure.

I called up Polizeirat Dr. Josef Wiesinger, head of Section IIc at the Ministry of the Interior, which deals with Nazi crimes. Wiesinger has often helped me with my investigations. I told him—rather boastfully, I'm afraid—that I had found the Gestapo man who arrested Anne Frank.

"He's a Viennese policeman named Silberbauer," I said.

Wiesinger didn't call my bluff. "What's his first name?"

"I don't know his first name."

"There must be at least six men called Silberbauer on the Vienna police force," he said. "Which one do you want?"

"That should be easy to find. All you have to do is go through their service records. I want the man who was with Section IV B 4 in Amsterdam in August 1944."

"That was nineteen years ago," Wiesinger said skeptically.

"Your records go back that far, don't they?"

"All right," he said. "Submit a written request to my office."

On June 2, 1963, I mailed a detailed report. Several weeks went by. When I went to see Wiesinger in July about something else, I asked again about Silberbauer. He said the files of all policemen called Silberbauer were "still being examined." In September, when I was back from my vacation. I called him again. I was told that "So far nothing concrete had become known."

On October 15, Sijes and Taconis came from Amsterdam to dis-
cuss several war-crimes cases in Holland with me. We went to see
Dr. Wiesinger. Once more I asked him about Silberbauer. My
Dutch friends, I said, would be eager to get some news.

"Sorry," said Dr. Wiesinger. "We are not yet ready with this matter." I noticed a certain edge in his voice but wrote it off to impa-
tience or overwork. I was wrong.

On the morning of November 11, *Volksstimme,* the official organ
of Austria's Communist Party, came out with a sensational story. *Inspektor* Karl Silberbauer of the Vienna police force had been suspended "pending investigation and possible prosecution" for his role
in the Anne Frank case. The communists made the most of their
scoop. Radio Moscow broadcast that the capture of Anne Frank had
been unmasked "through the vigilance of Austria's resistance fighters
and progressive elements." *Izvestia* later praised the detective work
of the Austrian comrades.

I telephoned Dr. Wiesinger. He was embarrassed. "Naturally we
would have preferred to have the story disclosed by you, and not by
the Communists. How could we know that Silberbauer was going to
talk? He was supposed to keep his mouth shut."

I decided not to keep mine shut either. I called a Dutch newspaper editor in Amsterdam and gave him the story. It made front-
page news all over the world. I received more cables and letters
than I had after Eichmann's capture. There were radio and TV in-
terviews. Paul Kraler, now in Canada, told the world about how the
Franks had lived up there in the attic. And in Switzerland, Mr.
Frank said that he had always known that their Gestapo captor had
been an SS man named Silberbauer.

Everybody was excited except the Austrian authorities, who said
they didn't comprehend "what all the fuss was about," as one high-
ranking official said to me. The journalists wanted to talk to Silberbauer, but the Minister of the Interior refused to release pictures of
Silberbauer and tried to keep him incommunicado. I didn't go along
with this. I gave Silberbauer's private address to a Dutch newspaperman. I thought the Dutch were entitled to at least one exclusive
interview. When the Dutchman came to see Silberbauer, he found
the police inspector (the second-lowest rank in the Austrian police)
in a very angry mood. He said he'd been railroaded.

"Why pick on me after all these years? I only did my duty. We've just bought some new furniture, on installment, and now they suspend me. How am I going to pay for the furniture?"

"Don't you feel sorry about what you did?" the reporter asked.

"Sure I feel sorry. Sometimes I feel downright humiliated. Now each time I take a streetcar I have to buy a ticket, just like everyone else. I can no longer show my service pass."

"And what about Anne Frank? Have you read her diary?"

Silberbauer shrugged. "Bought the little book last week to see whether I'm in it. But I am not."

The reporter said: "Millions of people have read the diary before you. And you could have been the first who read it."

Silberbauer looked at him in surprise.

"Say that's true. I never thought of it. Maybe I should have picked it up from the floor."

If he had, no one would ever have heard of him—or of Anne Frank.

When Dr. Wiesinger had told me, on October 15, "We are not yet ready with this matter," he already knew that *Inspektor* Karl Silberbauer, attached to First District Police Headquarters, had admitted that he had been in charge of the Gestapo posse, that he had personally arrested Anne Frank and the other people in the attic in Amsterdam, on the morning of August 4, 1944. I asked Dr. Wiesinger why he had kept this information from me. He said he'd had "orders from above" to keep the matter a secret.

After the capitulation of Germany, Silberbauer had fled from the Netherlands and returned to Vienna. Since he had left the Vienna police force in 1943 to join the SS, he had to submit to "denazification" proceedings in 1952. He was cleared and returned to duty with the rank of inspector.

For a month after Silberbauer's confession his superiors had done nothing. On October 4 he was suspended from service and was ordered not to mention a word about the whole matter, pending investigation. A month later, Silberbauer complained to a colleague that he'd had "some trouble because of that Anne Frank." The colleague, a member of the Communist Party of Austria—there are some Communists in Vienna's police force—reported the story to the Communist organization of former concentration-camp inmates. At a meeting on November 10, another man told the story. The following morning *Volksstimme* had its scoop.

The Austrian authorities found no evidence that Silberbauer was guilty of the deportation of the Franks. A spokesman for the Interior Ministry said that the arrest of Anne Frank "did not warrant Silberbauer's arrest or prosecution as a war criminal." He had only obeyed orders. Disciplinary proceedings followed, because Silberbauer had concealed from the denazification board the fact that he had worked for the Jewish Affairs Section of the Gestapo in Holland.

Mr. Frank, asked to testify, said his captor had "only done his duty and acted correctly."

"The only thing I ask is not to have to see the man again," said Anne Frank's father.

A police review board exonerated Silberbauer of any official guilt. He is back on the Vienna police force, assigned to the *Erkennungsamt* (Identification office).

Incidentally, Silberbauer had been working at police headquarters during all those years I'd been looking for him. It's a ten-minute walk from my office to headquarters. Probably we'd met in the street. And also, across from our Documentation Center there is a big textile store with a sign reading SILBERBAUER. A second such store, also called SILBERBAUER, is next to the entrance to our building. Of course, Silberbauer doesn't matter at all. Compared to other names in my files, he is a nobody, a zero. But the figure before the zero was Anne Frank.

Chapter 11

A PROFILE OF
SIMON WIESENTHAL (Continued)
Wiesenthal, Neo-Nazism,
and Denazification

Simon Wiesenthal's spectacular involvement with the case of Anne Frank brings up the whole question of neo-Nazism, not only in Germany and Austria but in other parts of the world as well. Obviously, the young people in Linz who claimed that the story of Anne Frank was fabricated had been systematically indoctrinated, and their example is not too dissimilar from that of George Lincoln Rockwell, the American Nazi Party leader who claims that the entire story of the German extermination of the Jews is a falsehood propagated by Jews.

Wiesenthal considers the term *neo-Nazism* inaccurate because it oversimplifies the issue. Clearly, he says, some of Hitler's ideas have survived Hitler. Political splinter groups, not only in Germany and Austria but also elsewhere, are playing with modern forms of ultra-nationalism. In Germany the vociferous organ of these groups is the *National Zeitung*, with a weekly circulation of 130,000. At the 1965 general election, the extreme National-Demokratische Partei (NDP) got 600,000 votes, about two per cent of the total vote. Despite its innocuous name, the party's tendencies are nationalist rather than democratic. Prior to the election, some party leaders made a pilgrimage to the Bavarian town of Landsberg, where the Führer wrote *Mein Kampf* while he was in prison, and the NDP men put wreaths on the graves of several Nazi war criminals buried

184

there. Perhaps it is no accident that there are always fresh flowers on the grave of Hitler's parents near Linz.*

The collapse of the Hitler regime came too fast for the Nazis. Financially they were well prepared for the end, having managed to put aside enormous amounts of money and other assets. Ideologically, and so far as a future organization was concerned, they had made few preparations. No general policies existed for a revival of the ideas of Nazism; no shadow hierarchy of a future party had been set up. Hitler and his followers had believed in total victory and suffered total defeat.

But the chance came faster than even the most optimistic of the hard-core Nazis had anticipated. Until the beginning of the Cold War, the Allies had made serious attempts at seeing justice done. In Nuremberg, the leading Nazi criminals were given a fair trial, although a segment of the population in Germany and Austria does not seem to think so. There was no time to deal with the small fry, the people who arrested, tortured, and killed the victims; that would come later. It never came. Instead there was the blockade of Berlin and the beginning of the Cold War in 1948. The realities of power politics became more important than the need for moral retribution. In West Germany, denazification was slowed down and ended. All Nazis became good Nazis—provided they were prepared to resist the new enemy, communism. In East Germany, the situation was not very different; there former Nazis enlisted in the fight against the West. The East Germans often point out that no former Nazis occupy high posts in the DDR (German Democratic Republic). There *are* former Nazis in East Germany, though not so many as in West Germany.

The fact is that both East and West used the Nazis for their own purposes. The perceptive ex-Nazis quickly seized the opportunity. Files were removed and traces disappeared; names were changed, identities eradicated. War-crimes prosecutions tapered off; sentences were commuted. A man who would have been sentenced to death in 1947 got off in 1948 with a life sentence, which was commuted in 1950. Many decent people became resigned to the idea that they

* In the 1966 land elections in Hesse and Bavaria the NDP got about 8 per cent of the total vote. Its leaders claimed they would win 40 seats in the Bundestag election in 1969.

would have to get used to living among murderers. An American major once said to Wiesenthal: "The enemy of yesterday will become the enemy of tomorrow if we leave him alone." Wiesenthal has never forgotten these words.

But he thinks there is an important difference between the 1920s, when Hitler prepared for his *Kampf,* and the 1950s, when the postwar Nazis thought *Der Tag* might come again. Hitler emerged at a time of widespread disillusion after a lost war, economic depression, and widespread unemployment. The bitter, disenchanted people of Germany were ready for anything and anybody. Today a new Hitler, if he exists, is handicapped by the prosperity of an affluent society and a slow, gradual strengthening of the democratic processes in Germany. People are politically lazy, looking toward the middle of the road rather than toward the extremes, more interested in their standard of living than in risky political adventures. But democratic ideas are slowly gaining.

Today the men behind what is called neo-Nazism haven't tried to form a large political movement; they know there is no basis for it. Instead they have tried to set up small, elite tactical groups that they expect to be the cadres of a future movement, if and when prosperity should end and a new world crisis should plunge people into despair and fanaticism. At that point, they hope, millions of disappointed people will be ready to follow them. This new nationalistic movement is not limited to Germany and Austria—which is why, Wiesenthal says, the term *neo-Nazism* is not correct. The movement has support in Western Europe, in the Arab countries, in South America, even in Great Britain and the United States—where anti-Semitic tendencies have been reported not only among the noisy but unimportant few hundred swastika-waving Nazis or the Ku Klux Klan, but also among members of the John Birch Society and even among respectable Young Republicans. Wiesenthal has evidence that the World Union of National Socialists, a group founded in America, has several hundred members in various European countries.

All these people are in touch with each other, which is no problem in these days of perfect communications. It is no accident that the editors of both the pro-Nazi *National Zeitung* in Germany and *American Opinion,* the official Birch Society magazine, have claimed —as Rockwell does—that it was a lie that the Nazis killed six million

Jews. These groups are active in many places. German Nazis are trained in Cairo; South Tyrol bomb-throwers get instruction in Belgium; the Croatian Ustachis have a training camp in Australia.

They are hard to pin down. It is more difficult to destroy a few isolated elite groups than to fight a popular movement. The elite groups may be dissolved by the authorities, but the groups are well prepared for such a contingency and disappear under a different guise and a harmless-sounding name. The Nazis were predominantly a national German movement; the new Nazis are a world movement on an international basis, held together by certain general ideas such as anti-Semitism. And an international movement can be fought only on an international scale. The new Nazis have found sponsors in unexpected places, among Texas millionaires and rich South Africans, among the immigrant descendants of former Nazis and Fascists in South America and wealthy Arabs. The movement seems divided into a Nordic group and a Latin group, but its members speak a common political language. Wiesenthal does not believe there is acute danger now, but there are latent perils in the future. Basically, he says, the new nationalist movement is an "inner emigration" that will become decadent unless it is able to invoke powerful new motivations. "We should expect the movement to continue to form small, efficient cells, which hope to act as fuses for a future bomb. But the bomb has not yet been built. Perhaps it will never be built," says Wiesenthal.

Wiesenthal is often asked why he continues to work in Vienna when he is primarily concerned with the crimes of the SS, an organization started in Germany and mostly run by Germans. He explains that for one thing since 1958 the West Germans, through their Central Agency of the State Administrations of Justice for the Prosecution of National Socialist Crimes of Violence, set up in that year at Ludwigsburg, have been energetic in tracking down Nazi criminals. In many cases concerning Germans he has had the sympathetic, active cooperation of the West Germans. There existed no similar prosecuting agency in Austria until 1963. In the early 1960s, Wiesenthal's continuous efforts, abetted by a segment of Austrian public opinion and press, were uncomfortable reminders to the Austrian government that if something were not done, Austria's image in the world might be damaged. In 1962, Wiesenthal informally brought together several Austrian legal officials with some of his friends in Ludwigsburg. When Franz Olah became Austria's Minister of the Interior in 1963, he notified Wiesenthal, two days after taking office, that a newly created section at the Ministry, Section IIc, would henceforth deal with the prosecution of Nazi crimes.

Ever since the Moscow Declaration of 1943, when the four Allied powers proclaimed their aim of "liberating Austria," the Austrians have emphasized that despite the four-power occupation from 1945 to 1955 Austria was a "liberated," not an "occupied," country like Germany. Austrian politicians, educators, and inhabitants in general made the most of this distinction. A generation of young Austrians grew up after the Second World War in the belief that their country was the "first victim of Hitler." There is no widespread feeling of guilt about Nazi crimes, since they were carried out "under German orders." Years after the Germans had begun to make restitution payments to the Jews, the Austrians maintained that they didn't have to pay anything to Nazi victims in Austria, since they were not responsible. On the contrary, they claimed *they* should get restitution from the Germans, whose fault the whole thing was anyway. And although Adenauer said "If the Austrians want something, we'll send them the bones of Hitler," the Austrians later did get 321 million marks as restitution for victims of the Nazi regime. When the Austrians at long last decided they would have to make some sort of restitution payments, they first paid money to the persecutors, not to those who had been persecuted. Millions of schillings were paid to Austrian Nazis to compensate them for the loss of jobs and property after the end of the war. Only much later were restitution payments made to Jews in Austria whose properties and jobs had been taken away by the Nazis.

Austria was invaded by Hitler's army on March 11, 1938. Newsreels showing the arrival of Adolf Hitler in Vienna prove that he received a welcome more enthusiastic than any he got in Germany. The largest crowd in Vienna's history, more than four hundred thousand people, cheered the Führer for leading Austria "home to the Reich." Nor was the enthusiasm of the Austrians for Hitler limited to the crowd in Vienna's Heldenplatz. On April 10, 1938, the Austrians overwhelmingly voted for the *Anschluss* with Germany. Every tenth

Austrian was a member of the Nazi Party—a ratio higher than in Germany. Between 1945 and 1947, when all Austrians who had been members of the Nazi Party had to register, 611,720 Austrians admitted membership in the Party.

Since then, Austria has made a number of phenomenal achievements. In 1955, the four powers signed the Austrian State Treaty, giving the country its freedom and promising to guarantee its permanent neutrality. Austria is the only country that was partly occupied and voluntarily abandoned by the Red Army. With the help of an industrious and gifted people, beautiful scenery, and over a billion dollars' worth of American aid, the Austrians made Austria a showcase of industry, tourism, and culture.

Looking at the country in which he has lived since the end of the war, Wiesenthal sees a less cheerful image. Although the Austrians accounted for only eight per cent of the population of the Third Reich, *about one third of all people working for the SS extermination machinery were Austrians. Almost half of the six million Jewish victims of the Hitler regime were killed by Austrians.* Such unpleasant facts are naturally not printed in the beautiful travel folders. An Austrian, *Gauleiter* Odilo Globotschnigg from Vienna, was in charge of the four Polish death camps of Treblinka, Sobibor, Maidanek, and Belzec, where more than two million Jews perished. About twenty-five leading members of Globotschnigg's staff were Austrian—among them the notorious Herrmann Höfle, who comitted suicide after the war in prison, and Franz Stangl, commandant of Treblinka. Ernst Kaltenbrunner, the feared Gestapo chief of the Third Reich, was Austrian. So was Adolf Eichmann. Many members of Eichmann's staff were Austrian, among them Franz Novak, his master of logistics, and Alois Brunner, who was active in Slovakia and Greece. In the Netherlands, two Austrians, Arthur Seyss-Inquart and Walter Rauter, directed the expulsion and annihilation of 110,000 Dutch Jews. Of the five thousand names on the list of war criminals active in Yugoslavia, where two million people were killed, 2499 are Austrians. In Northern Europe various large ghettos were run by Austrians, including Franz Murer in Wilna and Eduard Roschmann in Riga (Roschmann now lives as Fritz Wegener in South America).

For reasons that have never been clearly explained, the SS command assigned large numbers of Austrians to the states of the former Austrian monarchy—Poland, Yugoslavia, Slovakia. Perhaps the Germans expected the Austrians to be more familiar with the mentality and the language in these countries. Over a thousand Austrian policemen were assigned to the German *Schupo* and the notorious *Einsatzkommandos*—traveling execution squads going all over Europe as licensed exterminators of human beings. Many of these men are again working for the police in Austria, including some who are now under criminal investigation by public prosecutors. Meanwhile, they perform their duties and carry their weapons. "If the Austrian authorities don't dare suspend these men who are accused of murder, why aren't the men transferred to the post office or to another department where they don't carry weapons?" Wiesenthal has asked in public. He has never received an official answer.

The Germans called the Austrians *ostmärkische Schlappschwänze,* "weak sisters from the *Ostmark*" (Hitler's name for his beloved homeland). The Austrians tried to prove by extreme brutality that they could be more efficient than the Germans. They succeeded completely. The *Kristallnacht* * of November 9, 1938, the beginning of the systematic extermination of the Jews, was much worse in Vienna than in Berlin. All synagogues were burned down and thousands of Jewish stores were plundered. The streets were covered with pieces of shattered shop windows glistening in the moonlight. "The only Jews not punished during the *Kristallnacht* were those who were overlooked," reported the Innsbruck *Gauleiter* later to Party headquarters in Munich. (The shining exception among the Nazis was an Austrian SS man who suddenly realized the enormity of these crimes and went at great personal risk into the homes of Jews to warn them; he is now one of Wiesenthal's unpaid helpers.) It was in Vienna's Rothschild Palais that Eichmann began his activities and trained his special staff.

Since the end of the Second World War, Austria has been governed by a coalition of its two large parties, the conservative People's Party ("the Blacks") and the Socialists ("the Reds"). These two parties had fought each other bitterly in the 1930s. The civil war culminated with the "black" Chancellor Dollfuss ordering artillery to shell the "Red" workers' homes in Vienna. Four years later both the

* See Appendix.

Blacks and the Reds were swallowed up by the brown Nazis. Later the leaders of both parties met as prisoners in the concentration camps of Dachau, Buchenwald, and Mauthausen. They decided to make up and build a new state together. The coalition succeeded admirably during the four-power occupation, but it became somewhat brittle after Austria regained its sovereignty after 1955. Power and patronage, money, and influence are evenly divided in a political *proporz* (proportional) system that often ignores the intentions of the voters. In all national elections since 1949 the popular vote has been almost evenly split between the two big parties. Nearly everything is under the control of the two parties: the big banks, heavy industries, the federal railroads, radio and television networks, an airline, the salt, tobacco, matches, and liquor monopolies.*

Through the years, the two big parties have run neck and neck, competing for every vote. This is where the power of the former Nazis comes in. In 1949, 497,653 "less implicated" ex-Nazis were again permitted to vote in a general election. It is no secret that half a million former Nazis may tip the precarious balance of power. No Austrian political leader in his right mind would dare antagonize this powerful segment of the population by speaking out against Nazi criminals or in favor of more trials, particularly at election time. And there is almost always some election coming up in Austria.

After 1955 most Nazi war criminals were granted amnesty by various presidential decrees. Other pending proceedings were suspended by the courts. The preparation of a war-crimes trial takes from two to four years, and the Ministry of Justice claims not to have enough prosecutors familiar with such problems. A large number of Nazi trials in Austria have ended with acquittals, though the judges left no doubt in the minds of the jurors that they considered the defendants guilty. Jan Verbelen, SS *Führer* from Belgium, sentenced there *in absentia* to death for the murder of 101 persons, was found "not guilty" by a jury in Vienna in 1965, where he now lives as a free man. At the trials of Franz Murer in Graz (1963) and the brothers Johann and Wilhelm Mauer in Salzburg (1966) the people in the courtroom applauded the defendants. Practically the entire Austrian press—though not the entire Austrian populace—was

* The coalition came to an end in March 1966, when the People's Party won the national election, and Dr. Josef Klaus became Federal Chancellor.

shocked by the acquittal in Salzburg. *Die Presse* called it "a shame for Austria"; *Neues Österreich* spoke of "an insult for millions of victims." Psychologists have told Wiesenthal that jurors whose past is sometimes not immaculate subconsciously hope to acquit themselves in acquitting the defendant. After the Mauer trial Wiesenthal discovered that the foreman of the jury was a former SA man. Austrian juries usually acquit a murderer who claims that he acted under duress.

Austria does not recognize sentences pronounced by courts outside Austria. Austrian Nazis who were punished with prison sentences elsewhere for their crimes and later returned to their homeland are considered blameless and could, in fact, become members of a jury in a Nazi trial. Many responsible Austrians feel that a reform of the jury system is overdue. If the jurors identify themselves with anyone, it will be the visible defendant rather than his invisible victims. Austria has not really tried to conquer its tarnished past. Forty-two former SS men at Auschwitz, among them three camp doctors, now live peacefully in Austria, unmolested by the authorities.

"The attitude is quite different from the attitude in West Germany," says Wiesenthal. "And there is a startling difference between the number of pending cases and of arrested suspects. Early in 1966, there were 1120 proceedings pending in Austria against people accused of Nazi crimes. Only 3 out of the 1120 were arrested, less than three-tenths of one per cent. In Germany, more than fifteen per cent of all suspects are in jail."

The leading officials of Section IIc of the Austrian Interior Ministry and the State Police—the security branch of the police—have shown much understanding for Wiesenthal's work, but their hands are often tied by Austria's political system. As a result, Wiesenthal often encounters masterful inactivity when action is needed. Investigations are slowed down and trials postponed. SS men convicted of crimes and sentenced to life have had their sentences shortened and have later been set free. Some were freed by district attorneys because the incriminating facts were not considered "sufficient for an indictment" according to paragraph 90 of the Austrian criminal law. Others can no longer be indicted because their crimes fall under the statute of limitations.* Certain SS men were let off with light sen-

---

* See Appendix: Statute of Limitations.

tences after the war before the full weight of their crimes became known, because incriminating documents and witnesses were found only much later. They are safe: a man cannot be punished twice for the same crime.

"The slow and hesitant prosecution of Nazi crimes in Austria cannot be compared with the energetic way it is done in Western Germany," Wiesenthal said recently. "In Germany, my efforts are appreciated. In Austria, they are unhappily tolerated, and that's why I am going to stay here. When I submitted a memorandum about Austrian Nazi activities to Chancellor Klaus in 1966, he later admitted to me that he'd had 'a sleepless night.' These gentlemen are always lathering their faces. When will they start shaving?"

Chapter 12

BEYOND REASON

1

[Shortly after the war, I was notified in Linz that thousands of Jewish prayer books had been found in the cellar of a sixteenth-century castle in the Austrian province of Styria. A committee of five of us went to Styria to investigate. The castle was situated in a secluded, wooded region—a forbidding structure, gray, somber, dilapidated. An old caretaker took us into the damp cellar and switched on a dim electric bulb. After our eyes became used to the pale light, we saw huge heaps of black books—Bibles, prayer books, Talmuds. Thousands and thousands of them, like piles of black coals and bricks of coke. The prayer books had been brought here from Jewish homes and houses of worship all over Europe. The masters of the Third Reich had planned to distribute these books later among libraries, universities, scientific institutes. They were to become historical curiosities—relics of a race that no longer existed. Some day, it was thought, they might be as valuable as Assyrian papyrus rolls or Cretan figurines.

For a long time we stood there, unable to say a word. Each of us thought of the countless tragedies symbolized in this damp cellar —of the devout men and women from whom the prayer books had been taken.

The youngest member of our commission was a young Jew from

Carpathorussia who had told me that he had lost his entire family. He walked past the heaps of books, picking up one and than another, touching it with his lips, putting it gently back on the heap. Suddenly I heard a gasping sound. I turned around. The young man had a prayer book in his hand. He stood looking at the first page, his face white. He swayed, and collapsed on the floor.

We ran to him. One of us had a little brandy. He opened his eyes and took a sip. His hands were shaking. I picked up the prayer book and opened it. On the first page, I saw what I thought was a woman's handwriting. She must have written in great excitement:

> They've just come into our town. In a few minutes they will be in our house. If someone finds this prayer book, please notify my dear brother. . . .

There was some white space left. Underneath followed what seemed to be a last-minute postscript, written in haste, almost illegible.

> Do not forget us! And do not forget our murderers! They. . . .

The writing trailed off. I closed the book and looked at the young man. He was still pale, but he was quiet now. "If you don't mind, I would like to keep the book," he said. "It belonged to my sister. She died at Treblinka."]

2

The letter had been dictated in a hospital room in Frankfurt am Main. The nurse who had typed it explained that her patient, Frau Keller (as I shall call her) was coming along nicely, but she could not yet write herself. Frau Keller had tried to commit suicide by slashing her wrists, and she had almost succeeded.

Frau Keller was eager to get in touch with Herr Wiesenthal after reading his name in the papers. She'd asked the nurse, who had never heard of Herr Wiesenthal. But the nurse assured her patient that "all Jews know each other." She'd mailed the letter to a friend in Israel asking him to forward the letter to Herr Wiesenthal, whom he certainly knew. Actually, the man didn't know me, but the letter reached me anyway.

Frau Keller implored me to come and see her in Frankfurt if I ever happened to be there. There was a great sense of urgency in her request, though the letter did not say what it was all about. Enclosed was a picture that had been cut from an illustrated German magazine. It showed a man standing on the brink of a mass grave, about to be executed. Behind him stood a German soldier about to fire his gun.

I met Frau Keller in the quiet garden of her suburban home one afternoon in October 1961. Indian summer was in the air. From somewhere came the laughter of children. It was peaceful and pleasant except for the white bandages on Frau Keller's wrists and her unnaturally white face. She was about forty-five, with dark-blond hair, attractive in a homely way. In her eyes there was still the aftereffect of shock. She spoke an unfamiliar German dialect; later she told me that she'd come from East Germany in 1948.

"Thank you for coming," she said. "I *have* to talk to someone who understands my problem. The people here listen but they don't want to understand. On the contrary——"

For a while we both sat in silence. People often need time before they are able to talk. It is so hard to tell some things to a stranger. The picture from the illustrated magazine was lying on the small table between us.

Frau Keller had come to Frankfurt in 1948. She soon found work, and a few weeks later she'd met Keller. He seemed a quiet, nice, decent man. He had a good job in a factory. He was well liked there. "He didn't drink and didn't run around with women," Frau Keller said. "When he asked me to marry him, I accepted at once. It wasn't the great passion for both of us. But we were both lonely and not very young, and with some patience and understanding we thought we could make it work. I knew nothing about him, but you know how it was in these early years after the war. One didn't ask many questions. We were married in 1952, and bought this house. We put down the first installment, and paid off so much every year. He did a lot of things in the house; he could fix everything. We both loved the garden. We didn't see many people. My husband didn't like to meet new people, and that was all right with me. There was one thing I noticed: he never talked about the war. When I asked him, he said he'd been in it, like everybody else, and he gave a tired shrug, as though he didn't want to remember."

One morning in January 1961—over a half a year after the capture of Eichmann, just after a local newspaper had published a report about the "annihilation campaign" in the East—her husband had said goodbye to her, as usual. Taking his lunchbox containing a sandwich, an apple, and a newspaper, he had gone to work. He had not come home that evening.

Frau Keller didn't sleep all night. In the morning she called the factory. They said they had planned to call her. Was her husband sick? He had not reported for work yesterday morning. They checked with the hospitals and notified the police. It was assumed that Keller had become the victim of an accident. But the search of the hospitals remained negative. The police asked Frau Keller whether her husband had any enemies. She told them that they had known very few people. At the factory there was no explanation for his departure. Keller, his co-workers said, had been withdrawn—a "loner"—but he'd always been like that. His name was listed in the police file of missing persons, and that was the end so far as the authorities were concerned.

The neighbors, of course, kept talking. The consensus was that Keller had gone off with another woman. Frau Keller didn't believe it. Her instincts told her that her husband was not involved with somebody else; she would have sensed it. But where could he be? She began to search for a clue, went over the talks they'd had lately, tried to find whether he'd said something that had a meaning she hadn't grasped. But she always ran up against a blank wall. There had been no hidden letters, no one had come to see him, he wasn't nervous, he had slept well, had said little.

She checked with the missing persons bureau, but they had heard nothing. A police officer told her, not very tactfully, that "lots of men run away from their wives every week, and there's nothing we can do about it." After that Frau Keller didn't go back to the police, and she avoided talking to the neighbors. She didn't like to be pitied or ridiculed. She knew exactly what they were thinking. Besides, there was no time for gossip. She had to take a job again to pay her husband's debts. The factory refused to give her anything, and she couldn't expect any government pension so long as she had no proof that her husband was dead. During those months Frau Keller learned that life in the welfare state can be quite brutal.

Months went by, and she'd come to think of her husband as dead.

She was tired from her work, and she knew she wouldn't be able to keep the house and the garden; it was too expensive. On April 17, 1961—a day she will never forget—she went to the hairdresser in her suburb. While she sat under the dryer, she looked idly at an illustrated magazine.

Mechanically she turned the pages. She saw an illustrated article about executions of Jews in Winniza, the Ukraine. A picture showed a mass grave with many dead bodies and some, according to the caption, still alive. Below was a picture showing an execution. The victim stood at the rim of the grave. Behind him stood a German soldier photographed the moment he shot the man. He was a heavy-set man with glasses, in a field-gray uniform. Half a dozen other soldiers looked on grinning.

Frau Keller stared at the face of the soldier who was about to shoot. Her shock was almost like the impact of a bullet. No, there could be no doubt.

"Yes, Herr Wiesenthal. It was—the man I later married."

She'd uttered a cry, and the magazine had slid down from her knees. People came running. They thought she'd fainted under the dryer. She didn't tell them anything; how could she explain to them what she'd just seen?

"The magazine was several months old," Frau Keller said to me. "It came from a lending library. If I hadn't been at the hairdresser's that week, I wouldn't have seen it all. It is no coincidence, Herr Wiesenthal, that I saw the picture that day. Only—I can't explain it. It is beyond reason."

I agreed. "Are you absolutely sure that you're not making a mistake?"

"Absolutely, I've looked at the picture so many times through a strong magnifying glass. He was twenty years younger then, but he hasn't really changed. I recognized not only his face but I know the way he holds his head and extends his arms." She shook her head determinedly. "No—it was he."

She clasped her hands. "When I got home, I collapsed. I wished I could die. How could I go on knowing that I had spent nine years with a murderer? I looked at his face again through the magnifying glass. His face shows no emotion while he shoots. Perhaps he shot hundreds or thousands of men in cold blood. I know today that he didn't *have* to shoot them. He was young in 1941, too young to be forced. Perhaps he volunteered. I turned the page and looked at the mass grave, and I thought maybe he shot all the other people too. And then I remembered his hands that had touched me and taken me. It was as though I had helped him to do these terrible things."

She was staring into space. "I come from a devout Christian family. All my life I've tried not to harm any human being, even an animal. And now I feel that everything was in vain. There is no sense in anything I've done. I've lost hope. Until I read the reports about the Eichmann trial, I had not really known much about these things. Now I know. And my husband was one of them."

She had telephoned a plain-clothes officer at the local police, whom she'd known for years, and asked him to come to her home. She'd shown him the picture and said she wanted to notify the police.

The officer had looked at her coldly. "Do you want to tell me that you're going to denounce your own husband?"

She was speechless. She hadn't expected such an answer. She tried to explain what she felt. Certainly he was her husband, but he was a murderer. She'd fought hard and long with her conscience. She could not keep this terrible secret to herself.

"Frau Keller, you must be crazy," the police officer had said.

"But don't you understand?" She'd been desperate. "There was that report about atrocities in the newspaper that day he disappeared. There must have been something in the paper that frightened him. He knew they'd caught Eichmann. He wanted to disappear without telling me a word. Because he must have done terrible things."

"I still think you're crazy, Frau Keller. Do you want to see your husband in prison? Don't you understand that if you keep your mouth shut for a while, the whole thing will be over, forever? Before long, these things will come under the statute of limitations. Then no one can touch him."

Now, as I sat there, Frau Keller was still staring into space.

"Herr Wiesenthal," she said, without looking at me, "the police officer was only concerned about my husband. The thought crossed my mind that he too may have been a Nazi. Perhaps he still is a

Nazi. These people all help each other. He got up and said, 'You know, I really ought to notify the office of this case,' but the way he said it and looked at me I knew he would never tell them a word. He went out without saying goodbye. He considered me a traitor. I cannot tell you how miserable I was. Almost automatically, I stepped into the bathroom and—well, you know what I did."

She had survived only because the mailman happened to come along a few minutes later. He had heard a faint noise from the bathroom and found her lying there. He had called the ambulance that got her to the hospital.

"Frau Keller, this is not coincidence either."

"Yes, I know. I will have to live with it. But it is hard to be so utterly alone. I rechecked with the police, and they discovered that all his personal papers were made out in a false name. We don't even know his real name."

Suddenly she took my hand. "Tell me—have I done the wrong thing? Should I have kept quiet, as the police officer said?"

"You've done the right thing, Frau Keller. Much later you will know that there was nothing else you could have done."

For the first time there was some light in her eyes, and I said, "Did you try to find out his real name?"

She shook her head. "I hoped the police would help me. But they were not helpful at all. They asked *me* who I was, as if *I* had done something! They acted as though I had made up the whole thing. . . . So you see, I had to talk to someone who would believe me."

"I believe you."

There was little I could do. I notified the prosecutor of the case and gave him the name of the police officer who had advised Frau Keller to keep quiet. But it is impossible to find an unknown member of a military unit that took part in the execution of Jews in Winniza in the Ukraine late in 1941. There were several SS and *Wehrmacht* units involved. We don't know the names of the men who volunteered as executioners. We don't even know the real name of Frau Keller's missing husband. He remains one of the murderers among us.

Chapter 13

BUSINESS FIRST

One night in December 1946 I was waiting impatiently for a special courier from Bratislava. I'd already begun to collect material against Adolf Eichmann and the members of his staff, and in Bratislava, the capital of Slovakia, Dieter Wisliceny, one of Eichmann's closest collaborators, had recently been sentenced to death. In the death cell, Wisliceny had made up a list of Eichmann's staff members and had set down various other details concerning his former boss. Wisliceny claimed to know where Eichmann was then hiding. At last the courier came with a list of names. One of Eichmann's top aides had been stationed in every major city in all German-occupied countries. I put down the names of Eichmann's men next to the name of each city on a map of Europe. There were Rolf and Hans Guenther in Prague; Dannecker in Paris; Alois Brunner in Athens; Seidl and Burger in Theresienstadt; Hunsche in Budapest; Anton Brunner in Vienna; Erich Rajakowitsch in The Hague; and Wisliceny in Bratislava.

I drew fine lines between the cities with the names of these men. The body of a giant spider emerged. Eichmann was the spider's head. The spider's web had been destroyed, but many of the men who had formed its legs had escaped and were still at large.

Eichmann's deputy Rolf Guenther was probably dead; his brother, Hans Guenther, had disappeared. Seidl, Dannecker, and Anton Brunner were dead. Alois Brunner lived in Damascus. Anton Burger was hiding somewhere in Germany. One name on the list meant nothing to me: Dr. Erich Rajakowitsch. I paid no attention to him. There were more important criminals to be caught. The name Rajakowitsch kept showing up in various documents that I read in the months that followed. His exact duties in Eichmann's organization were not clear. He'd originally been a lawyer in Vienna, representing wealthy Jewish clients who, conveniently for him, did not return. That was all I knew about him at first. I found out that he had joined the SS, worked in some capacity for Eichmann, served in the East, and disappeared. Some people said he was probably dead. Others told me that Rajakowitsch was a smart fellow who was perhaps hiding out under an assumed name in a safe place—an Allied internment camp. Certain people said quickly that they had never heard of him. Had I been more experienced in those early days, I would have known that these people knew exactly where Rajakowitsch lived.

Patiently I collected more data. Erich Rajakowitsch had been born in 1905 in Trieste (at that time part of the Habsburg monarchy), the son of a *Gymnasium* professor. At the age of eighteen he came to Graz, breeding ground of so many Nazis, and studied law there. In 1934 he had married Anna Maria Rintelen, the daughter of Dr. Anton Rintelen, Austria's ambassador to Rome during the Dollfuss regime and one of the most notorious illegal Nazis in Austria. Later Rajakowitsch moved to greener pastures in Vienna, opened his legal practice, after Hitler's invasion joined the Party, was given membership card No. 6,330,373—not exactly a low number, but Herr Doktor Rajakowitsch soon made up in zeal what he lacked in priority. In Rajakowitsch's personal file there is an entry from the year 1939:

> SS-Candidate Rajakowitsch at this time acts as legal adviser to the Central Agency for Jewish Emigration in Vienna, and also in Prague and Berlin. In this function he meets all demands and does his work purposefully, quickly and efficiently. During a four-week action in Poland he proved himself versatile in all situations. Personally he shows a clear conception of life, has an

energetic appearance and proves incontestable national-socialist behavior. His character recommends him well for promotion to SS-Führer.

(signed) *Eichmann*
SS-Hptstuf.

The Vienna Agency for Jewish Emigration under Eichmann became the model for similar agencies all over Europe. It was located in the Rothschild Palais on Prinz Eugen Strasse. Eichmann and Rajakowitsch often met in the rooms where, on Sunday, March 13, 1938, Baron Louis von Rothschild, official head of the House of Rothschild, had been arrested by six steel-helmeted men who were told to wait until the Herr Baron had finished his leisurely lunch. They waited; Nazi protocol had not foreseen such an eventuality. The Baron was marched off to a cell in Vienna's police prison, and later interned at the Gestapo Hotel "Monopol." The Nazis asked $20 million for him, the highest ransom in history. They took less.

In October 1939 Rajakowitsch volunteered for the SS and was sent to Nisko, Poland, where, on Eichmann's initiative, the first concentration camp was set up. Reinhard Heydrich supported the plan to concentrate the Jews before they were sent to extermination camps. According to the bill of indictment,

> The Jews were told that the Führer had promised them new homes. There were no houses in Nisko but the Jews were permitted to build some. The wells in the area were said to be contaminated, but if they would bore for water they might find some. About one fourth of the Jews who arrived with the first transport were ordered to proceed by foot toward the east. Those who attempted to return would be shot.

By 1940 Rajakowitsch was a big wheel in Eichmann's organization. He was one of the instigators of the so-called Madagascar Plan, a blueprint for the deportation of all Jews from Europe to the island of Madagascar, which the Germans expected to get from the French after conclusion of a peace treaty with defeated France. The Madagascar Plan contains for the first time the ominous phrase *the final solution of the Jewish problem.*

For a while Eichmann was quite interested in the project. Rajakowitsch became the official "Madagascar expert" of Referat IV

B 4. Once he accompanied Eichmann on a trip to the Tropical Institute in Hamburg, where they studied the climate and living conditions of the island. The project was later dropped when it appeared that no peace treaty would be concluded with the French.

In April 1941 Dr. Rajakowitsch was made SS *Obersturmführer* and was sent by Reinhard Heydrich to Holland to set up yet another Agency for Jewish Emigration, "that should become the model for the solution of the Jewish problem in all European states." The solution, according to the prosecutor's bill of indictment, "was nothing but the badly camouflaged economic plunder of the Jews in Holland." A so-called *Vermögensverwaltungs und Rentenanstalt* (Administration of Property and Pensions) was founded, and the *Herr Doktor* became one of its trustees. After the expulsion of all Jews from Holland, Rajakowitsch volunteered for the *Waffen* SS in 1943, went through a course "for Germanic officers" in Bad Tölz, Bavaria, and was sent to the Eastern Front.

During the Eichmann trial in Jerusalem, the name of Rajakowitsch was heard again. Speaking of his activities in the Netherlands, Eichmann had said, "When I talked to Rajakowitsch five years ago, in 1955 . . . he confirmed to me some details of the operation. . . ."

Thus Rajakowitsch had been alive in 1955. He had been, perhaps still was, in Argentina; he'd been close to Eichmann. As the trial developed, Rajakowitsch's part in the Eichmann organization became clear. From the documents about the extermination of the Jews in Holland it was evident that Rajakowitsch belonged on the top of my list. The text of the bill of indictment that was ultimately issued against Rajakowitsch in Vienna in July 1964 explains why:

On October 1, 1941, there had been 140,000 Jews registered in occupied Holland. A few hundred later committed suicide; others died in concentration camps in Holland. Approximately 110,000 were deported after July 1942 to Poland, where they were killed. After the liberation only 5000 Jews returned to the Netherlands.

In 1941 SS *Standartenführer* Dr. Wilhelm Harster was named *Subkommissar* for the Jewish problem. His office at The Hague ordered the deportations that began abruptly in July

1942. Between the head office of Referat IV B 4 in Berlin and the branch office in The Hague there was much personal contact. Eichmann himself came to Holland to discuss all important questions. On August 28, 1941, Harster issued a secret decree in which he created the *Sonder-Referat Juden* (SRJ), which means "Special Department Jews." Its aim was "the final solution of the Jewish problem."

On August 12, 1942, Rajakowitsch, at that time in charge of Referat IV B 4 at The Hague, Holland, sent a teletype message to the commander of the SD in Paris, asking that the Dutch Jews interned in France be "evacuated" at once. Thereupon the commander ordered the deportation of eighty-three Jewish men, women, and children of Dutch nationality, in six transports, from Camp Drancy near Paris to Auschwitz. There they were handed over to officials of the concentration camp in accordance with "the final solution of the Jewish problem."

Among the eighty-three Jews there were seven children, from three to ten years old, without parents. The youngest of them was three-year-old Ruth Layner. The International Committee of the Red Cross in Geneva has informed us that of the eighty-three Jews only one survived "the hell of Auschwitz": Arthur Salomons from Amsterdam who was liberated by the Allied troops in Buchenwald where he had been brought from Auschwitz.

Dr. Rajakowitsch was an accomplice to murder according to Paragraphs 5, 134, 135, and 136 of the Austrian Criminal Code. He should be punished according to Paragraph 136.

Punishment under Paragraph 136 is life imprisonment.

On October 1, 1961, a few months after the Eichmann trial, I once more took up my work at the Documentation Center in Vienna. My first case was that of Dr. Erich Rajakowitsch. I submitted to the public prosecutor in Vienna all the facts that had become known about him during the Eichmann trial and all the documents concerning his activities in the Netherlands. The prosecutor studied the material and considered it important enough for a preliminary inquiry. A new warrant was issued for Dr. Erich Rajakowitsch, "address unknown."

Where could he be? Almost automatically I thought of South America. Eichmann had been there; others were still there. There was also a possibility that Rajakowitsch had been abroad but had later returned to Spain, Italy, Germany, or Austria.

I began by making cautious inquiries among Rajakowitsch's former professional acquaintances—lawyers, judges, court officials. Like other prominent lawyers in Vienna, he had administered the assets of former Jewish clients who had not returned. Some lawyers later tried to trace the heirs of such clients. Some didn't. It appeared that Rajakowitsch had made no such efforts.

During the winter of 1961, as more information reached my office, I was able to trace the postwar career of this formidable lawyer. After the capitulation he'd briefly been in an American prisoner-of-war camp, and then had escaped. For a while he was hidden in Styria by his former wife (they had been divorced in 1944), who later married the former NS *Gauhauptmann* of Styria, Professor Arnim Dadieu, now the man in charge of the German Institute for Rocket Research in Stuttgart (*Forschungsinstitut für Physik der Strahlantriebe*).

The British had looked for Rajakowitsch but didn't find him, though he lived in the very heart of the British zone—in Graz, the capital of Styria. In 1947 he had moved to Trieste, his native town, investing large funds in the firm of Enneri & Co. ("Import, Export, Representations, Commissions"), cable address: RAJARICO.

In 1951 and the following year, Rajakowitsch went to South America. He visited several countries and thought of settling there, but returned to Europe. In Austria, I discovered, a warrant had been issued for him in 1952, in connection with his "Aryanization" activities, but Rajakowitsch had come there several times in the 1950s, unworried about a possible arrest. He was right: the case was dropped by a court in Graz "for lack of evidence." Legally, he was a free man again. On August 22, 1953, he changed his name from Rajakowitsch to Raja. He gained control of Enneri & Co. and transferred its headquarters from Trieste to Viale Bianca Maria 31 in Milan, the commercial and banking capital of Italy. The Trieste office became a branch of the firm. Raja took an elegant apartment in Corso Concordia 8, Milan. He kept his Austrian citizenship. (At the time the earlier warrant had still been out for Rajakowitsch, the Austrian Consulate General in Trieste had issued him a valid passport in the name of Raja. The shortened name may have turned the trick.)

Enneri & Co. was a very interesting enterprise. Founded after the war by Conrado Enneri from Istria and Emil Felix from Austria, the firm specialized in trade with the Iron Curtain countries. It had dealings with a Raoul Janiti from Trieste, who had been investigated by the Italians for smuggling strategic goods to the Communist part of the world. One of the secretaries of the firm was Signora Giuliana Tendella, who became Raja's second wife in 1957. Enneri & Co. soon developed excellent business relations with the Soviet Union, Poland, Czechoslovakia, Hungary, and East Germany. Dr. Raja made several trips to Moscow, Prague, Warsaw, Posen, and East Berlin, where he and his Ohsorbermfahror was hospitably received by the Communist bureaucracy.

Raja seemed to have made a tidy fortune trading with the former enemies of Hitler's Germany; the partners in these deals had no political scruples. Raja was especially popular with former SS *Kameraden* in East Germany who had since become faithful members of the Communist Party. He became general representative of the Socialist republics' iron, graphite, and lignite interests. Enneri & Co. imported iron, graphite, and lignite as well as wood and glassware into Italy, exported ship's engines to East Germany and medical supplies to Hungary. Business first.

Raja was on good terms with the managers of several Italian steel plants and became interested in processes for manufacturing seamless oil pipe which the Soviets needed badly for their pipelines. Italian newspapers later reported that the Italian intelligence services began to observe Raja's activities, since there might be a possible connection between several cases of industrial espionage in Italy and the export of forbidden strategic goods. Fishing in troubled waters paid off handsomely. At the time of his arrest, Raja was reported to be a dollar millionaire. He owned a beautiful mansion, Villa Anita, in Melida, near Lugano, Switzerland.

I wrote to Dr. Louis de Jong, director of the Dutch State Institute of War Documentation in Amsterdam, that I knew the present address of Rajakowitsch and asked for material about the doctor's activities in the Netherlands. Dr. de Jong assigned one of his top aides, historian B. A. Sijes, to put together a file on Rajakowitsch's part in the "final solution of the Jewish problem" in Holland. In March 1962 I gave the prosecutor in Vienna a complete dossier on Rajakowitsch.

Incidentally, much of the information about Rajakowitsch (except that on his activities in Holland) came from a bank in Vienna. It wasn't difficult: I presented myself as a businessman interested in the credit rating of the firm of Enneri & Company. The bank did a fine job. They even supplied me the license-plate number of Rajakowitsch's car, the number of people working at his office and in his home, the names of firms he did business with, and other details. Banks can be useful institutions.

I found evidence that Rajakowitsch had often come to Vienna, until the second warrant had been issued there in 1961. After that he stayed away. In March 1962 I went to Milan to discuss the case with the Italian authorities. When I gave my information on Rajakowitsch to a Colonel Marnaro at the Palazzo de Giustizia, he shook his head in astonishment.

"How did you find out all these things? How many agents have you working for you in Italy?"

"Colonel," I said with mock surprise, "you wouldn't want me to reveal professional secrets, would you?"

I met the General of the Carabinieri in Milan, who asked, "So you are the man who had his fingers in the Eichmann affair?"

I nodded.

"Signor Wiesenthal," he said very quietly, "where is your ship? Or your private plane?"

I had to assure him that I wasn't going to kidnap Rajakowitsch.

The Italians sympathized with my work, but said they couldn't arrest Rajakowitsch. He was not an Italian citizen; he had not harmed any Italian citizen; his activities had taken place elsewhere. A delegation from various Jewish organizations went to intervene with the Minister of Justice in Rome. The Minister studied the case and said he might issue a warrant for sixty days against Raja-Rajakowitsch, *if* the Austrian Ambassador would officially request it. This meant that the Austrian Ambassador would have to get instructions from the Foreign Ministry in Vienna, which in turn would have to be asked to intervene by the Ministry of Justice.

Entering the dark labyrinths of Austria's bureaucracy, I walked into the Ministry of Justice in Vienna, trying to find out who was in charge of the case (which was not easy) and whether they would ask the Italian Ministry of Justice, through proper diplomatic channels, to extradite Dr. Erich Raja.

It seemed a direct question, but all I got were oblique answers. I was told that the investigation was "still pending." Definite conclusions "had not yet been reached." Instead of unbureaucratic action, there was bureaucratic evasion. The mills of Austrian justice, never fast, seemed to be grinding especially slowly in this case. The Attorney General told me he was very busy right now. Besides, he was leaving almost immediately on his Easter vacation.

"*Herr Generalanwalt,*" I said, "*I wish you a Happy Easter. For Herr Doktor* Raja I am going to *make* a Happy Easter."

There was only one way out of this legal impasse: to bring the case before the largest possible forum. I called Dino Frescobaldi, the Vienna correspondent of Milan's *Corriere della Sera*, on the afternoon of April 8, 1963, and gave him the story.

Two hours later, the editor of the *Corriere* in Milan sent a reporter to the home of *Dottore* Raja. The reporter was received by Rajakowitsch's son, who asked what it was all about. The reporter said they were going to print a big story about *Dottore* Raja and asked for a statement. He was asked to wait a moment, please. The son went to see his father and came back.

"My father will be at your office tomorrow morning," he said. The reporter went back to his office. The editor of the *Corriere* later admitted that he'd made a mistake in alerting Raja. By midnight the Raja story had been taken over by the wire services and was all over Italy. The next morning Dr. Raja was seen at his bank soon after it opened. I later heard rumors that he'd withdrawn about a hundred million lire in cash—$150,000. He stepped into his red Fiat 2000 coupé, drove away—and disappeared.

By that time Dr. Raja had become a front-page story all over Europe. Many papers printed his picture—a dark-blond man with a bland, longish face, a high forehead and bright eyes, who seemed to look at the reader with a somewhat ironic expression. A *Corriere* reporter telephoned me that Raja had crossed the Italian-Swiss border at Chiasso. I put a call through to the United Press in Zurich and asked them to notify the Swiss police of Raja's arrival in Switzerland. The Swiss looked for him at his villa in Melida, but didn't find him there. The next morning, the police at Lugano were notified by the chambermaid in a local hotel that she'd seen the *Corriere della Sera* with the picture of Dr. Raja, and that she was sure he was staying at the hotel.

The Swiss police informed Raja that he was considered an "undesirable alien." He was asked to leave the country *immediately*. Raja drove back to Chiasso, but the Italian border guards kept the barrier down as the red Fiat drove up and told the *dottore* that he was most unwelcome. During the following days, three of Switzerland's neighbors refused to let Raja in: Italy, France, Germany. And the fourth neighbor, Austria, was waiting for him with a warrant. It was not a very pleasant prospect for the wealthy lawyer.

For a while people in various places reported to me that they had seen the elusive Dr. Raja, but when we checked on his whereabouts, he was gone again. It was, as one Italian paper put it, a modern version of the Rossini aria "Figaro here, Figaro there." In Lugano, Raja told the Swiss police that he was going to Vienna "to sue Wiesenthal."

At last he went to see his lawyer in Zurich. They telephoned Raja's Viennese lawyer, a Dr. Dostal, who advised Raja to come to Austria and face the music. Over the United Press wire from Zurich to Vienna came word that Raja was going to take the next plane at Kloten Airport for Vienna.

Reporters, TV crews, radio people, and officials rushed out to Schwechat Airport. The Raja story had become a European sensation. Bets were laid whether he would come to Vienna and give himself up or try to escape, possibly to South America. I joined the "reception committee" at Vienna's airport as the Swissair Caravelle set down. The plane landed. Dr. Erich Raja was not among the passengers. Frantic telephone calls were made. Raja had boarded the Caravelle in Zurich, but in Munich, during a short stopover, he had disappeared.

I went back to my office, where I received an urgent phone call from a top official of the Munich police.

"We need your help, Herr Wiesenthal. Where is Raja? The whole force has been ordered into action. The Minister of the Interior is furious. We've got to get Raja—or the press will get us."

I told them to guard the border crossings between Bavaria and Austria, and while I was at it, suggested that they take a close look at the record of Raja's former boss in Holland, ex-SS *Brigadeführer* Dr. Wilhelm Harster.

"I'm afraid this is going to make your Minister even more furious. Harster is now an *Oberregierungsrat* at the Bavarian Ministry of the Interior in Munich."

I gave the Harster story to the Vienna correspondent of the *Deutsche Presse Agentur*. Twenty-four hours after the German papers printed it, ex-SS *Brigadeführer* Harster was suspended from duty. He was arrested in January 1966. The Harster case created a political scandal in Munich. On June 25, 1943, Dr. Wilhelm Harster, Major General of the German police, head of the German Security Police and SD in Holland, had reported to Hitler's *Reichskommissar* Seyss-Inquart: "Of the 140,000 Jews who were reported in the Netherlands, the 100,000th Jew has been removed from the nation. . . . On Sunday, June 20, during a special action in Amsterdam, 5500 Jews were seized within twenty-four hours."

After Harster was arrested, it became apparent that members of all leading political parties in Bavaria (CSU, SPD, FDP, and the Bavaria Party) were among his superiors at the Ministry of the Interior, where he'd held an important position since 1956. Harster had publicly declared that his superiors were "well informed about my record." At least five important officials at the Ministry had suggested that the former SS *Führer* be given a top position at the Ministry, whereupon the Minister signed the appointment. The Minister later admitted: "I suppose somebody tried to 'manage' something without really informing me." Some of the implicated officials pretend they can no longer remember what happened. The trial against Raja's former boss is now in preparation.

While the Bavarian police were nervously looking for Raja, I went to see the Attorney General at the Austrian Ministry of Justice. He had just returned from his Easter vacation. I asked him whether they were going to arrest Raja if he came to Austria.

The Attorney General was evasive. Much depended on whether the material against Raja was deemed "sufficient." There was a warrant out for him, but for the time being "only a preliminary inquiry" was planned. One would have to await its results.

"*Herr Hofrat,*" I said, "this happens to be Passover. Here is my prayer book. I was on my way to the synagogue to say the prayer for the dead. With your permission, I would like to say the prayer right here in your office for the 110,000 dead Jews of Holland."

He was very annoyed. "What do you want me to do?"

"I want justice. You've seen the material against Raja. You know he ought to be arrested."

"And if he turns out to be innocent?"

"Right now the whole world is watching you, waiting for you to take action. I honestly believe it will be better for the prestige of Austria if Raja were arrested and perhaps later released than if he is permitted to run around freely and make a mockery of Austria's justice."

I bowed to the *Herr Hofrat* and left. The following day Raja arrived by car from Munich. He had not been stopped at the Austrian border, although he was on the "wanted" list and both the German and Austrian police were looking for him. He walked into Vienna's court building, where an examining judge was waiting for him. Raja was still a free man.

Later in the morning I talked again to the Attorney General. He told me that Dr. Raja was being interrogated.

"And . . . ?" I asked.

"I believe they're ready for him. Go take a look."

I walked through the corridor of the courthouse. Two detectives stood in front of the door that led into the office of the examining judge; they were going to arrest Raja the moment he came out of the office.

Late in the afternoon of April 23—a few hours after Raja's arrest in Vienna—a representative of the East German Trade Institute, *Interkammer,* was seen removing from *Interkammer's* showcases at the Milan Trade Fair several articles belonging to the firm of Enneri & Company. Also removed was a photograph that showed Raja with officials of *Interkammer* and high-ranking members of the Soviet trade mission in Rome. It was noticed that the Communist Party in Italy, which had previously called Raja "the murderer of Anne Frank" and "Eichmann's henchman," were conspicuously silent about his arrest. According to the non-Communist papers, the Italian authorities were investigating a possible collaboration between ex-SS-man Raja and the Communist Party of Italy. Some Italian papers wrote that Enneri & Company had paid commissions on its Eastern trade deals to the Party.

Nikolai Svetailov, a member of a Soviet trade mission in Rome, who had often negotiated with Raja, was recalled to Moscow. The papers reported that in Moscow Raja had been a close acquaintance of Valentin Khrabrov, a high-ranking official concerned with the coordination of scientific research. Some people remembered that Raja was on friendly terms with the second husband of his first wife, Professor Arnim Dadieu of the Stuttgart Rocket Research Institute.

The Roman newspaper *Il Tempo* wrote on August 1, 1963:

> Italy's Communists are deeply concerned about the investigation of the former Eichmann aide, Rajakowitsch. He had become a Soviet agent after the war and had close contacts with the leading officials of the Communist Party of Italy, especially with the Party's foreign-trade experts. They say they accepted him only after the comrades from the Soviet trade mission in Rome had guaranteed Raja, calling him "a good patriot and genuine friend of the German Democratic Republic, and of the Communist Party."

The trial of Rajakowitsch took place in Vienna in April 1965. It was noted in the courtroom that the defendant behaved with conspicuous arrogance (the "energetic appearance" his friend Eichmann had liked). He was cocksure, refused to answer questions, and several times visibly annoyed his defense lawyers. Once he told the jury that his monthly income was about ten times that of the average juror. On another occasion he ridiculed the prosecutor and offended the judge. The jury pronounced him guilty. The court sentenced him to two and a half years in prison.

In October 1965, Dr. Raja was quietly released. He now lives in Austria, and he is well advised to stay there. The Dutch still have a warrant out for him. If Raja should ever try to leave Austria, the Dutch will ask for his extradition and bring him before a court in the Netherlands. Raja seems satisfied to live the life of a retired prosperous lawyer and businessman. It was always "business first" with him, and business has paid off. His son Klaus now manages the firm of Enneri & Company.

[After the arrest of Dr. Erich Raja, I was invited to speak in Amsterdam at a meeting of former members of the Dutch Resistance. Raja had been notorious in Holland, and the case had caused considerable comment.

On the morning after my lecture, I had a telephone call from a Dutch woman. She said she was downstairs in the hotel lobby. Could she see me for a minute? I went down and met an elderly woman with gray hair and soft, blue-gray eyes. She had been at the meeting. As she listened to me, the past came back. After a sleepless night, she'd talked with her husband, and now she was here. She said they were "ordinary people." Her husband was foreman in a large factory. Four of her five children were alive, and all had good jobs and were doing well.

"We never had much, but we always like to help other people who have even less. When we read, back in 1920, that there was a movement in Holland to bring over hungry Austrian children for a few months, we registered at once. My husband said there was always enough to eat for the whole family; one more mouth wouldn't matter. A few weeks later I waited at the railroad station when the long train arrived, and the children got out. Each had his name written on a small card around his neck. They looked frightened and starved. 'Our' child was a thin little boy named Hansi. His face was pale and his eyes were very large. Hansi had never known what a real meal was. He was six years old and very shy, but he soon made friends with our children. And he learned to eat. The first day he only stared at all the milk, butter, eggs, meat and vegetables. He said he'd never seen so much food in his life."

Hansi gained weight quickly. When he left Amsterdam two months later, he looked like any normal boy of his age. He often came back during the following years. They treated him like their

sixth child. Hansi called them "my Dutch foster parents." He sent
them many letters. At Christmas, and on his birthday, they sent him
gifts. One day they received a wedding announcement, and then
there were no more messages. A year later, the war broke out. They
wondered what happened to Hansi. He was a healthy boy and must
have been drafted into the army.

One morning in April 1942, there was a knock at the door.

"I was alone at home and when I opened the door I saw a man in
a black SS uniform. I cried out. Only a few days earlier some of
these SS men had come into our quiet, nice, clean street and carried
away some neighbors—Jews. It was terrible, and the shock was still
in my bones."

She had asked the SS man: "What do you want?"

He'd laughed. "Auntie, don't you recognize me? It's me—Hansi."

Hansi! In the black uniform with that terrible sign on the collar.
Was he among the SS men who came to arrest their Jewish neighbors? All over Amsterdam they had rounded up people in recent
days.

"What's the matter, Auntie?" he said. He asked to come in.

She barred the door. Something snapped in her.

"I couldn't help it, Mr. Wiesenthal. I said, 'I'm no longer your
aunt. And you won't come into my house—not in that uniform. Get
out!' And I banged the door shut after him. . . . My heart was
beating fast. How often I'd hoped to see Hansi again. But it would
never have occurred to me he would return as an SS man. . . .

"I watched him through the window. He stood in front of our
house, and then he gave a shrug and spat, and he walked off in his
black boots. I can still hear the sound of those boots, which we in
Amsterdam had come to identify with murderers.

"A few weeks later I had a letter from him. Very short, and not at
all like the Hansi we had known. He said it was regrettable that we
Dutch didn't understand the new times, that the Führer had glorious ideas and . . . Oh, what's the use? My husband tore the letter
to pieces."

Hansi was never mentioned again, as though by mutual agreement, One day in 1946, a letter came from a woman whose handwriting they didn't know. She wrote that she was Hansi's widow. He

had been killed in action somewhere in Russia. She was alone with her two children. Things were very bad in Vienna, and there was so little to eat. The children were hungry.

"It was the old story all over again. I showed the letter to my husband. You can't remain impassive when small children are hungry. We decided we would send them food packages, but we couldn't have them in our home. Too much had happened. None of our Jewish neighbors had come back alive. And we know of others who died. . . . Here we had nourished these Austrian children, trying to make them strong and healthy. And then they had come back as SS men, doing all these terrible things."

She was quiet for a while and then she said: "There is something else I must tell you. One of my boys was in the Dutch Resistance. He didn't come back either."

She got up. "I would like to know. . . . That's why I came. You may have a list . . . of these people. I would like to know what Hansi has done."

She gave me her address and left. I too was wondering what Hansi had done. "We had nourished these children and then they came back as SS men. . . ."

A year later I found his name on a certain list which wasn't exactly a list of honor. I didn't write her.]

Chapter 14

THE OLD BARON
COULDN'T FORGET

Chronologically, my story of Baron Evert von Freytag-Loringhoven starts one day in the summer of 1963, on a train to Berlin. But its beginning really goes back to the morning in the early spring of 1943 when two members of the Polish underground smuggled a fifteen-year-old Jewish boy into my wooden shack at the Eastern Railroad Repair Works in Lwow, Poland.

I remember well how the boy called Olek looked when I first saw him. He seemed terribly frightened; his blue eyes were wide with fear. He had red hair and thin lips, and his skin was sallow. The Poles said that Olek had spent the past few weeks hiding in a dark cellar. This was the first day in more than a month he'd seen the sun. He was the sole survivor of the entire Jewish population of Chodorow, a town in Galicia that had been wiped out by the Nazis. Three thousand men, women, and children had been murdered; only Olek remained alive. A Christian neighbor had saved him and concealed Olek behind a heap of coal in his cellar.

Now the Gestapo was searching all the houses again. The neighbor had handed Olek over to the underground. They gave him false papers that identified him as a Christian, but they said there was nothing else they could do. I kept Olek in my shack a few days and spoke to the manager of a building firm working inside the Repair

217

Works. I explained that Olek was a Polish youngster who had lost his parents. The manager agreed to take him on as an apprentice so he would eat in the canteen and get a place to sleep. Before Olek left my shack I made it clear to him that he would have to be very careful if he wanted to stay alive.

"You must tell *no one* that you are a Jew," I said.

"Not even another Jew?" he asked.

"No. Not even another Jew. And don't make friends with the Jewish prisoners who work at the railroad yards. Promise?"

He promised.

Olek survived the war. I saw him again in 1946, in Linz; he'd come from Poland and was waiting to join one of the illegal transports to Palestine. Three years later, when I first visited Israel, I heard that Olek had joined the *kibbutz* of the former ghetto fighters of Warsaw, some thirty kilometers north of Haifa, and I went to see him.

We've been warm friends ever since. On my trips to Israel I always spend a few hours or a day at his *kibbutz*. He took back his old name, Jitzchak Sternberg, and was elected secretary of his *kibbutz*. He is married and has two healthy children. He no longer resembles the frightened boy who came to my hut in 1943.

In April 1964, he invited me to come to his *kibbutz* and tell the people there something about my work. After my talk, I was called to the telephone. A man named Heinz Jacob, who lived in a neighboring *kibbutz*, had just heard I was there, and wanted to talk to me. It was very important   could he come over at once?

Heinz Jacob told me he had been born in Germany and had emigrated to Palestine with his parents in 1933. He was blond, blue-eyed, very German-looking. He was deeply sunburned and had the strong hands and slow movements of a farmer. Late in 1963, he had gone to Germany, his first return to the country of his birth, to check on his family's restitution claim for property taken by the Nazis. On a train to Berlin he shared a compartment with a tall, distinguished-looking German of about seventy. They began to talk. The man asked Jacob where he was from. When Jacob said he was from Israel, the older man looked surprised—and pleased.

"You don't look like a Jew, Herr Jacob." The old German introduced himself as Baron Evert von Freytag-Loringhoven.

Jacob laughed. "Many of our young Israelis don't *look* Jewish, if that's what you mean. Most children in our *kibbutz* are blond and blue-eyed—like children from Scandinavia or Texas. But they *feel* Jewish. That's what matters."

The Baron nodded. He said he'd never met an Israeli before; he'd spent much of his life in the isolation of the countryside. He had grown up on a feudal estate belonging to his family in Latvia. That, of course, was before the Bolsheviks expropriated the big landholdings in 1919. The Baron had known many Jews in Riga. He said they had been the most cultured people in the city, had loved architecture, music, the arts.

In 1919 the Baron had escaped to Germany, where he later inherited two estates in East Prussia, at Grodno and Merakowo, which he managed until 1945. Then the Russians came after him once more.

They talked about how they had both run away, the German nobleman from the Russians, the German Jew from the Germans. The Baron told Jacob that his brother had been an officer in the Kaiser's army and later in the *Wehrmacht*.

"The rule in our family for centuries has been that the oldest son would take over the estates and the others had to serve in the army. My brother was an ardent National Socialist before Hitler came to power. Like many officers, he'd felt humiliation after the First World War. He thought the National Socialists would recreate a greater Germany—"

The Baron gave a resigned shrug. "My poor brother soon became disillusioned. When he saw what the SS did before and during the war, my brother became an active enemy of the regime. He joined the patriots against Hitler on the twentieth of July 1944. You've heard about the abortive *coup?*"

Heinz Jacob nodded. He wondered why the old aristocrat, obviously a reticent man, was telling all this to a casual stranger on a train.

"My brother procured the explosives for Count von Stauffenberg's bomb. You know what happened. My brother committed suicide. Perhaps it was better—they would have hanged him too in Ploetzensee Prison in Berlin. I was arrested by the Gestapo in Berlin and spent several months at the Alexanderplatz Prison, but I was released through the intervention of a friend, a high-ranking Nazi.

After the war, I had to hide once more when the Russians came looking for me. A Polish officer, who had been in the Stutthof concentration camp near Danzig, saved my life. It's all very strange, isn't it? In September 1945 I managed to get false papers and finally reached the small place in Hesse where my widowed sister lives. Now I manage a small farm. Not a big one, but farming is the only thing I know."

The Baron leaned over. "Herr Jacob, I do not believe in coincidences. Neither would you, if you had lived my life. It cannot be just a coincidence that you and I met in this compartment. I hardly leave my farm nowadays. You are the first Jew I've met in years. I know about the terrible things we Germans did to the Jews because I've seen them with my own eyes. saw them kill innocent women. . . . Until today, I've never talked to anyone about it, but I still see these things in my nightmares. I cannot forget my secret, and I don't want to take it with me to the grave."

He put his hands across his eyes. "I can see a Jewish woman who worked on my farm in Merakowo. A very cultured lady from Prague. And I remember the young woman from Budapest who was a doctor and had set up a makeshift hospital in the little school in Grodno. Not older than thirty. Very pretty. I said I would try to hide her and perhaps she would have a chance of escaping later on. She said thanks, but she wanted to stay with her patients. In the end she was killed with them. I like to think that at least some of them were saved, and if I had their addresses would so much want to help them."

The Baron looked at Jacob. "Give me your address. I cannot talk about it today. But I'll write to you."

Now we sat in the small garden, surrounded by the citrus groves of the *kibbutz*—Sternberg, Heinz Jacob, and I. Jacob gave me the letters from Baron Freytag-Loringhoven.

"It's all in there, the whole story. We write each other all the time. You see, when he started to talk about 'the terrible things,' as he called them, I thought automatically of you. I said to the Baron: 'This might be of some value to Simon Wiesenthal,' and I told him of your work. The Baron looked startled and said: 'Now I know this isn't a coincidence. One of the work camps where some of the worst things happen is called Wiesenthal, in a small village near Thorn. I beg you to get in touch with this man Wiesenthal and give him the material.'"

I did not sleep that night. It was very quiet outside. Through the open window of my small guest room came the scent of Israel, a mixture of orange blossoms and flowers that I would recognize any time with my eyes closed.

I was reading the letters from the old German aristocrat, containing what he called his "terrible secret." The worst part of it is that he might never have told it if he hadn't met and liked a young Jew. I often wonder how many other secrets remain untold.

One day in November 1944 a trainload of twenty-eight hundred Jewish women arrived in cattle cars at the railroad station of Merakowo, near Thorn in what is now Poland. The stationmaster, a man named Zacharek who is still in Merakowo, remembered the transport well and later told Baron Freytag-Loringhoven about it. The women were weak and emaciated; some were half-dead. Their journey had been long and awful. Most of them came from Hungary; others were from Poland, Czechoslovakia, Romania, Holland, Austria, and France. They had already been in various concentration camps in Latvia and Lithuania and had later been brought in small freighters across the Baltic Sea to Danzig, and from there to the Stutthof concentration camp. Next they were sent to Merakowo. From the railway station in Merakowo the women were brought to the large estate near Grodno, about a mile away, that then belonged to the Baron. He later testified to one of my co-workers:

From Grodno the women were taken to four work camps: Malven, near Strassberg; Grodno, near Thorn; Shirokopas, near Kulm; Wiesenthal, near Thorn. Leader of the transport was SS *Obersturmführer* Ehle. In Grodno the women were ordered to dig antitank trenches. They lived in tents which had been vacated by members of the *Hitlerjugend*, who were previously digging trenches in the region. Some women were sent to work on the surrounding farms. About 135 of them were sent to my estates and worked in the stables or harvesting the potatoes in the fields.

Most of the women had almost no clothes when they arrived.

Many covered themselves with two old military blankets; they wore one around their shoulders and draped the second around their hips like a skirt. They were so hungry that they ran out into the fields and ate the leaves of sugar beets. Women who were too weak to work were killed by SS men, who would beat them with bludgeons on the backs of their necks. SS *Kommandant* Ehle later told me that this was a very practical method. He said; "No postmortem examination will ever establish the cause of death."

The women were killed on a small peninsula in the Sea of Grodno. They were thrown by other women into a mass grave, and finally these women were also killed. Every day Ehle gave orders to kill from 8 to 20 women. On January 16 or 17, 1945 —shortly before the Russians arrived—they killed 118 women. At that time a boy was born to one of the women. I tried to save the child with the help of two Polish workers. It was impossible. Ehle found the mother and the child. I saw with my own eyes how he killed the mother and the child. . . .

And so the chronicle of horror went. One woman was ordered to kneel for two hours on the frozen river "until her knees were fastened to the ice."

The guards were Germans and Ukrainians; the Baron called them "the worst imaginable rabble on earth." When a woman happened to be a few minutes late for work, they would invent "all sorts of sadistic punishment." As always when there is horror, there was also heroism, such as that of the woman doctor who refused the Baron's offer of help.

Baron Freytag-Loringhoven hid two other women in his house, a seamstress from Budapest and a woman from Prague, the wife of a furrier. His Polish foreman concealed a nineteen-year-old Jewish girl from Lodz. Ten women worked in the stables, where they took care of the young cattle. The Baron ordered that they be given milk and potatoes, though he knew that this had been strictly forbidden by Ehle. One prisoner, the wife of a mill-owner near Prague, gave him a list containing 500 names of women prisoners. Later, when Freytag-Loringhoven lived under an assumed name in Poland, he was searched by a Russian soldier, who took the list away from him and tore it up. The Baron continued:

On January 18, 1945, the remaining women were driven away. According to rumor they were taken to Danzig where they were pushed into the sea. . . . There are many others things that I saw and am willing to confirm. *This is the truth.* I wish I could find out whether any of the women survived and I wish them all good on earth.

I put down the Baron's letters. I had come here to visit a young friend, to see the children and the groves of the *kibbutz.* Even here I couldn't get away from the past.

There were two questions. First, was Ehle alive and would we find him? Second, would Baron Freytag-Loringhoven stick to his story in court? Time and again I'd had experience with witnesses who refused to talk before a judge or a district attorney. Often the testimony of a single witness is not considered sufficient to bring a man to trial. But Baron Freytag-Loringhoven would be a very strong witness. He had no personal motive for testifying except to serve justice; he was not a Jew; he had not previously known personally the man he was accusing. It was not a case of one man's accusation against another man's defense. The old principle *in dubio pro reo* ("When in doubt, find for the defendant") could not be applied in this case. Ehle had been an SS *Obersturmführer* in a concentration camp. It was a matter of common knowledge that such men didn't spend their time writing poetry or playing chess. The old German aristocrat could not be accused of prejudice toward the accused. The crimes had been committed on his estate. He had been an eyewitness.

I put the letters into my brief case. If we could find Ehle, we might have a strong case.

After my return from Israel I asked Michael Lingens, one of my fellow workers in Vienna, to contact the Baron. Lingens' mother, a Christian, daughter-in-law of the police chief of Cologne, had been sent to Auschwitz because she had helped Jews. Lingens' mother is now president of the Auschwitz Committee.

Lingens talked with Baron Freytag-Loringhoven, and later Frau Lingens went to see the old man. He agreed at once to testify in court. He said it was his duty. He did not want to die with such a terrible burden on his conscience. We wrote to the Jewish Historical Institute in Warsaw and asked them for documents or names of witnesses, but there were none. A similar request sent to the Israeli police was equally unproductive. Even the Israeli experts on Nazi crimes had never heard of the mass murder of the fifteen hundred women in Grodno. He wrote a report and sent it to the German Central Agency of Justice in Ludwigsburg.

A Prosecutor Rückerl was assigned to the case. Since the women had come from KZ Stutthof, he began by looking up the names of the guards in Stutthof. On the list was the name of *Obersturmführer* Paul Ehle. Ehle now lived in Kiel, where he worked as a mechanic. No one there had the faintest idea of his past.

"What bothers me most about this case is that we knew nothing about it," reported Rückerl. "If you hadn't notified us, the Baron might have died with his secret." I told him that even in Poland and Israel the files on Nazi atrocities revealed nothing about it.

"I'll contact Baron Freytag-Loringhoven," said Rückerl. "What he writes in his letters to Jacob will be considered only 'information' by a court. To interrupt the statute of limitations we need the Baron's sworn testimony. I am going to see if I can find a photograph of Ehle. If the Baron can identify it, we'll really have a strong case."

Baron Freytag-Loringhoven testified a few weeks later, confirming everything he'd written in his letters. The file was sent to the District Attorney in Kiel and former SS *Obersturmführer* Paul Ehle was arrested. He didn't try to deny his crimes. He would have been tried and, I believe, convicted if he hadn't died in prison in September 1965.

In November 1965, twenty years after the crimes in East Prussia, Polish authorities announced that they had found on the small peninsula in the Sea of Grodno the mass grave Baron Freytag-Loringhoven had described.

Chapter 15

A BRIDE FOR
DR. BABOR

Nowadays people come to me with all sorts of problems connected with the Nazi regime. They consider me a kind of general practitioner able to cure all the ills tracing back to the dark years no one likes to remember. Often they have only a vague idea what my work is. They've read something in the paper, they remember my name, they hope I can help them, advise them, protect them; they know I won't report them to anyone. The case of Dr. Karl Babor is a typical example. I might never have heard about it if a Jewish mother in an Austrian town hadn't read something about Wiesenthal in the paper and told her daughter to come and see me.

The girl's problem had had its origins several months before she came to see me. I shall call her Ruth, though this is not her name. She still lives in Austria. Ruth was about twenty-five years old when I met her, one day late in 1963, young and pretty and vivacious— dark hair, dreamy eyes, and a figure of the sort that Austrians politely call *vollschlank* ("full-slim"). Ruth told me she was an incurable romantic who had the idea that life should be an exciting adventure. She later admitted frankly that the whole thing had started because she had wanted a little excitement, which was something she did not have in the small Austrian town in which she lived with her mother. Her office job bored her, and so did the young men whom she met at infrequent parties. Two years earlier she'd visited her brother, an engineer in Kenya. Her brother had taken her on safaris into the bush. She'd loved everything about it—the strange sounds of the jungle, the animals, the atmosphere and the mystery. When she came back after three months, life in her native town seemed unbearably dull and routine at the office drearier than ever. When she typed the twenty-fourth or twenty-fifth letter that began *Dear Sir: We beg to inform you* . . . she felt almost a physical revulsion toward her typewriter. Such was her state of mind when she read a classified ad in the "Marriages" column of the Vienna *Kurier*. It was a rainy Sunday afternoon and Ruth had nothing else to do. The ad read:

> Physician, 42, excellent position overseas, wishes to exchange letters with nice girl. Purpose: marriage. Write to Box No.———

"I knew right away that *overseas* meant Africa," Ruth told me. "I cannot explain it; it was more than a hunch; I sensed it. I told my mother I was going to answer the ad, and she laughed. Mama knew me. But she thought there was nothing wrong in writing a letter, 'as long as you don't expect an answer.' Mama is not an optimist. Anyway, I wrote the letter and mailed it on Monday morning on my way to the office, and I thought about it for a few days. But then there was no answer, just as Mama had predicted, and after a while I forgot all about it."

Three weeks later, there *was* a letter for her, from a Diplom-Ingenieur Babor in Vienna.

Ingenieur Babor wrote in a courtly, old-fashioned style. He said he had read her letter carefully and would like to have the privilege of meeting her. He wanted to tell her all about his son Karl, a well-known doctor in Addis Ababa, Ethiopia. Karl was doing very well. Among his patients were several members of Emperor Haile Selassie's family.

"I talked it over with Mother," Ruth said to me. "We decided there was no harm in talking to this polite old man. Not that I thought of him as my future father-in-law. It was still something of a joke. The girls in the office said, 'Watch out, Ruth, in a year you're going to have a husband and a big house in Addis Ababa, and dozens of servants and automobiles. You'll be asked to dine with the Emperor, you lucky girl!' And everybody would laugh. Because they knew that I was *not* lucky. I'd fallen in love before—always with the wrong men. Either they were in love with somebody else or, worse, they were already married. At the office they called me the *unlucky* girl."

The following week Herr Ingenieur Babor paid a call on her. He was an elderly gentleman of quiet charm, very much as his letter had indicated. He seemed very pleased when he saw Ruth, and paid her a compliment. He said he'd received a stack of letters "this high"—he held up his hand six inches above the table—but he'd liked her letter best. He added, with Viennese gallantry: "And I may say that I like *you* even better than your letter."

He and his wife lived quietly in Vienna, he told her. Their only son, Karl, had gone to Ethiopia with his wife, a former Baroness Babo—"very curious, the similarity of our names"—who had died there in an automobile accident in 1960. His son's only daughter, Dagmar, was now twenty years old and was studying in Paris. Dr. Karl Babor was a gynecologist, "the best in Addis Ababa," his father said, who worked at the Menelik Hospital (which the Soviets had donated to Ethiopia) and also had a modern private clinic, with X-ray equipment and a laboratory. Once in a while he was invited to the Emperor's palace.

"Since the death of his wife our son has been very much alone," said the old man. "He cannot leave his patients and come to Europe, and so I suggested placing that ad in the Vienna paper. I said perhaps he would find somebody." He smiled at Ruth. "And I wouldn't be surprised if he *had* found somebody."

"Herr Ingenieur," Ruth said quickly. "I must repeat to you what I wrote in my letter. I am Jewish. . . ."

"But my *dear* young lady, that makes not the slightest difference. We are Catholics. We have always been liberal in our feelings. In our house anti-Semitism was unknown, believe me." He looked at Ruth. "You will write him directly, won't you?"

That was the beginning of a long, intensive mail romance. Every Monday morning the postman would wave a long airmail envelope with beautiful stamps (the postman would say: "If you don't need the stamps—") sent by Dr. Karl Babor, Box 1761, Addis Ababa.

After a few weeks, Babor enclosed his photograph. Ruth saw the picture of a dark-blond, medium-sized man with sad eyes, rather slim and youthful. He wrote that he was very lonely. His daughter spent most of her time in Paris. The bush was nearby and he loved to hunt, but it wasn't much fun going there alone. After two months he sent "hand kisses" to his "dear Ruth." She wrote back "Dear Karl." She thought she knew him quite well. At the office they were no longer joking about her going to Africa.

Karl's father asked her to come to Vienna for a day, and took her to a theater and to an inn where they drank wine and talked about Karl. Ruth was surprised that Ingenieur Babor didn't introduce her to his wife.

"When I asked about her he was evasive," she told me. "I supposed his mother had never liked the idea of a marriage ad. Meanwhile, Karl and I kept writing each other. His letters were kind and affectionate."

About a year after his first letter Dr. Babor invited Ruth to come to Addis Ababa. He wrote he'd made arrangements for her ticket from Vienna to Addis Ababa and return—"in case you shouldn't like it here—which I hope will not happen." He said he had also asked his daughter Dagmar to meet Ruth in Vienna "so that you and the girl can come out together."

After a few days, Dagmar arrived and came to see Ruth. They liked each other at once. Dagmar was a pretty girl with sad eyes. "I supposed that the child had never had much affection at home," Ruth told me. A week later the two flew from Vienna to Addis Ababa. Dr. Babor was waiting at the airport. He was polite and kissed her hand, and he embraced Dagmar. But he wasn't at all what Ruth had expected. There was something strange, almost frightening, about him.

"He wasn't as I had visualized him from his letters," Ruth said to me. "Strange and withdrawn. Almost sinister."

He was a very bad driver. On the road from the airport to the city he twice almost caused a head-on collision when he drove on the wrong side of the road. She asked, half-jokingly, whether he wanted to kill himself, and he said, very seriously, that he'd tried to do that for years. Ruth thought he was overworked and momentarily depressed. She knew that white men in Africa often suffer dark moods. But she was startled when he said with grim satisfaction that he'd had five automobile accidents in the past two years. She gave him a curious glance. How had he been able to keep his driver's license?

"My dear, I am well known at the Emperor's palace. I am the greatest doctor in Addis Ababa."

He stopped the car in front of a dark, deserted-looking house. The place was cool and Ruth wanted to relax. It had been a long flight and she was tired.

"Let's go into the bush for an hour," he said.

"Now?" She was surprised.

"Why not? It's only a short ride. Just change your shoes. I'll take my gun."

The bush was a few miles away. Again Ruth was captivated by the magic of Africa, but this time it was difficult for her to enjoy it. Karl drove like a madman. She got frightened. She said she would have to get out of the car if he kept driving like that.

"He laughed," Ruth said. "He laughed as though I'd said something funny. I was becoming a little afraid of him."

"Don't be silly," he had said. "This is not the Ringstrasse, where you can get out and take the next streetcar." He laughed again. He said he was going to take her to his favorite river: "It's infested with crocodiles." She thought he was joking. But he stopped the car and told her to come along, and they walked down the narrow path to the river. She saw the crocodiles in the dark, muddy water.

"Aren't they lovely animals?" he said. Ruth moved away.

"Let's go back," he said. "I want you to meet my best friend in Ethiopia."

"We stopped in front of the local police barracks and walked in. An old lion was lying under a tree. I was terrified, but Karl said there was nothing to be afraid of, that the lion was like a domestic animal and they were good friends. And then he put his hand into the lion's mouth. When he came back, I saw that blood was trickling down his arm. I said, 'My God, he bit you!' Karl chuckled, and said, 'I don't mind. He's my best friend. . . . Come on, let's go home.'"

The living room of Dr. Babor's house was damp and chilly. There was nothing to eat, and the icebox was empty. Dagmar opened a can of corned beef. Dr. Babor said he was tired, and he went up to his room without apology. There was an uncomfortable silence. Dagmar said her father's depressions were getting worse all the time.

"He must have had some frightful experiences during the war. He never talks about it. But it bothers him terribly. As long as Mother lived, he was much quieter. Sometimes he was almost happy, but since then—" She gave a helpless shrug. "He needed Mother very much. Then came the accident. And now—you've seen him. I'm frightened."

Ruth cautiously inquired about the automobile accident. Mrs. Babor had been driving the car one dark, moonless night when she hit a parked car. Her husband had sat next to her. The accident was never really explained. It appears that Mrs. Babor had made no attempt to turn and avoid a head-on collision, nor had she applied the brakes. It was as though she had *wanted* to hit that parked car. She'd been killed instantly, and her husband was badly hurt.

Ruth did not sleep that night. She thought of Karl's nice, affectionate letters—and of his brutal eyes, of the way he'd acted when he pushed his hand into the lion's mouth. She was glad she didn't have to see him at breakfast. He had gone to his clinic early. She went out with Dagmar. When they came home, late in the afternoon, he was sitting in the living room staring straight ahead. He didn't rise when they came into the room.

Ruth went up to her room. Downstairs there was an argument. She heard Dagmar complain that she was hungry and could find nothing to eat in the house. Then there was Dr. Babor's voice, shouting something Ruth didn't understand, and Dagmar's voice shouting back at her father, and suddenly there was quiet. After a while Ruth saw him leave the house and get into his car. He came back half an hour later with some food, but he didn't sit down with them for dinner. Dagmar said that her father ate almost nothing.

The next night, the wife of a local official brought a sick baby to Dr. Babor. Dagmar opened the door. The woman said that the baby was feverish and she couldn't reach her children's doctor. Would Dr. Babor look at the baby?

The girl came in and said a patient was outside with a baby. He jumped up.

"His eyes were bloodshot and his face was almost distorted with hatred," Ruth told me. "It was horrible. He shouted at Dagmar that he wouldn't touch the child; he hated children; let them die. 'I've never treated a child and never will. Out with them!' Dagmar stood transfixed, silently pleading with me, and I said: 'Karl, you are a doctor, aren't you? That child is sick. Please go out and take care of the baby.'"

"Then he turned on me. He told me not to interfere. He said he needed no advice from a dirty, fat Jewess. I was speechless. He screamed at me: 'Don't stare at me like that! I hate children. I hate all human beings. People ought to be gassed—killed as quickly as possible. We don't need people. Animals are much better than people. Animals must be spared!'"

He turned away and ran out into the night. The woman left with her child. The old servant told Ruth that Dr. Babor had probably gone to the zoo. She asked what he was doing at the zoo, now, at night? The servant said when Dr. Babor was "ill and worried," he liked to go and play with the leopard in the zoo. He liked to strike him and would put his hand into the beast's mouth. The next morning Ruth noticed that Babor's left hand was bandaged.

"I knew he was a sick man," she said to me. "I told him quietly that I was going back to Vienna. He went into a wild rage. He shouted that I had no right to talk to him like that. No one must talk to him that way. He was a great man, an important man, the greatest doctor in Addis Ababa. I smiled and said quietly: 'Karl, I think you are the worst fool in Addis Ababa,' and walked away. Then I heard the sharp intake of his breath, and turned around. He'd got up, and his eyes looked as though they were filled with blood. I sensed that he might strangle me. Something made me shout: 'Get out, you brute! Get out of here at once! Don't dare touch me!'"

"It was strange. The moment I shouted at him, he moved back. His shoulders hunched; his figure seemed to collapse. He made me think of an inflated rubber doll when you let the air out. He turned around and left. Not a word. The old servant waited until Babor had gone. Then he come in and bowed to me deeply. I had shouted at his master, and now I was stronger than his master. The servant told me that Babor's wife had always slapped his face when he got

'one of these attacks,' and then he would be silent and 'very nice.'
The servant grimaced. I telephoned the airport and made a reserva-
tion for the first flight out the following day."

The next morning, the plane was to leave at ten. When Ruth came
down with her bags, Dagmar told her that she and her father had
been invited to the Emperor's palace for breakfast and they couldn't
take her to the airport.

"In Addis Ababa a white woman cannot ride alone in a taxi," Ruth
explained to me. "God knows where these native drivers would take
me. I said to Dagmar. 'I'm sorry, but you and your father will have
to drive me to the airport first; then you can go to your Emperor.'

"Then I heard a sound in the doorway and saw him. He stood
there, motionless. He slowly came toward me. I thought he was
going to kill me. I acted out of reflex. I slapped his face hard—twice,
three times, I don't remember. He stood there and let himself be hit.
I think he actually enjoyed it—that was the worst part of it. He said
I should beat him, he didn't deserve anything else, he was no good,
he wanted to die, he'd wanted to die ever since his wife was killed."

Ruth closed her eyes. "Oh, it was terrible—all this in front of his
daughter. Afterward there was no problem. They took me to the airport. Dagmar cried. She'd wanted me to stay. He didn't say goodbye
to me, and I was glad. They drove off to have breakfast with the
Emperor, and I walked toward the plane. When I was in my seat I
called the stewardess and asked for something to eat."

From the airport in Vienna Ruth went to see Babor's father to tell
him what had happened. An elderly woman who was obviously the
doctor's mother opened the door, but when she saw Ruth she
quickly called her husband and left them alone.

"I was very much upset. I told him he should never have let me
go there. Didn't he know that his son was very sick and should be in
an asylum? How could Karl be a doctor when he refused to treat
children and said he hated people? He'd said that people should be
gassed, that he loved only wild animals. . . . I told him everything.
The old man apologized. He said Karl had suffered a breakdown
during the war and they'd hoped he was better now. He so much
needed somebody who was strong and energetic and would take
care of him.

"Yes," Ruth had said. "A fat, dirty Jewess who would beat him."
"I'm sorry, my dear. I hope you'll be able to forget the whole
thing," said Diplom-Ingenieur Babor.

But she couldn't forget it. She saw Dr. Babor in nightmares. She'd
gone back to her boring job at the office, and she made more typing
mistakes than ever. People said she looked changed. She couldn't tell
them what had happened. It was like something you read in a bad
book, but it didn't actually *happen* to people. Only her mother knew
everything, and her mother was worried. One night when Ruth
came home, her mother said: "I think you ought to tell the whole
story to someone who will understand it. I read something about
Simon Wiesenthal in the paper. Why don't you go to Vienna and
talk to him?"

Now Ruth gave a helpless shrug. "I know the whole thing sounds
unbelievable, Herr Wiesenthal. But it's true. I swear it's true."

I said I knew it was true. "I've known Dr. Karl Babor for years. I
saw him long before you did."

While Ruth had been telling me her story I'd been thinking of
something else. There is a certain scene on the stage of my memory
I shall never forget. It is a small room with dark-gray walls. The entrance is on the left side. The exit is in the middle of the back wall.
The exit leads straight into the crematorium of the Grossrosen concentration camp, near what was then Breslau (Wroclaw), Poland.

On the otherwise empty stage is a small table with several
syringes and a few bottles filled with a colorless liquid. There is one
chair. The faint smell of burned flesh is in the air. The year is 1944.
The time might be any time of day or night. This is the antechamber
of the Grossrosen crematorium. There are no gas chambers in this
concentration camp. The crematorium is served by a Russian
prisoner called "Black Ivan" because constant smoke has blackened
his face and his hands. Ivan looks really terrible, but few inmates
ever see him while they are still alive. By the time "Black Ivan" gets
to them, they no longer know any fear. He carries their ashes to a
nearby field where the camp gardeners plant vegetables for the
camp kitchen, for fertilizer. I know all this because I was a prisoner
assigned to work in the vegetable garden.

Now a young man stands in the middle of the room. He wears a white doctor's coat on top of his SS uniform. Most prisoners have seen the young "doctor" before; he is a member of the "selection committee." When the transports arrive, the prisoners are ordered to walk down the ramp and stand at attention in front of a small table. The "doctor" at the table moves his index finger to the right (life) or to the left (death). An SS man makes a sign on a list. The "doctor" takes a second look at the human wreck before him. "Open your mouth! Wider!" He nods. The prisoner is not entirely worthless. Three gold fillings. The "doctor" marks a big black cross with a thick wet pencil on the prisoner's forehead. "Abtreten!" All marked people must register at the camp office. The gold fillings in their mouths are registered in duplicate. They no longer own them but are permitted to use them while they're alive. Who says the SS are inhuman? They wouldn't remove a man's teeth while he is alive.

Soon the prisoners who have been directed to the left will stand again in front of the young man in the white medical coat. He is highly skilled at his job. He fills the syringe, tells the patient (who is stripped to his navel) to sit down on the chair. The patient is held by two SS men. The young man quickly steps in front of him, injects the lethal needle into the heart with a sharp thrust. The syringe contains phenolic acid.

"Herr Doktor Babor" is well liked by his SS superiors, who call him *Herr Doktor* although they know that when he joined up he was still only a medical student who had completed six semesters at Vienna University. "I always like to give them a little more than the lethal dose, just to be sure," he has told them. The "Doktor" is a very humane man. Sometimes prisoners are frightened when he administers the phenolic *coup de grâce*, but they haven't got much time to think. Other patients are waiting. The bodies of the dead are speedily dragged out through the exit door. A little later people outside will see smoke come out of the chimney.

After Ruth had told me her story, I sat for a long, long time at my desk. How often had I seen the smoke come out of the chimney while I worked in the camp garden? It was only the will of God that I had not had to sit down on the chair in front of "Herr Doktor" Karl Babor.

There is no extradition treaty between Austria and Ethiopia. In most African countries the statute of limitations for murder is ten years. According to Ethiopian law, Babor's crimes could no longer be prosecuted.

I looked up Babor's postwar history. He had been in an Allied internment camp, one of the "little fish" who had done "nothing serious." In 1947 he spent several months in Vienna's Landesgericht Prison, but the evidence against him was "not sufficient" and he was released. Babor was lucky. His case never went beyond a preliminary investigation. There were many other more urgent cases.

In 1948, Karl Babor resumed his medical studies at Vienna University. The following year, having passed his exams, he received the degree of Doctor of Medicine in the Great Hall of the University. He solemnly swore "to serve all humanity." Dr. Babor did his internship at the Gersthof Municipal Hospital in Vienna, and later practiced medicine in the lovely town of Gmunden, in the Salzkammergut. He is said to have been quite popular with his patients there. But Dr. Babor didn't feel safe in Gmunden. One day in 1952, two men came to his parents' apartment in Vienna and asked for him. They were former inmates of the Grossrosen concentration camp. When Babor's father told them his son was not there, the men went to the police and made an accusation against the doctor. And so it was perhaps no coincidence that Babor shortly afterward disappeared from Gmunden with his wife and daughter. The following year the Austrian authorities obtained more evidence on Babor's wartime activities. He was accused of having caused the death of an unknown number of people by poisonous injections. A warrant was issued for him. His address was by now unknown; he was believed to be somewhere in South Africa.

Since I knew that no Ethiopian court would try Karl Babor and that he would not come to Vienna voluntarily to stand trial, there remained only one possibility of forcing him to do it. I notified the Vienna correspondent of *The New York Times*. The resulting story had repercussions in America and Ethiopia. The Ethiopian Embassy in Washington hastily called a press conference to inform the public that Dr. Babor had never been the official physician of His Majesty the Negus. It *was* admitted that he'd treated members of the Imperial Household.

When my report was published by a Frankfurt newpaper, the editor received a letter from a German history teacher who wrote:

After the end of the war in 1945, my wife Ingeborg, her mother (since deceased), and her sister came to Austria and lived at the Hotel Post, in Stuben am Arlberg. A few houses away lived one Karl Babor, with his wife Helga and their daughter Dagmar, from Vienna. Babor walked on crutches; he told me he had been wounded at the end of the war. Early in 1946, my wife and her family moved to Zug, a small village near Lech am Arlberg, where they lived in an old *Wehrmacht* hut that now belonged to a local peasant. A little later they were joined by Babor and his daughter, who stayed with my wife's family until late in 1946. Understandably, people living together in such a small place become close to one another. Karl Babor told my wife and her relatives that he had been *Lagerarzt* [camp doctor] in several concentration camps.

My wife was then twenty-two, knew nothing of what had really happened in these camps and thought that "camp doctors" had normal humanitarian functions and duties such as other doctors. Later she worked as nurse in the Sanatorium Helios in Davos, which had been taken over by the Jewish Relief Committee. People from concentration camps who were suffering from tuberculosis were treated there. The horrors which her patients described to her, and the facts that my wife later discovered about these years—I teach history—opened her eyes. She feels now that she must contribute to the conviction of Karl Babor—something she can do because she knew the man quite well. She is willing to give all her information to Herr Wiesenthal, and asks you to forward this letter to the Documentation Center since she does not have Herr Wiesenthal's address. . . .

The New York Times story also had repercussions in Addis Ababa. German and Austrian correspondents asked Dr. Babor to defend himself against my accusations. At a press conference Babor indignantly told the correspondents that he had "never been active in any concentration camp. He admitted, however, that he'd been in Breslau as a *Truppenarzt* (military doctor).

"Dr. Babor, why don't you sue Wiesenthal for libel?" asked one of the reporters.

"I can't afford it. I would have to fly to Vienna, and I haven't got the money."

When I read about this in German and Austrian papers, I cabled Babor: PLEASE CLAIM YOUR FLIGHT TICKET ETHIOPIAN AIRLINES ADDIS ABABA STOP ROOM AND BOARD IN VIENNA PROVIDED STOP WIESENTHAL. I didn't consider it tactful to add that room and board would be provided free of charge in the Landesgericht county jail by the Austrian authorities, who still had a warrant out for him. I gave the cable to the local newspapers. I wanted to be sure Babor couldn't say he hadn't received it.

There was no answer to my cable. Babor did not want to come to Vienna. He decided to make another journey. He wrote his will, paid his bills, meticulously put all his papers in order, and drove out into the bush, to his favorite spot near the crocodile-infested river to which he had taken Ruth on her first evening in Addis Ababa.

There he stopped the car and took off all his clothes and put them into his car. He carried only his gun. Slowly he waded into the river, surrounded by the animals of which he was so fond. He kept going until the water reached almost to his breast, and then he shot himself in the heart.

Perhaps he had hoped the crocodiles would notice him, but they didn't. A few days later American tourists on safari saw the body floating in the dark river. They reported their discovery to the Ethiopian authorities. The police investigation established beyond doubt that Dr. Karl Barbor had committed suicide. A Nazi paper in Germany printed an exclusive news story to the effect that "Wiesenthal's agents" had killed Babor. The funeral took place a few days later. Many members of the Austrian and German colony were present.

Chapter 16

THE EXTERMINATION
OF THE GYPSIES

I noticed the telegram simply by chance one day in September 1954 in Prague, as I looked through various Nazi documents. It was from Gestapo headquarters in Berlin, dated October 13, 1939, and addressed to the Gestapo office in Mährisch-Ostrau in the Protectorate of Bohemia-Moravia (today Moravská-Ostrava, Czechoslovakia). It was for the attention of Lieutenant Wagner and "for immediate delivery to SS Captain Eichmann" and said:

> SS COLONEL NEBE CALLED ON 12.10.39 [October 12, 1939] AND ASKED FOR INFORMATION. WHEN CAN HE SEND THE BERLIN GYPSIES? I ASKED HIM TO BE PATIENT FOR A COUPLE OF DAYS UNTIL I CAN FIND OUT WHERE SS CAPTAIN EICHMANN IS AND ASK HIM TO GET IN TOUCH WITH SS COLONEL NEBE. IF THE TRANSPORT OF THE BERLIN GYPSIES IS TO TAKE MUCH LONGER, THE CITY OF BERLIN WILL HAVE TO BUILD A SPECIAL CAMP FOR GYPSIES AT GREAT COST AND STILL GREATER DIFFICULTIES. SS COLONEL NEBE ASKS THAT YOU PHONE HIM. [Signed] BRAUNE

The next message was another telegram, stamped *URGENT*, dated October 16, from Eichmann, *SD Donau* (the Gestapo Security Office in Vienna,) addressed ATTENTION CAPTAIN GÜNTER, GESTAPO MÄHRISCH-OSTRAU:
238

REGARDING TRANSPORT OF GYPSIES BE INFORMED THAT ON
FRIDAY, 20.10.39, THE FIRST TRANSPORT OF JEWS WILL DE-
PART VIENNA. TO THIS TRANSPORT, 3–4 CARS OF GYPSIES ARE
TO BE ATTACHED. SUBSEQUENT TRAINS WILL DEPART FROM VIEN-
NA, MÄHRISCH-OSTRAU AND KATOWICE [POLAND]. THE SIMPLEST
METHOD IS TO ATTACH SOME CARLOADS OF GYPSIES TO EACH
TRANSPORT. BECAUSE THESE TRANSPORTS MUST FOLLOW A
SCHEDULE, A SMOOTH EXECUTION OF THIS MATTER IS EXPECTED.
CONCERNING A START IN THE ALTREICH [Germany proper]
BE INFORMED THAT THIS WILL BE COMING IN 3–4 WEEKS.
[Signed] EICHMANN

I had gone to Prague to look at the Nazi documents that had been
found in four iron-bound chests on the bottom of the lake of Černé
Jezero in southern Bohemia. While I was there the Czechoslovak authorities showed me the archives that had been left by the Gestapo
in Moravská-Ostrava and found recently. This was the first docu-
mentary evidence I had seen of the extermination of the Gypsies.
Apparently the program was directed by Adolf Eichmann; the man
directly responsible was called Braune.

It was no secret, of course, that the Gypsies had been considered
racially inferior after Hitler came to power in Germany in 1933.
Three years later a special "research" department was set up by the
SD for the "investigation" of the Gypsies; it was somewhat similar to
the department of Jewish Affairs, for which Eichmann had worked
since 1937. The Nuremberg laws concerning Jews had earlier been
amended to include Gypsies. Marriages between Gypsies and Germans were forbidden. In September 1939, after the beginning of the
war with Poland, Himmler had decreed that all Gypsies living in
"Greater Germany" must be evacuated to Poland. This decree
affected about thirty thousand Gypsies; two thirds of them lived in
Germany, the rest in Austria's Burgenland province and in Bohemia-
Moravia.

I had known that some concentration camps had contained special compounds for Gypsies. A large camp for Gypsies had been set
up in Auschwitz Birkenau; during the big Auschwitz trial at Frankfurt am Main in the early 1960s the extermination of the Gypsies
was mentioned briefly.

I began to investigate the matter, since no one had done it before.

The Gypsies are not well-organized people; they move from one place to the next; many of them are illiterate. They have no Documentation Center, and no one particularly cared what happened to them until I found, by chance, the documents in the Gestapo archives of Moravská-Ostrava.

Two days after Eichmann had sent to the Gestapo office in Mährisch-Ostrau his telegram about the first transports of Gypsies, a teletype "conversation" between Captain (SS *Haupsturmführer* Walter) Braune in Berlin and SS Captain Günter in Mährisch-Ostrau took place. (We have copies of the conversation on the stationery of the Gestapo.) The exchange reads, in part:

I WOULD LIKE TO ASK THAT YOU INFORM COLONEL NEBE OR MAJOR WERNER THAT WE HAVE NOT BEEN ABLE TO REACH THEM. IN THE MEANTIME WE HAVE SENT THE MESSAGE THERE. THE NEXT TRANSPORT FROM MÄHRISCH-OSTRAU IS EXPECTED TO LEAVE ON WEDNESDAY 25.10.39. PERHAPS GYPSIES CAN BE INCLUDED IN THE TRANSPORT. GÜNTER

Captain Braune in Berlin replied GEHT I.O. *I.O.* means *in Ordnung*—"OK." Braune added:

I WILL INFORM COLONEL NEBE OR MAJOR WERNER. WHAT'S NEW THERE? MY STATISTICAL TABLES ARE KILLING ME.

Captain Günter replied:

HERE WE GET OFF THE FIRST TRANSPORT OF 901 JEWS TO NISKO [POLAND] TODAY. I AM GOING SOON TO KATOWICE. THE NEXT 1000 GO FROM THERE EARLY FRIDAY. HAS MISS LEITNER ALREADY ARRIVED THERE?

Braune:

YES. HAS MISS LUKASCH GOT THERE?

Günter:

YES. I CAN BE REACHED IN MÄHRISCH-OSTRAU AS BEFORE. MY DEPUTY IS PARTY COMRADE BRÜNNER WHO IS COMPLETELY INFORMED ABOUT EVERYTHING.

Braune:

WHEN IS CAPTAIN EICHMANN COMING HERE?

Günter:

PROBABLY EARLY NEXT WEEK. COLONEL MÜLLER WANTS TO PUT
A PLANE AT HIS DISPOSAL.
HH! ["HEIL HITLER!"] GÜNTER.

Braune:

HH! BRAUNE.

We made copies of all documents that related to the deportation
and extermination of the Gypsies. The originals remain in the
Czechoslovak State Archives in Prague. In June 1965 I sent the entire file to the First Prosecutor Schüle at the Ludwigsburg Central
Office. No one there or in Bonn had known anything about this little-
documented side of the Nazis' genocidal campaign. I was able to
identify *Hauptsturmführer* Braune. He had been assigned the job of
the extermination of the Gypsies by SS *Oberführer* Nebe, head of
the SS *Reichskriminalpolizeiamt*. Other SS men mentioned in the
documents were First Lieutenant Wagner, Captain Günter, Major
Werner, Colonel Müller, Heinrich Müller (Eichmann's superior), a
Party member named Brünner, and two women identified as Leitner
and Lukasch.

It is not now known whether Braune, the man chiefly responsible,
is alive.

Since 1964, we have found in various Jewish archives all over the
world bits of material dealing with the extermination of the Gypsies,
but many details remain unknown. It is not clear, for instance, exactly where the Gypsies were murdered. Many were sent to ghettos
with the Jews, especially in Warsaw, Lublin, and Kielce, Poland.
Often they were deported with the Jews and killed on the spot by
SS gunmen. In the reports of the SS extermination commandos in
the Ukraine we have found many references to killed Gypsies.

The deportation of Gypsies from North Germany did not get
under way until May 1940. Then followed transports from Bavaria
and the Burgenland province of Austria, near the border of Hungary. After the German invasion of the Soviet Union, *Einsatzgruppe*
D had orders to annihilate all Gypsies in the Ukraine and in the
Crimea. In 1942, deportations from western and southwestern
Europe continued, and the Gypsies were sent to various concentra-

tion camps in Poland. The final act probably took place in 1944, in the gas chambers of Auschwitz. No one will ever know how many Gypsies were murdered. There were perhaps hundreds of thousands in the Nazi-conquered lands of Europe.

In my report to the Central Office at Ludwigsburg I suggested that the evidence may be sufficient to open a new series of prosecutions for genocide.

Chapter 17

THE GALLERY
OF TEARS

The letter was from New Zealand. The handwriting was hard to read, but the meaning was clear: The old lady who wrote me knew this was not the sort of case I usually became involved with, but she had not known where to turn. She had sent many letters to Vienna in the past years, but no one would tell her anything. She had been taken away in 1939. They had come to her apartment in Vienna's First District. "They gave me exactly five minutes to get my coat and handbag," she said. She had no cash, and she'd already turned in her jewelry. There was only the apartment, with the lovely things in it:

> I'd made so many sacrifices to keep the apartment exactly as my parents left it to me—the Meissen, and the snuff boxes which Father had collected, the Biedermeier chests, the vitrine with the three Sèvres figurines, the old candlesticks, and the silver. During the inflation in the 1920s, when we were cold and hungry, I had to sell some of the things to buy food and coal. But I'd sold none of the paintings. And there was the one that I loved because I knew how much it had meant to my father. . . .

In the doorway she had turned for a final look. That was the last time she had seen her treasures. When she returned in 1946, there was nothing left. A well-known Nazi had moved into her apartment a few weeks after she'd gone. Shortly before the end of the war the Nazi and his family had fled, taking many things with them. No one could tell her what had happened to these things—people were busy looking for other people. No one cared about Meissen and snuff boxes and candlesticks. Later she emigrated to New Zealand, where she was supported by distant relatives.

> I got over the loss of all my things; other people lost much more. But I *would* like to know what happened to that painting. A rich friend would like to buy it. He promised to let me keep it as long as I live. And the money would help me. I'm getting old and there are bills to pay. . . .

She had written to various agencies in Vienna, requesting information about her painting. It took her two years to track down the place where they kept the "ownerless" paintings: at the Hofburg, in storage rooms managed by the *Bundesdenkmalamt* (State Monument Office). She wrote there, and was told to submit various documents, otherwise they were not permitted even to inform her whether the painting was there.

This was not the first time I'd heard about such paintings. Earlier a local lawyer had called me. A refugee from Vienna, now living in England, had asked him to try to get back a valuable painting that was being kept in the Hofburg.

"It's strange," the lawyer said. "I seem to be running into a curtain of fog. Everybody acts as though I wanted to steal something. I think you ought to look into the matter, Wiesenthal. I have a hunch somebody is hiding something behind these paintings."

Somebody was. As I began to investigate, in a field in which I had no previous experience, the results were most interesting. At the end of the Second World War confusion was confounded regarding the Continent's art treasures. The Nazis had organized the greatest art robbery in history. After Hitler, Göring, and Ribbentrop had shown surprising interest in the arts, "collecting" became a major Nazi status symbol and leisure activity, more profitable than hunting and fishing. The Führer himself was the leading art collector, making grandiose plans to give to his beloved home town, Linz, the greatest art collection the world had ever seen. It would easily dwarf the

Louvre, the Uffizi, the Prado. It would also be the greatest art bargain in history. An *Einsatzstab* (special staff) under Hitler's indefatigable cultural expert Alfred Rosenberg was created, with the purpose of plundering art treasures in the Nazi-occupied countries. The staff members were recruited among curators, art experts, and dealers.

Nazi "collections" were created either by outright confiscation or under a smoke screen of legality. A friend in Holland recently told me about the second method.

"It was known that I owned a beautiful Franz Hals. Not many of them were in private hands. Rosenberg's experts came to see me one day in 1941, with two friends from the Gestapo. They looked at my Hals and liked it. Naturally. They proposed that they buy it for the Führer's future museum a great honor and a spectacular privi lege for me to contribute to the super-museum. They showed their appreciation by offering me what they called 'a fair price.'"

My friend laughed. "In the 1930s, during the Depression, the painting had been appraised at 150,000 marks. Now they offered me 1500 marks. They said they didn't want to take advantage of me. One of the Gestapo men said that so far as *he* was concerned that was 1500 marks too much. He gave me sixty seconds to think it over. I accepted."

"Suppose you'd turned them down?"

He laughed again. "I know a man who was stubborn. The Gestapo took his painting, and took him along too. He never came back."

After the war, restitution experts tried to bring order into the chaos. Paintings stolen from museums and public galleries were easily identified and returned. It was less easy in the case of private collections whose owners had disappeared. The hardest problem involved paintings that had belonged to individuals who had owned only one or two or three. They haven't kept exact records, the way big collectors do.

The West Germans made an effort to trace the missing owners or their legal heirs; they also returned to Austria paintings that belonged to Austrians. The Austrians were slower. They handed over art treasures to rightful owners who could prove their ownership, but they made no effort to find the people who had owned the paintings, drawings, sculptures now stored at the Hofburg or their heirs. They knew that the owners had been persecuted for racial or political reasons. But they claimed that many cases were "complicated." Sometimes the former owners had "sold" art works under extreme pressure, as my Dutch friend had "sold" his Hals. The courts would have to decide whether such a "sale" was legal. A painting might have been requisitioned by a Nazi after the deportation of the Jewish owners, then later "requisitioned" by other people after the hasty departure of the Nazi. It was indeed complicated.

I began by studying the list of the more important staff members of *Einsatzstab* Rosenberg, who had had the job of plundering treasures. I was not too surprised to see that some of the men who took part in the great art robbery were again leading officials in museums and ministries; others had become prosperous art dealers. Two members of Rosenberg's staff are now respected dealers in a large city in southern Germany. One of the highest officials in Vienna's *Bundesdenkmalamt* had been NS *Gaukunstwart* (a sort of artistic *gauleiter*) in Carinthia. He was a member of a flying SS commission that traveled through Yugoslavia making selections for the Führer's museum.

I tried to establish exactly how many paintings were kept at the Hofburg and what kind of paintings. It wasn't easy. There were lists, but they were guarded like atomic warheads. I called up Frau Dr. P., the *Staatskonservator* (State Curator), and asked for an appointment. Who was I? What was it I wanted to know?

"I would like to get a list of the ownerless paintings sequestered at the Hofburg."

There was a long pause. "Who sent you to me?"

I explained that my mission was on behalf of some of the owners. Frau Dr. P. quickly said she was very busy and asked me to come in "about in ten days."

I went back then. Frau Dr. P. asked me what specific painting I wanted to know about. I said I wanted to know about *all* paintings.

"But that's impossible. We cannot disclose such information to private citizens."

I asked if she would prefer that I inform the press. She could always deny the story, I said.

At the mention of press, the State Curator stiffened. The whole thing was really not in her department, she said. She told me to go to the Finance Ministry.

At the Finance Ministry, the leading official didn't even talk to me. I was asked to see the subofficial in charge, a charming Austrian. He offered me a seat and a cigarette, and told me he was so glad to meet the *berühmte* (famous) Herr Wiesenthal.

"You mean the *berüchtigte* [notorious] Wiesenthal," I said.

He became less jovial. What could he do for me? I have reproduced the dialogue to the best of my recollection:

W: "How many paintings do you keep for unknown owners?"

Subofficial: "Well, it's hard to say. One would have to make an up-to-date inventory. There are constant changes, you know. We keep not only paintings for racially or politically persecuted owners, but also much stranded Hungarian and Czechoslovak property that arrived here during the war."

W: "How many belong to racially or politically persecuted people—two hundred? three hundred?"

Subofficial: "I'd say much more!"

W: "Two thousand?"

Subofficial: "Well, that's too much."

W: "Are there any valuable paintings among them?"

Subofficial: "It depends on what you call 'valuable.' There is nothing in the Rembrandt class."

W: "But there are some pretty good ones?"

Subofficial: "Well, yes."

W: "Why didn't you ever publish a list of these paintings? That would give their owners all over the world a chance of applying for restitution."

Subofficial: "But my *dear* Herr Wiesenthal, one doesn't have to publish such a list. The trade and the collectors know all about the more important paintings. *Das spricht sich herum* [that gets around]."

W: "Suppose it doesn't get around to a small town in New Zealand where an old Jewish lady lives on charity? She could sell her painting and enjoy the last years of her life."

Subofficial: "Hmm."

W: "I know that you returned some paintings to people who

proved their ownership. But paintings not claimed by 1968, I gather, will become property of the state."

Subofficial: "Now, what would *you* suggest?"

W: "I suggest that a catalog of all paintings and other art works be made. You know how much blood and tears is attached to these works. The catalog should be printed and sent to every Austrian consulate all over the world. People will have a chance to look at it and see whether their property is stored at the Hofburg."

Subofficial (wringing his hands): "Do you realize what that means? We would be drowned in a flood of letters."

W: "That will please the Austrian philatelists."

Subofficial: "You don't understand. The whole thing is *kompliziert* [complicated]. We've started negotiations with the Hungarians. We're going to talk to the Czechs. We haven't got the time to deal with each individual owner. We just haven't got the personnel."

I encountered similar reticence at the state department for *Vermögenssicherung* (securing of property). They said that a catalog of the paintings would create a veritable "paper war," and there would be lawsuits. One couldn't "just show" these paintings to people who pretended to be their owners.

"You don't know what happened after the Allied troops departed in 1955. We turned back sequestered property to the alleged owners. Then other people claimed the same property. Goodness, you have no idea what went on. Strangely enough, they were always fighting about the valuable things. No one wanted the bad stuff."

I said: "Does that mean that you want to wait until these things become property of the State?"

"Applications for restitution were to be made until the end of 1956. Later applications cannot be considered."

And if the owners hadn't known about the time limit? Oh, that was just too bad. But there was nothing one could do now.

There remained only an appeal to the highest government officials and to the people of Austria. I wrote letters to the Finance Minister, the Minister of Education, and the Minister of Foreign Affairs. "I am convinced that the Austrian Republic is not interested in profiting from art treasures covered with blood and tears." I wrote finally.

I sent all of my information on the matter, with copies of my letters, to the press. For a while no one printed anything. A high-ranking government official indicated to me that "the whole complex matter" was under consideration.

In October 1965 Vienna's *Express* printed an exposé on "The Gallery of Tears." Some of the other papers followed suit. The Foreign Minister, Dr. Bruno Kreisky, wrote me that he supported my suggestion for making up a catalog of the art treasures to be sent to Austria's consulates all over the world, where the presumptive owners could get all the needed information.

And on April 16, 1966, Dr. Wolfgang Schmitz, the Finance Minister, wrote me that he and the Education Minister had looked into the matter thoroughly:

> The solution of the problem that you brought up will be a new federal law that will probably be called *Kunstgut-Bereinigungsgesetz* [law for the disposition of art treasures]. I've already given orders to prepare a draft of such a law. It will enable people to present their claims within a certain time after the law becomes effective. I hope that you will agree with this intention. . . .

Maybe it won't be too late for the old lady in New Zealand.

Chapter 18

A PROFILE OF
SIMON WIESENTHAL *(Concluded)*
Wiesenthal in the Vineyard

Not long ago, Simon Wiesenthal received a letter addressed *Simon Wiesenthal, Manager, The Research Institute for Nazi Crimes, Munich.* The German postal clerk in Munich had crossed out *Munich* and forwarded the letter to Vienna. To people all over the world, Wiesenthal is exactly what the sender of that letter called him: a one-man research institute. Most people who write to him have never seen him. They write not only about crimes but also to ask for help in restitution cases, to complain about unsympathetic officials and anti-Semitic neighbors, and to trace relatives and friends who disappeared during the war. Wiesenthal is an address, a symbol, the last court of appeal for the minority who have not yet forgotten the past, and the uncomfortable prompter for the majority who prefer to ignore the past. Many letters are simply addressed *Wiesenthal, Vienna.* Some contain clues that will initiate a new case; others provide a missing part of an old puzzle.

Almost every letter contains a tragedy. Sometimes it is apparent that a man has begun to write a letter and, while he writes, the tragedy becomes alive before his eyes and the handwriting becomes difficult to read. Some letters end abruptly: "Forgive me, but I cannot go on." Sometimes people write because they know a secret they don't want to possess alone any longer.

"Unfortunately, they often write too late," Weisenthal says. "They assume, quite wrongly, that I know everything."

But he is often cheered up by people who think he knows almost everything. When he arrived at the airport in Frankfurt am Main recently and displayed his passport, a German official winked and asked with a smile: "Is one of *them* hiding here?" Another German official, on a train at the German border station of Passau, looked at Wiesenthal's passport and said: "*The* Wiesenthal. I presume?" The people in the compartment laughed.

"They stared at me as though I were a soccer player or a secret agent," Wiesenthal says. "They were intrigued but not resentful."

Never having studied law, Wiesenthal does not think within the narrow legal terms that often seem to inhibit people with formal training. His theories are often unorthodox, but nearly always logical, and his searching questions often baffle legal experts. In 1964, Wiesenthal began to study a list of eighteen hundred judges and public prosecutors, most of whom are now in high legal positions in Germany and Austria. All of them had administered justice during the Hitler regime in Germany, Austria, and the German-occupied countries. Almost all had signed death sentences "in the name of the Führer" in a shocking travesty of justice. For instance, a Catholic priest who had fired his cook for stealing was denounced by her to the Gestapo for listening to the BBC; he was sentenced to death. An Austrian woman was executed because she gave a Yugoslav prisoner of war a suit. A Polish forced laborer who helped to clean up the site of a bombed building was sentenced to death and hanged for keeping a small piece of chocolate he had found on the floor.

"I have no personal motive for going after these jurists," Wiesenthal says. "But in a democracy the legal branch of the government is the safeguard of continuity, the citizen's protection against arbitrary acts by the Executive. A rotten judiciary is the handmaiden of dictatorship. In Germany and Austria, justice was administered in the name of injustice. In the German-occupied countries the situation was even more complicated." For instance, he points out, after the German invasion of the Netherlands, Queen Wilhelmina and her government went into exile in London, and the Dutch army capitulated, but there were no collaborators among judges or other officials, so the German judges and prosecutors who followed the Ger-

man troops began to administer justice under what was called
Besatzungsrecht—occupation Law. "The Germans had invaded the
Netherlands illegally," says Wiesenthal. "How could they establish
law based on an act of lawlessness? If I break into my neighbor's
home, do I have the right to sentence him to death because he re-
sists my attack? This is exactly what the German jurists in the
Netherlands did when they sentenced Dutchmen to death."

If Wiesenthal's thesis should be tested and confirmed in court, the
German jurists who handed out improper death sentences under the
Nazi regime could be indicted as accomplices to murder. "Even if
they pretend to have acted under duress or under specific orders,
they may be personally acquitted by a jury, but the situation of ob-
jective illegality remains," says Wiesenthal. Such opinions, expressed
with unshakable belief, do not endear Wiesenthal to the legal or
political authorities. There have already been too many judicial
scandals in postwar Germany and Austria. Dr. Christian Broda, Austria's former Minister of Justice, once got so exasperated by Wiesenthal's probing into the doubtful past of some Austrian jurists that he
banged his fist on his desk and shouted that he would tolerate "no
further interference."

Wiesenthal remained calm under the outburst of ministerial
wrath. "Herr Minister," he said quietly, "you cannot shout at me. I'm
not here on behalf of a wealthy client who pays me a lot of money
to represent his interests. And I was not appointed as the lawyer for
six million dead people. No such appointment exists. But I've
worked for over twenty years for the memory of these people, and I
believe I've earned the right to speak for them. Will you deprive me
of this right?"

The Minister was silent. After a while he said: "I'll concede this
right to you. But only to you, Herr Wiesenthal."

Like many celebrated trial lawyers and prosecutors, Wiesenthal has
an inborn sense of drama and loves a colorful phrase. He often
makes statements that have a slight touch of the theatrical when
they are printed, but they sound completely convincing when he
speaks. At a meeting of former concentration-camp inmates in Israel
he said: "At the end of the last war the power of our suffering had
the force of an emotional atomic bomb, but we traded this for a box

of matches by going after material restitution instead of devoting our strength to moral restitution."

With perfect timing, Wiesenthal often breaks up a tense situation by injecting irony. Not only German and Austrian officials, but also members of Jewish organizations fear him as something of an *enfant terrible*. He was one of a delegation of Austrian Jews negotiating with that country's government about the amount of restitution to be paid for forty-eight synagogues and houses of worship that had been destroyed under the Nazi regime in Austria. In an undignified effort to haggle, the Austrian officials first offered three and a half million Austrian schillings ($140,000) and gradually went up to 10 million ($400,000). At that point Wiesenthal, unable to keep quiet, told them the story of a friend in a refugee camp who had lent ten schillings to a fellow inmate at a time when ten schillings was a small fortune. Later the lender tried in vain to get back the money. Finally, when the borrower had received a visa and was about to go abroad, he came back to Wiesenthal's friend and wanted to repay the money. "My friend and I were playing chess," Wiesenthal continued. "My friend looked up and said, 'Please keep your money. I don't want to change my mind about you for ten schillings.'" The Austrian officials did not like the allusion. After long negotiations they paid 30 million schillings ($1.2 million), a great deal less than the value of actual damage, estimated at 164 million schillings ($6.35 million).

Wiesenthal was just as ironic at a recent meeting of the former members of Austrian resistance movement, to which he belonged. He bitterly criticized the membership for their weak role in present-day Austrian politics. "I don't understand you," he said, glaring at them. "You were not afraid of some brutal SS *Führer*, but now you worry about some second-rate local politicians. I think it's quite a comedown for our organization."

Wiesenthal's friends consider him a latter-day Biblical prophet who makes no compromises, with either himself or anyone else. The life of a prophet is never an easy one. Wiesenthal goes around giving people unpopular warnings and telling them unpleasant truths. His relations with many people are often hampered because he reminds them too much of the past. He is something of a symbol, and people feel uncomfortable in the presence of a symbol. Bruno

Marek, Mayor of Vienna, told him recently: "Herr Wiesenthal, you sometimes make life very difficult for us but we need you: you are the voice of our conscience vis-à-vis the Jews." Wiesenthal seems to be almost everybody's conscience. Jews who didn't suffer personally under the Nazi regime—because they lived far away or were lucky enough to get away in time—are slightly awed when they first meet him. Many regard him with a mixture of admiration and consternation.

"Wiesenthal talks, and a cold draft seems to go through the room," a Jewish acquaintance says. "I didn't know that such men existed outside of the Old Testament. He is the watcher and the warner, and he's been right so often that no one dares ignore him." He is a most impressive public speaker. One of his old friends says: "Sometimes Simon steps out of himself and performs the part of Wiesenthal, the Voice of the Conscience, but Wiesenthal the performer is only an intensified expression of Wiesenthal the man. He is not an actor playing a part, but a sort of priest preaching with terrific intensity. He loves to argue out complicated problems."

Wiesenthal often argues with former SS men, who are coldly hostile in the beginning and visibly confused when they leave him. "The trouble with Wiesenthal," says a former SS *Führer*, "is that he believes in what he says, thinks everything out in advance, and then tells it to you in the clearest possible way. He is too well prepared for all the answers and arguments you may have."

Even people who were with Wiesenthal in the concentration camps are slightly awed by this fervor. "Simon can be a bit *unheimlich* [eerie,]" one of them said recently, "but we need him. If there were no Wiesenthal, one would have to invent one." Wiesenthal realizes that he seems "eerie" to many people—a somewhat mystical man who has been close to death often and now takes considerable risks to carry out what many people think is a dangerous mission. His heritage of mysticism, which comes from generations of mystically minded ancestors, helped him survive his long, dark journey through the concentration camps. He had long talks with his fellow inmates about the key to Jewish mysticism—the problem of guilt and punishment. He feels that the whole of Jewish history is in essence the story of guilt and punishment. As a child he was often told by his deeply religious grandmother that there was a higher divine justice. Human justice would make many errors, she said, but there was an inexorable logic in the higher justice. He says the thought gave him great strength. He believed the Jews in the concentration camps would all die, but in the end their torturers would die too and have to account for their crimes before the court of higher justice.

"The concentration camp did strange things to men," Wiesenthal says. "No man remained the same. I've seen atheists become deeply religious men and religious men turn away from God. Many devout Jews tortured themselves with the question 'Was our guilt so deep, so terrible, that we were given such punishment?' Even if they were guilty, without knowing it, they couldn't perceive why small, innocent children deserved such punishment. Those children could not be guilty. It was impossible to escape a sense of mysticism when you felt constantly surrounded by death. For instance, SS men tore down the gravestones in the Jewish cemeteries in Lwow and used them as pavement of the main road in the concentration camp. They thought they would humiliate us by forcing us to walk across the tombstones of our parents and grandparents with the Hebrew signs. They only made us more aware of our strength. They made even the doubtful believe again. The doubtful and the weak began to realize that some day all this would end, and then the SS men would be held responsible.

"I've seen SS men throw a Torah at each other. A devout Jew touches the Torah, the Mosaic Law, only with his prayer scarf. The SS men would cut the Torahs into small pieces and throw them out on a garbage dump. To have to see all this and not lose one's belief in a higher justice a man had to be very strong; but *if* he believed he was stronger than ever. The concentration camp made atheists out of the doubtful, but it also made the believers more deeply religious than before."

Wiesenthal's preoccupation today is no longer the discovery of Nazi criminals. Of the 22,500 names on his list, he has brought to justice some nine hundred in the past twenty years—only a fraction. He has no hope of apprehending all he considers guilty of Nazi crimes, or even half or a third of them. The wheels of justice turn slowly; often it is several years from the time Wiesenthal submits a case to a prosecutor until the opening of the trial.

Time has become Wiesenthal's enemy, one he cannot beat. No prosecutor will work on a case that is not properly documented. No court of justice will sentence a criminal without evidence, either documents or the testimony of at least two witnesses. After twenty years, people's memories fail them and they confuse places, times, and incidents. A skilled defense lawyer who cross-examines a nervous witness may upset the structure of evidence Wiesenthal has worked hard to set up. Worst of all, witnesses die. For Wiesenthal, finding witnesses has become a biological problem. A person who spent several years in concentration camps hardly has the life expectancy of the average citizen. His daily food ration was a bowl of watery liquid called soup and a tiny piece of bread. The prisoners had to work fourteen hours a day in rain and snow, wearing rags. Sometimes they had no shoes. They often had to bury their own friends and relatives. The physical exertion was aggravated by mental and emotional suffering. Perverted SS guards would force the prisoners to "fertilize" a vegetable camp-garden with the ashes of their dead brothers. In the Grossrosen camp, healthy-looking prisoners were selected to break in new shoes for soldiers on daily twenty-mile marches. Few prisoners survived this ordeal for more than two weeks.

In contrast, the SS men in the concentration camps had special SS food, plenty of liquor and plenty of women, their own hospitals and doctors. Compared to their comrades at the front, they had an easy life. Most of them are in fairly good health today, while most of those among their victims who survived are sick people, suffering from diseases of the heart, the lungs, the kidneys. Wiesenthal is bothered by circulatory ailments and painful attacks of spondylitis, a deformation of the vertebral column caused by frequent beatings. A few years ago he went to consult a specialist who didn't know him.

The doctor shook his head. "Were you a boxer in your younger years? You seem to have taken plenty of punishment."

"I've taken punishment, but not in the ring," Wiesenthal said drily. He knows that often the criminals survive the witnesses, and in a few years there will be no living eyewitnesses to what happened in the death camps of the SS.

"The trouble with many witnesses is that they remember facts but forget dates," Wiesenthal says. "During the trials of seven of my 'clients' I've seen reliable witnesses discredited by the defense because they were not certain of a date or gave a wrong date. The defendant could prove that he hadn't been there at that time, so naturally he couldn't have committed the crime. The acquittal of Franz Murer was such a case. The witnesses described crimes they had seen with their own eyes. They gave details proving that they had been there. They remembered that the defendant had often worn a long leather coat. They described the crimes exactly because they had seen them in their mind's eye so many times and wouldn't forgot them as long as they lived. But they were not quite sure what day it was, or what month, and some even mixed up the year. Was it 1942 or 1943? They hesitated. The jury, which had no sympathy for the witnesses, was delighted."

Early in 1966, Wiesenthal appeared as a witness at a trial in Saarbrücken. The judge asked him to testify only on what he had seen with his own eyes, not what he'd heard from others. Wiesenthal told the court that this was impossible.

"I couldn't make a mistake about a major crime that I've seen with my own eyes," he told the judge. "When one sees a friend killed before his own eyes he doesn't forget it. But I wouldn't be so sure when minor details are concerned. In such cases I cannot always distinguish between what I've seen myself and what I've heard from others who were also there, and it is possible that their stories fuse with my own memories. There are certain things I can swear I've seen. There are other things which I believe happened but I couldn't confirm them under oath." Wiesenthal was later told by both the judge and the prosecutor that his explanation had made his testimony absolutely credible.

The worst witness is one who claims to remember everything. "After twenty years the human instinct of self-preservation acts like a filter or a screen, keeping back certain things one doesn't want to remember," Wiesenthal says. "Some people have better memories than others, but it is inconceivable that anyone should remember with absolute certainty something that happened twenty years ago.

The most valuable witnesses are those who tell the judge once in a while: 'Sorry—this is something I cannot remember exactly.'"

Wiesenthal likes to be among young people and often accepts invitations to speak at meetings of fraternities, Catholic or Protestant youth organizations, and similar groups. He is convinced that the young generation will decide "whether we've won or lost the future."

"In my talks with these young people I try to immunize them against many ideas they grew up with at home and in school. The older people may have forsworn their allegiance to Nazism, but in their subconscious they cannot get rid of all the Nazi Party baggage they have carried all these years. Frequently the young people tell me that their parents and teachers often try to justify the Hitler regime—and themselves—by playing up its positive achievements."

The young people were told that Hitler did away with unemployment. Besides, look at all the wonderful *Autobahnen* that were built under the Nazi regime! The young people were not told about the slave laborers who built the autobahns, or that full employment was the price paid for preparing the Second World War. But the young people find out about these things elsewhere, and then they ask their fathers and teachers why they didn't tell the truth. Often Wiesenthal, as a member of the older generation, is forced to explain the problems of his generation to the young. He knows that at the end of the war many people in Germany and Austria were bitterly disillusioned by the Nazi regime, and ready for a vigorous democratic re-education.

"If the people who accepted Hitler and his regime had been taught as children that you cannot wipe out whole nations because they are different from you, many of them would have hesitated. Hitler might never have come to power. But these people didn't have the advantage of being talked to the way I talk to their children now. And the confused Allied postwar attempts at re-education didn't help the older generation much, either."

"They still think they were right, most of them," says Wiesenthal. "But the young people are different; they ought to have a decent chance. They must learn that the innocent people have to dissociate themselves from the guilty ones. They must make a clean break. It's not easy. Most young people in Germany and Austria have grown up without ethical leadership, with no positive ideals. They're still being held responsible for the sins of their fathers. When they travel to other countries where the Nazis committed atrocities, these German and Austrian youngsters are asked unpleasant questions. Sometimes, because of their belligerent attitudes, they are thrown out and asked not to come back. It isn't fair. They should be told the truth, and they should be given a chance."

The young people often consider Wiesenthal a romantic figure, although he assures them soberly that his job involves mostly patient digging and careful deduction, and not much romance. After his talks, young boys and girls sometimes come to him to offer their help. Some come out of idealism; they feel that by helping Wiesenthal in his search into the past they could do something "important," something "to lead us out of the vacuum in which we exist," as one young man explained it. Wiesenthal rarely accepts such offers because he feels that the youngsters might be thrown into serious conflict with their environment. In a few cases Wiesenthal has accepted the help of those who seemed deeply dedicated to the idea of atonement or had strong personal reasons for wanting to help, such as the young man he calls Alex.

There is often very hot give-and-take in Wiesenthal's talks with the young. He may be reminded that "it was the British who invented concentration camps during the Boer War" or be asked whether the horrors of Hitler's death camps are not balanced by the horrors of Stalin's death camps. Sure, the *Kristallnacht* must have been terrible for the Jews, say his questioners, but wasn't Katyn terrible for the Polish officers who were killed by the Russians? The English complain about Coventry and the V-2s that struck London, but what about the British and American bombs that destroyed the beautiful city of Dresden?

Wiesenthal tries to give logical answers to such questions. "I tell them that I condone no crime, no matter who committed it. But no man can carry the world's weight on his shoulders. I cannot investigate all crimes. For reasons I assume my listeners will understand, I have decided to investigate Nazi crimes—most of them committed against Jews, but some committed against non-Jews. I have investigated crimes against Gypsies, against Italian soldiers, against Dutch and Danish patriots."

He explains to his listeners that no crime can be "balanced" by another crime. "You may remember the murder, a few years ago, of a young dancer at the Vienna Opera House. She was brutally killed backstage by an unknown man. He got away and was caught months later. The Vienna Opera murder created widespread excitement. Suppose the murderer had defended himself in court by saying that other, worse murderers had not yet been caught and punished—why should *he* be punished? No man with a sane appreciation of right and wrong would accept such a defense. The truth is that murder can never be excused by another murder. One cannot 'balance' crimes as one balances a pair of scales or the accounts in bookkeeping. After the war, I was often told by Nazis that they had been kept a year or two in Allied prisoner-of-war camps, just as I had been kept in their concentration camps. Consequently they thought we were *quitt*—even. Aside from the fact that a concentration camp was somewhat different from an Allied prisoner-of-war camp, there remains the truth that history is inexorable. History does not permit the equalization of crimes."

Wiesenthal is often asked by his young friends, both Gentile and Jewish, how it could happen that millions of people—Jews, Poles, Yugoslavs, others—let themselves be dragged away like cattle to the slaughterhouse, without trying to resist. Hundreds of thousands walked into the gas chambers guarded by just a few SS men. Why didn't the vast majority of victims at least make an attempt to revolt against the tiny majority of executioners?

"The young people who now ask these questions were born after the war and grew up in freedom," he says. "They never really learned what fear meant. The victims of the Nazi regime had been numbed by shock long before they stepped into the gas chambers. The SS succeeded in killing their victims' instinct of survival. Many of them no longer wanted to live; they were tired of torture. A young German once said to me: 'Even animals in the jungle fight for survival—why didn't you people fight for life in the jungle of the concentration camp?' I explained to him the difference between the jungle and the camps. The jungle is a brutal society, but a free society where the stronger species kills the weaker one. In the concentration-camp society that was ruled by the SS, the weaker species was reduced to subanimal status. They registered our gold teeth. They stripped us naked. They branded our wrists. They shaved a strip in the center of a man's hair. [They called it *Freiheitstrasse*— Freedom Street.] They did many other things, until they had squeezed out of men the last reserves of human dignity."

His young listeners, who seem to have given such matters a lot of thought, also ask Wiesenthal why the Jews didn't "do something" after the war. A former SS man once said to him: "Most of us expected the survivors of the concentration camps to start a blood bath among the SS, and take justice into their own hands. The world would have been shocked, but many people might have understood."

Wiesenthal explained that the Jews have always had a high regard for the sanctity of human life and didn't think that murder would expiate murder. The ex-SS man was not convinced. "Aren't you sure, Wiesenthal, that it wasn't just weakness?"

"I was a member of the group that prepared the conspiracy of July 20, 1944, against Hitler," another German told him. "If we had won, we would not have treated the Nazis with kid gloves. We would have arrested as many as we could find and put them before the regular courts. Some of us would have made short work of the SS and the Gestapo. The Jews missed their chance. Now you mustn't complain that you have to live among murderers."

Wiesenthal admits that the historical chance of moral retribution *was* missed. "The survivors of the camps were too weak, too apathetic for any concerted action. We were hardly able to walk; some of us were more dead than alive when we were liberated. Still, this is not a valid excuse. Later on, when we were physically stronger, everybody wanted to get away from the horror of the past as quickly as possible. A few found jobs. Others made a few schillings buying and selling PX cigarettes. Some wanted to emigrate and spent their days sitting in the anteroom of the nearest American consulate. Life was cruel, but life had to go on. And so the job of retribution was mostly left to those who never suffered in a concentration camp, the lucky ones who had got out in time. They were our spokesmen—and they didn't care about moral restitution; they were interested in material restitution. They talked about money, not about bringing to justice the men responsible for the apocalypse. Our critics have a point. It's too late now. Many murderers will remain among us."

Chapter 19

TWO CANDLES

When I was a young student, I often spent a few weeks in the Polish mountain resort of Zakopane in the Carpathians. In summertime there were the woods, sunshine, peace. In winter there was good skiing. Today, Zakopane is again a popular place for skiers. Not far away is the small town of Rabka. And there once lived a little Jewish boy named Sammy Rosenbaum. I first heard of Sammy Rosenbaum one morning in September 1965, when a Mrs. Rawicz from Rabka came into my office in Vienna. I was looking for witnesses who might testify at a trial that was to be held in Germany in connection with Nazi crimes at Rabka.

Mrs. Rawicz had known Sammy Rosenbaum well. He had been "a frail boy, with a pale, thin face and big, dark eyes, who looked much older than his age—as so many children do who learned too early about life and never laughed much." Sammy was nine years old in 1939, when the Germans came to Rabka in the early days of the Polish campaign, and life became a nightmare for the Jews there. Until then life had been fairly normal—if it ever could be called normal for a poor Jew in Poland. Sammy's father was a tailor who worked long hours and made little money. People like the Rosenbaums were fair game for the authorities, and in Poland the hunting season lasted twelve months a year.

263

The family lived in two musty rooms and a tiny kitchen in an old, dark house. But they were happy, and very religious. Sammy learned to say his prayers. Every Friday night he would go with his father to the synagogue, after lighting the candles at home. Mother and Sammy's sister Paula, three years his senior, stayed at home and prepared dinner.

That sort of life became only a memory after the Germans occupied Poland. In 1940, the SS set up what it called a "police school" in former Polish Army barracks in the woods that surrounded Rabka. It was not an ordinary school; it was a training center for future cadres of SS killers. This was the early phase of extermination. Executions were carried out by platoons of SS men who shot their victims. Sometimes they had to shoot fifty, a hundred, perhaps a hundred fifty people a day. SS men at Rabka were being hardened so they would not break after a few weeks of duty. They had to become insensitive to the sight of blood, to the agonized shouts of women and children. The job must be done with a minimum of fuss and a maximum of efficiency. That was a *Führerbefehl*—the Führer's order.

SS *Untersturmführer* Wilhelm Rosenbaum from Hamburg was made school commander. Rosenbaum was a true SS type: cynical, brutal, convinced of his mission. He would walk around town with a riding crop. "When we saw him in the street we got so frightened that we would hide in the nearest house entrance," the woman from Rabka remembered. Early in 1942, SS man Rosenbaum ordered all Jews in Rabka to appear at the local school to "register." The Jews knew what that meant. The sick and the elderly would soon be sent away. Others would have to work for the SS, the *Wehrmacht*, wherever they were sent.

Toward the end of the registration, SS *Führer* Rosenbaum appeared in the schoolroom, accompanied by his two deputies, Hermann Oder and Walter Proch. (Both were among my first postwar "clients." I found Proch in 1947 in Blomberg-Mondsee, a village near Salzburg. He was sentenced to six years in prison. Oder, also an Austrian, was arrested in Linz in the big villa he had "requisitioned" from the former Jewish owner. He was later released by the Americans and is now a prosperous businessman in Linz. SS *Führer*

Rosenbaum disappeared after the war but remained near the top of my private "Wanted" list.)

In the schoolroom in Rabka, SS *Führer* Rosenbaum looked through the list of names. "Suddenly he beat his riding crop hard on the table," the woman from Rabka told me. "Each of us winced as though we had been whipped. SS man Rosenbaum shouted: 'What's that? Rosenbaum? Jews! How dare these *verdammte Juden* have my good German name? Well, I'm going to take care of it!'" Perhaps SS *Führer* Rosenbaum would be surprised to discover that his good German name is generally considered a Jewish one, though there are, of course, people called Rosenbaum who are not Jewish.

He threw the list back on the table and strode out. From that day on everybody in Rabka knew that the Rosenbaums would be killed; it was only a question of time. People in other places were known to have been arrested and executed because their name was Rosenberg, or because they were Jews and their first name happened to be Adolf or Hermann.

By that time, frightening rumors were being whispered in Rabka about the police school. Practice executions were said to be taking place in a clearing in the woods. Examinations were held, with the SS students shooting people while with clinical detachment SS *Führer* Rosenbaum and his deputies observed the students' reactions. The living targets for these examinations were Jews and Poles who had been rounded up by the Gestapo. If a student flinched, he would be taken out of the execution squad and sent to a front-line outfit.

Mrs. Rawicz knew what she was talking about. After the registration she'd been sent to the police school as a charwoman. "When the SS men came back from the clearing in the woods I had to clean their boots, which were always covered with blood."

It was a Friday morning in June 1942. The eyewitnesses, two of whom now live in Israel, cannot remember the exact date, but they know it was a Friday. One of the witnesses had been working in the house across from the playground behind the school. He saw what happened. Two SS men escorted "the Jew Rosenbaum," his wife,

and their fifteen-year-old daughter Paula. Behind them came SS
Führer Rosenbaum.

"The woman and the girl were marched around the corner of the
schoolhouse and then I heard some shots," the witness has said under oath. "I saw how SS man Rosenbaum began to beat our Rosenbaum with his riding crop. He shouted: 'You dirty Jew, I'll teach
you a lesson for having my German name!' Then the SS man took his
revolver and shot Rosenbaum the tailor. He shot him twice or three
times. I couldn't count the shots; I was too horrified."

Earlier, the SS men had come for the Rosenbaums in a small
truck. Rosenbaum, his wife, and their daughter were around the
table in the front room having breakfast. Sammy was already at a
large stone quarry in nearby Zakryty, where he'd been sent as a
forced laborer after his twelfth birthday. All Jewish men had to
work, and Sammy was now classified as a man. But he was weak and
undernourished and couldn't do much except sort out the stones and
put the smaller ones on a truck.

The SS sent an unarmed Jewish policeman to the quarry for
Sammy. They often sent Jewish policemen to arrest other Jews when
they were too busy with their curriculum at the police school. The
Jewish policeman later told the Jewish charwoman at the school exactly what had happened. He'd gone out to Zakryty in a small
horsedrawn cart. He'd stopped the horse and waved at Sammy
Rosenbaum. Everybody in the quarry stopped working and stared
—the Jewish laborers and the two SS men who guarded them.
Sammy put the big stone he held in his hands on the truck, and
walked toward the cart. Sammy knew what was going to happen.

Sammy looked up at the Jewish policeman. "Where are they?" he
asked—"Father, Mother, and Paula. Where?"

The policeman just shook his head.

Sammy understood. "They're dead." His voice was low. "I've
known for a long time that it was going to happen. Because our
name is Rosenbaum."

The policeman swallowed, but Sammy didn't seem to notice.

"And now you've come for me." He spoke matter-of-factly. There
was no emotion in his voice. He stepped up and sat down on the
seat next to the Jewish policeman.

The policeman was unable to say a word. He had expected the

boy to cry, perhaps to run away. All the while he was riding out to Zakryty the policeman had wondered how he could warn the boy, make him disappear in the woods, where the Polish underground might later help him. Now it was too late. The two SS guards were watching with guns in their hands.

The policeman told Sammy what had happened that morning. Sammy asked if they could stop for a moment at his house. When they got there, he stepped down and walked into the front room, leaving the door open. He looked over the table with the half-filled teacups left from breakfast. He looked at the clock. It was half past three. Father, Mother, and Paula were already buried, and no one had lit a candle for them. Slowly, methodically, Sammy cleaned off the table and put the candlesticks on it.

"I could see Sammy from the outside," the Jewish policeman later told Mrs. Rawicz. "He put on his skullcap, and started to light the candles. Two for his father, two for his mother, two for his sister. And he prayed. I saw his lips moving. He said *Kaddish* for them."

Kaddish is the prayer for the dead. Father Rosenbaum had always said *Kaddish* for his dead parents, and Sammy had learned the prayer from his father. Now he was the only man left in his family. He stood quietly, looking at the six candles. The Jewish policeman outside saw Sammy slowly shaking his head, as though he'd suddenly remembered something. Then Sammy placed two more candles on the table, took a match and lit them, and prayed.

"The boy knew that he was already dead," the policeman said later. "He lit the candles and said *Kaddish* for himself."

Then Sammy came out, leaving the door open, and quietly sat down on the cart next to the policeman, who was crying. The boy didn't cry. The policeman wiped away the tears with the back of his hand and pulled the reins. But the tears kept coming. The boy didn't say a word. Gently he touched the older man's arm, as if he wanted to comfort him—to forgive him for taking him away. Then they rode out to the clearing in the woods. SS *Führer* Rosenbaum and his "students" were waiting for the little boy.

"About time!" said the SS man.

I told Mrs. Rawicz from Rabka that I had known about the SS police school since 1946. Several years earlier I had given the authorities in Hamburg all the facts and testimony in the case against SS man Wilhelm Rosenbaum. Now there would be testimony for an additional case.

"Where is SS man Rosenbaum now"? she asked.

"Wilhelm Rosenbaum was arrested in 1964 and is now in a prison in Hamburg awaiting trial."

She gave a sigh. "What's the use? They are all dead. And the murderer is alive." She signed the affidavit. "It makes no sense."

No tombstone bears Sammy Rosenbaum's name. No one might have remembered him if the woman from Rabka had not come into my office. But every year, one day in June, I light two candles for him and say *Kaddish*.

Chapter 20

THE KILLERS
OF GALICIA

[Nowhere else have the Jews suffered so much for so long as in my native land of Galicia, traditionally the land of pogroms. Galicia was the eastern outpost of the Austro-Hungarian monarchy, situated along the western border of Czarist Russia; later it became part of the Polish Republic; today it belongs to the Ukrainian Soviet Socialist Republic. In an area about the size of Indiana, there lived about 3.5 million people, among them 800,000 Jews.

As a boy I often listened as my maternal grandfather told us children many stories about the pogroms—sad and wistful stories that often had a bitterly ironic twist. I remember the story about Grandfather's Jewish friend who ran the village pub in a small place in Galicia populated by Ukraninian peasants and a few Jews. One of the best customers was the local priest, who loved his *schnapps* but didn't like to pay for it. One Saturday night, when the priest was asked to pay his weekly bill, he said he had no money and left the key to the church as security. He promised to pay on Sunday, when he would get money from the peasants. Then he staggered home.

On Sunday morning the peasants came to attend Mass and couldn't get into the church. They woke up the priest.

"The dirty Jew at the village pub has locked you out. Go get the key!" he told them.

The enraged peasants marched to the tavern, beat the Jewish

owner half-dead, broke everything, got drunk, and celebrated Sunday by carrying out a small pogrom.

Life was hard for the Jews in Galicia, but they loved the country. There was an abundance of fruit and vegetables, of meat and poultry, of butter and eggs. A family could live well for $10 a month. Some lucky ones had "rich" relatives in America, who sent them a five-dollar bill every month. The spiritual climate of the oppressed Jewish minority was exhilarating. The Jews, most of whom lived in the towns, escaped into a world of learning, of books, music. About 6000 Jews lived in my native town of Buczacz. Even poor people saved all their money to send the children to the local *Gymnasium,* a secondary school in which we learned Latin and Greek. Between the two World Wars more than 200 young people from Buczacz went to the university or a technical college in Lwow or Warsaw. Many scientists, artists, musicians, and writers came from the area. Samuel Joseph Agnon, the Israeli poet who was co-laureate of the Nobel Prize for Literature in 1966, was born in Buczacz.

After the beginning of the Second World War. all the Jews in Poland suffered, but the Jews in Galicia suffered the most. During the Soviet occupation, from September 1939 until June 1941, many Jews were arrested as bourgeoisie or members of the intelligentsia; or because they were Zionists or owned property. Many Poles and Ukrainians were also arrested as "nationalists." Unfortunately there were some Jewish commissars among the Soviet officials. After Hitler invaded the Soviet Union on June 22, 1941, the Soviets left Galicia in a great hurry. Instead of taking along the people they had imprisoned—Jews, Poles, Ukrainians—the Soviets shot most of them. Naturally, Ukrainian agitators told the peasants that "the Jews shot your people," which led to new outbreaks of anti-Semitism. The vanguard of the invading German armies were units made up of pro-German Ukrainians who, for revenge, started a wave of pogroms. I knew Jews who had been in Soviet prisons, had managed to escape, and were later killed by Ukrainians "because they killed our people." Either side the Jews were on was the wrong side.

Early in 1942, at the Wannsee Conference in Berlin, the Nazis decided to make occupied Poland (the "General Government") the center of their genocidal activities. The 3.5 million Jews of Poland would be killed in their own homeland, with the consent and sometimes the cooperation of a great many Polish fellow citizens. Poland was the ideal country in which to set up the death camps. The SS and the Gestapo could rely on voluntary helpers who had been brought up in the East-European tradition of brutal anti-Semitism.

In none of the other occupied countries (Czechoslovakia, Belgium, Holland, Denmark, Norway, France, Italy, Greece, Yugoslavia) would most of the native population cooperate with the executioners. Even in Austria and Germany relatively few people among the civilian population knew the whole truth about the death camps, although many knew a little. On the whole, the dark secrets were well kept.

In Poland there were no secrets. The trains that transported the freight cars full of victims to the extermination camps appeared in the official railroad schedules. The Polish population knew about the concentration camps. They saw the wretched prisoners in their striped dungarees as they were taken to work. They complained about the stench from the chimneys of the crematoriums in the vicinity of their houses.

Modern slavery was introduced in Galicia in 1941 when the Germans moved in. A minor Gestapo member or a low-ranking SS man knew that in Galicia he could pillage and plunder, torture and kill, and there would be no questions asked. Even the Nazis had to stop some of their own criminals. The govenor of Lwow, SS *Führer* Lasch, was arrested because he had confiscated too much Jewish property for himself.

In my private files I have a photostat of a bill that reads "6 ropes @ 8.80 zloty" and, underneath, "Paid." Six ropes for the twelve members of the Jewish Council in Lwow, who were executed on September 1, 1942, by order of SS *Oberscharführer* Oskar Waltke, head of the Gestapo's Jewish Affairs Section in Lwow. Waltke, who was tried in Hannover, in November 1962, cynically denied everything when I presented in court photographs that had been taken secretly at the execution of my friends in the Polish underground. I also presented the bill for the ropes. With incredible cynicism, Waltke's boss, *Obersturmführer* Leitmayer, had sent the bill to the new members of the Jewish Council. The successors of the dead men paid—knowing that they would soon be executed too. Waltke was finally sentenced to eight years in prison.

There was no law in Galicia except the law of the SS. After the German invasion, the Jews from all the villages and small towns were concentrated in ghettos in the larger cities. The native Ukrainian population cooperated actively with the Gestapo and the SS. Many Ukrainian auxiliary policemen were even more brutal than the SS. (In France, where the Germans were often unable to distinquish Jews from Frenchmen, the Gestapo imported Ukrainians, who found the French Jews for them.)

In Galicia the persecution of the Jews was carried out with incredible cynicism. In some cities the Jews had to pay for the bullets with which they were shot; we have proof of this. The brutality of the SS in Galicia surpasses everything the Nazis did elsewhere. I have spent years tracing the crimes in Galicia. A two-line news item in *Jüdische Rundschau,* a small magazine published in Basel, Switzerland, which I saw in the spring of 1958, started me on a search through a huge tangle of crimes. The scope of the forthcoming Galicia trial will surpass the Auschwitz trial in Frankfurt am Main.]

The 1958 news item in *Jüdische Rundschau* said that an SS man named Richard Dyga had been arrested in Waldshut, a small town in Baden-Württemberg.

The name Dyga brought back to me the memory of a scene that had happened on the morning of July 19, 1944, in the Lwow-Janowska concentration camp. I took the phone, called Waldshut, and asked for the prosecutor in charge of the case against Herr Dyga. He was Dr. Wilhelm Angelberger, who turned out to be a man who understood such problems and had the energy to cope with them. I asked him how Dyga had been arrested, and he said it had really been by mistake. A woman in Hannover had accused a certain man called Dyga of war crimes. This Dyga had turned out to be the wrong man, but while the Germans checked the case, they found evidence against SS man Richard Dyga. I told the prosecutor that with my own eyes I'd seen Dyga commit murder at least once.

"Do you think you would recognize Dyga today, fourteen years later?"

"I believe I would."

Dr. Angelberger asked me to come to Waldshut. At the prison there, we walked down a long corridor on the second floor. Windows looked down on the prison courtyard below. It was a dark winter day. A dozen prisoners walked in a circle. All wore short overcoats and woolen caps. I glanced down for a second and said: "Dyga is the third from the left. But tell him to take off his glasses. He didn't wear glasses when I knew him."

"Let's go to my office," Dr. Angelberger said.

Dyga was brought in. He hadn't changed; the same blank eyes, the same vicious mouth. He was a *Volksdeutscher* (expatriate German) from Silesia, who spoke Polish. Like other *Volksdeutsche* from the Sudeten land, Slovakia, and Yugoslavia, he had an un-German, Slavic name and a strong inferiority complex that made him want to prove himself 150 per cent German. This he had done by being especially brutal to the prisoners.

Dr. Angelberger asked Dyga whether he knew me.

"No."

"Of course Herr Dyga doesn't know me," I said. "There were thousands of us prisoners, and an SS man didn't look us in the face. But perhaps Herr Dyga will remember how we escaped together, prisoners and SS men, from Lwow toward the west, how we set up Construction Staff 'Venus.'"

He smiled. "Yes. We even had another one called 'Merkur,' I think."

"That's right. I'm going to remind you of a few more things, Herr Dyga. Be sure to interrupt me if I say something that isn't true."

He nodded.

I said: "I remember the final rollcall at the Janowska concentration camp, on July 19, 1944. You told the prisoners that those unable to march would be taken on a wagon. Several horsedrawn vehicles stood behind the barracks."

Again Dyga nodded.

"An old Jewish woman raised her hand. Her legs were badly swollen. Her husband, next to me, said to her: 'Don't tell them! Be quiet!' but she said: 'I cannot walk, I haven't got the strength.' . . . She told you she had pains in her legs and you took her out of the group to the spot behind the barracks where the wagons stood, and then we heard a shot. I saw the woman fall. I took the old man in my arms and pressed my hand to his mouth so he wouldn't scream, because you would have shot him too."

"What do you have to say, Herr Dyga?" said the prosecutor.

"*Herr Staatsanwalt*, that woman was unable to walk, so I—" Dyga stopped in the middle of the sentence. He realized he'd said too much.

"Herr Dyga, you've already made a confession, right now."

Dyga protested that he'd confessed nothing.

"Herr Dyga," I said, "this is only the beginning. I have many other things to tell you. My memory is better than yours. . . ."

That was the beginning of what will be one of the biggest trials in the history of German justice, the Galicia trial. I stayed in Waldshut three days. The confrontation with Dyga had brought back to me all the details of what I had seen. The case is particularly close to my heart: I lost my whole family in Galicia.

Dr. Angelberger provided me with a room and a secretary. For three long days I dictated—names, dates, locations, events. I remembered sixty-eight names, with some mass murderers among them: Blum, Kolonko, Heinisch, Lohnert, Wobke, Rokita, Gebauer. Dr. Angelberger introduced me to *Kriminalmeister* Faller, a very able German police inspector. After my return to Vienna we corresponded further. From our files I put together material concerning Lwow. I began to collect the testimony of witnesses I had known. They in turn found other witnesses. I submitted a whole album of photographs. Many of the pictures had been found after the liquidation of the Lwow concentration camp. For some reason, quite a few SS men liked to be photographed next to people they had executed. I have photos of SS executioners standing proudly next to the dangling bodies of two men they had just hanged. There are other even worse photographs. These pictures were useful: now the criminals had faces, and many witnesses, seeing these pictures, remembered vividly what had happened to them. During the years after 1958 I collected from eyewitnesses more than 800 affidavits. Thirty-six of the sixty-eight criminals I had remembered were eventually tracked down. Half of them are now in jail waiting to be tried.

The chief defendants will not be in the dock when the Galicia trial begins, however, SS *Brigadeführer* Dr. Otto Gustav Wächter, the former police chief of Vienna, and his deputy, SS *Brigadeführer* Friedrich Katzmann from Darmstadt, are dead. Wachter was one of the five Nazi agents who planned and carried out the assassination of Austrian Chancellor Dr. Englebert Dollfuss on July 25, 1934. At the beginning of the Second World War, he was named governor of the Cracow district in Poland, and later he was sent to Lwow. I saw him early in 1942, in Lwow ghetto. He was personally in charge on August 15, 1942, when four thousand elderly people in the ghetto were rounded up and sent to the railway station. My mother was among them.

Wächter escaped after the war with the help of *ODESSA* and was given refuge in a religious college in Rome by Slovak priests who didn't know his identity. His escape had been planned well; he even took his archives along from Bavaria. In 1949, Wächter became very sick and wasn't expected to live long. He told the people in Rome who he was, asked to see his wife, who lived as Lotte Pohl in a nearby refugee camp, and asked to see a priest. He was given the sacraments by Bishop Alois Hudal, the Austrian rector of the German Catholic Church in Rome, and died. He is buried in Rome. Later, an Austrian aristocrat who occasionally helped me asked Bishop Hudal to release Wächter's files. The Bishop refused.

Wächter's chief of police was SS *Brigadeführer* Friedrich Katzmann. When he came into the Lwow concentration camp, we knew that soon thousands of people would be sent to their deaths. He was a small man with a pale, anemic face and hard, thin lips. His eyes were dark and lusterless. No one ever saw him smile. He wrote a long report on *Einsatz Reinhard,* the action that killed 2.5 million people in Poland as retribution for the killing of Reinhard Heydrich by Czech partisans in 1942. At the end of his report, Katzmann writes: "Galicia, which once had 800,000 Jews is now *judenrein* [cleared of Jews]." End of report.

After the war Katzmann disappeared. I followed up many clues, but did not find him. In the fall of 1956, I received an anonymous letter from Darmstadt. The writer suggested that I look for a salesman in Germany called "Albrecht," who was said to be a vicious Nazi criminal. There are many salesmen in Germany known by this name, and I threw the letter away. Three years later, when I talked to *Kriminalmeister* Faller, he mentioned Katzmann, and said he had reason to believe that Katzmann was hiding somewhere in Germany under the alias Bruno Albrecht.

"In Darmstadt," I said, instinctively, and I told him about the anonymous letter. A few days later, Faller informed me that "Bruno Albrecht," a salesman, had died on September 19, 1957, at the Alice Hospital in Darmstadt. Told by the doctors that he didn't have much time, he asked to see a priest and confessed that he was the former SS *Brigadeführer* Friedrich Katzmann. He asked to be buried under his real name—just like his boss, Otto Wächter.

Compared to Wächter and Katzmann, the criminals mentioned in this chapter are only small fry. I remember SS *Untersturmführer* Wilhaus, commander of Lwow-Janowska concentration camp. He was a perfect sadist. He lived in a house inside the camp with his wife and his daughter, a blonde six-year-old named Heike. One morning several Jewish laborers were putting up a building near his house. Eyewitnesses saw Wilhaus on the balcony of his villa with his wife and Heike. He pointed at the masons as they bent down, working on the brick wall. They must have reminded Wilhaus of the figures used as targets on the shooting range, for suddenly he took his gun, aimed carefully, and fired. A man fell. Heike thought this was a wonderful game. She clapped her hands. Papa aimed carefully again and hit another target, killing a man. Then he handed his gun to his wife and told her to try. She did. Down went the third Jewish mason.

Wilhaus' various brutalities are detailed clinically in the manuscript of a book written by the late Professor Tadeusz Zaderecki during those years. Professor Zaderecki, a Polish Christian, had studied Judaism, spoke Hebrew, and was familiar with the Jewish community in Lwow. He had many Jewish friends and suffered deeply for them. When the German atrocities began, Professor Zaderecki decided to keep a record of all the things he saw and heard; this was to be his monument to the dying Jews of his beloved city. Professor Zaderecki often slipped furtively into the ghetto, talked to the Jews, and secretly made notes. His book contains dates, names, locations. The Jews themselves had no time to record the brutalities; survival was a full-time job. Professor Zaderecki is dead, but the Polish underground saved his manuscript. I had it translated and submitted it to the prosecutor in Waldshut. It has been of great value in the prosecution of SS criminals in Lwow.

From the manuscript, I learned why Wilhaus had suddenly been transferred from his post as commander of the concentration camp. The office of the Lwow-Janowska concentration camp was in touch with various firms in Lwow that delivered food, building materials, coal, barbed wire, and other necessities. An employee of one of these firms was a Polish engineer who was a member of the Polish underground. One of his cousins, a Polish woman, was a prisoner at the concentration camp. The underground knew all about Wilhaus' brutalities. A special meeting of the underground cell decided that Wilhaus would have to die. Some members volunteered to shoot him, but this might have led to terrifying reprisals. Then the engineer remembered that his firm had several letters from the office of the concentration camp, complete with official seal and Wilhaus' signature. One of the underground members, an expert penman, wrote a letter and signed Wilhaus' name. "Wilhaus" asked the Fuhrer's Chancellery in Berlin for a transfer to the Eastern front. It ended with "As a German and an SS man, I feel this is my duty to my Führer and my *Vaterland*."

A few weeks later, Wilhaus was summoned to the Chancellery, where he found himself, much to his surprise, sitting across from *Reichsleiter* Martin Bormann. The *Reichsleiter* told Wilhaus that the Führer had been much pleased with Wilhaus' letter. Yes, said Bormann, the *Untersturmführer* had given a commendable example of *Pflichterfüllung*—"fulfillment of duty." The Führer had kindly consented to Wilhaus' request.

"Here are your travel orders to the Eastern front," said Bormann. "Congratulations. *Heil Hitler!*"

"*Heil Hitler!*" said SS *Untersturmführer* Wilhaus, and staggered out.

He fell in action near Danzig, late in 1944. I ultimately discovered his wife in Saarbrucken, and notified the German authorities. They questioned her about her shooting exercises in the Lwow concentration camp against living targets. Frau Hilde Wilhaus is now in prison in Stuttgart, waiting to be tried.

At the Eastern Railroad Repair Works in Lwow in 1943, there were always a few hundred Jewish forced laborers. One of them, a quiet little man named Chasin, worked in the stable next to the German canteen. Chasin's job was to take care of a few horses. He was given special permission to sleep in the stable. Chasin's wife had been killed in the spring of 1943 during one of the SS annihilation actions in the ghetto. Their eight-year-old son escaped and was hidden by neighbors. Somehow word was sent to Chasin that the child was alive in the ghetto. Chasin obtained a pass to the ghetto and smuggled his son into the Ostbahn Works. There was a big oat bin in the stable, a sort of wooden crib with a lid on top. Chasin put his boy into the crib and drilled a few holes in its sides so that the child could breath. The boy stayed there almost three months. Only at night, after the Germans had gone home did Chasin permit his child to come out for a breath of fresh air. Eugen Jetter, the German inspector in charge of personnel, knew about the child, and so did other Germans, but they kept the secret.

One day in the summer of 1943, *Oberinspektor* Peter Arnolds discovered the secret. Later I was told that a Polish woman working in the kitchen, who brought a little food to the child once in a while, had inadvertently mentioned it to Arnolds. He was much feared among the prisoners. If a forced laborer didn't greet him with proper respect, Arnolds would slap the man's face. Most of the German officials at the Railroad Works treated us correctly and despised Arnolds, but there was nothing they could do about him.

Arnolds alerted the SS guards at the Janowska concentration camp and told them about the boy in the stable. SS *Scharführer* Schonbach, a member of the camp's special execution commando, came to the Repair Works. I saw him meet Arnolds in front of the German canteen.

I ran into the stable. Chasin stood weeping next to the body of his son, which had been thrown on top of the manure heap behind the stable. Chasin told me that Arnolds and Schonbach had come into the stable, and Arnolds had opened the crib and pointed to the child. Schonbach took the boy out, lifted him up, and told the father to turn around. He shot the child, threw the body on the manure heap, and said to Chasin: "Throw one of the horse-blankets over the body. Quick!" Arnolds and Schonbach stayed two hours at the canteen and got drunk. My immediate boss, *Oberinspektor* Adolf Kohlrautz, later told me: "Of course, Arnolds had to get drunk to forget the whole thing."

For years after the war I'd been looking for Arnolds, without success. In January 1958, when I had some business in Düsseldorf, Cologne, and Frankfurt, I discovered accidentally that Peter Arnolds was now a high-ranking official of the German Federal Railroads in Paderborn. I notified the court in Paderborn, and the district attorney there asked me to come there and confront Herr Arnolds.

The confrontation took place in the office of the district attorney. I accused Arnolds of being responsible for the death of the little Jewish boy. Arnolds didn't deny it. Finally he said: "Herr Wiesenthal, maybe we could come to an agreement in this matter."

"Herr Arnolds, there can be no agreement when the death of a child is the issue."

Then Arnolds told the district attorney an involved story. It wasn't really he who had told the SS about the child in the crib. It had been done by one Schulze, the manager of the German canteen. Conveniently for Arnolds, Schulze was dead and could not defend himself. I found another key witness, *Inspektor* Eugen Jetter, one of the German officials at the Lwow Repair Works. Jetter admitted that he had known about the little boy in the crib, as had many others, and had kept his mouth shut. He told the district attorney that it was common knowledge at the Repair Works that Arnolds had handed the boy over to his murderer. After his testimony, Jetter, who now lives in Stuttgart, began receiving anonymous phone calls at night. Strange voices called him *"Judenknecht"* (slave of the Jews) and hung up.

Reluctantly the authorities had to suspend the case against Arnolds. He is lucky. Of the twelve hundred Jews who worked at the Lwow Repair Works at the time, only three survived—and I have not been able to find the other two, who might serve as witnesses against him. SS man Schonbach, however, was arrested by *Kriminalmeister* Faller. Schonbach admitted at once that he'd shot the little boy. He is now in jail.

And there was Richard Rokita, the deputy camp commander in Lwow who later went to Tarnopol, also in Galicia, in furtherance of his career as murderer. He killed several hundred or perhaps a thousand Jews there; he probably doesn't know how many himself. We called Rikita "the friendly murderer." He never beat anyone, never screamed at prisoners. He shot them politely. He was something of an artist. He had played the violin in his native Kattowitz, Upper Silesia (now in Poland), and he loved music. When he came to the Lwow concentration camp, the first thing he did was to organize a special camp orchestra. There were some first-rate musicians among the prisoners. Rokita assigned Sigmund Schlechter, a well-known Jewish composer from Lwow, to write a "death tango." The camp orchestra played the death tango while executions were carried out. Executions with musical accompaniment are often carried out on the operatic stage, but at Lwow they fired real bullets while the music played.

Once Rokita walked through the camp and saw an old, weak Jew. The Jew saluted. Rokita greeted him amiably, threw a piece of paper on the ground, and told the old man to pick up the paper. The Jew bent down, and Rokita shot him. As I said, a friendly murderer.

Rokita was high on my list, but I couldn't find him. I didn't know whether he was alive. If he was, he would probably again be a musician.

In the fall of 1958 I took a train to Geneva. In the dining car, I sat across from a Danish officer. We started to talk. It turned out that we had both been at the Grossrosen concentration camp at the same time in 1944. After the war he had been in the British Zone of Germany. We talked about the old days and I mentioned Rokita. The Danish officer asked what Rokita looked like.

"He had a broad face, big eyes, and pouting lips. He played the violin quite well."

"That's strange," said the Danish officer. "I believe it was in the Hamburg officers' club in 1947 or 1948—there was a German band playing. Of course, I cannot be sure—it's such a long time ago. But I believe there was a violin player who looked like that."

I made a report to Prosecutor Angelberger. We began to look for Rokita in northern Germany, but couldn't find him. On my next visit to Waldshut, I discussed the case with *Kriminalmeister* Faller. He told me he'd made inquiries among the musicians' unions in Hamburg, Lübeck, and Bremen. There was no Rokita among the members. Then he'd talked to musicians and described Rokita. One day a musician came to see him. The musician knew a man corresponding to the description, but his name was not Rokita. He was called Domagala.

"Then I began to look for Domagala," said Faller. "No luck; no such name on the lists of the musicians' unions. The police didn't have the name either."

I had an idea. "Let's try the *Krankenkasse* [government health insurance office]. Everybody likes to carry health insurance today— even murderers."

That night Faller called, "You were right. There is a man called Domagala in Hamburg, and he does carry health insurance. He's no longer a musician. He's a night watchman. I hope to find him tonight. I'll let you know."

Two hours later, *Kriminalmeister* Faller stopped a night watchman in a Hamburg factory who was known as "Domagala."

The man admitted at once that his name had been Rokita and that he had been in Lwow and Tarnopol. He told Faller that he no longer played the violin. It was a smart idea for him to take a job as night watchman. There was little chance of his being recognized by one of his former victims. It might have worked if he hadn't tried to carry health insurance. He may need it. He was arrested and thrown into prison, but he got sick and had to be temporarily released for medical care.

The massacres at Stanislau form one of the most moving chapters in the tragedy of Galicia. In 1939 Stanislau had almost 100,000 inhabitants. Half were Jews, the other half Poles and Ukrainians. According to the schedule of *Einsatz Reinhard*, German-ruled Poland was to be *judenrein*—"cleansed of Jews"—by the end of 1942. In Stanislau, the schedule was carried out to the minute.

On October 12, 1941, the Jewish districts were surrounded and approximately twenty thousand Jews were driven together near the Jewish cemetery. Everybody had to hand over money, jewelry, fur coats, and finally clothes. The naked Jews were driven in front of two large ditches (*Panzergraben*—tank traps) and shot with submachine guns. According to a bill of indictment ultimately handed down in Salzburg against the SS men in charge of this crime, two brothers named Johann and Wilhelm Mauer:

> The action began in the early morning and lasted until darkness. Motorized vehicles were posted around the cemetery and their lights illuminated the liquidation. At least 12,000 Jews were murdered. The rest were driven back, stark naked, into the city. . . .

The brothers Mauer were among the worst sadists in Stanislau. They were *Volksdeutsche* from Poland and had all the complexes of such "inferior" Germans. The few survivors of Stanislau told terrible stories about the brothers, but unfortunately they gave their name as Maurer, with an extra *r*. Consequently Prosecutor Sichting in Ludwigsburg, who investigated the case, was looking for two men named Maurer.

In 1963 I met Sichting, who told me that his investigators had found lots of Maurers but none who had been born in Poland. I suggested that the name of the brothers might be Mauer instead. The Prosecutor asked me to make a search in Austria. I contacted a committee that keeps track of *Volksdeutsche* in that country. Yes, two brothers, Johann and Wilhelm Mauer, were in Salzburg working for the Evangelical Auxiliary Service, a charitable organization. Johann was "refugee adviser"; Wilhelm was in charge of a youth home—perfect jobs for two mass murderers. One of my helpers went to the Salzburg police and found out that the brothers had been born in Poland. He brought back a picture. Looking at it, I remembered that I had actually encountered Johann Mauer after the war, when he'd worked for a Protestant charity and I was doing something for a Jewish refugee organization. Unfortunately I hadn't then known about his past.

I checked with Sichting, and submitted all the material against the brothers to the district attorney in Salzburg. The arrest of the Mauers caused a local sensation. The trial against them, early in 1966, became one of the most scandalous chapters in the annals of Austria's postwar justice.

It seemed almost impossible to form a jury, so many people asked to be excused on account of sickness or for other reasons. Strange things happened in the crowded courtroom of the beautiful festival city of Salzburg. The audience applauded the defendants and laughed when Jewish witnesses were sworn on the Bible. All witnesses recognized the brothers; the testimony was very convincing. After many hours of deliberation, the jury admitted that the defendants had committed murder, but ruled that they had acted under duress, executing orders from above. The court had to acquit the defendants. But the presiding judge informed them, in accordance with the Austrian penal code, that the verdict of the jury was "an obvious error," and therefore there would be a new trial against them. Until then, the defendants would remain in prison.

The verdict at Salzburg and the anti-Semitic behavior of the courtroom audience created shock waves throughout Austria. *Wiener Zeitung* spoke of a "shameful verdict." Catholic and Socialist students marched through Vienna carrying placards reading *Austria, National Park for Nazi Criminals.* I didn't help matters when I discovered—too late, unfortunately—that the foreman of the jury had been an illegal Austrian Nazi and an SA man. The new trial of the Mauer brothers took place in Vienna in November, 1966. Johann Mauer was sentenced to eight years in prison, and Wilhelm Mauer to twelve.

Chapter 21

THE THIRTY-SIX RIGHTEOUS

While Franz Murer directed the annihilation of the 80,000 Jews of Wilna in 1942, another Austrian happened to be present. His name was Anton Schmid, from Vienna. He was forty-two, a *Feldwebel* (sergeant) in the regular *Wehrmacht*. Like many other Austrians, he had been drafted into the *Wehrmacht*.

Schmid was not the drill-sergeant type. He was a quiet man who did a lot of thinking and said very little; he had few friends among his army buddies. Only one picture exists of him. It shows a thoughtful face, with soft, sad eyes, dark hair, and a small mustache. His army unit was in Wilna during the worst months of Murer's extermination activities.

Anton Schmid was a devout Catholic who suffered deeply when he saw other people suffer. He was also a man of exceptional courage. His story might never have become known except for various pieces of testimony in our files on Murer. Among the 250 survivors of the Wilna ghetto, there are several whose lives were saved by Anton Schmid. They later told me his story.

Many Germans in Wilna secretly condemned Murer's atrocities, but they dared not do anything. Schmid decided it was his Christian duty to help the oppressed Jews. He became a secret one-man relief organization. He would slip into the ghetto, at great personal risk, bringing food to starving Jews. He would carry milk bottles in his pockets and deliver them for babies. He knew that thousands of Jews were hiding elsewhere in Wilna, and he acted as a courier between them and their friends in the ghetto. He carried messages, bread, drugs. He even dared to steal *Wehrmacht* guns, which he gave to Jewish resistance fighters.

"He did all these things without ever waiting for anyone to thank him," a survivor told me. "He did it out of the goodness of his heart. To us in the ghetto the frail, quiet man in his *Feldwebel's* uniform was a sort of saint."

The inevitable happened. The Gestapo discovered, during the first days of April 1942, that Schmid had tried to smuggle five Jews out of the ghetto and bring them to the nearby Ponary forest, where they hoped to hide. He was arrested. In the morning a German court-martial sentenced him to death.

Two hours later Schmid wrote to his wife, Stefi, and his daughter:

> Received your two letters. . . . Am glad that all is well with you. I must tell you what fate awaits me, but please, be strong when you read on. . . . I have just been sentenced to death by a court-martial. There is nothing one can do except appeal for mercy, which I've done. It won't be decided until noon, but I believe it will be turned down. All similar appeals have been turned down.
>
> But, my dears, cheer up. I am resigned to my fate. It has been decided from Above—by our dear Lord—and nothing can be done about it. I am so quiet that I can hardly believe it myself. Our dear God willed it that way, and He made me strong. I hope He will give you strength, too.
>
> I must tell you how it happened. There were so many Jews here who were driven together by the Lithuanian soldiers and were shot on a meadow outside the city—from 2000 to 3000 people at one time. They always threw the small children against the trees—can you imagine? I had orders (though I didn't like it) to take over the *Versprengtenstelle* [dispersal place] where 140 Jews worked. They asked me to get them away from here. I let myself be persuaded—you know I have a soft heart. I couldn't think it over. I helped them, which was very bad, according to my judges. It will be hard for you, my dear Stefi and Gertha, but forgive me: I acted as a human being, and didn't want to hurt anyone.

When you read this letter, I will no longer be on this earth. I won't be able to write you any more. But be sure that we shall meet again in a better world with our dear Lord. I wrote an earlier letter on April 1, enclosing the picture of Gertha. This letter I'll give to the priest. . . .

Four days later, on April 13, Anton Schmid was executed. He died with five Jews he had tried to save. He was buried in a small soldiers' cemetery in Wilna. Two days later, the priest, Father Fritz Kropp, sent Schmid's last letter to his widow in Vienna:

Monday, the 13th, at 3 P.M. your dear husband had to depart [wrote Kropp]. I was with him in the last hours. . . . He prayed and remained strong to the very end. His last wish was to tell you that you too must remain strong. . . .

The name of Anton Schmid appeared in several diaries of Jews who were later killed in the ghetto of Wilna. All describe his kindness and courage. A few of the survivors remember him well. I began to collect their testimony. One day my friend Dr. Mark Dvorzecki from Tel-Aviv, whose testimony about Wilna during the Eichmann trial had helped convince the Austrians that Murer would have to be tried, came to see me in Vienna. He gave me the address of Anton Schmid's widow.

I went to see Frau Schmid, a tired, elderly woman who runs a small store and has very little money. Her married daughter Gertha lives with her. They told me that life had not been easy for them in 1942, when it became known in their district that *Feldwebel* Schmid had been executed because he'd tried to save some Jews. Some neighbors even threatened Frau Schmid, the widow of a "traitor," and told her to go elsewhere. A few people broke the windows in her home.

I asked Frau Schmid whether she had a wish. Yes, she said; she would like to visit the grave of her husband in Wilna. This was not easy to arrange, for until 1965 Wilna was closed to civilian tourists by the Russians. I told the story to the Soviet Ambassador in Vienna and asked him to get permission for the family to go to Wilna. I said the Documentation Center would finance the trip. On October 29, 1965, Frau Schmid and her daughter and son-in-law took the train to Minsk and from there they took a plane to Wilna. The Documentation Center has arranged that a tombstone be placed on the grave of Anton Schmid, with the inscription

HERE RESTS A MAN WHO THOUGHT IT WAS MORE IMPORTANT TO HELP HIS FELLOW MEN THAN TO LIVE.

Frau Schmid showed me an earlier letter from her husband, dated April 1, 1942. He was already under investigation by the Gestapo. "Everybody must die someday," he had written. "One can die as an executioner or as a helper [*Helfer*]. I want to die as a helper."

An old Jewish legend, often cited in Hassidic teachings, has it that there are thirty-six righteous men on earth, unknown to others and themselves unaware of their mission. The legend goes back to Isaiah 50: "Glory to those who trust in Him." Him in Hebrew is written LO; these two letters, according to the Hebrew system of numeration, in which certain letters also stand for certain numbers, stand for the number 36. Also, according to the Babylonian Talmud, "The world has not less than thirty-six pious men who receive daily the face of God." The thirty-six righteous men, according to these teachings, are mostly poor, simple, ordinary people—workers, farmers, water-bearers, and so on—but "the world is supported by them." They are "the vessels into which the suffering of the whole world flows. . . . If even one of them were not here, the world would perish with suffering." They never make themselves known to other people. They appear at times of dire need, during great catastrophes, perform their duty, and die.

Chapter 22

THE OTHER SIDE
OF THE MOON

[One day in April 1945, shortly before the end of the war in Europe, a transport from Hungary arrived at the Mauthausen concentration camp. Most of the people were weak and emaciated; it seemed that they had already been written off by the camp management, for they were sent directly to the death block where I then lay.

Among the new arrivals was a noted Hungarian rabbi. It was rumored that he'd succeeded in smuggling a small Hebrew prayer book into the concentration camp. I admired the rabbi for his courage. He must have known that the SS punished anyone who was caught bringing in any possessions, even an old toothbrush or a piece of broken mirror.

The rabbi came into our room the next day, walking from bed to bed. Many of the starved people were too weak even to sit up. I expected the rabbi to talk to them and give them a little comfort. Instead he said he would lend his prayer book to each man for fifteen minutes. The "lending fee" would be one fourth of a man's daily soup ration. You must realize that one bowl of watery liquid was all we got in twenty-four hours. Yet many were glad to give up part of their meager food ration for fifteen minutes with the prayer book. It was a small, black book, and they would hold it between their palms. They were too weak to read, but the book brought back memories of their childhood, the Friday-night service at the syna-

288

gogue, the voice of the cantor. The little book would take them back into the living room where the candles were lit for the Sabbath, and a delicious smell drifted in from the kitchen. One of the dying men in our room was a judge who had converted to Catholicism, but now he too rented the little book and spent fifteen precious minutes with his memories, and then he gave the rabbi one quarter of his soup ration.

Actually, the rabbi died before anyone else. The excessive quantity of soup was too much for his weakened digestive system. He was taken away, but people hardly noticed it. I wondered what had happened to the prayer book.

After our liberation we were taken to the rest camp of Bindermichl in Linz, where we were under the care of American doctors. The Americans built a small synagogue inside the rest camp. For the opening service, in April 1946, a Torah was brought from America, and an old rabbi from there arrived to say the first prayers.

I told my friends I was not going to attend the service. I couldn't tell them that I didn't want to see a rabbi ever again. I couldn't forget the greedy man who had bartered faith for food. Instead of comforting the dying he had filled his stomach with their soup. I had had enough of such men.

That night Rabbi Silver came to see me. He was a small man who wore an American Army uniform without insignia. He had a small white beard, and his bright eyes shone with great kindness. He must have been at least seventy-five, but his mind was sharp and his voice was youthful. He told me he'd been born in the Ukraine, the country of pogroms, and had emigrated as a boy to America, the country of hope.

He put his hand on my shoulder. "So they tell me you're angry with God?" he said in Yiddish, and he smiled at me.

I said not with God, but with one of his servants, and I told him what had happened.

He kept smiling. "And that's all you have to tell me?"

"Isn't that enough, Rabbi?" I asked.

"*Du Dummer* [you silly man]," he said. "So you look only at the bad man who took something from the good ones. Why don't you look instead at the good men who gave something to the bad one?" He touched me with his outstretched palm and left.

I went to the service the next day. Ever since I have tried to remember that there are two sides to every problem, although sometimes it is as difficult to see the other side as it is to see the other side
of the moon.]

1

I often think of old Rabbi Silver when I am faced with a complex
problem that offers no simple answers. I thought of him one morning in September 1965, when Frau C sat across from me. She wore a
tweed suit and carried a small overnight bag. She'd spent the whole
night on the train from Germany. Her hair was disheveled. She'd
taken a taxi directly from the station to my office.

"I had to see you, Herr Wiesenthal. I couldn't wait. I need your
help in my restitution case. And I must talk to someone who believes
me. No one does, because my story is so hard to believe."

Her story is true, though. I later checked all the facts carefully.
Frau C is the Jewish wife of a former German SS general.

She was sixty when she came to me, and there were deep lines of
suffering in her face. But I believed her when she told me that she'd
once been a pretty girl—and a pretty wild one too. She had inherited her temperament from her mother, an actress in Vienna. She
became a minor actress herself, was playing small parts in Munich
in 1934 when she met *him*—we'll call him Hans. Their love affair
was passionate and carefree. They agreed not to talk about the
future. She knew that he went regularly to some sort of office, but
she didn't inquire too closely about it. She was just grateful that he
was working; a great many people were unemployed in Munich and
in the rest of Germany in 1934. Only when the doctor told her that
she was going to have a child did she begin to ask a few questions.
Hans took her in his arms and told her she must not cry. He had to
make a confession: he was with the political section of the SS. That
was the "office."

"I didn't cry," Frau C told me. "I was terrified because now I, too,
had to make a confession. I had told him my father was dead. I'd
lied to him. My mother was a Catholic; my father, my *illegitimate*
father, was a Jewish lawyer in Berlin. That meant I was not an

'Aryan,' as he'd thought. I was half Jewish. As an SS man he could never marry me. But Hans refused to concede defeat; he was a wonderful man. He said we could give the child to an SS home and live together unmarried. I said I wanted to bring up the child myself. Hans went to Berlin and talked to my father, who told him that his name appeared on no document in connection with me. That meant that I could pass as an Aryan and we could marry. Actually it wasn't easy, and Hans had to argue for two years until the SS permitted him to marry; I suppose they had their doubts since officially I had no father. But I was blond and I have blue eyes. If I had looked more Jewish, they would never have given their permission."

They were happy with their little girl. They had a large apartment in Munich. Hans was driven in an official car every morning to the Dachau concentration camp, where he was in charge of the political department.

"The most terrible things had not yet happened," continued Frau C. "Hans always managed to avoid those special courses in how to hunt and torture and kill people. Yes, they had such courses even then. But the years went on, and things became worse. Hans saw too much and knew too much. He'd been promoted to SS colonel, and he asked for a transfer to Hamburg. There was a small concentration camp in Neuengamme nearby, and he was put in charge. He thought he would be on the sidelines there, but he was mistaken. Neuengamme was an extermination camp; between 1938 and 1945, 55,000 people from France, Denmark, Norway, the Netherlands, Austria, Belgium, the Soviet Union, and Germany died there. All the transports from Hamburg and the northern part of Germany ended here. Our house was not far from the camp. I tried to help the prisoners in little ways—asked Hans to send some to work in our home and gave them food. Then the Gestapo found out about it and we got orders to move our residence to Hamburg, where they gave us a large apartment. I believe from that time on I was always under surveillance. They knew I wasn't to be trusted."

With the beginning of the Allied bombing attacks that eventually destroyed the inner city of Hamburg, Frau C spent her nights in the air-raid shelter. There she noticed a girl named Esther, who kept apart from the other people and talked to no one.

"I *knew* she was Jewish and I had to help her," Frau C said. "It was like a compulsion. It was also a crazy thing for the wife of a high-ranking SS man to do." She gave a shrug.

The young Jewish woman was very shy and very reluctant to talk to Frau C. A few nights later, after Frau C had brought her a new thermos bottle, having noticed that Esther's was broken, they became friendlier. Esther lived in a tiny room in an attic where some Christian neighbors were trying to conceal her. Her mother had already been taken to Ravensbrück concentration camp, and she knew that *they* would come for her soon. She was terrified because she was expecting a child.

"I took her to my apartment. My husband was away. No matter what happens, I said to myself, her child must be born. The child must live. But one night the Gestapo came for her. I pleaded with them, and they said she could stay at the apartment for the night but at five in the morning she would have to be at Biberhaus, where the transport left for Ravensbrück. After they'd gone, we packed a few things and went to the railroad station. There was a midnight train for Munich. I still had an apartment there. When we got to Munich I realized I needed documents for Esther. I went to Regensburg and stole my sister-in-law's passport. Then I told the people in Munich that Esther was my sister-in-law. Next, I informed my husband that I was pregnant. I explained that I had kept it a secret for a while. I said it was safer in Munich than in Hamburg. Hans was relieved, I think. He'd had much trouble with his SS superiors in Hamburg because I talked too freely."

Hans was very happy about the news. He hoped it would be a boy this time. Their daughter was now six, and lived with her paternal grandmother in a villa in Regensburg. Hans sent his wife beautiful things for the baby; he hoped that everything would go well with her and the child. When Esther's time came, Frau C put her into a private clinic which treated only the wives of high-ranking officers.

"There was only one way of doing it," said Frau C. "I registered Esther under my own name. I sold some jewelry to pay for the doctor and the hospital. My husband couldn't understand why I didn't go to the large SS hospital near Munich where I would have everything free. I explained to him that I wouldn't be happy to give birth to my child in a place which was officially under SS jurisdiction. He understood. The child was born on August 28, a lovely little boy who didn't know that something was very wrong with him: he was a Jew. I took him home while Esther remained in the clinic. I knew I was risking my life, but I didn't care very much; the child was much more important."

She hoped that Esther would soon join them, but there were postnatal complications. The doctor was worried about her. In the meantime Hans had been granted special leave to see his child. He arrived with his friend Weiss, who worked in the headquarters of the Dachau concentration camp. Frau C watched them as they admired the sweet little boy. They lifted him from the cradle and played with the baby and became like little boys themselves.

"If they'd known that the little boy was Jewish . . . I couldn't bear to pursue the thought. Goodness, you should have seen my husband! He was beside himself. Had the child packed in silk and woolens and took him for a ride to Tegernsee. Can you imagine what went on in my heart? I was glad when his leave was over. I hoped Esther would get well and come home soon. But one night they called me from the clinic—and that night she died in my arms. I had to tell the truth to the doctor. He had to report her death, and Esther had been listed under my name! Officially, I had died that night—and there I stood in front of him. He took the phone and called the Gestapo."

The Gestapo came two hours later for Frau C. She tried to talk her way out of the dilemma; said she hadn't known that Esther was Jewish, that she'd cared only about the child, that she wanted to adopt the little boy. They didn't believe a word of it. If she'd wanted a boy so badly, they said she could have adopted one of the illegitimate SS children—that's what the German wife of a good SS man was expected to do. They kept her five days and beat her mercilessly but she stuck to the truth that her husband had not known about it. She was sent to the nearest concentration camp.

"And the child?" I asked.

"They killed him before my eyes. He was just ten weeks old." She sat with her hands in her lap, very tired. "Naturally, they found out all about me—about my Jewish father. Hans had protected him until then. They came for my father, too, and . . . well, you know.

As for my husband, they apparently believed me when I said he was not implicated, for they kept him in his job."

She spent eighteen months in the concentration camp, until she was able to escape to Holland not long before the end of the war. After the war she and her husband were reunited and went back to Munich.

"That was the worst time. The Americans arrested my husband and treated me like a criminal. For them I was the wife of an SS general. The Jews and the concentration-camp people hated me. And the former Nazis despised me because they knew I was Jewish. There was no friend wherever I looked; no one believed me. Even now they still ask me 'Why did you do it?,' but all of them mean different things. The Jews mean why did I marry an SS man? And the Nazis mean why did I help a Jewish woman when I was the wife of an SS *Führer?* And the West German authorities have refused my application for economic restitution although I was a prisoner in the concentration camp. . . . Poor Esther wrote me a letter from the clinic shortly before she died. She predicted exactly what would happen to me. 'No one will have mercy on you. Wherever you turn, you will be hated.' "

"And your husband?"

"After the scandal became known, some of his *Kameraden* told him that he should have shot me. He didn't shoot me. Never uttered a single word of blame. In fact, he and his friend Weiss were the only ones who were decent: two SS men who were commandants of concentration camps." She bent forward and took my arm. "Does it make sense to you? Does anything make any sense?"

2

Herr Direktor D is a respected citizen in a large German city. A man with an important position, substantial income, a nice home, the right friends. Every morning the chauffeured Mercedes comes for him, and every night he is brought back home in style. The neighbors take off their hats and bow deeply to the *Herr Direktor.* Though he has been in the city only a few years, it didn't take him long to join the right club, get invited to the best parties, appear every Monday among the subscribers at the local theater: a man of some distinction locally. True, some people have asked "Where does he come from? What did he do before this?" But any *Menschenkenner* (judge of men) can see that *Herr Direktor* D is a successful member of Germany's new *Wohlstandsgesellschaft* (prosperous society). Who cares where such a man comes from? The thing that matters is not what he is, but what he represents.

I wonder what the friends and neighbors would say if they knew that *Herr Direktor* D had had a successful wartime career as deputy commander of a notorious concentration camp and had been personally responsible for the death of at least thirty people. These are the cases I know about. Only God knows how many more there were. In 1963, I had at last found this man after a search that had lasted two years and led through two continents. I knew his real name, his background, his crimes. And that was all—I could do nothing to bring him to trial.

The public prosecutor in D's city had said to me: "I've examined your evidence and it's a shocking case. I say this although I should no longer be shocked, after my experiences in the past few years. But most of the material is based on hearsay information. We must have eyewitnesses."

"It's not easy to find eyewitnesses from such small camps after more than twenty years, *Herr Staatsanwalt*."

"I know, but this man has powerful friends. Unless we get a very strong case, the indictment might become a boomerang. Go and get me the testimony of a trustworthy eyewitness, and I'll prosecute."

So the long search for eyewitnesses began. Most of the people I found knew a lot, but had not seen enough themselves. They had never seen the man kill somebody. People were beaten to death in the camp and everybody knew that D had done it—but no one had actually been present. D preferred to do his beating at night, in the privacy of his apartment.

"There are two people who would know," a former prisoner told me. "One is Max, who was the *Häftlingsdoktor* [prisoners' doctor] in the camp. The deputy commandant called him when people were dying or dead. And Helen would know too. She worked as private servant in the apartment of the deputy camp commander."

It took a long time to find the addresses of these two people. I'm concealing their real names for reasons that will become obvious a little later. Max practiced medicine in Paris. Helen lived somewhere in Germany. I wrote to them, explained the importance of their testimony. There was no answer.

I wrote again, then once more. Not a word. That was unusual. People often refuse to testify, and sometimes they may have very painful reasons, but at least they try to help me somehow. Max and Helen were Jewish. They couldn't be interested in protecting an SS criminal.

Meanwhile *Herr Direktor* D was picked up every morning by his chauffeur. He had a valid passport; if he noticed that we were after him, he might get away, and that would be the end of the case.

One day I met a friend who lives in Paris. I casually mentioned Max. My friend knew him well. He said Max led a very lonely life, saw no one except his patients, was strange and withdrawn and "a little frightening sometimes." I told him the story. My friend shrugged.

"That doesn't surprise me. Max is the last man who would want to walk into a courtroom and testify. He once told me he wants to forget everything, if one can ever forget."

"Go and explain to him that we have a duty toward our dead," I said. "So many people carry out their duties toward the living. No one thinks of his obligations toward the ones who cannot speak up any more. It's too late to bring them back to life. But not too late to bring someone like D to justice. Moral restitution is stronger than material restitution. It's too easy to say that one doesn't want to remember."

I said much more to my friend and asked him to repeat everything to Max. I felt very strongly about it and I was very bitter.

A few weeks later I had a short note from Max. He suggested that we meet somewhere, but not in Austria or Germany; he wouldn't come there. We made a date and met in Switzerland.

He'd told me he was fifty; he looked much older. His eyes were very dark and almost lifeless. He spoke haltingly, as though every word were an effort. He never smiled. I agreed with the friend who had called the doctor "a little frightening."

"I know what you think of me. Your friend told me what you said, and you are right, in principle. But when I tell you my story, you will agree that I am, unfortunately, the exception. I cannot testify in court."

"So much depends on it."

"I know, but first listen. Everything that the people from our camp say about this man is true. In several instances I was there when he got through with his victims. Some of them were beyond help. This man was a sadist who tortured and killed for no reason at all. You know the type."

He spoke with clinical detachment. I said I knew the type very well.

"He was always correct to me. Perhaps because he realized that I knew so much. He still needed me, and in due time I believed he would shoot me. I was certain of it, and he had no doubt that I knew. On that basis there was an uneasy truce between us. And there was another reason. In the women's compound, which we male prisoners were not permitted to enter, was my fiancée. Yes, Helen. We came from the same town in Poland, we had gone to the same school, we'd fallen in love as students. She was even then the prettiest girl. She is still very beautiful."

His voice almost faltered, and I was afraid he wouldn't go on.

"Naturally, he noticed her. He was a great man with women, always boasted about his ways with them. He knew about Helen and me, and he derived much pleasure from torturing me. He took her out of the camp and installed her in his apartment as his personal servant. He would tell me how nice it was to come home to Helen. How she kept the apartment nice and spotless, cooked his meals, cleaned his shoes. It was much worse than if he'd beaten me to death, as he beat others."

One day two friends planned an escape and asked Max to come along. He said he was not going to leave without Helen. They thought he was a fool. His days at the camp were numbered. Everybody knew that. It would only be a matter of weeks or months before the deputy commander shot him. If Max escaped with them, he might later help Helen from the outside. There was at least a fighting chance. The Polish partisans were in the woods. He owed it to the girl to try to escape.

"We got away," he said. "We joined the partisans, and when we linked up with the Russians we all joined the Red Army. I volunteered for front-line service. Once I was back in the region, I thought I would try to do something for Helen. In my dreams I saw myself entering the camp with my unit and triumphantly liberating Helen."

He gave a tired shrug. "It didn't quite turn out that way. I was sent into the interior of the Soviet Union, where I worked in a hospital. I did everything possible to get sent back to the front. They kept me there; they needed me. When the war was over, I tried hard to leave Russia. But not until 1950 was I finally repatriated. In our home town, I found out what happened to Helen.

"When the Red Army had approached, the camp was liquidated. A few got away, but almost all male prisoners were killed. Of the women only Helen survived. He took her with him when he escaped. He changed her name, gave her false papers. Yes, there is no doubt: he saved Helen's life. But . . . she had had a child by him. People told me she disappeared after the war. Probably went to Germany, but no one knew whether she was still alive and where she might be."

He got up and paced the hotel room where we sat, a tired, prematurely aged man with dead, hopeless eyes.

"It took me years to find her. She'd changed her name, but at long last I obtained her addresss. There was no telephone, so I walked up to her apartment and pressed the button. A young man opened the door. I'd prepared myself during these long months for the moment when I would see Helen again. But I was not prepared for this. The boy in front of me looked exactly like his father. I've never seen a more startling example of family resemblance. I stood there transfixed; I was unable to move. Then I pulled myself away. I could not go in. Not with this boy around. I turned and was about to leave, and then I heard a door being opened and saw Helen.

"She came out into the hall and I looked into her eyes. One short second and I knew everything, and so did she, although not a word was said. She loved me; she'd always loved me, just as I shall never cease loving her. We stood there, and the second lasted an eternity. Then the boy moved. I realized he still stood between us. She introduced us. I admired her self-control. She managed to say a few casual words, then sent him away under some pretext, and we were, at last, alone."

"I'm told that you are not married."

"No, and I shall never marry. There was never, and never will be, another woman in my life. I love Helen as much today as when we were in separate compounds of the camp and looked at each other through the barbed-wire fence when the guards weren't watching. Just looked and prayed that some day there would be no fence between us. Now the fence is gone, but—"

He took my hand. "Don't you understand? I cannot marry the mother of this boy who reminds me of a murderer. I could never— never—get used to his presence. It might even hurt the only thing I've left in my heart—my love for Helen. I stayed all day long. We talked; mostly we cried. Then I went away, and I've never seen her since, and never will again. So now you know why I cannot step into the witness box. I couldn't conceal my bitterness when I see that man. The hatred would show, and the defense would make the most of it. I'll swear that all the accusations against him are true, and perhaps that will help you more than my personal testimony in court. But I shall not be there."

A few days later I visited Helen in Germany. Max was right—she was still very beautiful; she had the genuine feminine loveliness that grows on one. She looked younger than Max, although there was a similar sadness in her eyes. I told her that I'd seen Max and asked her why she hadn't answered.

"Because I cannot testify in court."

"I'm told that you know a lot."

"I've seen terrible things. There were beatings in his flat and . . ." She put her hand over her eyes. "I'll never forget it. Afterward they would carry them over to the little shack where Max treated them, *if* they were still alive. The memory doesn't give me a moment's peace. I know your job. Herr Wiesenthal. You have a right to know all these things. But there is something else."

She went out and came back with a young man. He was about twenty, tall and blond. He looked exactly like the photographs of his father. I realized what Max must have felt when he saw the boy— and knew that the boy was innocent, couldn't be blamed. He stayed with us for a few minutes, then kissed his mother's hand and went off to class at the nearby university. Helen said he was a good boy and a good son, devoted to her.

She had watched me when I first saw the boy—and she knew instinctively that Max had told me everything.

"My son doesn't know who his father was," she said. "He thinks that his father died during the war. His father has never seen the boy. He doesn't know that I'm alive, that there was a child. I didn't know it myself when he and I fled from the camp, shortly before the Russian troops came. He saved my life. He got me false papers as an Aryan. He gave me some money, and then he went on toward the West. He wanted to be captured by the Americans. I prayed that God would take the child from me. But God decided otherwise. He made me give birth to the boy, and he made the boy his father's image. Perhaps to punish me. Why did I let him take me to his apartment? Why didn't I stay with the other women in the camp and die with them? Why does one have that terrible urge to survive?"

She stared at me. What could I say? I told her that people had done worse things in order to survive. But she didn't listen.

"There were moments when I wanted to strangle the baby. But I couldn't do the same things that his father had done. I could not kill. . . . Do you now understand why I cannot testify? You must not even tell them that I'm alive. His lawyers would force me to appear in court, make me swear that he saved my life. He doesn't know the price I'm paying for that." She avoided looking at me when she asked: "Did Max talk about me?"

"He told me everything."

"And now . . . ?" There was fear in her eyes.

"I've never dropped a case yet when I had witnesses. But this case depends on the testimony of Max and you. You two have suffered enough. Nothing will be done about this case."

Chapter 23

ONE CENT PER BODY

I first came upon the name *Franz Stangl* in 1948 when I was shown a secret list of decorations awarded to high SS officers. Most of the recipients were given the *Kriegsverdienstkreuz* (Cross of Merit) for "bravery beyond the call of duty," "giving aid to comrades under fire," or "escape under especially hazardous circumstances." But after certain names on the list there is just the penciled notation "Secret Reichs Matter," followed by *für seelische Belastung*—"for psychological discomfort." The coded Nazi terminology meant "for special merit in the technique of mass extermination." Franz Stangl's name was followed by both the notation and the special remark.

The next document I saw bearing his name was this list of articles delivered to RSHA Berlin by the administration of the Treblinka concentration camp near Warsaw between October 1, 1942, and August 2, 1943:

> 25 freight cars of women's hair
> 248 freight cars of clothing
> 100 freight cars of shoes
> 22 freight cars of dry goods
> 46 freight cars of drugs
> 254 freight cars of rugs and bedding

> 400 freight cars of various used articles
> 2,800,000 American dollars
> 400,000 pounds sterling
> 12,000,000 Soviet rubles
> 140,000,000 Polish zlotys
> 400,000 gold watches
> 145,000 kilograms golden wedding rings
> 4,000 karats of diamonds over 2 carats
> 120,000,000 zlotys in various gold coins
> several thousands strings of pearls
> (Signed) *Franz Stangl*

Stangl had been the commander of Treblinka. Of the 700,000 people known to have been taken there, about forty are now alive.

Late in 1943, there had been no more victims. Poland was considered *judenrein*—rid of Jews. Most of the Jews from Austria, Germany, and the Nazi-occupied countries had been liquidated. Smaller jobs were done in such places as Dachau and Mauthausen.

For the Nazis there remained a problem: What could be done with several hundred high-ranking SS technicians of mass extermination? In Nazi terminology they were "secret bearers, first class," which meant that they knew far too much for their own or the Party's good. Evidence could be destroyed by opening mass graves and burning bodies, tearing down the death barracks, and blowing up gas chambers and crematoriums. At Treblinka all that was done. Now as many as possible of the witnesses had to be eliminated. Many of the "secret bearers, first class" were sent to a theater of operations in which they were not expected to survive—Yugoslavia, for instance. The Yugoslav partisans never took Germans alive. Consequently, the Nazi high command sent many of the SS mass murderers to fight the Yugoslav guerrillas. (The cynicism of the Nazi system is frequently evidenced in its terminology, and the Nazi leaders had a colloquialism for the elimination of their own men who were sent to a front from which they were not expected to return: *zum Verheizen*—"to incinerate.")

I discovered in 1948 that Franz Stangl was among the few German survivors of the Yugoslav front. At the end of the war he had returned to Austria and joined his wife and children. Frau Stangl worked as a governess. But Franz Stangl didn't enjoy his liberty very long in Austria. He was subject to automatic arrest as a former SS *Obersturmführer;* with many other SS men, he was brought to Camp Marcus W. Orr in Glasenbach, near Salzburg, by the Americans. He underwent a routine investigation. No one knew that he was the former commander of Treblinka. He was questioned, and gave routine answers about his wartime service. Then he went back to his bunk, lay down, smoked an American cigarette, and talked with fellow SS officers about escaping.

Stangl spent two years at Camp Glasenbach. I was often there during the period I worked for the War Crimes Commission, the CIC, and the OSS. The internees were well fed and sunburned, and they led a pleasant life. They had amusing company from another part of the camp, where the wives of high-ranking Nazis and some former women concentration-camp guards were interned. Before Stangl was able to carry out any escape plans, he was transferred from Camp Glasenbach to the regular prison in Linz. It had been discovered that he was a former Austrian police officer who had worked in Castle Hartheim, the Nazi training school for scientific human extermination described in the next chapter. The Austrians were going to try him, but there were many cases, and the courts were busy.

The prisoners were often sent out to clear away rubble and help rebuild bomb-damaged structures. I later heard that Stangl was with a group of petty criminals who worked at rebuilding the state-owned VOEST steel combine in Linz. The prisoners were not heavily guarded. Why would they want to run away? They got more food in the prison than outside. At the nearby Enns bridge, Soviet soldiers guarded the frontier of the Soviet Zone of Austria. Surely, no prisoner would be foolish enough to run away *there.* But on the evening of May 30, 1948, Franz Stangl was not among the prisoners with whom he'd marched out in the morning. No one had seen him escape, but no one got very excited about it. A notation was added to his file and the file thrown on top of many other files. Neither the American authorities nor the Austrian press was informed.

When I ultimately learned that Stangl had vanished, I decided to check on his family. By the time I found their address in Weis I was told by neighbors that Frau Stangl and her three daughters had left Austria on May 6, 1949. After her husband's escape, Frau Stangl had found a job at the local American library. Meanwhile (I found out later) Franz Stangl had been brought to Damascus, Syria, through the good officers of *ODESSA*. He found a job, made plans for his wife and children to join him. He knew a wealthy Indian woman in Damascus who often traveled to Switzerland. She promised to hire Frau Stangl as governess for her two children. The Syrian Consulate in Berne, Switzerland, would issue the necessary visas.

One day in 1949 three men from Schenker & Company, the well-known Austrian forwarding agents, came to Frau Stangl's apartment, wrote DAMASCUS in large letters on the sides of two large wooden crates, and took the crates away. Frau Stangl said goodbye to friends and neighbors, promised to write soon, and left with the girls for Switzerland. In Berne she received visas for Syria and disappeared.

By late in 1949 much had become known about the Treblinka death camp and the activities of Franz Stangl. He was by then classified as among the worst of the missing Nazi criminals. There was a lot of talk in Weis. Frau Stangl's friends and neighbors told me that she hadn't written so much as a post card. Some people said all the business about Damascus was just to fool the police. They had heard from "somebody" that the Stangls were "probably" in Beirut, Lebanon. I wrote *Damascus, or possibly Beirut* on the index card of Nazi criminal Franz Stangl, and put his file among those on high-priority unfinished cases. I knew, however, it wouldn't be an easy case. The Syrians were not likely to extradite a Nazi criminal.

Nothing happened until one day in 1959, when a German newspaperman came to see me. I'd known him for years. He had just traveled for his paper through various Arab countries, and he brought me a list of Nazis living there. "Incidentally," he said, "Franz Stangl is in Damascus. I didn't meet him, but I talked to some people who were absolutely sure. They said he worked as a garage mechanic."

After Eichmann's seizure in Argentina in May 1960, the German journalist made another trip to the Arab countries to report on people's reactions. When he came to see me a few months later he said Stangl was no longer in Damascus. "He seems to have disappeared a few days after Ben-Gurion announced Eichmann's capture," said my friend.

Ben-Gurion had told the Parliament of Israel and the world at large that Eichmann was now in a prison in Israel, without giving any details. There was much speculation in the world press about the successful *coup*. A German news magazine reported that Eichmann had been brought to Israel with the help of certain pro-Israeli members of the Druses, a tribe living near the Syrian-Israeli border. The story was fiction from beginning to end, but it seemed to have alerted Stangl. The German journalist was told that Stangl had left Damascus in a great hurry. I crossed out *Damascus* on his file card and wrote *Address unknown.*

On February 21, 1964, an Austrian woman came to my office in Vienna, very much agitated. She had read a statement I had made to the press the preceding day, mentioning among others Franz Stangl and his crimes. She was crying. "Herr Wiesenthal, I had no idea that my cousin Theresia was married to such a terrible man. A mass murderer! It's terrible. I couldn't sleep all night."

Frau Stangl was her cousin!

"Where is Theresia now?"

"Why—in Brazil, of course."

She shut her mouth and stepped back, looking at me. She realized that she had said too much. I tried to draw her out cautiously, but she would say nothing else. I didn't want to break my usual rule and ask her name. It is well known in Vienna that I never insist on finding out the names and addresses of people who come to me voluntarily and give me information. I had to let her go.

Next day, a seedy-looking character came to see me. He had shifty eyes and seemed unable to look me straight in the face. When he talked, he rubbed his chin nervously. I wasn't surprised when he admitted that he'd been a member of the Gestapo. I was less than surprised when he assured me that he had done "nothing bad." I often wonder who is to blame for all the bad things that were done; no one admits having done anything.

"They made me join," he said. "What else could I do? I'm just the little guy who gets pushed around."

I said nothing. It was the usual preface.

"I read the story in the papers. About Franz Stangl. Because of men like Stangl we little guys have had endless trouble since the end of the war. I have had jobs, but after a while they find out what you've done, and they fire you."

"I thought you'd done nothing bad," I said.

He was angry. "That's not what I meant. But when they hear I was with the Gestapo . . . Well, you know how it is."

"Yes, I know."

"The big men—the Stangls, the Eichmanns—they had all the help they needed. They were taken out, and given money and jobs and false papers. Who helps guys like me? Look at my shirt, my suit. No job, no money. Can't even afford a little wine."

I didn't want to argue with him, though I thought there was a smell on his breath. Maybe it was Scotch. Or rubbing alcohol.

"Look," he said when I kept silent. "I know where Stangl is. I can help you to find him. Stangl didn't help me. Why should I cover up for Stangl?"

He squinted at me sidewise.

"But it's going to cost you money."

We had, at last, got to the point.

"How much?" I asked.

"Twenty-five thousand dollars."

"You might as well ask for 2 million. I haven't got that kind of money."

He gave a shrug. "All right. I'll make you a special price. . . . How many Jews did Stangl kill?"

"No one will ever know exactly how many died while he was in charge at Treblinka. Perhaps as many as 700,000."

He knocked his fist on the table. "I want one cent for each of them. 700,000 cents. Let's see—that's $7000. A bargain, really."

I had to keep my hands on the desk. I was afraid I would lose control and slap his face. I'm no longer shocked by cynicism after all these years, but this man's arithmetic was too much for me. I got up.

"Well?" he asked.

I wanted to throw him out, but I sat down again. Perhaps this was my only chance of finding one of the most vicious criminals of all.

"I won't give you a penny now. But if Stangl gets arrested on the basis of your information, you'll get the money."

"Who guarantees that the bargain is kept?"

"No one guarantees it. And if you don't like it, get out!"

"All right," he said. "You don't have to get excited. I shall tell you exactly where Stangl is now employed. But I don't know what name he's living under. Is it still a deal?"

"Go ahead."

"Stangl works as mechanic in the Volkswagen factory in São Paolo, Brazil."

This information turned out to be correct. Stangl is still working in São Paolo; we have his present address. And he is still on the "Wanted" list of the provincial court in Linz, Austria, which issued the original warrant against him. I once saw a photograph of Stangl. It shows him holding a riding crop as he drives people into the gas chamber at Treblinka. If this man should be brought to justice, I won't mind paying $7000 to a former Gestapo member.

Chapter 24

SCHOOL FOR
MASS MURDER

One day late in May 1961, a middle-aged Austrian woman came to see me in Linz. It was shortly after the capture of Adolf Eichmann, and the local papers had written at length about my part in the search for him. Now all sorts of people came to tell me things I didn't want to know and to sell me things I didn't need. Some offered their special knowledge, others came to ask for my advice. I wasn't sure why the woman had come to see me. She was unkempt and unattractive. She wore a sloppy pullover and her unwashed hair hung down on her forehead—not exactly the sort of woman who might have been expected to tell me about a love affair, but that's exactly what she did. Bruno Bruckner, originally a night guard at the Linz stockyards, was an enthusiastic amateur photographer. He had lived with the woman and promised to marry her. Then he'd met someone else. . . .

I was listening abstractedly, wondering when she would get to the point.

"—and in 1940 Bruno worked for the Nazis and became a special photographer at Castle Hartheim."

Hartheim! I was very much on the alert now.

"Do you mean Castle Hartheim in Alkoven?"

"Yes," she said. "Just half an hour by car, on the highway to

Passau. Were you ever there? During the war the Nazis turned Castle Hartheim into a sanatorium. That's where Bruno was working as a photographer. He would come to see me in Linz twice a month. Always had lots of money. That was when he started to go around with this woman and—"

"Yes, I know. What was he doing in the sanatorium?"

"Well, he was told to make pictures of the patients. The pictures were sent to Berlin. It was a big secret, but he got drunk and told me all about it."

"What sort of pictures did he make there?"

Suddenly the woman got up. Perhaps I had asked too much.

"Why don't you ask Bruno?" she said venomously. "He was a Nazi, all right, and you go after Nazis, don't you? Here is his address. He can tell you all about the nice experiments they made him photograph in Hartheim." And she left.

I had first heard about Hartheim during my final weeks at the Mauthausen concentration camp. The crematoriums were busy and sometimes an oven broke down, and an expert "from Hartheim" would come to fix the machinery. And sometimes groups of prisoners were sent "to Hartheim"; they never came back. Somebody told me that Hartheim was the name of an old castle not far from Mauthausen. *Hartheim* seemed synonymous with *death,* but I didn't give it much thought. Lying on my bunk in the death block, I was too weak to think.

In 1947, several SS guards from the Mauthausen concentration camp were tried before an American military court in Dachau. I had helped prepare the evidence against some of the SS men, and I was in the courtroom. One of the defendants testified that he'd been sent to Mauthausen "from Hartheim." He was sentenced to death. No other mention was made of Hartheim.

The next time I came upon the name of Castle Hartheim was in a report on the Nazi regime's euthanasia program. Most of the facts are known, so I shall recapitulate them only briefly here. The first mention of euthanasia—which the Nazis called *Gnadentod* (mercy killing)—occurs in January 1940. By order of Adolf Hitler, three men met in Brandenburg: *Reichsleiter* Philip Bouhler, Reichs "Health" *Führer* Dr. Leonardo Conti, and Hitler's private physician Dr. Karl Brand. Their orders were to make plans for *Vernichtung lebensunwerten Lebens.* This phrase, which exists in no other language, can be inadequately translated "destruction-of-lives-not-worthy-of-living." The project was top secret and was directly under the control of the Führer's Chancellery, the staff of which was under the control of Rudolf Hess and, after Hess' defection, of Martin Bormann. Bormann appointed a committee of medical experts under Professor Dr. Werner Heyde, a professor of psychiatry at Würzburg University. Heyde was responsible for the deaths of at least 100,000 people. He disappeared after the end of the war under the name Dr. Sawade, was caught in 1962, and committed suicide in prison shortly before he was to be tried.

During the initial phase of the euthanasia program, certain groups of people—the mentally retarded, the incurably sick, the very old—were the victims, having been classified as *Unnütze Esser,* "useless eaters." The theory was that they consumed valuable food and produced nothing; so they had to die. Most of them were Christians—German and Austrian patients in hospitals and asylums. No Jews were among them; most Jews had already been sent to the concentration camps. The Nazis considered euthanasia a quasi-ethical sort of murder, and reserved it for members of their own race. Officially, the program was listed under the code *T4*—the euthanasia experts had their headquarters in an elegant villa in Tiergartenstrasse 4, Berlin.

The decision whether human beings were to live or die was made by doctors known as T4 experts. They received the personal files of "potential useless eaters" from hospitals and asylums in Germany, Austria, and other countries. These doctors gave a perfunctory look at these files without bothering to look at the patients. When a file was marked with a cross, the death sentence had been pronounced.

Next the files were sent to a special transportation office and sturdy attendants would bring the doomed men and women to the nearest "clinic" or "sanatorium" for a swift death by injection. Four such institutes are mentioned in the reports on euthanasia that I have studied. Three were in Germany: Hadamar, near Limburg; Sonnenstein, near Pirna, Saxony; Castle Grafenegg, Brandenburg. The fourth was Castle Hartheim, near Linz.

After the hospitals and asylums had been relieved of many "useless eaters," the operation was expanded under the code *14 f 13.* It now covered German and Austrian inmates of concentration camps who were sick or invalid, often as a result of forced labor. (Austria's former Federal Chancellor, Dr. Alfons Gorbach, an invalid, was selected for Castle Hartheim, but was saved by his calligraphic handwriting and was sent to work in the office of the Dachau concentration camp.) Action 14 f 13 began in 1941 and lasted until the end of the war. After 1943, many French camp prisoners were sent to die in Hartheim.

After reading the report, I drove out to Castle Hartheim, which is situated in the peaceful village of Alkoven, about twelve miles from Linz, surrounded by green fields and softly rolling hills. Castle Hartheim was a rather forbidding sixteenth-century Renaissance structure with four towers and many rows of windows. Through the gate I walked into a large courtyard surrounded by beautiful colonnades. The castle was at the time inhabited by *Volksdeutsche* refugees from the East. I knew they wouldn't be able to tell me much, having come here after the war. I walked into the village and talked to a few people there, but they became reticent when I asked about Hartheim. They said it had been "some kind of sanatorium," gave a shrug, and walked away. I got back into my car and drove to Linz. I probably wouldn't have thought of Castle Hartheim again if a jealous woman hadn't come to tell me about Bruno Bruckner, who had photographed certain "experiments" at the mysterious castle.

I began to investigate the unfaithful Bruno. He was now working at a state-owned chemical plant in Linz, and he was still said to be an enthusiastic amateur photographer. In our files there was mention of a certain SS *Obersturmführer* Bruckner who, according to the testimony of survivors from some concentration camps, had been a courier between the camps and Berlin. One of the duties of this SS *Obersturmführer* Bruckner was to deliver to Berlin gold and jewelry taken from Jewish prisoners. There was no description of the SS man. I gave what material I had to the Linz police, and a police officer was sent to interview Bruckner. There was no specific accusation against him, and we had to move cautiously. I suggested to the police officer that he start talking about gold and jewelry, and later switch unobtrusively to Castle Hartheim. The police officer did this very well. Bruckner emphatically denied having ever been in the SS. He had been "a simple *Wehrmacht* soldier." He had never been a courier for the SS, never carried any gold or jewelry. In fact, he said, he had not even obtained any sort of war "loot" himself.

"I didn't even bring a camera back from the war," Bruckner said. "And it's no secret that nearly everybody came home with a couple of cameras. Not to mention other things."

The police officer had nodded. "But you have some cameras now?"

"Sure. I had them long before the war."

"What kind of pictures did you take in Castle Hartheim, Bruckner?"

Bruckner seemed so relieved that the subject of gold and jewelry had been dropped that he admitted everything.

"Medical pictures. They made some experiments down in the cellar and I photographed them through a peephole in the door."

He hadn't volunteered for the job, he said. One day in 1940 a man from the Nazi *Gauleitung* in Linz had asked him whether he was able to run a first-class darkroom. Bruckner had said that he would love to run such a darkroom. A few days later he'd been asked to come to the *Gauleitung*, where he'd been interviewed by two men. He had to sign a statement that he would talk to no one about his work. The following day he was fetched by a Herr Lohthaller who drove him out to "Sanatorium Hartheim." On the way Bruno Bruckner had asked what he would have to do there.

"Don't ask me," Lohthaller had said. "They will tell you."

At the castle, Bruckner was taken to Captain Christian Wirth, the commander. Bruckner described Captain Wirth as "a nice man after working hours but very strict while you were on duty. He wouldn't hesitate for a moment to shoot a person if something went wrong." Wirth told Bruckner that he would have to take "three photos of each patient," showed him the darkroom—which indeed was a first-class one—and showed him where he would sleep.

Bruckner photographed about thirty patients a day, sometimes more. It was hard work. "Some patients were raving mad and had to be restrained by male nurses. Once or twice a patient got away before they could be given the lethal injection and jumped at me. It was tough. And the worst part was that I couldn't eat anything. There was a terrible stench in the air from the cremation ovens. It remained with us day and night. After a few days I went to Captain

Wirth and said I couldn't stand it. I asked to be released from the assignment."

Captain Wirth had not been pleased with this request and had given Bruckner three choices: "Either you stay here and keep your mouth shut, Bruckner, or you'll be sent to Mauthausen. Or, if you prefer, you will be shot here at once." Bruckner dejectedly went to his room. That night Captain Wirth sent him a bottle of *schnapps*. Bruckner got drunk, and after a while he forgot the stench in the air.

Gradually Bruckner found out more about Hartheim. It was not easy, because people were very secretive and told him not to ask any questions if he wanted to stay alive. But he was no fool. He noticed that the two doctors in charge, Dr. Rudolf Lohnauer from Linz, the chief physician, and Dr. Georg Renno, deputy chief physician, didn't like his making the pictures. But he had his orders from Wirth. After a few weeks Wirth had told him to go down in the cellar and make some pictures of the latest "experiments."

"What sort of experiments?" asked the police officer.

"Patients were now being killed by gas. I had to make close-ups of them during their death struggle. Later I had to photograph their brains too. Wirth called them 'scientific material' and sent them to Berlin. I was not permitted to keep any of these pictures. Next to the experimental room there was the crematorium. I didn't ask any questions. It was a good job. I was paid 300 marks a month, and made a little money on the side taking pictures of the employees, with Captain Wirth's permission. The food was good. And there was always plenty of liquor. And at night there were lots of parties. Everybody was sleeping with everybody else."

Bruno Bruckner did his job and kept his mouth shut. Later Captain Wirth was transferred; his successor was a Franz Stangl. And some time in 1941, it was all over for Bruno, unfortunately. The *Wehrmacht* drafted him and sent him to the Eastern Front.

"Was there anything else you noticed while you were in Hartheim?" the police officer asked.

"Yes," Bruckner said. "One thing I couldn't figure out. About thirty or thirty-five patients were gassed every day in the cellar. Yet they had at least eighty employees, and some came down to the cellar to watch. What did they need eighty people for?"

I was able to answer Bruckner's question a few weeks later, after a thorough investigation. Castle Hartheim was not only a euthanasia institute, as I had assumed until Bruckner's interrogation. Hartheim was much more.

There were certain facts, seemingly unrelated. Wirth, the commander of Castle Hartheim, was later in over-all charge of the three Polish extermination camps of Belzec, Sobibor, and Treblinka, where a million and a half Jewish men, women, and children were gassed between 1941 and 1943. His successor in Hartheim, Franz Stangl, later became commandant of Treblinka. Gustav Wagner, another Hartheim alumnus, later commanded the Sobibor camp; he is probably hiding now under another name in Argentina. Hartheim's chief doctor, Dr. Rudolf Lohnauer from Linz, after the war committed suicide with his whole family. His deputy, Dr. Georg Renno, was arrested in Frankfurt in 1963, and will be tried there. Finally, a great many SS men who did technical jobs in the gas chambers and crematoriums of various concentration camps had spent some time in Hartheim—or in one of the three other euthanasia clinics.

The terrible truth is that the euthanasia centers were regular schools of murder. I deal only with Hartheim, which was easily accessible to me, but similar material exists about the three other places in Germany. All of them were training centers for Hitler's genocide program.

This discovery answers questions that have perplexed historians and criminologists since the end of the war: how were people selected and trained to carry out the murder of 11 million people, and how did they keep their secrets so well that they were not known for years after the end of the war? Obviously, men assigned to the gas chambers, who had to watch the deaths of tens of thousands of people day after day and week after week, would have to be trained technically *and* psychologically, otherwise they might collapse under the continuous stress.

In 1947, I began to discuss the problem with various experts who had studied the files of the Nazi annihilation machinery. I asked historians, criminologists, doctors, and the people at the Yad Vashem Institute in Jerusalem: How could it be explained that there had never been a breakdown in the extermination machinery at the death camps? We knew that at the Wannsee Conference in January

1942, the Nazis had determined upon the methodical extermination of 11 million Jews in Europe, and that various methods of genocide had been tried out. We knew that there had been mechanical breakdowns. Once Himmler was present when experiments using the exhaust gases of submarine engines for extermination had proved highly unsatisfactory. Himmler had been furious, and there had been draconic punishment. Machines broke down, but the people handling them never did. How could it be that the people operating the gas chambers and ovens were more reliable than the machines? Had they been trained mechanically *and* psychologically to stand the terrific strain? The question bothered me for years. The Nazis had known that time was running out for them. Plans already existed for the annihilation of the Gypsies, the Poles, the Russians. That meant the machinery of genocide had to be kept running at high speed. All facts pointed toward the conclusion that special cadres of technically skilled and emotionally hardened executioners were trained somewhere. Castle Hartheim and the other euthanasia centers were the answer.

Hartheim was organized like a medical school—except that the "students" were not taught to save human life but to destroy it as efficiently as possible. The deaths of the victims were clinically studied, precisely photographed, scientificaly perfected. (At later trials in Germany it was proven that at the death camps of Belzec, Sobibor, and Treblinka special photographers also made pictures of people being killed.) Various mixtures of gases were tried out to find the most effective one. Doctors with stopwatches would observe the dying patients through the peephole in the cellar door of Castle Hartheim, and the length of the death struggle was clocked down to one tenth of a second. Slow-motion pictures were made and studied by the experts. Victims' brains were photographed to see exactly when death had occurred. Nothing was left to chance.

The "students" first watched the experiments; later they carried them out themselves. Each "student" was selected by high-ranking Nazi officials, the so-called *Gau-Inspekteure*. Security was so tight that in this matter the *Gau-Inspekteure* were personally and directly responsible to Hitler's Chancellery. The Nazis realized that there must be no slip-up. Germans and Austrians were being killed, and there could be trouble. Despite all precautions, slip-ups did ultimately occur in the "sanatoria" of Sonnenstein and Grafenegg. There was talk among the population, and these places finally had to be closed. In Hadamar and Hartheim, the organization was perfect. The places were secluded. There was no talk.

No one will ever know exactly how many people were murdered in the Renaissance castle with the beautiful colonnade. No memorial for the victims of Hartheim, most of them Austrian and German Christians, has been built. The records of the registry office have not been found. At the Dachau trial in 1947 people testified that from thirty to forty human guinea pigs were "treated" in the cellars every day. That would account for about 30,000 people in three years. Toward the end Hartheim became just another place of extermination. When the executioners in nearby Mauthausen became too busy, the surplus victims were sent to Hartheim.

Hartheim graduates later became teachers of future cadres of scientifically trained killers. After some practice, the "students" became insensible to the cries of the victims. The "teachers" would watch the reaction of their "students." It was a brilliant psychological touch to use Germans and Austrians as victims in the basic training for mass murder. If a "student" did not break when he had to kill his own people, he would have no moral scruple about exterminating thousands of *Untermenschen*. A "student" who couldn't take it was sent to the front, where his commander would assign him to a *Himmelfahrtskommando*—suicide squad.

I submitted my dossier on Hartheim to Dr. Christian Broda, then Austrian Minister of Justice. On February 20, 1964, I was able to tell the press that the Minister had assured me, in the presence of Attorney General Dr. Franz Pallin, that my material would be handled immediately "so that this new knowledge can be used in the course of all pending proceedings." The files contain the names of several Austrian citizens who had been active in Hartheim. As I write this, in the summer of 1966, they are still at liberty.

Chapter 25

WHERE IS BORMANN?

The whereabouts of Martin Bormann remains the biggest unsolved Nazi mystery. Hitler's chief deputy has occasioned more rumors and legends, more spilled printer's ink than any other Nazi leader. The question "Is Bormann dead?" is always good for another cover story in any German mass-circulation magazine. No other prominent Nazi has been declared dead and then revived so many times. Witnesses have claimed that he was buried in May 1945 at the fairgrounds in the Moabit section of Berlin, after his escape from Hilter's Chancellery. West Berlin police dug up the area in 1964 and found nothing. Several years ago he was reported buried in Asunción, Paraguay. The exhumation of the grave in question revealed the body of a Paraguayan citizen named Hormoncilla.

After the war, Bormann was said to have been seen in an Italian monastery, in Moscow, in the Tyrol, in Australia, and in many South American countries. In 1947 he was said to be in Egypt, in 1950 in Southwest Africa, the following year in Chile, in 1952 in Spain. Once he was reported to have escaped from Germany across the Alps. It was also claimed that he was taken in a German U-boat from Kiel to Tierra del Fuego, the world's southernmost settlement. In October 1965 the Italian press agency ANSA learned from one Pascuale Donazio, "a prominent personality of the Fascist regime,"

317

that Bormann was living in the jungle of Brazil's Matto Grosso. Unfortunately, the sensational stories about Bormann always fizzle out like fireworks, and after a moment of glare there is again complete darkness. No one yet has been able to claim the reward of 100,000 marks ($25,000) that the prosecutor's office in Frankfurt am Main will pay for information leading to the capture of Martin Bormann.

I became interested in the Bormann mystery only after the Eichmann trial. Being so late, I had the advantage of having at my disposal the accumulated experience of all people who had worked on the Bormann case—the police, prominent jurists, historians, criminalists.

What makes the mystery of Martin Bormann so fascinating? He is much better known today than when he was in power, overshadowed by the more colorful figures of Goering, Goebbels, Himmler. A great many people in the Third Reich had never heard of him. Many people didn't even know what he looked like. After the flight of Rudolf Hess to England in 1941, Bormann became the *Führer's* deputy. He was closer to Hitler, and more powerful, than any other prominent Nazi.

I've spent many hours studying the photos of the enigmatic Bormann—a heavy-set man with a bull neck and a nondescript, impassive face, strangely empty and rather brutal. When I discussed the Bormann legend in Frankfurt with Fritz Bauer, who prosecuted at the Auschwitz trial, he called Bormann "the typical *Bierkopf* [beer head]." Bormann has the *Dutzendgesicht* (dime-a-dozen face) one sees in many *Bräustüberln* in Bavaria, where men sit around drinking beer and discussing politics, and where arguments are often settled by the strength of the voice rather than the weight of the facts.

Josef Wulff, the Jewish historian, calls Bormann "Hitler's shadow," implying that Bormann was the *Führer's* omniscient, passive *alter ego*. I believe the Nazis who called Bormann "Hitler's evil spirit" were closer to the truth. He was the head of the enormous, closely knit Nazi Party organization. Below the *Führer* were 19 *Reichsleiter* and, one notch below, 41 *Gauleiter*. (There were 40 *Gaue;* a forty-first *Gauleiter* represented the Germans abroad, the *Auslandsdeutschen.*) Underneath the *Gauleiter* were 808 *Kreisleiter*, then 28,376 *Ortsgruppenleiter*, who were in charge of whole towns or of certain parts of a large city. There were 89,378 *Zellenleiter*—but the word *cell* is misleading, for a NSDAP cell might consist of four or six, or even eight, city districts. On the lowest level there were several hundred thousand *Blockleiter*, each a small god to the people living in his immediate neighborhood.

After the beginning of the Second World War, when Hitler became fascinated by major strategy problems, Martin Bormann was put in charge of the Party apparatus. He was *Reichsleiter* in Germany, Hitler's secretary, chief of the "Party Chancellery of the *Führer*." All the top-secret orders passed his desk—the orders leading to the annihilation of the Jews and other "inferior" races, the persecution of the Church, the mass murders in euthanasia institutes and concentration camps. Bormann decided who was permitted to see Hitler, and he kept away people who might have had a moderating influence on the *Führer*. A great many orders signed by Hitler bore the imprint of Bormann's mind. At the Nuremberg trial, Goering admitted that many documents bearing the signature of Hitler were conceived and written by Bormann.

Bormann was the typical inflexible, inhuman Nazi Party boss. Born in 1900 in Halberstadt, he began his political career when he was eighteen and after the lost First World War joined the *Freikorps Rossbach*, one of the fascist groups that opposed the Weimar Republic. Convicted of a murder, he went to prison. Later he was decorated by Hitler with the *Blutorden* (Blood Order) for his illegal activities. By 1928 he was already a paid Party official assisting Hess. Bormann married the former Gerda Buch, whose father became the Nazi Party's highest Justice. The Bormanns had seven children. At one time Bormann considered legally introducing polygamy into Germany after the war—as proved by his draft of a decree that would have forced every SS man to have three wives. With his computer-like mind, he calculated the enormous losses of German men during the war and such a surplus of women in postwar Germany that polygamy seemed the only method of making up for the losses in twenty or thirty years. All the Nazi establishments set up for the obligatory mating of approved Aryans were influenced by Bormann's primitive notions.

He developed his thoughts in his letters to his wife, who thoroughly approved. Bormann told his wife all about affairs with his various mistresses. (The Bormann letters were published in London in 1954.) On January 21, 1944, Bormann wrote his wife about his latest conquest, a woman he called M (recently identified as Manja Behrens, an actress now performing in East Germany):

> You thought M must be a very unusual girl. No, sweetie, she is not an unusual girl—but I am an incredible *Kerl* [rascal]. I fell madly in love with her . . . and I took her in spite of her protests. You know my willpower, against which M couldn't defend herself very long. Now she is mine and I feel doubly and very happily married. M suffers from terrible pangs of conscience about you. Which is pure nonsense, of course. I got her with my willpower. . . .

Frau Bormann answered on January 24:

> You will have to see that M gets a child in a year, and the next year I must have a child so that you will always have one wife who feels up to it [*die auf dem Damm ist*]. Then we'll gather all the children in the house on the lake and live together, and the wife who is not pregnant at the moment can always come to the Obersalzberg or to Berlin to be with you.

At the very base of the Bormann mystery is not the question of where he is hiding now. The key to the mystery is whether Bormann managed to survive the night of May 1, 1945, after he left the Reichs Chancellery and was beyond doubt seen alive by several witnesses. Bormann belonged to the small group of Nazis who, after the arrival of the Red Army in Berlin, escaped into the *Führerbunker,* Hitler's private air-raid shelter below the Chancellery. Of the top Nazis, only Bormann and Goebbels were there after Hitler's suicide on April 30, 1945. Goebbels announced that he was not going to survive the Third Reich and committed suicide, killing his wife and children. Bormann had a phial of prussic acid, but said he would try to get away. He ordered General Krebs, the last chief of staff of the *Wehrmacht,* to go to the Russian lines and offer the surrender of the Reichs Chancellery in return for a safe conduct for the defenders. Marshal Vassily Chuikov demanded unconditional surrender.

Bormann decided they would try to break through the Soviet chain of tanks closing in from all sides on the Chancellery. He was in radio communication with Grand Admiral Doenitz in Schleswig-Holstein, who had been named Germany's *Reichspräsident* by

Hitler. At half past four on the afternoon of May first, all those still in the bunker were told to get ready. Radio commentator Hans Fritzsche, in the nearby Propaganda Ministry, considered the plan "complete madness" and threatened to go to the Russians and offer the capitulation of the entire government district. Bormann asked Fritzsche not to do this and, under pressure from Fritzsche, promised to order the *Werwolf*—the guerrilla groups that had been formed to fight on after the defeat—to refrain from further action. Fritzsche and State Secretary Naumann went into the garden of the Chancellery, where Bormann arrived a minute later. According to Naumann's testimony, Bormann wore a field-gray uniform with the insignia of an SS general and a dark leather coat. He gave the order to several SS leaders to dissolve the *Werwolf* organization.

At 10 P.M. the defenders began to file out of the bunker. Bormann was in a small group with Naumann, Reichs Youth Leader Artur Axmann, Hitler's driver Kempka, and the Führer's physician Dr. Stumpfegger. Near the Friedrichstrasse railway station they came to the Weidendammer Bridge, leading across the Spree River. On the other side of the bridge were Russian tanks. Bormann's plan was to try to break through the line of tanks with the help of some German tanks and armored vehicles.

Driver Kempka told the Nuremberg tribunal:

> The German tanks began to move across the bridge, following the lead tank. Bormann walked behind the lead tank. This tank was hit, I suppose by a *Panzerfaust* thrown from a window, and exploded. Where Bormann stood, there was a darting flame going up.

Reichsjugendführer Axmann later said:

> The German Tiger tank, which carried a lot of ammunition, blew up. The terrific air pressure knocked me over. Instinctively, I sought cover in a bomb crater. There were several men there: Bormann; Hitler's surgeon, Dr. Stumpfegger; Dr. Naumann; Goebbels' aide Schwaegermann; and my own aide, Weltzin. All were unhurt. We discussed how we could get out of Berlin.

They walked back to Friedrichstrasse station, went up onto the railway embankment, crossed a nearby railroad bridge over the Spree, and followed the tracks until they almost reached the Lehrter station, which was already occupied by the Soviet troops. According to Axmann, Bormann and the others went down from the embankment to the street, where they encountered some Russian soldiers. Bormann and the other men had already taken off their insignia of rank. The Russians, perhaps thinking these men were from the *Volkssturm*, Hitler's hastily formed and ineffective civilian defense corps, offered them cigarettes and paid no attention to them. Then, Axmann continued:

> Bormann and Dr. Stumpfegger left our group and walked quickly toward Invalidenstrasse. The rest of us followed later. In Invalidenstrasse there was much shooting. As we had almost passed the bridge across the tracks of the Lehrter station, we saw two men lying on the ground. We knelt down next to them. Perhaps we could help them. They were Martin Bormann and Dr. Stumpfegger. An error is impossible. Their faces were visible. They were lying on the back, arms and legs spread out. I touched Bormann. No reaction. I bent over him. No breath. I saw no wounds or blood. The shooting continued. We had to go on. . . .

There are other witnesses. Most of them have testified many times. In their later testimony, the witnesses often refute details given earlier. Also, the testimony of the witnesses differs in many ways. Hitler's chief pilot, Bauer, swore that Bormann had worn a brown uniform, without insignia, and a steel helmet. Naumann swore that Bormann had had a field-gray SS uniform and a Party cap.

Studying the testimony and its evaluation by experts—criminologists, historians, military men—I concluded that their evaluations failed to take into consideration something that seemed to me of the utmost importance: in such a situation, when it is a matter of life or death, it is every man for himself. As they walked together under the hail of Soviet bullets, *Reichsleiter* Bormann and Hitler's driver were no longer separated by an abyss of rank. They were two frightened men running for their lives. In such a moment no man pays much attention to the man next to him; no one tries to make accurate mental notes for future testimony. It was dark, and it is quite certain that the fugitives were not looking at the men to their right and left. They were trying to survive, not to observe.

Then there is the characteristically confusing matter of Bormann's diary. It is beyond doubt a genuine diary. It is now in Moscow, but there is a copy among the files of the East German authorities. The last two lines in the diary say

30.4. Adolf Hitler X, Eva B. X
1.5. *Ausbruchsversuch* [trying to break out]

Some people claim the diary was found on the ground. Others say it was found in the overcoat pocket of a dead man. The assumption is that the dead man must have been Bormann, for if the diary is genuine the dead body must be Bormann's. But I could mention a dozen cases in which prominent Nazis put their own identity papers into the pockets of dead men, hoping that this would prove that they, the prominent Nazis, were dead.

There is another important psychological point: the big Nazis I asked about Bormann are convinced that he is alive. The consensus is "He was always a smart fox, just the man to outsmart even death." Eichmann was convinced that Bormann was alive as late as 1960; Eichmann told the police investigators in Israel this. A prominent diplomat, one of my most reliable sources, tells me that there exists a Bormann Fund in Spain which finances neo-Nazi and Fascist activities.

The more or less sensational stories published about Bormann's escape begin with the time he supposedly left Germany, in the winter of 1945. A certain Peter Franz Kubainsky, who later was arrested in Innsbruck, admitted that on December 12, 1945, he had brought Martin Bormann from Reichenhall, Bavaria, to Salzburg, Innsbruck, and Nauders, near the Italian border. "However," said Kubainsky, "I did not know then that the man was Bormann, since he wore a small mustache and made a completely plain impression on me." Kubainsky claims that the man had Italian travel documents issued to him by a Vatican organization headed by Monsignore Heinemann, Via dell' Anima 4, Rome. Heinemann allegedly gave Kubainsky the address of a Josef Wolf, living near Castle Labers, in Merano, Italy, "where I channeled Bormann."

> As a matter of fact [said Kubainsky], I saw how Bormann was put by Msgr. Heinemann into the monastic garb of a Jesuit and so I saw how he boarded a ship in Genoa for Argentina. . . .

It is known to me that Bormann lives in Peru under the false name of José Perez and has an import-export firm that goes under the maiden name of Bormann's present wife. Bormann's first wife died in Italy in 1945.

Kubainsky's report does not stand up under close scrutiny. The Innsbruck police add a postscript: "He seems to be a so-called *Sensations-Journalist* [sensation-mongering journalist]."

Casting aside such dubious assertions, there seem to be some ascertainable facts that are much more interesting.

Item: Through the help of a Swiss friend, I read the testimony of a woman who is quite certain that she saw Martin Bormann in 1956 on a bus in São Paolo, Brazil. (Her report was later carefully checked by the German authorities.) This woman had known Bormann personally in Berlin and had talked to him several times at the Reichs Chancellery. After the war she lived in Lausanne, Switzerland. In 1956, she went to São Paolo to visit her daughter. Sitting in a bus, she looked up and, to her great surprise, saw Martin Bormann. "I addressed him in German, 'Herr Bormann! . . . You —here?' He looked stunned, got up without a word, stepped to the door, and got out even before the bus came to a full stop. Then he was gone."

Item: In May 1962, one of my co-workers got in touch with Frau Paula Riegler, formerly the housekeeper in Bormann's home in Pullach, Bavaria, who stayed with Frau Gerda Bormann until Frau Bormann's death in Merano in 1945. When Frau Riegler was interviewed by my man, she did not admit that she was still in contact with Bormann. But she was convinced that he was alive—in 1962. She told my helper that Bormann's former secretary, Else Kruger, was now married to a farmer somewhere in Austria, but she said she did not know Else Kruger's married name or her address. From Zurich I received other information about Else Kruger, who is said to have important contacts with South America.

Item: In 1962 I had a visit from an Italian journalist, Luciano Doddoli of Milan, who is employed by the newspaper *Espresso*. In 1960, Doddoli had been in Chile to report on the big earthquake there for various Italian papers. There he met a Professor Enrique Bello, who taught art at the University of Santiago de Chile. Professor Bello was searching for relatives who had disappeared during the earthquake. It was shortly after the capture of Adolf Eichmann; Doddoli and Bello were talking about former Nazi leaders who were said to be hiding under false names in Valdivia, in the southern part of Chile. Professor Bello told Doddoli that he'd met a woman who had "lived with Bormann from 1948 to 1951." He arranged a meeting between the woman and Doddoli. She called herself Keller and was working for a German-Chilean trading firm. Doddoli did not find out any facts about Bormann. Frau Keller told Doddoli "one could one day talk about this matter." Professor Bello said he thought "it might be a question of money."

Item: During my search for Dr. Josef Mengele, I received a letter addressed *Wiesenthal, Vienna,* from Port au Prince, Haiti. Johnny Sommer, a German who had spent the past forty years in South America, wrote that he was the former owner of a night club called the Ali Baba in Asunción, Paraguay, which he'd sold in 1963. He now owned the Roxy Bar in Port au Prince. We began to correspond. In May 1964 he sent me a group photograph made during the war, showing Hitler and his staff, about twenty-five people. There were no names on the picture. One man was indicated by an arrow. Sommer wrote: "This man, called Bauer, often came to my night club in Asunción with a certain Mengele, in 1961. Sometimes a Dr. Jung was with them. They often went fishing together in the Alto Paraná River." This information was later confirmed to me by other witnesses in Asunción. The man marked by the arrow is Bormann. The Jung family are rich landholders in Paraguay.

I noticed that in all reports on Bormann there is a conspicuous void. They either deal with the dramatic events of the fateful evening of May 1, 1945, or they deal with the reappearance of Bormann sometime in the fall of 1945, when various people are reported to have seen him. Where did Bormann spend the time from May first to late fall, and what was he doing?

On May 6, 1963, I appeared on the *Panorama* program of the German television network in Hamburg. I mentioned, among other things, the case of Martin Bormann, and called the "dark time" from May first to the late fall of 1945 the key to the Bormann mystery. A few days later I received a letter from a man I shall call Franz Rapp. He wrote that he had reliable information about "the dark time."

I met Rapp at the Hotel Dachs in Munich. He was fifty-four, a native of Bolzano in the Italian South Tyrol, where he was accredited as a court interpreter. In 1938 he had opted for German citizenship, as people of German descent there were allowed to do by Mussolini, and during the war had served in the *Wehrmacht*. After the war, he became the representative for Italian and Swiss firms selling coffee machines and household goods. He now lives in a small town near Heidelberg, Germany.

Rapp told me that in the late fall of 1961 he had been in Innsbruck, which was in his sales territory. There he met a man who shall be called Franz Holt, then forty-three, who later became his partner. Holt lived in Innsbruck as a lodger in the house of a woman I'll call Frau Hilde. The three became great friends. One night, after many glasses of wine, Holt nudged his friend. He said he was going to tell him his "big secret." Rapp said he didn't want to hear any secrets; he had noticed that Frau Hilde was trying to keep Holt from talking. But Holt was in high spirits and paid no attention to her. He said Rapp was his friend and partner, they were making good money together, and why shouldn't his friend know about his secret? He poured more wine and started to talk.

During the war, Holt's story began, he had been with an ambulance outfit. At the end of the war he was briefly a prisoner of war in a French internment camp near Innsbruck, and was soon released. Holt became an employee of the Austrian Red Cross in Tyrol. During the early summer of 1945 the Austrian Red Cross began to repatriate Austrian soldiers from Allied prisoner-of-war camps in Germany. The repatriation action was sponsored by the Catholic Church, and the Allies took a favorable view of it since they wanted to demonstrate that they considered Austria a "liberated" country, not an "occupied" country like Germany.

Holt was assigned to a Red Cross group that traveled to various camps in Germany, Italy, and France. The members of the mission were given identity cards in four languages (French, English, Russian, and German) that entitled them to enter any Allied prisoner-of-war camp. They collected Austrian soldiers—but not SS men or war criminals—and repatriated them.

In the fall of 1945, Holt told Rapp, he had been with his group in a camp in northern Germany near Flensburg, Schleswig-Holstein.

(Bormann had been trying to reach Grand Admiral Doenitz in Flensburg when he left the Führer's bunker.)

At the camp, Holt was approached by a *Blitzmädel*, a member of the *Wehrmacht's* women's auxiliary forces, who asked him to take her along to Austria although she was not an Austrian. She offered him a valuable diamond ring. Holt knew that the checks by the British were perfunctory, and agreed. She came again the following day, with another piece of jewelry. Would he consent to take along her brother, too? Holt looked at the jewelry and found it hard to resist. All right, he said, he would put them into the transport as Austrian returnees. They joined him the next day. The man wore a small mustache and glasses, but the glasses seemed to bother him. When he wanted to look at something, he always took them off.

When the transport reached Innsbruck, where the Austrian prisoners were to be interrogated and sent to their homes, Holt was again approached by the couple. They asked him to take them to Nauders, a village at the Austrian border, from which it was not far to both the Italian and Swiss borders. Naturally, they expected to pay for his services. This time they gave him a valuable brooch. Holt knew the border area well. He assumed the couple were not just brother and sister, but he didn't care as long as they rewarded him so well. To avoid the Allied border patrols in the area, Holt had to guide the couple through the woods, on remote paths, across a high mountain pass. It was October or November, Holt said, and already very cold. There was much snow on the ground. Often they got stuck in yard-high snowdrifts. The woman showed great strength: she kept going no matter how tired she was, and told the men to hurry up because they must not be caught by one of the patrols. They crossed the border into the Italian South Tyrol, where Holt was told to take them to one of the monasteries in the Vintschgau region. Only then, at the end of the journey, was Holt told whom he'd guided to safety. The man told him that he was *Reichsleiter* Martin Bormann.

"At the gate of the monastery," Holt told Rapp, "Bormann had rung the bell. The door had been opened. Bormann took a paper out of the inside of his pants, where it had been sewn. The doorkeeper read the paper and asked them to wait. After a while he came back and asked Bormann and the woman to enter. I thought that

Bormann's escape must have been well prepared in advance. Bormann turned around to me and said: "Franz, you've done something terrific. If you don't talk about it, you'll get some money every month as long as you live.' They shook hands with me and went in, and the door of the monastery was closed."

Analyzing the story Holt had told to Franz Rapp late in the fall of 1961 in Innsbruck, I concluded that it contained many credible elements. Most members of Bormann's group who tried to break through the Russian ring in Berlin succeeded in getting out. Why shouldn't "the smart fox" Bormann succeed? He had tried to reach Flensburg to talk to Doenitz, had found sanctuary under an assumed name in the safest possible place, a British prisoner-of-war camp. It was not improbable that he would carry some valuable pieces of jewelry, that he would try to reach a monastery in Italy, as so many prominent Nazis before and after him. He would be one of the most important travelers on *ODESSA*'s "monastery route."

I asked Rapp to talk to Holt and get more detailed information. Rapp wrote to Holt, suggesting there might be a lot of money in this proposition if he were able to supply particular facts. At their next meeting, Holt was very embarrassed and asked Rapp to forget the whole thing. He wasn't interested in money, he said. In fact, he might lose much more than he might gain. He implored Rapp not to tell the secret to anyone. I made an investigation in Innsbruck. The police confirmed that Holt had actually been with an ambulance outfit during the war, and later became an employee of the Austrian Red Cross. He *had* helped to repatriate Austrians from various German camps. And finally, according to Rapp, he still received a check every month from abroad, always from a different bank.

The next authentic detail in the Bormann mosaic was supplied by a small, fragile woman we shall call Bettina. She now lives in a quiet boarding house in Germany. She spent more than twenty-five years in Chile and returned to Europe because she was homesick. In October 1964, Frau Bettina wrote to the police in Vienna and asked for my address. Then she wrote to me. When she had lived in Chile, she said, Martin Bormann had bought a large piece of land in her immediate neighborhood. She knew from the newspapers that I might be interested, and proposed a meeting.

I was, of course, interested. Frau Bettina received me in her room and took out of a drawer a photocopy of a map titled *Kartenskizze Chilenische Schweiz*. "Chilean Switzerland" is in the south-central part of Chile. I had the impression that the map had been drawn by Germans in Chile for a certain purpose. It shows the area between the Pacific Ocean and Argentine border to the east. The area between the towns of Valdivia and Bariloche is marked with certain secret signs—triangles, rings, and squares, each with a number. Three of the triangles carry the signs *OD* and *UL*. It is a lovely region, with mountains and lakes, woods and rivers. There are beautiful spas and summer resorts—exactly the sort of landscape where an exiled wealthy German could live in pleasant seclusion. Could it be that the secret symbols had a military meaning?

I asked Frau Bettina how she got hold of the mysterious map.

"In the apartment house in Valdivia where I lived there was a German named Arturo Schwarz. He was a quiet, reticent man who talked to few people and often went away for weeks. He never told the neighbors what he was doing. For some reason he seemed to have confidence in me. Before going away, he would leave the keys to his apartment with me and ask me to keep an eye on the place and water the flowers.

"Then stories about Nazi criminals in South America began to appear in our newspapers. I began to wonder about my mysterious neighbor. He spoke German, had plenty of money, didn't do any regular work, and wanted to talk to no one. Could it be that he was one of these people who had good reason to remain anonymous? One day in 1960, while Herr Schwarz was away, a stranger came to me and told me that Herr Schwarz had suddenly died on a trip in Brazil. He asked me for the keys to Herr Schwarz' apartment. I said I couldn't find the keys, and asked him to come back the next day. When the man had left, I went into the apartment and looked around. There were a few books and a few papers on the table. I saw several copies of this map, and took one with me."

Some time afterward Frau Bettina made a trip to the small town of Osorno, halfway between Valdivia and Puerto Montt. Herr Schwarz had often talked about Osorno, where there lived many Germans who had arrived after the Second World War. Frau Bettina met a few of them.

"They behaved as if it were still 1938," Frau Bettina said. "I particularly remember a German lawyer who talked like Goebbels. Everybody I met seemed to have plenty of money, no particular work, and a nice home. All were retired, and talked constantly about the great Third Reich. Several people mentioned that Martin Bormann was living somewhere in the region. The lawyer in Osorno had purchased a piece of land for Bormann between Valdivia and the Argentine frontier. Everybody knew about it. If you look at the map, you'll see that this part of the region is marked by some of the secret symbols."

Frau Bettina's information tallies with information I have about former Nazis who live around Bariloche, on the Argentinian side of the frontier. It's a similar story. The Germans there own beautiful estates and much land. Mengele has often been seen there. There have been mysterious feuds between German groups, and sometimes there are gunfights, but the local police keep these things pretty much under cover.

The last piece of the mosaic was brought to me by a young student in Vienna. He telephoned me at my office one day in 1964 and asked me to meet him at a coffee house. There I found a pleasant, good-looking man of twenty-six, with melancholy eyes. He *had* to talk to me. Several months ago a beautiful young Brazilian woman, about thirty, had come to Vienna to study art.

"She's very beautiful," the young man said with a sigh. "She is from Curitiba, a town in the Brazilian state of Paraná."

I tried not to appear interested. In Paraná there are German settlements where some of my prominent "clients" are hiding. They are greatly admired there. The mentality is strictly Third Reich.

The Brazilian woman was married to the German owner of an import-export firm. He often came to Barcelona on business. On his last trip he'd permitted his wife to go on to Vienna. She had a nice voice and was crazy about taking singing lessons, "and Vienna is the best place for it," said the young man.

They'd met and fallen in love. The young man sighed again. I said nothing, but I kept wondering why he had called just me to tell me about his love affair with a beautiful Brazilian woman.

"I know her name, but she asked me to keep it to myself," he said. "It's a delicate situation. She doesn't get along well with her husband. She has to be careful. Well, one day we were together in a coffee house, and I read a Bormann story in one of the magazines. We began talking about it. These things fascinate me. My friend laughed and said she could tell me a *lot* about the subject. And she took a photograph from her handbag. It was made in 1964 and shows a group of people. One of them, a heavy-set, balding man, half raises his right hand while the picture is being taken, as if he wants to shield his face. Actually he is covering only his right ear. My friend said: 'Look at him. All the Jews and many Germans are after him. He was one of the biggest Nazis. My husband works for him.' "

I said nothing.

"You're probably wondering why I'm telling you," he said. "Well, I'm crazy about this woman. She left Vienna a few weeks ago to rejoin her husband in Spain. I know she loves me very much. She told me she has her own money. But he would never give her a divorce. He's one of these brutal *Kerle*."

I listened. I wasn't even surprised that a marriage triangle would lead me back to Martin Bormann. I've learned in the past twenty years to be surprised by nothing.

"Herr Wiesenthal, I am absolutely sure the man was Bormann. Of course I know Bormann only from the photographs in the magazines, but the man trying to shield his face looked exactly like the pictures I had seen of Bormann. Obviously my friend's husband must be a prominent Nazi, otherwise Bormann would not use him on international errands. We thought—that is, I thought, if I gave you his name, and you had him arrested the next time he is in Spain——"

He was silent.

"You get rid of the husband and could live with your Brazilian woman happily ever after?" I said.

"Exactly. And you might get Bormann's address in Curitiba. My friend will give it to you. . . . She would like to live with me in Europe."

There, for the moment, the matter rests. I promised the young man not to do anything that might embarrass the woman. He gave me her name. He will keep me posted when she and her husband come back to Europe.

But suppose I can provide evidence that Bormann lives at a

certain address in Curitiba—what will happen? Twenty-four hours later he would disappear. He can easily submerge in South America. He has money and a network of fanatically devoted helpers.

Many countries are interested in Bormann, but no country is *really* interested. Fritz Bauer, the prosecutor in Frankfurt, doubts whether any South American country would extradite him. The mystery of Martin Bormann—most probably now living near the frontier of Argentina and Chile as I write this, early in 1966—will degenerate into a simple biological equation. He is well protected. No country will want to attempt a second Eichmann case. Bormann will come to his end some day, and the reward of 100,000 marks will never be paid. Death needs no money.

Chapter 26

POSTSCRIPT

The stories of many of my cases are admittedly hard to believe, a fact that brings me to the prophecy of SS *Rottenführer* Merz. I never knew his first name, but I remember the man well.

It was one afternoon in September 1944 near Grybow, Poland, during the German retreat from the East. The Lwow concentration camp had been liquidated, its 200 SS guards had successfully "disengaged" themselves from the advancing Red Army, and I was one of the thirty-four survivors of the camp whom the SS men were "guarding" to give them a pretext for their westward retreat.

That afternoon *Rottenführer* (Corporal) Merz had invited me to come along on a walk to a nearby village. Food was scarce, and we were going to try to promote a few potatoes. I spoke Polish and Merz thought I would be helpful.

The day had been hot. We'd found two small bags of potatoes in the house of a peasant, and now each of us carried one bag on the way to the bivouac. That in itself was remarkable; normally I would have carried both bags. As we passed a brook at the edge of the forest, Merz suggested that we sit down for a while and relax.

Merz had been one of the few SS men who was always decent to the prisoners. He'd never beaten anyone, never shouted at us. He'd addressed us using *Sie,* the polite German form, as if we were human beings. Still, I was not prepared for what was to come.

"As a child, I was told a fairy tale about this boy who wants to go somewhere and utters a wish, and an eagle with enormous wings takes him there," Merz said to me. "Remember, Wiesenthal?"

"Well, I remember the one about the magic carpet."

"Yes, that's the same idea." Merz stretched out on his back and was staring into the hazy sky. We were enveloped by the rustling of the trees and the soft murmur of the brook. It was very peaceful and very unreal, the prisoner and the SS man relaxing in the idyllic countryside in the midst of the apocalypse.

"Suppose an eagle took you to America, Wiesenthal?" Merz asked me. "*Was würden Sie dort erzählen* [What would you tell them there]?"

I was silent. Was he trying to trick me into saying something foolish?

Merz guessed my thoughts. He smiled. "Don't be afraid. You can talk frankly."

"*Herr Rottenführer,*" I said diplomatically, "I really never thought of it. How could I get to America? I might as well try to get to the moon."

I was playing for time. Admittedly Merz was the exception, a *good* SS man. But he was an SS man; how could I trust him?

"Just imagine, Wiesenthal, that you were arriving in New York, and the people asked you, 'How was it in those German concentration camps? What did they do to you?'"

I didn't answer. I was sure of Merz now. I trusted him. But it was hard to answer.

I said—haltingly, I remember—"I believe . . . I believe I would tell the people the truth, *Herr Rottenführer.*"

Was he going to shoot me? I'd seen SS men shoot people for much less reason.

Merz was still looking up into the sky. He nodded, as if he'd expected my answer.

"Yes. I've thought about it—many times. I've seen what has happened to your people. I'm an SS man, but sometimes I wake up in the middle of night, and I don't know whether it's a dream or the truth."

I said nothing. It was safer to let *him* talk.

"You would tell the truth to the people in America. That's right. And you know what would happen, Wiesenthal?" He got up slowly and looked at me, and he smiled. "They wouldn't believe you. They'd say you were crazy. Might even put you into a madhouse. How can *any*one believe this terrible business—unless he has lived through it?"

APPENDIX

Abwehr. The counterespionage service of the *Wehrmacht* (the German armed forces), headed by Admiral Canaris. Canaris was arrested and executed in 1944 as an Allied spy, and the *Abwehr* was disgraced.

Argentina. At the end of the First World War, while Germany and Austria went through a political and economic crisis following their defeat, many people emigrated from both countries to Argentina. Not unexpectedly, most of the new emigrants were radical nationalists who refused to live in defeated Germany "under the chains of Versailles."

With customary diligence, the new immigrants built schools, factories and other enterprises, published newspapers and magazines, gained considerable political influence. In a remarkably short time they held key positions in their adopted land. But they always remained in spiritual and political touch with the *Heimat.* By the time their homeland had been taken over by the Führer, many Germans and Austrians in Argentina rallied to Hitler's support. The Nazis knew the importance of the *Auslandsdeutschen,* these Germans abroad. The NSDAP was well organized in Argentina. At the beginning of World War War II, the Argentine Nazi Party had 60,000 members. *Gauleiter* Bohle in Berlin, responsible for all Germans abroad, was represented in Buenos Aires by his deputy, Heinrich Korn.

The *Auslandsdeutschen* missed no opportunities in Argentina. They had shipping lines, cultural institutes, a student-exchange program, a special news service, Transozean (to compete with Reuters and the American wire services), and newspapers and magazines supported by Goebbels' Propaganda Ministry. And the military attaché at the Argentine Embassy in Rome, Juan D. Perón, learned German in order to be able to read the original edition of *Mein Kampf*. On October 17, 1943, Perón led his *descamisados* (shirtless ones) in his march against Buenos Aires, imitating the strategy of Mussolini. He imitated other things, too, when he was elected President in 1946. He had special flying commandos, organized somewhat like the SS *Rollkommandos*. His private secretary was the son of a German Nazi.

After the war, the Nazis sent experts and money to Argentina. Perón himself, according to an investigation made in Buenos Aires after his downfall, was given around $100 million. Buenos Aires became the terminal port for the vast clandestine Nazi travel organization *ODESSA*. The Germans took over hotels and boarding houses, provided the new SS immigrants with identity papers, had excellent connections with the highest government officials. At one time a group of Argentinian Germans were plotting to fly to Germany and liberate the Nazi criminals interned at Landsberg Prison.

Gestapo. Geheime Staatspolizei [Secret State Police], the Party's security organization that operated inside and outside Germany.

Gleichschaltung. The complete coordination of all political and other activities by the Nazis.

Kristallnacht [Crystal Night]. On November 7, 1938, *Legationssekretar* Erwin von Rath, a diplomat at the German Embassy in Paris, was assassinated by Hershel Gruenspan, a Polish Jew. By way of reprisal, Reinhard Heydrich ordered all synagogues in Germany and Austria burned and destroyed on the night of November ninth. Jewish stores were looted. It was the beginning of the end of the Jews in these countries. The Nazis remember the *Kristallnacht* because the streets were covered with broken pieces of glass from the smashed shop windows of Jewish stores, hence the name.

NSDAP. Nationalsozialistische Deutsche Arbeiterpartei [National Socialist German Workers' Party], founded by Hitler in 1919 out of a small political group called the German Workers' Party. In this book usually called the Nazi Party.

RSHA. Reichssicherheitshauptamt; could be termed the Interior Ministry of the SS, comprising all intelligence and counterintelligence services.

SA. Sturmabteilungen, the brown-shirted storm troopers, founded in 1921, originally divided into groups of a hundred men.

SS. Schutzstaffel [Security Guard], originally Hitler's personal body-guards in 1923, recruited from the toughest members of the SA, to become *Ordner* at political meetings. In 1929 Himmler was told by Hitler to build the SS organization into the elite corps of the Party.

SD. Sicherheitsdienst, the elite of the elite; the intelligence service of the SS under Reinhard Heydrich.

Statute of Limitations. Neither the Bible, Roman law, nor canon law knows a statute of limitations for crimes. Anglo-Saxon law, handed down to modern Britain and the United States, is based on the principle *tempus non occurrit regi* (the passage of time has no influence on the prosecution of crime). In England and in the United States there exists no statute of limitations for murder. The Austrians solved the dilemma by restoring an old Austrian law that did not recognize a statute of limitations for murder.

In Germany the great debate took place in 1964, when the government seemed willing to let the statute of limitations lapse. Under the pressure of world opinion the question arose in West Germany whether the existing twenty-year statute of limitations should be extended. Nearly 70,000 Nazi criminals had been sentenced by then, but prosecutions were still pending against 13,000 suspects. These prosecutions would be dropped if the statute were applied. Three out of four letters reaching the Bundestag in Bonn were in favor of letting the law lapse. ("There must be an end to this thing. . . . One cannot treat a nation like a juvenile delinquent. . . .") Dr. Ewald Bucher, West Germany's Minister of Justice, opposed the extension of the statute. He claimed that nearly all important Nazis had already been caught and indicted. Bucher formerly was a member of Hitler Youth and of the Nazi Party. Bucher, a member of the rightist Free Democratic Party (FDP) which formed a coalition with Ludwig Erhard's CDU, was under strong pressure from his party colleagues. The FDP needed the votes of the German rightists and neo-Nazis.

Most of the German press and almost the entire intellectual and political leadership of West Germany disagreed with Bucher. Bucher was presented by Wiesenthal with a collection of 360 letters from

German and Austrian politicians, scientists, artists, jurists, and writers in favor of an extension of the law. There were letters from Agustín Cardinal Bea, Protestant Bishop Hans Lilje, Banker Hermann J. Abs, Professor Carl J. Burckhardt, Nobel Prize winners Max Born and Werner Heisenberg, among others. After an agonizing debate, the Bundestag voted to consider September 21, 1949—the day West Germany began to manage its own postwar affairs—the starting date for the twenty-year statute of limitations. This means that the statute of limitations is extended until September 21, 1969.

Even if the statute of limitations were extended indefinitely it would never be possible to prosecute all Nazi crimes. Take Auschwitz: at least 6,000 SS men served at various times as guards, technical personnel in gas chambers and crematoriums, medics, office workers. Only 900 are known by name. Of these, some 300 were handed over to the Poles, and of the remaining 600 the location of half is known, but not in every case is there a witness who will testify in court. In the concentration camps, the victims did not know their torturers by name. Some top criminals were known—the Mengeles and Stangls. But the anonymous cogs in the machinery of extermination, the little men who shot a few people here and there, turned on the gas, injected lethal doses of phenolic acid—where are they now? Walking around at liberty, probably healthier than their victims who survived, and perhaps sleeping better.

Wannsee Conference. On January 20, 1942, Reinhard Heydrich convened a meeting of fifteen top-ranking Nazi bureaucrats in the Berlin suburb of Wannsee. It was here that "the final solution of the Jewish problem" was settled: deportation to the East, forced labor, and mass execution. Adolf Eichmann was among the lowest-ranking Nazis present, but it fell to him to see that the "final solution" was efficiently carried out.